# WOMEN, POWER AND RESISTANCE

## An introduction to Women's Studies

**edited by**
**TESS COSSLETT, ALISON EASTON**
**and PENNY SUMMERFIELD**

**Open University Press**
Buckingham • Philadelphia

Open University Press
Celtic Court
22 Ballmoor
Buckingham
MK18 1XW

and
1900 Frost Road, Suite 101
Bristol, PA 19007, USA

First Published 1996

A catalogue record of this book is available from the British Library

ISBN    0 335 19390 0 (pbk)    0 335 19391 9 (hbk)

*Library of Congress Cataloging-in-Publication Data*
Women, power and resistance: an introduction to women's studies/
    edited by Tess Cosslett, Alison Easton, and Penny Summerfield.
        p.    cm.
    Includes bibliographical references and index.
    ISBN 0-335-19391-9. – ISBN 0-335-19390-0 (pbk.)
    1. Women – Social conditions.    2. Women in popular culture.    3. Sex
role.    4. Gender identity.    5. Feminism.    6. Patriarchy.
7. Feminist theory.    I. Cosslett, Tess, 1947–.    II. Easton, Alison, 1943–.
    III. Summerfield, Penny, 1951–.
HQ1121.W8855    1996                                                              96-22705
305. 41–dc20                                                                            CIP

Typeset by Type Study, Scarborough
Printed in Great Britain by Redwood Books, Trowbridge

For Lancaster University's Women's Studies students –
past, present and future

# Contents

# Notes on contributors

*Sara Ahmed* is lecturer in Women's Studies at Lancaster University. She is the current convenor of Part One Women's Studies, and also teaches a third year Women's Studies course on gender, race and colonialism, as well as MA Women's Studies courses on feminism, psychoanalysis and deconstruction, and on feminism and post-colonial theory. She has published articles recently in journals such as *Social and Legal Studies*, *Hypatia* and *Australian Feminist Studies*.

*Sarah Beresford* has been a lecturer in law at Lancaster University for three years. As well as lecturing on the law degree course, she also lectures on law and families in the Part One Women's Studies course. She has previously published in *Family Law* and is currently writing her first book.

*Tess Cosslett* is a senior lecturer in English at Lancaster University. She lectures on fairy tales on the Part One Women's Studies course, and teaches a module on women's auto/biography as part of the Women's Studies MA. She has written on female friendship in Victorian fiction, and on the representation of childbirth. Her most recent book is *Women Writing Childbirth* (1994). She also writes poems.

*Kathleen Cross* is currently writing her PhD thesis at Lancaster University on the reproduction of whiteness in popular texts about the Human Genome Project. Her other main (pre)occupation is singing, playing guitar and writing songs.

*Rosemary Deem* is Professor of Educational Research and Dean of Social Sciences at Lancaster University. Her undergraduate teaching covers gender, 'race' and youth, as well as gender and educational organizations; her postgraduate teaching includes an MA module on women and leisure. Her most recent book is *Active Citizenship and the Governing of Schools*, with Kevin Brehony and Sue Heath (1995).

*Alison Easton* has taught at Lancaster since 1973 and is now senior lecturer in English. She specializes in nineteenth-century American literature and women's writing, and is author of *The Making of the Hawthorne Subject* (1996). She was co-director of Lancaster's Centre for Women's Studies 1991–94, and first convenor of the introductory Women's Studies course.

*Janet Finch* is Vice-Chancellor of Keele University. She previously taught at Lancaster University, and was a member of the Centre for Women's Studies. Her academic discipline is sociology, and much of her published work is on family concepts and issues. Her most recent book is *Negotiating Family Responsibilities* (1993), co-authored with Jennifer Mason.

*Consuelo Rivera Fuentes*: Chilean writer (some poetry books published), EFL teacher, activist of her dreams (sometimes defeated by activists of night-mares); pursuing MPhil/PhD in Women's Studies/Sociology at Lancaster University. Hobby: writing poems with and about other women. Her article, '*Todas Locas, Todas Vivas, Todas Libres*: Chilean Lesbians: 1982–1995', is being published in M. Reinfelder (ed.) *Amazon to Zami: Toward a Global Lesbian Feminism* (forthcoming).

*Ruth Henig* is head of the History Department at Lancaster and has wide-ranging interests in nineteenth and twentieth-century European and Asian history. She has lectured in the Part One Women's Studies course about women's involvement in local and national politics, drawing on her own experience as a Lancashire County Councillor for the past 14 years.

*Hiroko Kawanami* is a lecturer in Buddhist Studies at Lancaster University. She lectures on women in Buddhism in the Women's Studies Part One course, and teaches an MA module on women in Indian and East Asian traditions in the Department of Religious Studies. She is currently working on a book on Buddhist nuns in Burmese Buddhism.

*Wendy Langford* teaches Women's Studies and Sociology at Lancaster University. She has recently completed her PhD on the relationship between romantic love and gendered power. Her publications include: 'The Sexual Politics of Loving Too Much: Discourses of Popular Advice on Heterosexual Relationships' (1993), and 'Snuglet Puglet Loves to Snuggle with Snuglet Piglet: Alter Personalities in Heterosexual Love Relationships', in L. Pearce and J. Stacey (eds) *Romance Revisited* (1995).

*Steph Lawler* is a lecturer in Sociology at Durham University, where she teaches undergraduate and postgraduate courses in feminist sociology. She previously taught in the Centre for Women's Studies at Lancaster University. She is the author of '"I never felt as though I fitted": Family Romances in the Mother–Daughter Relationship', in L. Pearce and J. Stacey (eds) *Romance Revisited* (1995).

*Lynne Pearce* is a senior lecturer in English at Lancaster University where most of her teaching is in the area of feminist theory and women's writing, both at undergraduate and postgraduate level. Her most recent book is *Reading Dialogics* (1994) and she is now working on a volume entitled *Feminism and the Politics of Reading*.

*Santi Rozario* is a lecturer in Sociology and Anthropology at the University of Newcastle, New South Wales. While visiting Lancaster University in 1995 she co-taught a module on women in Indian and East Asian religious traditions for the MA in Women and Religion. She is the author of *Purity and Communal Boundaries: Women and Social Change in a Bangladeshi Village* (1992).

*Gabrielle Russell* is an independent film maker currently lecturing on film video and animation at Leeds College of Art and Design, where she also teaches Media Studies. She recently lectured on the representation of women in film for Lancaster University's Department of Sociology and Centre for Women's Studies, where she also supervises MA students in video production.

*Deborah Sawyer* is a senior lecturer in Religious Studies at Lancaster University. She lectures on church and organization in the Women's Studies Part One course; she also teaches an undergraduate course on Bible and Gender, and is coordinator of the MA in Women and Religion. She has published a translation and commentary on Jewish midrash, *Midrash Aleph Beth* (1992). Her study *Women and Religion in the First Christian Centuries* is being published by Routledge in 1996.

*Robbie Smith* is a tutorial fellow in Independent Studies at Lancaster University and also teaches History, Sociology and Women's Studies courses in Adult Education. She was convener and a lecturer in the Part One Women's Studies course for a year. Her paper, 'Feminists Before Feminism' (1994) was published by the Centre for Women's Studies, and she is currently researching the history of female sexuality.

*Carolyn Stone* is a lecturer in the Department of Educational Research at Lancaster University. She has lectured on women and morality in the first year Women's Studies course and teaches an undergraduate course which reflects her interests in philosophy, feminisms and women's education. She also (jointly with Penny Summerfield) teaches an MA module on gender and the curriculum.

*Kathleen Sullivan* is writing up her MPhil in Women's Studies and Sociology at Lancaster University. She is researching the interface between ecological responsibility and the care of radioactive materials. Her interests include: ecofeminism, permaculture and sustainability, non-violence, children and poetry. She is co-founder of the Institute for Deep Ecology Education, London.

*Penny Summerfield* is Professor of Women's History at Lancaster University. She was director and then co-director of the Centre for Women's Studies at Lancaster from 1989 to 1994. She teaches courses on women's history at undergraduate and postgraduate levels. She has published extensively on British women and World War II, notably *Women Workers in the Second World War* (1989), and also on the history of schooling and gender identities.

*Carole Truman* is a lecturer in Applied Social Science at Lancaster University and a member of the Centre for Women's Studies. Her teaching and research interests are in the areas of women, work and opportunity and also on the topic of social science research. Recent books include *Women in Business* (1993) and *Rethinking Social Research* (1994).

*Sue Wise* is a senior lecturer in Applied Social Science at Lancaster University. She teaches on feminist perspectives in social policy and social work, including equal opportunities policies and practices, and has published on a range of topics, including child abuse, and on feminist approaches to social science research. A recent book is *Breaking Out Again: Feminist Ontology and Epistemology* (with L. Stanley) (1993).

*Linda Woodhead* is a lecturer in Christian Studies in the Department of Religious Studies, Lancaster University. She lectures on women and Christianity on the Part One Women's Studies course, and teaches a module on women and sexuality in the Christian tradition as part of the Women's Studies MA. Her most recent publication is an article on 'Faith, Feminism and the Family', in the *Concilium* volume, 'The Family' (1995).

# Acknowledgements

This book, like the Lancaster University first year undergraduate course on which it is based, has been a collaborative project. The editors wish to celebrate everyone involved: the working group who planned the course in 1990–91; the teachers who have contributed over the years; the Centre for Women's Studies' officer, Janet Hartley, who administered the course from its beginnings; the university departments, faculties and administration which supported us; and the students who have taken and continue to take the course. We would also like to thank Jacinta Evans of Open University Press for her support and assistance in creating a textbook out of the course, and above all, the contributors to this volume.

**ALISON EASTON**

# Introduction
# What is Women's Studies?

So here you are with this book in your hand, starting a Women's Studies course or simply intent on discovering what Women's Studies is about. Some of you will have already studied in this area; for others it will be a completely new subject. But all of you will find yourselves being asked, sometimes eagerly and sometimes with incomprehension or hostility, 'What is Women's Studies?' One simple reason for the question is that Women's Studies is a comparatively new academic subject. The first Women's Studies course was taught in the United States in the late 1960s. In the 1970s the subject grew slowly, becoming a substantial presence in universities, colleges and adult education classes in more and more countries in the 1980s. In many places it is still establishing itself. At Lancaster where this textbook originated, there has been a Centre for Women's Studies since 1984, degrees since 1987 and this introductory course since 1991.

Why then is Women's Studies necessary, and in what ways is it different from other academic subjects? Pause for a moment and think about the things people say when they hear about your Women's Studies course or see you with this book. Have they said, 'Is it a proper subject?', or 'What about Men's Studies?', or 'Are they all lesbians?', or 'Can you get a job after studying it?', or 'Haven't women got equality now?', or 'Aren't they just man-haters?', or 'Do you have to be a feminist to do it?', or 'Aren't there worse things to worry about?' Perhaps you've also met up with those who are excited, committed, curious, supportive, envious – these voices are just as important.

In 1979 Adrienne Rich, American poet, civil rights activist, feminist and lesbian, set out this agenda for Women's Studies:

Suppose we were to ask ourselves, simply: What does a woman need to know to become a self-conscious, self-defining human being? Doesn't she need a knowledge of her own history, of her much-politicized body, of the creative genius of women of the past – the skills and crafts and techniques and visions possessed by women in other times and cultures, and how they have been rendered anonymous, censored, interrupted, devalued? Doesn't she, as one of that majority who are still denied equal rights as citizens, enslaved as sexual prey, unpaid or underpaid as workers, withheld from her own power – doesn't she need an analysis of her condition, a knowledge of the women thinkers of the past who have reflected on it, a knowledge, too, of women's world-wide individual rebellions and organized movements against economic and social injustice, and how these have been fragmented and silenced?

Doesn't she need to know how seemingly natural states of being, like heterosexuality, like motherhood, have been enforced and institutionalized to deprive her of her power? Without such education, women have lived and continue to live in ignorance of our collective context, vulnerable to the projections of men's fantasies about us as they appear in art, in literature, in the sciences, in the media, in the so-called humanistic studies. I suggest that not anatomy, but enforced ignorance, has been a crucial key to our powerlessness.

(Rich 1987: 1–2)

Though feminists in the 1990s might question Rich's unproblematic conceptions of autonomy and collectivity (Women's Studies never stands still), none the less this is an excellent summary of key issues: the untold history of oppression, survival and accomplishments; the pervasiveness of that oppression which continues to this day (we're not postfeminists because we don't live in a postpatriarchy); the central insight that, far from being 'natural', this state of affairs is socially constructed; and finally, the need to understand one's condition before one can change it. It is for this reason that we have made 'women, power and resistance' the key theme of this introductory volume.

Women's Studies is a vital part of the work of feminism – or rather feminisms, because 'feminism' takes many forms and assumes many different, at times contradictory positions, and in the past 30 years in particular it has been in a continual state of debate, evolution, conflict and change. Though this is a source of strength for Women's Studies, it makes it hard to define what feminism is. Most forms of feminism assert that existing relations between the sexes, in which women are subordinated to men, ought to be changed by giving women control over their lives. But such a general statement raises many questions: it is possible to generalize about 'woman' and 'oppression', what theories of power is one using, and what visions of the future might one have? One way of approaching the variety and contradictions of feminist principles and practice is to ask 'Where is feminism?' rather than 'What is feminism?' (Skeggs 1997). This way we can understand how feminist views and activism manifest themselves in differing ways according to the variety of situations women find themselves in – for example, in rape crisis centres, in an Indian village, or in women's magazines. Women's Studies is one of these manifestations, and one which constantly reflects critically on itself and demonstrates the enormous diversity of feminist understandings.

Rich called for a fully informed understanding of women's past and present condition, and we need to understand why women do not have this knowledge; why, until recently, has there been, for example, no history or psychology or sociology of women. You might like at this point to pause again and think about what your own educational experience tells you about this situation: what did your teachers think you ought to know, how were you taught, and how much did you learn about women? To complicate matters, gender cannot be the sole object of our study: knowledge and understanding of other bases for social division, such as class, race and sexuality, have also been absent from the study of society, culture and science. As we hope to show throughout this textbook, the study of women and gender always intersects with the investigation of these other structures of division and power.

It is helpful to think of this historical exclusion from scholarship and curricula in terms of a politics of knowledge. As Dale Spender explains in *Men's Studies Modified*, what we regard as knowledge is not 'universal' or 'true' or 'objective'. The idea that knowledge is 'value-free' turns out to be a device merely to legitimize mainstream scholarly knowledge (Spender 1981: 1–9). This kind of knowledge is socially constructed. It tends to serve the interests of those who have power. It is marked by the underlying beliefs of the social systems in which it is formed. It masks its operations with talk of 'human nature' and 'common sense'. In consequence feminist perspectives which challenge it will be deemed highly threatening.

So how does Women's Studies respond to these orthodoxies? I shall offer you a list of seven ways in which Women's Studies attempts to change the structure of knowledge and the ways in which we learn.

First, the study of women is not a self-contained body of knowledge which has been added onto existing subjects without altering them. Instead it radically revises whole academic fields. For example, in English Studies the exploration of women writers by feminist literary critics has changed in the ways in which male-authored texts are approached; and feminist historians have shown that male historians' preoccupation with turning points has concealed major continuities in the position of women.

Second, Women's Studies is interdisciplinary. This means that feminist scholars do not stay inside a single traditional discipline (a department of knowledge, for example sociology), but instead have been particularly active in fighting against this compartmentalization of knowledge. With so many influences on women's lives and conditions, we must relate knowledge from many different sources. For example, a study of childbirth involves not only medical science, sociology and anthropology, but literary studies and oral history. A study of the ways in which time/space is gendered brings together not only feminist historians and geographers, but also feminist sociologists, urban planners, psychologists, critics of film, literature and the visual arts, those working in cultural and media studies, and many others.

Third, unlike many mainstream disciplines which believe their work is

apolitical, Women's Studies openly and proudly acknowledges the necessarily political nature of *all* knowledge. This ensures that the politics of
Women's Studies is constantly under review and always evolving, for
Women's Studies is not a cosy in-group congratulating itself on a shared
sense of being right. We do well to keep remembering there is no correct
feminist position. You'll find within this textbook a variety of approaches
and positions, with each chapter introducing and participating in these
intense debates. The other vital aspect of Women's Studies' political nature
is its links with wider women's movements. Rather than believing in
knowledge for its own sake, Women's Studies asks what is knowledge *for*.
Some feminists outside colleges and universities worry whether academic
feminism is a distraction from the battle to change society, but those within
Women's Studies argue that there is a vital connection between knowledge
and action – a two-way relationship, each side sustaining the other. So, in
the final part of this book we'll be looking at some aspects of feminist
activism. We shall take it last both because its often disturbing issues need
the support of the understandings and perspectives which we hope the rest
of the volume will provide, and because Part IV focuses attention on
women as agents, that is on what women have and are currently doing to
resist oppression. This is the good news!

Fourth, Women's Studies recognizes the value of women's personal,
lived experiences and the skills and awarenesses which we accumulate
through everyday social interaction. Too often researchers have dismissed
what women have to say about their experiences, for example within the
family, or sexually. However, while feminist scholars have made what
women say about their experience a vital part of their study, this is not
unexamined experience. By listening to women, but listening thought-
fully, analytically and critically as well as respectfully, we transform the
construction of knowledge (see Stanley and Wise 1993). Furthermore, we
need to understand that 'experience' is not simply an individualistic
matter. What is subjective is also collective and shared; it is part of the
world of social and economic institutions, language and other cultural
practices, and is a continuous process by which we come to have a sense
of ourselves and our place in the social order.

Fifth, Women's Studies talks about women, not woman. Patriarchal
social structures often treat all women as a unified category, but Women's
Studies has learnt to recognize and examine differences between women,
to stress the fluidity of female identity and to reject the idea that all women
are essentially the same. So, if we hear ourselves saying 'women' (and we
all do it!), we need to stop and think who exactly we mean. Similarly,
saying 'men are . . .' or 'typical men!' can be unhelpful, since it plays into
ways in which feminine and masculine are often defined *against* each other
and so perpetuates patriarchal ways of thinking. In the early days of
Women's Studies 'women' was all too often unthinkingly used to mean
white, heterosexual and middle-class women, and women of colour, lesbians, working-class women, for example, were treated as special categories. The concept of 'difference', however, seeks to interrogate those
so-called norms which have come about as a result of present power

structures. So, when looking at race for example, we shall examine white-ness as well as what is called blackness, and when exploring sexuality, heterosexuality is as much a topic for analysis as lesbianism or bisexuality. Furthermore, as we take this sense of difference more and more on board, these categories themselves start to break down. Try describing yourself in class, race and sexual terms, and then notice how you begin to modify or refine those terms. Two other important categories of difference must be included, the historical and the geographical. We study women of differ-ent times and places not simply for elements in common, but equally importantly for the ways in which they differ.

Sixth, feminist researchers try hard not to treat the subjects of their research as an inferior object. Knower and known belong to the same uni-verse, and we gain from acknowledging this. Equality and cooperation are necessary in research; student and teacher in dialogue will also learn from each other.

Finally, there is the role of what is called theory in Women's Studies – or rather theories because there are many different, indeed competing ones. Jackie Stacey (1993: 50) offers a useful definition:

> The term 'feminist theory' generally suggests a body of knowledge which offers critical explanations of women's subordination. By 'criti-cal' I mean that the explanation does not seek to reinforce or legiti-mate, but rather attempts to undermine, expose or challenge, women's subordination. It also tends to operate at *some* level of abstraction, using analytical categories which move beyond the merely descriptive or anecdotal, and at some level of generalization moving beyond the individual case.

There has been debate about the value of theory, and students may shy away from it at first because exploring matters through abstract concepts is undeniably hard and probably unfamiliar. But the experiences we are trying to understand are complex, and theories help. At their best they free us from our blinkers, point out our own hidden assumptions, give us a clearer understanding and develop new forms of knowledge. Theories can be studied on their own, but they inform all aspects of Women's Studies, and in this textbook you'll be introduced to them through their application to a wide range of subjects. You will find that any specialized terms are explained within the chapters or in their endnotes.

To sum up, here is one working definition of Women's Studies. Women's Studies as academic discipline has at least three dimensions. It involves the study of the way gender relations have operated in social life in the past and the present. It encompasses the study of representations of women's experiences in, for example, literature, language and religion. It includes the study of concepts used to differentiate women and men, such as fem-ininity and masculinity. In addition it examines theoretical perspectives on all the above, particularly those drawn from feminist theory.

The first three parts of this textbook take up these three main dimen-sions. Rather than give you a general survey of each one, we shall intro-duce you to each of these key elements by a group of essays which explore selected aspects. The topics have been chosen as introductory, representative examples. They are not set up as *the* most important areas. All topics are important in Women's Studies, and here are 23 of them! Every year at Lancaster we include different material, depending on what expertise we have available, and in this way the course keeps evolving. We want to draw attention to the huge diversity of material which can be included in each section, and encourage you to think beyond these specific cases.

Central to the project of Women's Studies as defined above is the understanding that, in the words of Simone de Beauvoir (1972: 295), 'One is not born but rather becomes, a woman', that is to say, we can provide a social explanation for the differences between women's and men's lives. 'Gender relations', the key term here, refers to the ways in which social life, both in the past and the present, has created structures in which women and men have particular roles and rights. Patriarchy (in the original Greek, the rule of the father in a family or tribe) is the term now used by feminists for this systematic organization of male supremacy and female subordination socially, politically, economically and culturally, but as we shall clearly see throughout this volume, patriarchy is not one monolithic power structure, and instead takes many different forms and governs relationships in various ways.

This textbook begins with a section which examines the position of women in various social institutions and organizational structures, including work, the family, romantic love and educational and religious systems. The chapters in this part examine the production of gender inequality in these contexts. They also explore the ways in which power relations have been contested within these institutions, and how they have withstood these challenges.

Given the social construction of femininity, it is also important to distinguish between our experiences and the images we meet of these in the arts, media and other cultural texts, and we need also to explore how our experiences are affected by those images. (This is not a simple split between actuality and image, but a two-way influence). The key word here is 'representation', a term which again points to the cultural construction of experience, in particular, the processes by which cultures construct images and through these images create meaning. These processes also involve consumers, spectators and readers. Part II of this volume explores aspects of these issues through six examples.

Part III considers the way in which gender identities are socially constructed and their relation to biology, that is it explores ideas of what is 'feminine' (that is, culturally defined) as opposed to 'female' (biological sex). The crucial distinction explored here is between 'sex' (biological difference) and 'gender' (the social interpretations of that biological difference). Part III investigates how norms are constructed culturally in different societies and how these can be challenged.

The overarching theme throughout this textbook, structuring every essay, is Women, Power, Resistance. We shall be investigating first what is the nature of power in each area of study; second, how and why women have been and are excluded, subordinated and marginalized in different ways and in many areas of society and culture; and third (because this is not a course only about oppression), how women have found ways of resisting this subordination, both inside those power structures and outside them. The book's final part, 'Women and political change', focuses on the third element, resistance, looking at the historical development of feminism and at contemporary forms of activism both in Britain and internationally. These will again underline both shared experiences of oppression and also the differences among women and their politics. This course is about change. If it provides us with the knowledge that things are not 'natural' but constructed and gives us a comparative understanding of differences over time, space, race, class and sexualities, then we can see that change is not only possible but happening.

○ **Acknowledgements**

Many thanks to Beverley Skeggs for her helpful comments on a draft of this chapter.

○ **Questions**

> 1 In what ways does your experience of education (school, college, university) reflect a 'politics of knowledge'? To what extent have you seen feminist principles in practice?
>
> 2 What does 'feminism' mean to you? Write your response, and bring it to class or share it with interested friends.
>
> 3 What is meant by the 'politics of difference', and why is it important to feminism?
>
> 4 This chapter began with some awkward questions from imaginary (though all too real) speakers about Women's Studies. How would you now answer them?

○ **Further reading**

> Discussions of Women's Studies both as an academic project and in connection with wider feminist issues keep being updated and revised. A good place to start looking at major subject areas, issues and debates is Bowles and Duelli-Klein (1983), Richardson and Robinson (1993), the four anthologies edited by Gunew (1991), Humm (1992), Jackson et al. (1993) and Evans (1994), and the four

volumes in the Open University series by Bonner *et al.* (1992),
Crowley and Himmelweit (1992), Kirkup and Keller (1992) and Mc-
Dowell and Pringle (1992). Aaron and Walby (1991), Hinds *et al.*
(1992), Kennedy *et al.* (1993) and Griffin *et al.* (1994) continue
ongoing debates about feminist teaching and research. Rich (1980),
Langland and Grove (1981) and Spender (1981) are early explorations of pedagogical issues. Culley and Portuges (1985), Thompson
and Wilcox (1989) and Davis *et al.* (1994) continue exploration of this
area. Stanley and Wise (1993) is an important discussion of the
principles of feminist research. Introductions to feminism (both
theories and practical dimensions) include Jaggar (1983), Mitchell
and Oakley (1986), Barrett (1988), Humm (1989), and Lovell (1990).
Ramazanoglu (1989), Hirsch and Keller (1990) and Spelman (1990)
focus on issues of difference, with hooks (1984,) Lorde (1984), and
James and Busia (1993) addressing black feminisms. For readings on
lesbian issues, see the extensive list of references at the end of Robbie
Smith's chapter in this volume.

## References

Aaron, J. and Walby, S. (eds) *Out of the Margins: Women's Studies in the Nineties.*
London: Falmer Press.
Barrett, M. (1988) *Women's Oppression Today: The Marxist/Feminist Encounter* (rev.
edn). London: Verso.
Beauvoir, S. de (1972) *The Second Sex* (trans. and ed. H. M. Parshley). London: Penguin.
Bonner, F., Goodman, I., Allen, R., Janes, L. and King, C. (eds) (1992) *Imagining
Women: Cultural Representations and Gender.* Cambridge: Polity Press.
Bowles, G. and Duelli-Klein, R. (eds) (1983) *Theories of Women's Studies.* London:
Routledge.
Crowley, H. and Himmelweit, S. (eds) (1992) *Knowing Women: Feminism and Know-
ledge.* Cambridge: Polity Press.
Culley, M. and Portuges, C. (eds) (1985) *Gendered Subjects: The Dynamics of Feminist
Teaching.* London: Routledge.
Davis, S., Lubelska, C. and Quinn, J. (eds) (1994) *Changing the Subject: Women in
Higher Education.* London: Taylor and Francis.
Evans, M. (ed.) (1994) *The Woman Question* (2nd edn). London: Sage.
Griffin, G., Roseneil, S., Hester, M. and Rai, S. (eds) (1994) *Stirring It: Challenges for
Feminism.* London: Taylor and Francis.
Gunew, S. (ed.) (1991) *A Reader in Feminist Knowledge.* London: Routledge.
Hinds, H., Phoenix, A. and Stacey, J. (eds) (1992) *Working Out: New Directions for
Women's Studies.* London: Falmer Press.
Hirsch, M. and Keller, E. F. (eds) (1990) *Conflicts in Feminism.* New York: Routledge.
hooks, b. (1984) *Feminist Theory: From Margin to Centre.* London: South End
Press.
Humm, M. (1989) *The Dictionary of Feminist Theory.* Brighton: Harvester.
Humm, M. (ed.) (1992) *Feminisms: A Reader.* Hemel Hempstead: Harvester.
Jackson, S., Atkinson, K., Beddoe, D., Brewer, T., Faulkner, S., Hucklesby, A.,

Pearson, R., Power, H., Prince, J., Ryan, M. and Young, P. (eds) (1993) *Women's Studies: A Reader*. Hemel Hempstead: Harvester Wheatsheaf.

Jaggar, A. (1983) *Feminist Politics and Human Nature*. Brighton: Harvester.

James, S. M. and Busia, A. P. A. (eds) (1993) *Theorizing Black Feminisms: The Visionary Pragmatism of Black Women*. London: Routledge.

Kennedy, M., Lubelska, C. and Walsh, V. (1993) *Making Connections: Women's Studies, Women's Movements, Women's Lives*. London: Taylor and Francis.

Kirkup, G. and Keller, L. S. (eds) (1992) *Inventing Women: Science, Technology and Gender*. Cambridge: Polity Press.

Langland, E. and Grove, W. (eds) (1981) *A Feminist Perspective in the Academy: The Difference It Makes*. Chicago, IL: University of Chicago Press.

Lorde, A. (1984) *Sister Outsider: Essays and Speeches*. Freedom, CA: The Crossing Press.

Lovell, T. (ed.) (1990) *British Feminist Thought: A Reader*. Oxford: Blackwell.

McDowell, F. and Pringle, R. (eds) (1992) *Defining Women: Social Institutions and Gender Divisions*. Cambridge: Polity Press.

Mitchell, J. and Oakley, A. (eds) (1986) *What Is Feminism?* Oxford: Blackwell.

Ramazanoglu, C. (1989) *Feminism and the Contradictions of Oppression*. London: Routledge.

Rich, A. (1980) Toward a woman-centered university, in *On Lies, Secrets, and Silence*. London: Virago.

Rich, A. (1987) What does a woman need to know?, in *Blood, Bread, and Poetry: Selected Prose 1979–1985*. London: Virago.

Richardson, D. and Robinson, V. (eds) (1993) *Introducing Women's Studies*. London: Macmillan.

Skeggs, B. (1997) *Culture, Identity and Respectability*. London: Sage.

Spelman, E. V. (1990) *Inessential Woman: Problems of Exclusion in Feminist Thought*. London: Women's Press.

Spender, D. (ed.) (1981) *Men's Studies Modified: The Impact of Feminism on the Academic Discipline*. London: Pergamon.

Stacey, J. (1993) Untangling feminist theory, in D. Richardson and V. Robinson (eds) *Introducing Women's Studies*. London: Macmillan.

Stanley, L. and Wise, S. (1993) *Breaking Out Again: Feminist Ontology and Epistemology* (2nd edn). London: Routledge.

Thompson A. and Wilcox, H. (eds) (1989) *Teaching Women: Feminism and English Studies*. Manchester: Manchester University Press.

# PART I

## The social organization of gender relations

In the first part of the book, we explore some of the ways in which gender inequalities are institutionalized. We examine the family, romantic love, paid work, education and religion as social institutions in the sense of sets of relationships between people which are seen as fundamental for society, and in which arrangements are prescribed by culture and regulation. We ask how women are affected by the organization of gender relations in these social institutions.

Janet Finch considers whether the family is 'the source of all our discontents' as women. Wendy Langford takes a close look at the way power operates in the emotional relationship upon which families are supposed to be founded – love. One of the issues raised in the first two chapters of this part concerns the effects of economic equality on relations between men and women. Carole Truman reviews the potential for achieving such equality through paid work. Next Rosemary Deem introduces us to ideas about the ways organizations embody gender relations, focusing on educational organizations, from nursery schools to universities. As in the case of paid work, equal opportunities strategies may provide sites of resistance to the dominant theme of women's subordination in organizations. Deborah Sawyer also uses organizational models, though in relation to a different sort of social institution, Christian religion. Finally Hiroko Kawanami introduces us to the position of women within the Buddhist faith which dominates much of southern, central and eastern Asia.

# Women, 'the' family and families

When Edmund Leach (1968) first made the claim in 1967 that 'the family is the source of all our discontents' he was not viewing families through the lens of gender. Indeed when he wrote this the second wave of feminism was just beginning to gain strength in Britain and an analysis which places gender at the heart of our understanding of families was only just developing. But in the subsequent development of feminist thought Leach's description could be taken as an accurate summary of the writings of many feminists on this issue.

Certainly the dominant feminist thought of the subsequent 20 years saw entrapment in the family as fundamental to women's oppression (however defined), and resistance to such entrapment as essential to their liberation (Barrett 1980; Young *et al.* 1981; Edholm 1991). However this 'orthodox' feminist analysis has been increasingly challenged as representing the pre-occupations of white, middle-class women; as a consequence feminist analyses of the family have become more diverse and in some ways more muted. Feminist writers who represent the perspectives of women in the third world, or women of colour, or women who are physically less abled have all questioned whether the family is necessarily and inevitably the main source of women's oppression (Ramazanoglu 1989; Charles 1993). Of course what the terms 'oppression' and 'liberation' mean – indeed whether they are appropriate terms at all – are themselves debated. But for the purposes of this chapter I shall assume that most feminist writers would endorse the sentiments expressed by Mary Wollstonecraft two centuries ago when she wrote, 'I [only] wish women to have power . . . over themselves'.

Feminist thought has long seen the family as the major obstacle to most women's ability to have 'power over themselves'. In this chapter I shall build on the different strands in feminist thought in order to answer the questions: *Is* the family the source of all our discontents as women? Must families necessarily and inevitably be seen as the key to women's oppression, as orthodox feminist thought would have it?

## ○ 'The' family and families

My starting point for answering this question is that the word 'family' conveys a wide variety of different meanings in the English language. Sometimes it refers to the group of people who share the same household (as in 'family size' packets of cereal); sometimes it means parents and their children (as in 'starting a family'); sometimes it denotes the wider kin group, composed of people who can trace their relationships through a 'family tree'. We could go on extending this list.

In such circumstances, we need to think carefully about which aspect of 'family' we are focusing on when we ask questions about its impact on women's lives. Within feminist thought over the last 30 years, the argument that the family is fundamental to women's oppression has really been a critique of one meaning of 'family', namely the nuclear family household. This refers to a group based on a heterosexual couple, sharing a home with their own children whilst they are young but not with anyone else. Feminists have seen this arrangement as detrimental to women because 'the family' in this sense embodies a particular definition of gender relations, conventionally allocating to a man the role of breadwinner and to a woman the role of homemaker and making women both dependent upon and subordinate to men (McIntosh 1979).

It is of course not surprising that feminist critiques should have concentrated on this meaning of 'family', since in many ways it is the most commonly used meaning of the term. But more importantly it represents what we might think of as the *dominant form* of the family in Britain and societies like it.

By calling it the 'dominant' form of the family I am using that term in two senses. The first is statistical, referring to the 'dominant' form of household as the type of living arrangements experienced by the majority of the population. Is the nuclear family household the dominant form of family in this sense? That question is actually quite a complex one because we all change the types of household in which we live over the course of our lifetimes. If we take a snapshot of household composition at any given point in time, only a minority of the population is living in a household composed of a married couple plus dependent children. For England, the figure was 24 per cent in 1992 (*Social Trends* 1994).

However if we ask how many of the population have *ever* lived in such a household, the answer would be that almost everyone has lived in a classic nuclear family household at some point either as a child or as an adult or both. The great majority of women do marry and most also have children. For example, of women born in 1951, over 90 per cent had married at least once by the time they reached their fortieth birthday (*Marriage and Divorce Statistics* 1991). Most also have children, for example an estimated 78 per cent for women born in 1955 (*Birth Statistics* 1992).

On this basis it looks as if motherhood is still very popular. However are women rejecting marriage (or cohabitation with a heterosexual partner) as part of the package associated with motherhood? This again is a rather complex question to answer because we can say how many women are bringing up children without men, but we cannot be sure how many of those have positively chosen to live in this way. In 1991 there were just over one million women bringing up children alone in Great Britain (*Social Trends* 1994). Since the great majority of single parents are women who have been married but who are now separated or divorced, it looks as if we can say that most women at least are inclined to try the conventional package of marriage/cohabitation-plus-children even if it does not work out, for whatever reason. Certainly the figures do not really support the view that women are positively rejecting marriage or heterosexual cohabitation in large numbers. The popularity of remarriage after the first attempt has ended adds further weight to that conclusion.

There is also a second sense in which the nuclear family household is the 'dominant' form, and if anything this is of greater importance than its dominance in a statistical sense. The idea that a married couple plus their children is what counts as a 'real' family is a pervasive and powerful idea in our society (Bernades 1985). In terms of beliefs, values and images the dominance of this family form has by no means been undermined. If anything its dominance is growing, as politicians of various persuasions talk about 'strengthening family life'. Almost always this means strengthening *this kind* of family life, in which married partners stay together, in which parents' lives are focused around caring for and controlling their children and, often, in which women give priority to their role as mothers over other options (Abbott and Wallace 1992).

It is important therefore to distinguish between the use of the term 'the' family which carries this kind of ideological loading and refers to one particular form of family, and the use of the plural term 'families' which is more neutral and acknowledges that families may come in different shapes and sizes. If we look at it this way we can see that the orthodox feminist critique is actually a critique of 'the' family primarily, perhaps exclusively.

In the rest of this chapter I shall concentrate on exploring whether 'the' family is necessarily and inevitably detrimental to women and whether the same arguments apply to other family forms. I shall do this by considering first the situation of women who live inside 'the' family, moving then to women who live outside this particular family form.

## ○ Women inside 'the' family

What are the consequences for women who do live within the context of 'the' family? Does the family represent a major factor which restricts opportunities and which puts women into a position subordinate to men, as many feminists have argued?

In order to answer this question properly, we need to consider in a little more detail the distinctive form of gender relations characteristic of 'the' family. In other societies, at other historical times, there have been wide variations (Edholm 1991). So how did the relationships characteristic of 'the' family come to be the dominant form? Feminist scholarship, especially the work of feminist historians has been very important in uncovering the answers to these questions (Hall 1979; McIntosh 1979; Barrett 1980; Walby 1986). The analyses which they have produced links 'the' family and its distinctive gender relations with the industrial revolution. This brought fundamental changes in the way in which productive work was organized, bringing large numbers of people together into working units and employing them for wages. This meant a physical separation between the workplace and the home, with the wage packet as the main economic link.

This reorganization of economic life set the scene for a reordering of gender relations in a number of ways. There was economic pressure for women to concentrate on making sure that the male labour force was fed, cared for and prepared for their daily work, only taking on waged work themselves at times of labour shortage or acute family poverty. There was also moral and religious pressure for women to concentrate their efforts on the home, and to be a civilizing force on the unruly masses who lived in the growing new industrial towns, as they were perceived by those who held political and economic power. Third, the growing trade union movement increasingly pressed for women to be excluded from certain types of work and for men's wages to be high enough to cover the costs of maintaining a wife and children as well as themselves. As a consequence the physical separation between the home and the workplace came increasingly to be associated with a division of labour between women and men, and a separation of the world into 'public' spheres which were the province of men and 'private', domestic spheres which were the province of women.

My rendering of this story is inevitably a crude oversimplification. There are lively debates among feminist and other scholars about many of the details; but the broad parameters of this account have been widely accepted and have been very influential in shaping feminist thinking about the importance and the persistence of 'the' family.

The real debate focuses on questions of change and diversity. Are women still defined and confined by this dominant family form as much as they were in the past? Where women now are living 'inside' this family form, can they renegotiate its consequences in terms of gender relations? Must living in a nuclear family household mean inevitably that women are subjected to the power of men, as some feminists would argue?

These questions can be tackled in a number of different ways. One major focus of recent research has been concerned with the domestic division of labour, and how far it has been renegotiated by contemporary women living in heterosexual partnerships. Very few women now expect to be without an income of their own and wholly dependent on the male wage, except perhaps for a short period while they have very young children. This suggests that one of the key foundations of male power in 'the' family has been steadily eroded. Does this mean that women no longer have to specialize in being homemakers and can move as readily as men can between the public world and the domestic sphere?

The idea that contemporary marriages (and cohabiting partnerships) can work on the basis of equality and sharing is not new. The notion of marriage becoming a 'companionate' partnership can be traced certainly to the years immediately following the second world war if not before (Finch and Summerfield 1991). More recent evidence suggests that many couples still express commitment to an ideal of equal partnership but that this is not necessarily reflected in the way in which their lives are organized (Brannen and Moss 1988; Mansfield and Collard 1988; Pahl 1989; Morris 1990).

Perhaps the best test case of change within 'the' family comes from studies of male unemployment. Here we have a situation in which men no longer enjoy the responsibilities and rights associated with being the breadwinner – always seen as the key foundation of male power in 'the' family. Does this change mean that gender relations alter radically, that the division of labour changes and that women are no longer in a subordinate position? The evidence is ambiguous at best. Having reviewed a range of British and American studies on this issue, Lydia Morris (1990) has concluded that though being unemployed appears to free men to take a more active role in domestic work and organization, there is little evidence that men do exchange paid work for unpaid domestic work, except at the margins. Indeed there is evidence of male resistance to this because it might undermine their position in the household, which rests on their previous breadwinner status.

To summarize the discussion in this section, we can say that it is difficult to reach a clear conclusion on the question of whether living inside 'the' family necessarily and inevitably puts women in a subordinate position to men. Certainly the evidence suggests that less change has occurred in reality than would be implied by the rhetoric that marriage is now an 'equal partnership'. But this still leaves open the question: *can* women live within 'the' family without being placed in a dependent and subordinate position?

The answer to this question probably depends ultimately on whether we are talking about individual women, or women in general. Some individual women may well be resourceful enough to resist the form of gender relations conventionally associated with 'the' family and to ensure that they are neither defined nor confined by it. However to do this successfully, the conditions must be right. If a woman is to avoid economic dependence on a man's income she must be able to command a secure income of her own on the same scale as his. If a woman is to avoid being defined as the person who specializes in caring for home and children, she must be able to organize these matters in other ways – either by persuading her male partner to specialize in being the homemaker or by being able to pay someone else to be responsible for domestic and childcare tasks.

As soon as we start spelling out the conditions which make it possible to live in 'the' family, but under a different set of gender relations, we see that the conditions which would make it possible are not available to most women. The labour market still puts men in an advantaged position, making it difficult for most women to command a consistent and secure income comparable with that of a male partner. In 1993 the average female weekly earnings was about £220 per week, whereas the average for men was just over £300 (*Social Trends* 1994). Full-time childcare is available but at a price which many women cannot afford (Brannen and Moss 1988).

In other words our society, and others like it, is still organized in a way which presumes the dominant model of the family, including the gendered division of labour associated with that. Taking the position of women in general therefore, living within 'the' family does still imply a package which includes a conventional division of labour, albeit perhaps in a modified form.

## Women outside 'the' family

There are many circumstances in which women may live outside the dominant form of the family. Amongst the most common of these circumstances is being a single parent and bringing up children without a man. Simply living alone is another. Some women choose to live in partnerships with other women. Some women live in households which extend to three or more generations or include members of their wider kin group. In Britain this is most likely to apply to women of Asian descent. Any of these circumstances may be combined with an experience of close family ties outside the household, which means that women's experience of family life has many different dimensions (Finch and Mason 1993).

Thinking about these different circumstances expands our horizons in discussions about families and puts into a different perspective the question: is family life always and necessarily a key to women's oppression? We could go through each of these circumstances in turn, posing that question and probably answering it in slightly different ways. In this chapter I have chosen to focus on just one of the circumstances where women live outside 'the' family, the situation of women bringing up children as single parents.

The number of households headed by a single parent has been growing fast in Britain in the last 20 years. Most of these households are headed by women who have been in a married or cohabiting partnership which has now ended. In these circumstances women live in a household without a resident man but otherwise composed in the same way as 'the' family. What does the absence of a resident man mean for women's lives and opportunities? Does this version of a family overcome the negative consequences of 'the' family from the perspective of women?

On the surface it looks as if the absence of a resident man removes one of the main feminist objections to 'the' family, namely that each woman has a man able to exercise day-to-day control over her life. Certainly if a woman has been subjected to violence by her former male partner, his removal from the household has obvious positive consequences and means that she is no longer under the daily power of a man in the physical sense.

However it would be naive to presume that living as a female single parent automatically removes women from all the controls which a male partner might wish to exercise over them. As the French feminist writer Christine Delphy pointed out, divorce may simply mean that a man's control over his former wife takes different forms (Delphy 1976). Especially if they still have young children, they will be obliged to maintain a continuing relationship with each other and – in most circumstances where the care of the children is allocated to the mother – this means that a man still has the right to influence how his former wife organizes her life.

These points are illustrated in a number of studies of separated and divorced women including, for example, work on the consequences of the legislation operated by the Child Support Agency (CSA) in Britain. This is the government body with the responsibility to ensure that separated and divorced fathers pay maintenance for the upkeep of their children. In a study of women who potentially were clients of the CSA, it was apparent that many would prefer to live without the financial support collected by the agency because their male partners believed that paying maintenance gave them the right to dictate the terms on which their children would be raised (Clark *et al.* 1993).

This leads to another important point about the consequences of being a single parent: poverty. Though of course there is considerable variation in individual circumstances, in general there is a strong association between being a female single parent and having a low income. For single mothers, income from the state is often more important than income from the labour market, reflecting the severe difficulties of combining employment and childcare without the support of a partner. Around two-thirds of single mothers are dependent on income support at any given time, and about four-fifths have had to rely on it at some point while they were bringing up their children. This state benefit represents a minimum income level, and there is a great deal of evidence to suggest that bringing up children on a very low income makes it extremely difficult to create a lifestyle which meets basic standards of health and comfort (Graham 1993).

The underlying reason for the association between single parenthood and poverty is that a woman with the responsibility for bringing up children fits badly into a society whose economic and social arrangements still are based on the dominant model of 'the' family. The idea that one parent earns the wages whilst the other looks after the children simply cannot be made to fit the circumstances of single parents of either sex. Female single parents – who of course are the great majority – have the further difficulty that, even if they can solve the problem of doing paid work whilst also looking after their children, the income which most can command is very low.

We can see therefore that the dominant model of 'the' family has a significant and continuing impact on women who live outside it as single parents. At an individual level, separation from a male partner does not mean that a woman can be completely free of the gender relations which characterize 'the' family. At the level of material survival, most female single parents are bound to struggle because economic life is still organized to allow men to earn an income which will support a family much more readily than women can, and in a way which makes it difficult to combine the roles of breadwinner and carer for children. We can add to this a pressure at the ideological level, from which no single parent really can escape, which defines their circumstances as an inferior form of family life. Precisely because 'the' family is the dominant model in this sense the public image of single parent families is that they are not 'real' families. They are literally families with something missing. Thus at an ideological as well as a practical level the dominant form of family remains a potent force in the lives of those who live outside it as well as those who live within it.

○ **Conclusion**

So from a feminist perspective, can we say that the family does remain the source of all the discontents of women? Is it – in the sense which feminist writing has implied – the key to women's oppression?

In this chapter I have distinguished between 'the' family and other family forms and suggested that the gender relations characteristic of the dominant family form are indeed a key to understanding women's place in the social world. The real issue is how far this is changing, and whether it is possible for individual women to change it in their own lives.

It is possible to interpret the evidence about this change in different ways, and these differences would correspond to some extent to different positions in feminist theorizing. My own argument has been that the gender relations characteristically associated with 'the' family may have been modified somewhat in recent years but essentially they remain in place. They continue to have an important impact both on women who live inside and those who live outside 'the' family. Certainly some women try to establish different forms of gender relations inside as well as outside the dominant form of family life, and some achieve a notable measure of success. For them, Mary Wollstonecraft's desire that women should have 'power over themselves' may have been fulfilled. But ability to succeed requires commitment – a persistence in going against the grain of social life. It also requires circumstances which are particularly favourable, especially that they are favourable to a woman's establishing a clear and consistent economic independence. Realistically, one must conclude that such circumstances apply only to a rather small minority of women, even at the end of the twentieth century.

○ **Questions**

> 1 This chapter has used single parents as the example of women who live outside 'the' family. Select any other group of women who live outside 'the' family and consider whether the same arguments

apply. Does living in different circumstances remove all the constraints which 'the' family creates for women who live inside it?

2 Collect examples from your local newspaper of stories about both women and men taking part in public life (e.g. speaking at public meetings, taking the lead on behalf of their company, on the local council). Analyse the ways in which these stories are presented and consider: Do women's family roles seem to intrude into their public lives more than men's? If so, in what ways?

3 Read Chapter 2 'Settling down' in Graham (1993). In the light of this chapter, consider: Given that women now have the means to control their own fertility, why do the great majority of women still become mothers?

○ **Further reading**

There is no single book which covers all the material discussed in this chapter. Classic discussions of the argument that the family is the source of women's oppression are to be found in McIntosh (1979) and in Chapter 6 of Barrett (1980). More recent ideological movements which have reinforced 'the' family are analysed by Abbott and Wallace (1992). In relation to evidence about the reality of women's family lives, Morris (1990) provides a comprehensive summary of research on households up to the late 1980s; Abercrombie and Warde (1992) provide a collection of chapters which summarize and discuss 15 studies on families and households. Brannen and Moss (1988) discuss the particular situation of women trying to combine motherhood with paid work and Graham (1993) is concerned specifically with single parent families; both are accessible and interesting studies.

○ **References**

Abbott, P. and Wallace, C. (1992) *The Family and the New Right*. London: Pluto Press.
Abercrombie, N. and Warde, A. (1992) *Social Change in Contemporary Britain*. Cambridge: Polity.
Bernades, J. (1985) Do we really know what 'the family' is?, in P. Close and R. Collins (eds) *Family and Economy in Modern Society*. London: Macmillan.
Barrett, M. (1980) *Women's Oppression Today*. London: Verso.
*Birth Statistics* (1992) Office of Population, Censuses and Surveys. London: HMSO.
Brannen, J. and Moss, P. (1988) *New Mothers at Work: Employment and Child Care*. London: Unwin.
Charles, N. (1993) *Gender Divisions and Social Change*. Hemel Hempstead: Harvester Wheatsheaf.
Clark, D., Lewis, J. and Morgan, D. (1993) *Whom God Hath Joined*. London: Routledge.

Delphy, C. (1976) Continuities and discontinuities in marriage and divorce, in S. Allen and D. Leonard Barker (eds) *Sexual Divisions and Society*. London: Tavistock.

Edholm, F. (1991) The unnatural family, in M. Lovey *et al.* (eds) *The State or the Market*. London: Sage.

Finch, J. and Mason, J. (1993) *Negotiating Family Responsibilities*. London: Routledge.

Finch, J. and Summerfield, P. (1991) Social reconstructions and the emergence of companionate marriage 1945–59, in D. Clark (ed.) *Marriage, Domestic Life and Social Change*. London: Routledge.

Graham, H. (1993) *Hardship and Health in Women's Lives*. Hemel Hempstead: Harvester Wheatsheaf.

Hall, C. (1979) The early formation of Victorian domestic ideology, in S. Burman (ed.) *Fit Work For Women*. London: Croom Helm.

Leach, E. (1968) *A Runaway World? Reith Lectures 1967*. London: BBC.

McIntosh, M. (1979) The welfare state and the weeds of the dependent family, in S. Burman (ed.) *Fit Work For Women*. London: Croom Helm.

Mansfield, P. and Collard, J. (1988) *The Beginning of the Rest of Your Life*. London: Macmillan.

*Marriage and Divorce Statistics* (1991) Office of Population Censuses and Surveys. London: HMSO.

Morris, L. (1990) *The Workings of the Household*. Cambridge: Polity.

Pahl, J. (1989) *Money and Marriage*. London: Macmillan.

Ramazanoglu, C. (1989) *Feminism and the Contradictions of Oppression*. London: Routledge.

*Social Trends* (1994) Central Statistical Office. London: HMSO.

Walby, S. (1986) *Patriarchy at Work*. Cambridge: Polity.

Wollstonecraft, M. (1792/1975) *A Vindication of the Rights of Women*. Harmondsworth: Penguin.

Young, K., Wolkowitz, C. and McCullagh, R. (1981) *Of Marriage and the Market*. London: CSE Books.

# 2 | WENDY LANGFORD

# Romantic love and power

There is perhaps no subject to which the famous feminist slogan that 'the personal is political' is more pertinent than that of romantic love. People generally find it difficult to comprehend how the dynamics of their personal relationships, let alone the deeply felt experience of 'falling in love', could be determined by relations of power. On the contrary, love is more often held to be the very antithesis of power, concerned with a private world of cooperation, caring and mutuality. Love has even been heralded as the enemy of power, something which can save us from oppression. This supposed dichotomy between love and power has however been seen by feminists to map onto another supposed dichotomy between the 'private' and the 'public' which, it is argued, supports the mistaken belief that power only manifests itself in the public sphere of life (Meyer 1991). Through challenging such ideas, feminists have developed crucial new analyses of how 'personal' areas such as sexuality, marriage, motherhood, friendship, and personal relationships are socially constructed and organized in ways which benefit men at the expense of women. Viewed in this way, romantic love can be seen as an important political and theoretical issue.

## ○ Women's 'religion'

The idea that romantic love might threaten women's interests has been around since the nineteenth century (Leach 1981). Here however I will concentrate on more recent feminist ideas, inspired in particular by the French philosopher Simone de Beauvoir. In *The Second Sex* (1949/1988) de Beauvoir mounts a devastating analysis of the psychological processes involved in heterosexual romance. She proposes that woman is defined as 'Other' by man, as a passive object, destined for a life in the sphere of 'immanence', that is the concerns of everyday life. Man, on the other hand, has defined himself as the 'One', the active subject who is capable of 'transcendence', that is a life oriented towards freedom. While the woman is denied the possibility of her own transcendence, the ideology of romantic love teaches her that her life can be meaningful and significant through devoting herself to finding and keeping a man.[1] Instead of seeking her own freedom, the woman comes to 'desire her enslavement so ardently that it will seem to her the expression of her liberty' (de Beauvoir 1949/1988: 653). Furthermore, because seeking freedom through submission is paradoxical, women have to engage in a whole series of damaging manipulations and self-deceptions in order to go on believing it is possible, undermining themselves further and reinforcing their failure to achieve their own transcendence. Woman's tendency to 'humble herself to nothingness' before man leads de Beauvoir to conclude that love is like a religion for women.

## ○ False consciousness

Intellectually inspired by de Beauvoir, feminist writers in the early 1970s contributed to a radical politicization of romantic love. Some early 'radical feminists' developed de Beauvoir's insight that women 'in love' engage in fantasy and delusion. Appropriating a Marxist model of power relations, 'The Feminists' (1973) argued that romantic love is a form of 'false consciousness' which prevents women from recognizing the reality of their exploitation by the 'ruling class', defined as all men, and prevents them from bonding with their own 'sex class'. The desire to fuse romantically with men in a hopeless attempt to overcome their own powerlessness shows that 'the phenomenon of love is the psychological pivot in the persecution of women' (Atkinson 1974: 43). Romantic love should therefore be seen as 'a pathological condition' which should be replaced by basing close human relationships on the more equal model of friendship (ibid.: 44).

There are however a number of problems with seeing romantic love simply as a form of 'false consciousness' which benefits a hostile ruling class. In particular, by defining all men and women as simply oppressors or oppressed, this approach tends to characterize heterosexual love relationships as *only* about the oppression of women: '[f]or the woman, love is always self-sacrifice . . . [a] frenzied passion which compels a woman to submit to a diminishing life in chains' (Dworkin 1976: 105). Such a formulation of the problem leaves no room for us to develop understandings of how women are able to *resist* male domination. Moreover, if men are defined only as hostile oppressors, it becomes theoretically impossible for male behaviour towards women ever to be non-oppressive. If, as feminists, our concern is to change the balance of power between men and women, we must not only be able to identify love relationships as oppressive, but be able to distinguish the harmful dynamics between individuals from those which are not harmful.

Some feminists have argued that attempting direct change in heterosexual relationships is not worthwhile, and that resistance is only possible if women cease engaging in relations with men altogether and bond only with other women. Many women have found 'sexual separatism' to be a positive and empowering experience. For other feminists however, it is not seen as a necessary or desirable strategy, often because their feminism must involve struggling against dimensions of power other than gender. For example, resisting capitalist, imperialist and racist domination involves many feminists in making important political and emotional bonds with men, even though these relationships may not be equal (Kanneh 1993; Yuval-Davies 1993). Furthermore, even if avoiding romantic relationships with men could 'solve' the love/power problem in theory, feminism still needs to address the deep and compelling emotional desires which disrupt 'rational' political choices. For heterosexual feminists, the desire for love relationships with men often means struggling with contradictions which cannot be eradicated in any simple way.

A further problem with the 'false consciousness' theory of romance is that, while it does not explicitly exclude homosexual love, it is based on an assumption of heterosexuality. Within such a model, love between men can only be conceived of as a conflictual relation between those intent on domination, thus denying the capacity of gay men to 'fall in love' with each other and experience deep feelings of tenderness. Defining women as powerless victims, on the other hand, makes lesbian love appear to be power-free, thus failing to account for the realities of power struggles between women. Furthermore, if it is the case that in western patriarchal cultures, women's desire for freedom is mutilated into self-sacrifice under the delusion of romantic love, what implications might this have for lesbian relationships?

○  **Politics of the ego**

While these kinds of questions remain largely unanswered, another version of early radical feminist theory on love seems potentially useful. Instead of depicting men and women as oppressors and oppressed by defi-nition, this develops de Beauvoir's emphasis on the psychological dynam-ics occurring between lovers. Men's power over women is seen to rest on the culturally developed ability of the male ego to have power over the female ego (New York Radical Feminists 1971).[2] These 'politics of the ego' are based, not in any direct desire on the part of men to hurt women, but through men's need to derive their own strength and self-esteem by over-riding women's independent sense of self. 'Love' in the context of our patriarchal culture is synonymous with a kind of submissive, ego-boosting behaviour which women are expected to show men, but not vice versa. The culture produces men who are 'emotional invalids'. Men's inability to love can make them seem weak and hopeless to women, but in fact the resulting one-way emotional relationships underpin the system of sexual inequality: '[male] culture is parasitical, feeding on the emotional strength of women without reciprocity' (Firestone 1979: 122).

The theory of the 'politics of the ego' has certain advantages, not only in direct application to romantic love, but in allowing parallels to be drawn between the psychological power dynamics of love relationships and those of other kinds of relationships. Although the institutions and practices of society make it much easier for men to occupy the position of the 'One' (the subject) and determine that women occupy the position of the 'Other' (the object), in relation to men, this is not the only dimension of power. The dominant culture may also be seen to support the occupation of the 'One' position by, for example, white people, able-bodied people and those in higher class positions. Furthermore, social hierarchies are not always straightforward. For example, a refusal to occupy the 'Other' position or even a strategic attempt to reverse the dynamics may be understood as strategies of resistance. The theory therefore potentially allows us to understand society as a complex web of power relations which are enacted at the individual level in terms of who recognizes whose point of view and who defers to whom. Romantic love could be seen as one of many sets of cultural beliefs which determine the form of these individual human inter-actions in ways which benefit particular social groups over others.

For those seeking to change the balance of power in love relationships, the 'politics of the ego' approach offers a useful framework. Relationships can be judged not simply by who is having them with whom, but in terms of whether both partners are benefiting equally from the liaison. In par-ticular, while altruism might be seen as an important feature of love relationships, denying the self can be dangerous. The self-denial which heterosexual romantic love demands of women led Simone de Beauvoir to posit 'genuine' love as an alternative. This would be

> founded on the mutual recognition of two liberties; the lovers would then experience themselves both as self and as other: neither would give up transcendence, neither would be mutilated ... For the one and the other, love would be a revelation of self and enrichment of the world.
>
> (de Beauvoir 1949/1988: 677)

However, while such a view of love can seem very appealing, the desire to attain it carries inherent dangers for women. While 'real life' romance with men disadvantages women, it could be argued that striving for an equal and reciprocal romantic relationship, a 'genuine love', a 'true love', is an investment of emotional energy which women are already too keen to make. Indeed it may be the fantasy of attaining such an ideal love that blinds women most to their own deep-rooted investments in an unequal system of love.

## ○ **Reading the romance**

The prevalence of romantic fantasy was seen by feminists in the 1970s as a major contributory factor to current 'politics of the ego'. Popular ro-mantic fiction in particular was seen as 'titillating mush', constituting a form of 'sterile self-deception' (Greer 1970: 188). Ironically however, while feminists dismissed romance, the 1980s and 1990s have seen an unprecedented boom in the already huge sales of romance fiction. Moreover, the wide appeal of romance to women of different classes, educational levels, political beliefs, and sexualities showed that feminists could not afford to ignore what is a 'primary category of the female imagination' (Snitow 1984: 274). Research in the areas of feminist literary and cultural studies has therefore sought to understand why romance reading is so popular with women and what meaning it has in their lives.

While some writers continued to stress that romance is an ideology which teaches girls and women a particular type of subservient femininity (e.g. Christian-Smith 1990), others argued that such an approach wrongly assumes readers to be passive dupes who soak up everything they are told and then reproduce it in real love relationships. Instead, romance reading is seen to be such a compelling activity precisely because it offers women the chance to achieve in fantasy what they cannot achieve in real life. For example, textual analyses of Harlequin romances (the US equivalent of Mills and Boon), reveal that the reader is offered the fantasy of overcoming men's indifference and dominance through identifying with a heroine who succeeds in taming a cold, arrogant hero (Modleski 1982; Snitow 1984). The texts offer women a place where they can negotiate and symbolically resolve the conflicts, tensions and anxieties that are involved in trying to achieve successful love relationships in real life: 'on balance the contradictions in women's lives are more responsible for the existence of Harlequins than Harlequins are for the contradictions' (Modleski 1982: 57). However, while fantasies of turning distant and brutal men into tender and considerate lovers might make women feel better, this may in itself be problematic. Likening romance to tranquillizers, Modleski argues that ultimately it may increase women's problems by defusing their resistance to oppression within love relationships (1982: 57).

The conclusions drawn from textual analysis are confirmed by studies which look at readers themselves. Janice Radway, for example, found that women read romance for two main reasons: as a pleasurable escape from the psychologically and emotionally draining task of caring for others, and as a vicarious way of experiencing attention and emotional gratification which they did not get in the rest of their lives. Radway concluded that 'all popular romantic fiction originates in the failure of patriarchal culture to satisfy its female members' and thus functions as 'a utopian wish-fulfilment fantasy' (1987: 151).

## ○ 'Real life' love

Women's real life dissatisfaction with heterosexual romantic love relationships has been documented by studies which have found women to be generally disappointed and frustrated with the lack of emotional intimacy in their love relationships with men (Hite 1988; Mansfield and Collard 1988; Duncombe and Marsden 1993). Hite's study also included lesbian relationships which women reported as more satisfying, although paradoxically, too much closeness tends to cause difficulties between women (Lindenbaum 1985). While there is clear evidence of widespread unhappiness among heterosexual women, there has been a notable lack of feminist analysis of 'real life' love problems. Only Hite addresses how women's frustrations reflect power relations. She argues that men's refusal to talk about their feelings, their expectations of receiving more emotional support than they give, their unwillingness to really 'see' their female partners, and their assumption that they will take first place psychologically in the relationship, are all evidence of an 'unequal emotional contract' which allows men to use 'emotional withholding' as a strategy of maintaining dominance.

Developing such analyses is crucial because there are indications that power in love relationships is extremely difficult to identify (Komter 1991; Meyer 1991). It is largely latent, working insidiously through shaping the subjectivity of the less powerful so that they see their disadvantaged position as normal and natural. In a study of marriage in the Netherlands, Aafke Komter (1989: 214) concluded that inequality is largely sustained by hidden power 'reflected in everyday understandings and legitimations of the status quo'. Like other researchers (Mansfield and Collard 1988; Duncombe and Marsden 1993), Komter also found that regardless of evidence to the contrary, couples were keen to present their relationships to researchers as being equal. This confirms that how people see their own relationships cannot be taken as a reliable indication of the balance of power between themselves and their partner, and further suggests that people's desire to conform to egalitarian ideals of caring and sharing may itself serve to mask the unequal nature of love relationships and help to construct the apparent dichotomy between love and power.

While the emotional dynamics of power remain largely hidden and unresearched, the proliferation of popular romance has been paralleled by a proliferation of relationship advice books, likewise aimed at a female audience. Feminist textual analysis has revealed the general failure of this genre to address questions of gendered power (Jackson 1989; Langford 1993). While authors all agree that there is an epidemic of 'love misery', explanations range from the claim that it is women's fault for picking the 'wrong men' (Cowan and Kinder 1986) to the claim that feminism has itself caused the problems through making women 'close their hearts' to men (Jeffers 1990). Challenging current forms of 'love' is not generally on the agenda, and while there has not been any research which has addressed how women actually use such texts, it could be claimed that while romance fiction 'recycles' women's discontent into an investment in the fantasy of reciprocity, self-help advice recycles it into encouraging women to do all within their power to 'save the relationship', regardless of the personal cost to themselves.

○  **'Fiction' and 'reality'**

The contrast between real life disappointments and compensatory fantasies can suggest a particular relationship between fantasy and reality:

'sometimes girls live out romance as a kind of antedote to their real lives' (Connell *et al.* 1981: 167). Through 'embroidering on reality', girls can inject drama and excitement into what are 'really' boring and unsatisfying relationships with boys (ibid.). However, some writers have argued that we should not necessarily regard female dissatisfaction as being directly caused by the failure of males to meet pre-existing emotional needs. It has been suggested that while romance-readers do indeed seek compensation for their unsatisfying love relationships, the novels they read may themselves help to create their disappointments through helping to construct the expectation that happiness and emotional fulfilment can be found through romance (Ganguly 1991; Belsey 1992).

The idea that our emotional experiences, including love, are determined by the culture in which we live is a challenging one. It means holding onto the realization that however real our emotions are, they are nevertheless 'socially ordered, linguistically mediated and culturally specific' (Jackson 1993: 39). Stevi Jackson suggests that in making sense of this claim, it is useful to think about romantic love as a 'narrative':

> We can identify with love stories not because they record some pre-existing emotion, but because our cultural tradition supplies us with the narrative forms with which we begin to be familiarized in childhood and through which we learn what love is. Narratives are not only encountered in novels, plays and films – they are very much part of everyday cultural competences. We constantly tell stories to ourselves and others and we continually construct and reconstruct our own biographies in narrative form. Hence subjectivity is in part constituted through narrative.
>
> (Jackson 1993: 46)

Jackson argues that the reason falling in love can feel like 'getting to star in your own movie' is not because the movie reflects real life (although it might do) or because real life is influenced by watching movies (although it might be), but because both movies and real life are partly produced through larger cultural narratives (sometimes also called 'scripts' or 'discourses').

Narratives of romantic love are themselves culturally and historically specific phenomena which are constantly being produced, reproduced, challenged and changed. And ironically, while feminists have argued that romantic love as we know it is a set of ideas and practices which benefit men at women's expense, feminist research has revealed that it is women themselves who are most likely to express their sense of self and experience their emotional life through narrativized accounts of romantic love relationships. For example, Sharon Thompson (1992) found that in interviews with 25-year-old males about their relationships with females, tales of disconnected sexual episodes were all her respondents could muster. In contrast 'almost every girl over 15 could tell, in virtually one three- or four-hour breath, a story of her own that was imbued with the discoveries, anguish and elation of intimate relations' (Thompson 1992: 351). The stories had a highly polished quality which showed they were well rehearsed:

These were the stories that teenage girls spend hundreds of hours telling each other, going over and over detail and possibility as part of the process of constructing and reconstructing sexual and existential meaning for themselves.

(ibid.)

The lack of boundaries between 'fact' and 'fiction' was evidenced by the emotions girls expressed as they 'wept and glowed' in the telling of their stories (ibid.).

## The cultural politics of romance

The involvement of females in producing narratives of romantic love has clear political consequences. As well as the disadvantages which the 'politics of the ego' themselves might bring, there is the question of what girls and women are not doing while they are involved in romantic concerns. Sharon Thompson (1992: 352) concluded that the lives of the teenage girls in her study were prone to being 'ruined by love', not so much in terms of what actually happened to them in relationships with boys, but 'by a propensity to stake precious time and lose heart at the gaming table of romance'. A textual analysis of *Jackie* magazine similarly revealed that 'the girl is encouraged to load all her eggs in the basket of romance and hope it pays off' (McRobbie 1981: 118). Even highly educated women interested in pursuing professions and involved in a wide range of activities and social networks have been found to be seduced by a strong 'culture of romance' among their peers which led them to opt out of high status careers into marriage and low-paid jobs (Holland and Eisenhart 1990).

Moreover romantic culture does not only involve women's emotional investment in patriarchal social systems, but is a peculiarly western model of love relationship which is being exported all over the world. As Ganguly argues,

romance novels rarely ever deviate from a compulsive ethnocentrism in which exotic locations are merely idyllic backdrops for the tall, dark, handsome and *white* hero to conduct his love affair with the heroine who, no matter how 'exotic' her looks, is also, of course, Caucasian and Christian.

(1991: 141)

The white, western character of romance can be seen to fuel racist and imperialist beliefs about the superiority of particular kinds of relational arrangements, particularly the mythology that relationships based on romantic love are characterized by 'freedom' and 'choice' and are thus automatically less oppressive to women than 'arranged' marriages (Amos and Parmar 1981).

To give another example, romance in its popular manifestations is also clearly a heterosexual narrative which constructs love relationships between men and women as the 'natural' way to find fulfilment. Such beliefs contribute to the predominance of heterosexuality as a 'compulsory' way of life which has been highlighted as particularly oppressive to women. Not only are lesbians marginalized, but the stigma and silence around lesbian lifestyles deprives all women of the chance to form affectionate, sexual and political bonds with each other (see Rich 1980). Women seeking love relationships are thus culturally coerced into seeking primary bonds with men, and while all love relationships may be power relationships, the 'politics of the ego' in heterosexual unions are likely to reinforce and reproduce male social dominance in predictable ways, which are hidden by being seen as freely chosen 'love' relationships. For example, the idea that women's domestic work and childcare is a 'labour of love' hides the fact that men benefit from the appropriation of women's unpaid labour (Comer 1974; Delphy and Leonard 1992).

## Rewriting the romance

The fact that it is largely women who produce romantic narratives need not be seen as entirely negative. Whereas earlier writers argued that feminists should simply reject romance, the realization that we are unable to step outside of the narratives through which we experience our emotional lives has led to the development of new ideas about resistance. Recent critics have suggested that if romance is a script, feminists can be involved in rewriting it, producing new and more liberatory versions of old and familiar plots. Indeed, Lynne Pearce and Jackie Stacey (1995) argue that such rewriting is well under way, as feminists have challenged and transformed traditional romantic conventions of gender, class, ethnicity and sexual preference. Romance no longer embodies a common meaning or set of values, but has become 'a *fractured* discourse that addresses some of us very differently from others' (1995: 24). Moreover, it is not only feminists who are rewriting romance. Even within popular fiction, romance does not have a static form but changes and adapts in accordance with social and cultural changes, including feminist critiques (Jones 1986). Nevertheless, it should be remembered that most romantic fiction is still produced by huge and powerful commercial operations which represent politically conservative interests, and that most romances still carry the message that for women, it is only through a meaningful encounter with a man that self-realization can ensue. Thus while retaining optimism about the impact of feminism upon dominant cultural narratives, the politics of romance must remain a central concern for feminists.

## Conclusion: love, power and resistance

Feminism has challenged the love/power dichotomy and confirmed romantic love as a patriarchal narrative which implicates women emotionally in a system of relationships which disadvantages them, and which upholds heterosexist, racist and imperialist values. Claims that feminists should therefore reject romantic love altogether, or at least reject heterosexual love, have given way to analyses which foreground the complexities of the relationship between power and love and suggest that feminists should seek to rewrite the romantic script rather than reject it completely. Such a strategy of resistance deserves serious consideration, especially in view of the apparent attraction of the romantic ideal for many women.

Nevertheless, cogent arguments can be made against it. However the script is rewritten, there is no guarantee that the other actors will play their new parts, especially if their power partly depends on maintaining the current 'politics of the ego'. Moreover, even if feminists succeed in 'writing out' all the inequalities and omissions in romance, perhaps we should finally consider whether investing our energies in the promise of salvation through an exclusive encounter with one other human being is the best way to realize our hopes for a better world.

○ **Questions and exercises**

> *Small group discussions*
>
> 1  Discuss whether you think the dominant narrative of romantic love should be rejected or simply changed. How would you change it?
>
> 2  List as many examples as you can of how the 'politics of the ego' might operate in a love relationship.
>
> *Written assignments*
>
> 1  Read a Mills and Boon romance (or similar). Discuss why you think the story might appeal to women, and describe what changes, if any, you would make to it, and why.
>
> 2  Read a popular self-help book on love relationships. Discuss the view of love that is put forward in the text. How far are issues of power considered?

○ **Further reading**

> Meyer (1991) discusses the supposed dichotomy between power and love. Douglas (1990) is a good resource if you are interested in radical feminist and lesbian theories on love and sexuality. Pearce and Stacey (1995) is a useful collection of essays representing a wide range of contemporary feminist thought on the subject of romance. An interesting resource for looking at women's experiences of love relationships is Hite (1988), although the book is short on analysis.

## ○ Notes

1 I am defining ideology here as a body of ideas, beliefs and representations that determines the way people live. It creates a 'reality' which establishes an imaginary relation of the individual to the world, and serves the interests of a particular power group.

2 'Ego' is used here in the sense of a person's image of themselves, especially in terms of self-importance.

## ○ References

Amos, V. and Parmar, P. (1961) Resistance and responses: the experiences of black girls in Britain, in A. McRobbie and T. McCabe (eds) *Feminism for Girls: An Adventure Story*. London: Routledge and Kegan Paul.

Atkinson, T. (1974) *Amazon Odyssey*. New York: Links Books.

Beauvoir, S. de (1949/1988) *The Second Sex*. London: Pan Books Ltd.

Belsey, C. (1992) True love: the metaphysics of romance, *Women: A Cultural Review*, 3(2): 181–92.

Christian-Smith, L. (1990) *Becoming a Woman Through Romance*. London: Routledge.

Comer, L. (1974) *Wedlocked Women*. Leeds: Feminist Books.

Connell, M., Davis, T., McIntosh, S. and Root, M. (1981) Romance and sexuality: between the devil and the deep blue sea? in A. McRobbie and T. McCabe (eds) *Feminism for Girls: An Adventure Story*. London: Routledge and Kegan Paul.

Cowan, C. and Kinder, M. (1986) *Smart Women, Foolish Choices: Finding the Right Men, Avoiding the Wrong Ones*. London: Bantam Books.

Delphy, C. and Leonard, D. (1992) *Familiar Exploitations*. London: Polity.

Douglas, C. A. (1990) *Love and Politics: Radical Feminist and Lesbian Theories*. San Francisco, CA: ism press.

Duncombe, J. and Marsden, D. (1993) Love and intimacy: the gender division of emotion and 'emotion work', *Sociology*, 27(2): 221–41.

Dworkin, A. (1976) *Our Blood: Prophecies and Discourses on Sexual Politics*. London: Harper and Row.

The Feminists (1973) The Feminists: a political organization to annihilate sex roles, in A. Koedt, E. Levine and A. Rapone (eds) *Radical Feminism*. New York: Quadrangle Books.

Firestone, S. (1979) *The Dialectic of Sex: The Case for Feminist Revolution*. London: Women's Press.

Ganguly, K. (1991) Alien[ated] readers: Harlequin Romances and the politics of popular culture, *Communication*, 12: 129–50.

Greer, G. (1970) *The Female Eunuch*. London: Granada.

Hite, S. (1988) *Women and Love: A Cultural Revolution in Progress*. London: Viking.

Holland, D. C. and Eisenhart, M. A. (1990) *Educated in Romance: Women, Achievement, and College Culture*. Chicago, IL: University of Chicago Press.

Jackson, C. (1989) 12 steps to heaven, *Trouble and Strife*, 17: 10–17.

Jackson, S. (1993) Love and romance as objects of feminist knowledge, in M. Kennedy, C. Lubelska and V. Walsh (eds) *Making Connections: Women's Studies, Women's Movements, Women's Lives*. London: Taylor and Francis.

Jeffers, S. (1990) *Opening Our Hearts to Men: Taking Charge of Our Lives and Creating a Love That Works*. London: Piatkus Ltd.

Jones, A. R. (1986) Mills and Boon meets feminism, in J. Radford (ed.) *The Progress of Romance: The Politics of Popular Fiction*. London: Routledge and Kegan Paul.

Kanneh, K. G. (1993) Sisters under the skin: a politics of heterosexuality, in S. Wilkinson and C. Kitzinger (eds) *Heterosexuality: A Feminism and Psychology Reader*. London: Sage.

Komter, A. (1989) Hidden power in marriage, *Gender and Society*, 3(2): 187–216.

Komter, A. (1991) Gender, power, and feminist theory, in K. Davis, M. Leijenaar and J. Oldersma (eds) *The Gender of Power*. London: Sage.

Langford, W. (1993) 'The sexual politics of loving too much: discourses of popular advice on heterosexual relationships'. Occasional paper, Lancaster: Centre for Women's Studies, Lancaster University.

Leach, W. (1981) *True Love and Perfect Union*. London: Routledge and Kegan Paul.

Lindenbaum, J. (1985) The shattering of an illusion: competition in lesbian relationships, *Feminist Studies*, 2(1): 86–7.

McRobbie, A. (1981) Just like a *Jackie* story, in A. McRobbie and T. McCabe (eds) *Feminism for Girls: An Adventure Story*. London: Routledge and Kegan Paul.

Mansfield, P. and Collard, J. (1988) *The Beginning of the Rest of Your Life: A Portrait of Newly-wed Marriage*. London: Macmillan.

Meyer, J. (1991) Power and love: conflicting conceptual schemata, in K. Davis, M. Leijenaar and J. Oldersma (eds) *The Gender of Power*. London: Sage.

Modleski, T. (1982) *Loving with a Vengeance: Mass-Produced Fantasies for Women*. London: Routledge.

New York Radical Feminists (1971) 1969 – politics of the ego: a manifesto for New York Radical Feminists, in J. Hole and E. Levine (eds) *Rebirth of Feminism*. New York: Quadrangle/The New York Times Book Co.

O'Connor, P. (1991) Women's experience of power within marriage: an inexplicable phenomenon? *Sociological Review*, 39(4): 823–42.

Pearce, L. and Stacey, J. (eds) (1995) *Romance Revisited*. London: Lawrence and Wishart.

Radway, J. (1987) *Reading the Romance*. London: Verso.

Rich, A. (1980) Compulsory heterosexuality and lesbian existence, *Signs*, 5(4): 631–60.

Snitow, A. B. (1984) Mass market romance: pornography for women is different, in A. Snitow, C. Stansell and S. Thompson (eds) *Desire: The Politics of Sexuality*. London: Virago.

Thompson, S. (1992) Search for tomorrow: on feminism and the reconstruction of teen romance, in C. Vance (ed.) *Pleasure and Danger: Exploring Female Sexuality*. London: Pandora Press.

Yuval-Davies, N. (1993) The (dis)comfort of being 'hetero', in S. Wilkinson and C. Kitzinger (eds) *Heterosexuality: A Feminism and Psychology Reader*. London: Sage.

# 3  CAROLE TRUMAN

# Paid work in women's lives: continuity and change

The study of women's work, both paid and unpaid, has been and remains an important area for Women's Studies. This is because it is within the institution of 'work' that inequalities between men and women are at their most visible. In most Organization for Economic Cooperation and Development (OECD) countries, women earn considerably less than men within the formal economy. Patterns of gender segregation lead to women and men doing different sorts of jobs, in different parts of the economy, at lower levels within organizations, and with different working patterns. Much of women's work has been invisible – because it is within the 'informal economy' or because it is unpaid. 'Work', therefore, is a topic that has been of interest to feminists from a range of academic disciplines including history, sociology, economics, geography and psychology, and a variety of different perspectives. The approach taken in this chapter is to explore ways in which the labour market is gendered, and the impact that this has on women's opportunities in paid employment. Feminists have made important contributions to the study of labour markets, work and employment. They have shown that labour markets are in their very nature gendered and that gender permeates the concepts and definitions of what constitutes 'work', including skill, work time, wage differentials, and the allocation and labelling of work. In what follows, we shall review these issues, pointing where appropriate to current debates about them.

## ○ The conceptualization of work in women's lives

The period since the second world war has been one of apparent change in women's paid employment in Great Britain. In general, women's participation in paid work has increased dramatically and this rise is predicted to continue. According to government statistics, women account for nearly half the workforce in Great Britain in the 1990s (Department of

Employment 1993). The proportion is expected to rise towards the end of the century when it is predicted that women will outnumber men in paid work (Hakim 1993). However, despite more women working, the conditions and rewards for women employees remain second-rate compared to men.

A major area of difference between men's and women's work is around what actually constitutes 'work' in the working day and the working week. Feminists have pointed out that for women, the term 'work' includes waged labour, and also a variety of forms of unwaged labour associated with households and communities. Unwaged domestic labour, care of young and elderly dependants are features of many women's working lives (see for example, Oakley 1974; Finch and Groves 1983; Yeandle 1984). That women take on an unfair proportion of this work is seen by some to be a root cause of women's oppression (a recent analysis of these debates can be found in Delphy and Leonard 1992). Other authors argue that women are open to exploitation through unpaid work because of the discrimination they face in paid employment (for example, Walby 1986). The interaction between paid and unpaid work in women's lives is central to our understanding of the inequalities that women experience. Tancred (1995) argues that the sociology of work has failed to make adequate use of feminist reconceptualizations of 'work' as experienced by women. She argues that feminist perspectives help us not only to understand women's experiences of work, but can also illuminate the changing contours of men's work.

Apart from unwaged domestic and care work, many women also undertake considerable work in their local communities in the form of voluntary work. This may include organizing activities for children, helping neighbours, organizing jumble sales, doing meals on wheels and so on. This type of activity, which is often unacknowledged as work, is an important way in which women contribute to community life (Deem 1986). Internationally, women's vital role in food production has frequently been ignored by development aid programmes. This has contributed to malnutrition and starvation in parts of Africa where it is estimated that 80 per cent of food is produced by women (Women's Feature Service 1992; Epstein 1993).

If women's work is open to a variety of different definitions, then it follows that it is difficult to measure. This is true, not only across the division between paid and unpaid work, but also in trying to quantify women's involvement in different forms of paid employment. Women's part-time employment, temporary, seasonal and home-based work have all been systematically overlooked or underrecorded by census enumerators and in official statistics (Hakim 1980, 1993). In Pakistan, the term 'statistical purdah' has been developed, after the official census recorded only 147 egg producers. This is work traditionally carried out by women in many households and its scale is clearly unrecognized (Allen and Truman 1993: 2). Economists have noted the problems of trying to measure women's work – for example Joshi and Owen suggest that measuring female activity rates is as variable as measuring a length of elastic (1987). Given this misrepresentation and underrecording of women's work in official statistics, feminists have pointed to the need to draw upon a variety of sources in order to build up a picture of women's work.

○ **The wages gap and the gendered labour market**

Despite legislation, there remains a persistent gap between women's wages and those of men.[1] On average, women still earn only 70 per cent of men's full-time hourly earnings. When comparing women in full-time manual occupations with men, the gap widens with women earning only 63 per cent of men's average weekly earnings (EOC 1994). Whilst the inequality in wages is stark, using aggregate figures may be misleading since the gendered nature of the labour market means that it is not possible to make direct comparisons between men's work and women's work. This is because of a number of important differences between patterns of men and women's paid work. These differences include the prevalence of women in part-time work; 'horizontal occupational segregation' whereby the labours market is divided into 'women's jobs' and 'men's jobs'; the undervaluing of skill in women's work; 'vertical segregation' where men predominate at the top of organizational hierarchies and women predominate at the lower levels; and finally, the differential prospects of men and women in a changing labour market. The chapter will now go on to consider each of these areas in turn.

○ **The part-time predicament**

According to government statistics, women comprise 90 per cent of the part-time workforce in Britain. Part-time work also constitutes an important source of employment for many women: 44 per cent of all women are part-time workers, whereas only 6 per cent of men work part-time. It is predicted that as the number of full-time jobs declines, the growth in part-time work will continue because part-timers are seen as constituting a 'flexible' workforce (Beechey and Perkins 1987). Hurstfield (1987) discusses how definitions of what actually constitutes part-time work vary considerably and this makes it difficult to assess the impact of part-time working on individual workers. For example, measurement of part-time work focuses upon jobs rather than on workers, but women may undertake more than one part-time job in order to maintain their income. Whilst the wages of part-time workers make an essential contribution to household incomes, part-time jobs are usually paid at lower rates that their full-time equivalents. The gap in wages is greater for part-time workers, with women working part-time earning only 59 per cent of the average hourly earnings of men.

Part-time work has been heralded as convenient for women with other demands on their time or even as solving the problem of how women may devote themselves to both their homes and participate in paid employment. It is open to question whether part-time work actually provides

women with the flexibility to combine paid work with family responsibilities. Jobs such as cleaning are often performed outside of normal office
hours. This increases the length of the working day for women who in
many cases have already done a day's domestic work. 'Flexible' work of
this nature brings with it disadvantages for women who end up working
a double day of both paid and unpaid work.

What employers term as 'flexibility' may actually be experienced by
women workers as the casualization of work where individual workers,
rather than employers, carry the burden of irregular working. In shop-
work, Robinson notes that 'by replacing one full-time sales assistant with
two or three part-timers, employers can save as much as eight hours per
week' (1988: 52). Part-timers also provide a workforce who might be on
hand to cover peak times during the day or week when demand is high.
Their contracts may stress a *minimum* number of hours to be worked. In
practice, workers may be asked to work over these hours, but with no
entitlement to overtime rates. Some employers in the UK and the Netherlands have issued workers with 'zero hours' contracts. This means that the
worker has no right to any work at all, but the employer can call upon the
worker at any time to undertake paid work on demand (Holtmaat *et al.*
1989). In these cases, individual workers have a commitment to an
employer, but without any guarantee of remuneration.

Beechey and Perkins (1987) showed that where employers have a predominantly female workforce, part-time work will be used as a means of
achieving 'flexibility' in levels of service, production or output. In contrast,
where jobs are performed by men, flexibility is achieved by other strategies, such as the provision of overtime. Using this analysis, part-time work
may therefore be seen first and foremost as an employer strategy, rather
than something that is offered for the convenience of women.

Part-time workers do not enjoy the same rights and employment conditions as full-time workers; they do not have the same rights of access to
occupational pension schemes. Many part-time workers earn so little that
they do not pay National Insurance contributions. This means that they do
not build up entitlements to unemployment and sickness pay, or to a state
pension. In some cases, this means that in the long term part-time workers
may be worse off than those outside paid work, in receipt of state benefits. The Equal Opportunities Commission (EOC) sees government as
responsible for ensuring that part-time workers enjoy, pro rata, the same
terms and conditions of employment as full-time workers.

It is recognized that part-time jobs will grow because of economic growth
in sectors of work where women have been employed, namely the service
sector including hotels and catering, distribution, health and education
(Lindley and Wilson 1993). This is in contrast to sectors where men predominate such as heavy industry and manufacturing, which have been in
decline. The increase in women's involvement in the labour market and
particularly in part-time work thus needs to be viewed in the context of
gendered occupational segregation, that is the process by which the labour
market is divided into men's jobs and women's jobs. The segregated labour
market will now be explored.

○ **The segregated labour market**

Gender segregation of the labour market has been seen as one of the most important causes of the wages gap between men's and women's work (Hakim 1981; Walby 1988; Rubery and Fagan 1994). As we have seen part-time work contributes an important dimension of gender segregation. However, it is also important to recognize that the labour market is also racialized. Part-time work has been a feature for white women, but generally speaking black women tend not to be found in part-time jobs (Bhavnani 1994; Roberts 1994). Almost 70 per cent of working women from ethnic groups are full-time employees. It has been suggested that the reason for this difference is largely financial, since women from ethnic minorities often come from poorer households and therefore need a full-time wage. Whereas gender segregation describes how women do different jobs to men, we need to understand how race, ethnicity and culture also contribute to further segregation and inequality within the ranks of women workers (Brah 1994). This aspect of segregation is typified by minority ethnic women being found in ancillary jobs such as cleaners, domestic assistants and cooks, within the health service and in the lowest paid jobs in hotel and catering. Consequently, the wages of women from minority ethnic groups are only 75 per cent of white women's hourly pay (Roberts 1994: 10). Phizacklea (1988) describes how the labour market has developed and reproduced 'ethnic' niches within the larger body of women's work. Women from ethnic minorities are found in the jobs with the lowest status, for example, ethnic minority nurses are concentrated in the care of elderly people and in mental health.

That women do different jobs to men is undoubtedly a major contributory factor to the inequality in wages. The notion of 'skill' also forms part of this dynamic. Feminists have shown how the term 'skill' is socially constructed. This means that the level of skill designated to a job often depends on who is performing the job rather than what the content of the job actually involves. Perceived levels of skill reflect the level at which work is rewarded (Gallie 1988) but, 'far from being an objective economic fact, skill is often an ideological category imposed on certain types of work by virtue of the sex or power of the workers who perform it' (Phillips and Taylor 1980: 79). The relationship between gender and skill is socially constructed meaning that work done by women demands less skill and therefore has less worth. Glucksmann identifies how 'the skills that women brought to assembly work or learned on the job (dexterity, attention to detail, speed) went unrecognised and were discounted as innate sexual characteristics' (1990: 209). Rees (1992) points out that 'innate characteristics' associated with men (such as physical strength needed by labourers) may not be rewarded either, but the opportunities for men to develop time-served skills is greater and those skills then reap higher rewards. Furthermore, women are given much less opportunity to acquire new or more valued skills through formal training. Changes in gender segregation in the workplace are often associated with deskilling. For example, the introduction of new technology in the clothing industry has led to a greater

range of jobs being open to women. Cutting – traditionally a male preserve
– can now be fully automated and is an occupation where women might
be found (Truman and Keating 1988). However, Cockburn has shown how
the 'skilled' aspect of new technology often remains a male preserve:
'Women may push the buttons but they may not meddle with the works'
(1985: 11–12). The effects of changes in technology will be taken up
further in the final section of this chapter. Other authors have shown that
where women begin to enter traditionally male professions such as law
(Spencer and Podmore 1986) or medicine (Allen 1988) gender segregation
is not eliminated. Processes of resegregation usually occur whereby gender
inequalities are maintained (Rubery and Fagan 1994). For example,
women may develop different specialisms to their male counterparts, and,
as will be shown in the next section, gender differentials in income are
maintained.

## Careers and equality of opportunity

Gender segregation not only separates out women's from men's jobs
within the labour market as a whole, but it has also been shown to operate
within organizations with women concentrated at the lowest levels of
organizational hierarchies, and men concentrated at the top (Hakim 1979).
Despite over a decade of many larger employers offering 'equal opportunities', women remain underrepresented in the higher echelons of
organizations (Hansard 1990). The term 'glass ceiling' has been used to
describe the difficulties that women face in trying to develop their careers
and obtain promotion. This is a 'barrier so subtle that it is transparent, yet
so strong that it prevents women and minorities from moving up the
management hierarchy' (Evetts 1994: 6). Women from ethnic minority
origins are even less likely to reach managerial positions than white
women, and where they do enter management it is more likely to be in
the context of self employment or in small units in retail, catering or cleaning trades (Bruegal 1994).

Many feminists have noted how the whole notion of 'career' is gendered
and centred on male norms of continuous employment, full-time work
and progression through increasing levels of job responsibility (Dex
1985: 86; Beechey, 1987). The 1984 Women and Employment survey and
subsequent further analyses demonstrated how whilst many women are
more or less permanently attached to paid employment, their paid work
histories are also interrupted with periods of unpaid activity involving the
care of dependants (Dex 1984; Joshi 1984; Martin and Roberts 1984).
Despite the presence of the women's movement, it remains the case that
women rather than men take time out of paid work to care for children
(Gelb and Palley 1987).

A number of initiatives have been started to help women combine paid
work with family. For example, the 1990s have seen the emergence of so-
called 'family friendly' employment policies and initiatives such as Opportunity 2000 (Business in the Community 1993; Opportunity 2000 1993).

The purpose of such schemes is to reduce gender inequalities in employment by adopting employment practices that recognize the tensions
between paid and unpaid work. A range of 'family friendly' policies should
thus provide better career prospects for women, and should help employers make better use of women's experience and qualifications. Employers
should also see financial and other benefits from retaining experienced
staff, and thus reducing labour turnover which avoids the costs of finding
replacements (Holtermann 1995).

A number of organizations have noted the high costs of replacing staff:
Barclays Bank estimates that the replacement costs for a worker in the
senior clerical grade or above are £17,000. For less skilled positions, Boots
the chemists estimates that a 1 per cent annual turnover of staff costs is
equivalent to one million pounds (cited in Bruegel and Perrons 1995). Progressive firms have found that initiatives such as workplace nurseries and
career break schemes which result in women with children remaining with
their employers actually pay for themselves (Truman 1986, 1992; Opportunity 2000 1993).

Women who work for employers with 'family friendly' initiatives should
be in a position to experience greater equality of opportunity in paid work,
but there are also drawbacks. Although employers and individual women
may derive benefit from family friendly policies, one argument against them
is that because these policies are targeted at women, they fail to encompass
the wider problem of why it is women who undertake most of the caring
roles outside paid employment. It is possible that unless men begin to take
up family friendly initiatives, they will further reinforce women's role as
unpaid carers with unequal career prospects (Truman 1992).

There is plenty of evidence to show that even highly qualified women
experience gender inequality at work relative to their male equivalents.
Compared with men of similar standing, women with degrees, professional
qualifications and vocational qualifications are less likely to work in the
private sector – which is associated with higher salaries. Men with qualifications are likely to earn substantially more than qualified women: 63 per
cent of men had salaries in the top quartile of earnings, compared to only
40 per cent of women. At the lower end of earnings, almost 25 per cent of
academically qualified women in full-time work are in the lowest two
quartiles, compared to only 15 per cent of their male counterparts (Conti
and Dex 1995).

Family friendly policies are rarely available to all employees (Holtermann and Clarke 1992). The Local Government Management Board
(1993) found that although equal opportunities ideology is often thought
to be inclusive, not all employees are in reality given access to family
friendly initiatives. Consequently there is considerable debate around the
extent to which the pursuit of equal opportunities is an appropriate strategy for women. For example, bell hooks points out that 'equality' has
limited meaning if it only allows women to be exploited on the same basis
as men. She suggests that if 'poor women had set the agenda for the feminist movement, they might have decided that class struggle would be a
central feminist issue' (hooks 1986: 136). The class structure, she argues,

allows privileged women to be at odds with poor women. Ramazanoglu (1989) suggests that 'equal opportunities' are most appropriate for white, middle-class women where the only disadvantage they experience is based upon their gender. 'Equality of opportunity' may only serve those women who are already advantaged by the class structure and may obscure important differences between women. Some feminists believe that on balance, there is little evidence that campaigns for equal opportunities in the workplace have made a significant contribution to the wider women's liberation movement (Charles 1993). Despite recognizing good reasons for concern and scepticism. Cockburn makes the important point that:

> If equal opportunities initiatives did not exist we would have to invent them. Even those women who are bitterly disillusioned with the equality experience would no doubt begin anew the fight for fairness at work were it not already occurring. Not all women who experience discrimination, who are stuck in women's-work ghettos, will accept their subordination as inevitable. Women have a growing sense of their own worth . . . equality initiatives . . . involve a *struggle*.
> (Cockburn 1991: 16–17, emphasis in original)

Equal opportunities initiatives based upon alliances between women may be seen to be part of the feminist agenda for women's work in a changing labour market. It is to labour market change that we now focus our attention.

## ○  The changing labour market

As noted earlier in this chapter, more women are found in paid employment than ever before and they will soon outnumber men. This is indicative of underlying structural changes in the labour market. Feminists stress the importance of recognizing how the nature of labour market change is fundamentally gendered as well as racialized. In this final section, we assess the extent to which women's future experience of paid work will be subject to continuities and change.

Employer strategies aimed at increasing flexibility go hand in hand with cutting costs. The resulting casualization of work has a counter-effect to any real opportunity that might be created by changing working relations. The abolition of wages councils has removed protection for the regulation of wages in many industries where women predominate (OEC 1995). In manufacturing this casualization is typified by increased outworking or homeworking. Allen and Wolkowitz (1987) show how homeworking, rather than being primarily a convenient form of working for women, is highly exploitative. It provides poor levels of pay, no checks on working conditions and often pressurizes women to work to tight deadlines. Control of supply work is in the hands of manufacturers and any failure to meet their requirements can result in the loss of future work. Racism within casual employment networks by which news of work is spread by word of mouth, can mean that black women are excluded from employment opportunities. Mitter (1986) describes how a deterioration in conditions of women's work is taking place on a global scale that sweat-shop conditions facing women from ethnic minorities in the UK are not dissimilar to the equally poor conditions in developing countries. The global economy and so-called free trade zones mean that manufacturing bases can be switched easily depending upon where the cheapest labour forces are to be found.

Although the service sector is growing, authors such as Adkins (1995) have pointed to its reliance upon casual contracts of work. Bhavnani has identified that black women are underrepresented in growth areas of work and are 'more likely to take a share in rising unemployment' (1994: 12). This is because they are more likely to be employed in occupations that are in decline. Although demographic differences mean that there will be more black women entering the workforce, Bhavnani predicts that they will increase their employment levels, but only in deteriorating conditions of working relations.

The division between 'core' workers and 'periphery' workers may be seen most vividly in the case of the legislative framework that led to compulsory competitive tendering (CCT) in local government.[2] An EOC report (Escott and Whitfield 1995) showed that the extension of CCT to manual services has had a differential impact on women and men. Female part-time employees have been most affected by a decline in working hours in cleaning and catering. They are more likely to be involved in multiple job-holding, but because each job is technically with a different employer, they are excluded from employment protection. The numbers of hours worked in cleaning (predominantly done by women) declined by between 16 and 25 per cent following the introduction of CCT, while the hours worked by male refuse collectors remained largely the same. CCT provides another example of how the changing labour market is having a limiting effect on opportunities for women.

In contrast to the deskilling, deregulation and intensification of many forms of work, the growth of new technology is resulting in skill shortages. New technologies have become a pervasive feature of everyday life – from the increased use of computers, fax machines and so on in the office, to computer aided design (CAD) in manufacturing, and Electronic Point of Sale (EPOS) systems in retailing. Training has been seen as an important aspect of the growth of a technologically literate workforce. Authors such as Wajcman (1991) and Cockburn (1985) have both demonstrated how new technologies are products of inequality based upon class, gender and race relations, and that their introduction reinforces these inequalities. Although new technology means that many jobs are deskilled, Rees points out that higher level jobs in information technology could be made open to more women with the increased provision of women-only training. In countries like the Federal Republic of Germany there are signs that a progressive training ethos is beginning to lead to the desegregation of jobs previously segregated by gender (Rees 1992: 168).

In conclusion, this chapter has shown that structural changes in the labour market have led to increases in the *quantity* of women in paid work. Whilst the potential remains for women to benefit from more opportunities in paid work, there are, as we have seen, many factors which mitigate against any improvements in the overall *quality* of jobs done by women. We have observed continuity and change in differences between men's work and women's work, but it is important also not to overlook differences between women. Within the changing labour market, women's experiences of paid employment are marked not only by gender, but also by race, culture and ethnicity and class.

○ **Questions and exercises**

> 1 Using large pieces of flip-chart paper, ask an older female friend or relative to map out her work history. You should ask her to include paid work, but also to incorporate other definitions of 'work', such as care work, political work, community work and so on. Would you say that work is a central part of her life? What range of definitions of 'work' have been used?
>
> 2 Construct a job description for a person who is caring full-time for a relative. What qualities and/or experience might they need? How would you describe the skills that are required to care for a dependent person? Could these skills be developed equally by women and men?
>
> 3 Discuss ways in which you think men might be disadvantaged by gender-segregation in work.

○ **Further reading**

> There is a wide range of literature that deals with different aspects of women's paid work. Useful introductory texts include Dex (1985) and Rees (1992). For an overview of different definitions of work, see Beechey (1988) and Tancred (1995). Walby (1988) provides a comprehensive account of different aspects of occupational segregation. The situation of black women in paid employment is provided in Bhavnani (1994) and Westwood and Bhachu (1988). Phizacklea (1990) describes the way in which the clothing industry is segregated along lines of gender, race and class whilst Glucksmann (1990) provides a useful account of women in assembly lines between the two world wars. Issues relating to work, technological change and skill can be found in Chapter 2 of Wajcman (1991).
>
> Women's experiences within organizations, the barriers that they face, and the way that different forms of inequality interact, can be

found in Cockburn (1991). In particular, Chapter 1 engages with debates around equal opportunities campaigns and initiatives.

○ **Notes**

1 The British law governing sex discrimination at work is the Sex Discrimination Act, 1975, and the law on equal pay for work of equal value is the Amended Equal Pay Act, 1984. The Equal Opportunities Commission provides a range of useful guides to the law in Great Britain, Codes of Practice, and the difficulties relating to the implementation of the law.
2 Compulsory competitive tendering (CCT) has been used increasingly in the public sector under government legislation since 1980. Services which were traditionally provided by local authorities (and increasingly in the National Health Service) now have to be put out to market tender. In many cases, the new contractor might employ the same workers who were previously employed directly by the local authority or health authority.

○ **References**

Adkins, L. (1995) *Gendered Work: Sexuality, Family and the Labour Market*. Buckingham: Open University.

Allen, L. (1988) *Any Room at the Top? A Study of Doctors and Their Careers*. London: Policy Studies Institute.

Allen, S. and Truman, C. (eds) (1993) *Women in Business: Perspectives on Women Entrepreneurs*. London: Routledge.

Allen, S. and Wolkowitz, C. (1987) *Homeworking: Myths and Realities*. London: Macmillan.

Beechey, V. (1987) *Unequal Work*. London: Verso.

Beechey, V. (1988) Rethinking the definition of work, in J. Jensen, E. Hagen and C. Reddy (eds) *Feminization of the Labour Force: Paradoxes and Promises*. Cambridge: Polity.

Beechey, V. and Perkins, T. (1987) *A Matter of Hours: Women, Part-Time Work and the Labour Market*. Cambridge: Polity.

Bhavnani, R. (1994) *Black Women in the Labour Market*. Manchester: Equal Opportunities Commission.

Brah, A. (1994) 'Race' and 'culture' in the gendering of labour markets, in H. Afshar and M. Maynard (eds) *The Dynamics of Race and Gender: Some Feminist Interventions*. London: Taylor and Francis.

Bruegel, I. (1994) Labour market prospects for women from ethnic minorities, in R. Lindley (ed.) *Labour Market Structures and Prospects for Women*. Manchester: Equal Opportunities Commission.

Bruegel, I. and Perrons, D. (1995) Where do the costs of unequal treatment for women fall?: An analysis of the incidence of unequal pay and sex discrimination in the UK, *Gender, Work and Organisation*, 2(3): 113–24.

Business in the Community (BIC) (1993) *Corporate Culture and Caring: The Business Case for Family Friendly Provision*. London: BIC.

Charles, N. (1993) *Gender Divisions and Social Change*. Hemel Hempstead: Harvester Wheatsheaf.

Cockburn, C. (1985) *Machinery of Dominance: Women, Men and Technical Knowhow*. London: Pluto Press.

Cockburn, C. (1991) *In the Way of Women: Men's Resistance to Sex Equality in Organisations*. Basingstoke: Macmillan.

Conti, H. and Dex, S. (1995) *Highly Qualified Women*. Sheffield: Department for Education and Employment.

Deem, R. (1986) *Work, Unemployment and Leisure*. London: Routledge.

Delphy, C. and Leonard, D. (1992) *Familiar Exploitation A New Analysis of Marriage in Contemporary Society*. Cambridge: Polity.

Department of Employment (1993) *Labour Force Survey, Spring Quarter*. London: HMSO.

Dex, S. (1984) *Women's Work Histories: An Analysis of the Women and Employment Survey*. Department of Employment Research Paper No. 46. London: HMSO.

Dex, S. (1985) *The Sexual Division of Work: Conceptual Revolutions in the Social Sciences*. Brighton: Wheatsheaf.

Epstein, T. S. (1993) Female petty entrepreneurs and their multiple roles, in S. Allen and C. Truman (eds) *Women in Business: Perspectives on Women Entrepreneurs*. London: Routledge.

Equal Opportunities Commission (EOC) (1994) *Some Facts About Women*. Manchester: Equal Opportunities Commission.

Equal Opportunities Commission (EOC) (1995) *The Inequality Gap*. Manchester: Equal Opportunities Commission.

Escott, K. and Whitfield, D. (1995) *The Gender Impact of CCT in Local Government*. Manchester: Equal Opportunities Commission.

Evetts, I. (ed.) (1994) *Women and Career: Themes and Issues in Advanced Industrial Societies*. Harlow: Longman.

Finch, J. and Groves, D. (eds) (1983) *A Labour of Love*. London: Routledge and Kegan Paul.

Gallie, D. (ed.) (1988) *Employment in Britain*. Oxford: Blackwell.

Gelb, J. and Palley, M. (1987) *Women and Public Policies*. Princeton, NJ: Princeton University Press.

Glucksmann, M. (1990) *Women Assemble: Women Workers and the New Industries in Inter-war Britain*. London: Routledge.

Hakim, C. (1979) *Occupational Segregation: A Comparative Study of the Degree and Pattern of Differentiation between Men and Women's Work in Britain, the USA and Other Countries*. Department of Employment Research Paper No. 9. London: HMSO.

Hakim, C. (1981) Census reports as documentary evidence: the census commentaries 1801–1951, *Sociological Review*, 28: 551–89.

Hakim, C. (1993) The myth of rising female unemployment, *Work, Employment and Society*, 7(1): 97–120.

Hansard (1990) *Report of the Hansard Society Commission on Women at the Top*. London: The Hansard Society.

Holtermann, S. (1995) The costs and benefits to British Employers of measures to promote equality of opportunity, *Gender, Work and Organisation*, 2(3): 102–12.

Holtermann, S. and Clarke, K. (1992) *Parents, Employment Rights and Childcare*. EOC Research Discussion Series No. 4. Manchester: Equal Opportunities Commission.

Holtmaat, R., Hursfield, J. and Huws, U. (1989) *What Price Flexibility? The Casualisation of Women's Employment*. London: Low Pay Unit.

hooks, b. (1986) Sisterhood: political solidarity between women, *Feminist Review*, 23: 125–38.

Hurstfield, J. (1987) *Part-timers Under Pressure: Paying the Price of Flexibility*. London: Low Pay Unit.

Joshi, H. (1984) *Women's Participation in Paid Work: A Further Analysis of the Women in Employment Survey*. Department of Employment Research Paper No. 46. London: HMSO.

Joshi, H. and Owen, S. (1987) How long is a piece of elastic? the measurement of female activity rates in British censuses 1951–1981, *Cambridge Journal of Economics*, 11: 55–74.

Lindley, R. and Wilson, R. (eds) (1993) *Review of the Economy and Employment 1992/3: Occupational Assessment*. Coventry: Institute for Employment Research, University of Warwick.

Local Government Management Board (LGMB) (1993) *Equal Opportunities in Local Government*. London: LGMB.

Martin, J. and Roberts, C. (1984) *Women and Employment: A Lifetime Perspective*. London: HMSO.

Mitter, S. (1986) *Common Fate, Common Bond: Women in the Global Economy*. London: Pluto.

Oakley, A. (1974) *The Sociology of Housework*. Oxford: Martin Robertson.

Opportunity 2000 (1993) *Second Year Report*. London: BIC.

Phillips, A. and Taylor, B. (1980) Sex and skill: notes towards a feminist economics, *Feminist Review*, 6: 79–88.

Phizacklea, A. (1988) Gender, racism and gender segregation, in S. Walby (ed.) *Gender Segregation at Work*. Milton Keynes: Open University.

Phizacklea, A. (1990) *Unpacking the Fashion Industry: Gender, Racism and Class in Production*. London: Routledge.

Ramazanoglu, C. (1989) *Feminism and the Contradictions of Oppression*. London: Routledge.

Rees, T. (1992) *Women and the Labour Market*. London: Routledge.

Roberts, B. (1994) *Minority Ethnic Women: Work, Unemployment, and Education*. Manchester: Equal Opportunities Commission.

Robinson, O. (1988) The changing labour market: growth of part-time employment and labour market segmentation in Great Britain, in S. Walby (ed.) *Gender Segregation at Work*. Milton Keynes: Open University.

Rubery, J. and Fagan, C. (1994) Occupational segregation: plus ça change?, in R. Lindley (ed.) *Labour Market Structures and Prospects for Women*. Manchester: Equal Opportunities Commission.

Spencer, A. and Podmore, D. (1986) Gender in the labour process – the case of women and men lawyers, in D. Knights and H. Wilmott (eds) *Gender and the Labour Process*. Aldershot: Gower.

Tancred, P. (1995) Women's work: a challenge to the sociology of work, *Gender, Work and Organisation*, 2(1): 11–20.

Truman, C. (1986) *Overcoming the Career Break: A Positive Approach*. Sheffield: Manpower Services Commission.

Truman, C. (1992) Demographic change and 'new' opportunities for women: the case of employers' career break schemes, in S. Arber and N. Gilbert (eds) *Women and Working Lives: Divisions and Change*. Basingstoke: Macmillan.

Truman, C. and Keating, J. (1988) Technology, markets and the design of women's jobs, *New Technology, Work and Employment*, 3(1): 21–9.

Wajcman, J. (1991) *Feminism Confronts Technology*. Cambridge: Polity.

Walby, S. (1986) *Patriarchy at Work*. Cambridge: Polity.

Walby, S. (1988) (ed.) *Gender Segregation at Work*. Milton Keynes: Open University.

Westwood, S. and Bhachu, P. (1988) *Enterprising Women*. London: Routledge.

Women's Feature Service (1992) *The Power to Change: Women in the Third World Redefine their Environment*. London: Zed Books.

Yeandle, S. (1984) *Women's Working Lives*. London: Tavistock.

**ROSEMARY DEEM**

# The gendering of educational organizations

## ○ Introduction

In this chapter I want to look at women and education in a distinctive way, not by exploring the educational experiences of women and men and noting how and in what ways these differ, as is the case in much of the literature about gender and education (Weiner 1985; Measor and Sikes 1992; Wrigley 1992), but by considering the nature of educational institutions as organizations within which there are both students (or pupils) and workers (including teachers, teaching assistants, technical, secretarial and other support staff). This approach has several advantages: first it allows us to examine the kinds of cultural rules and assumptions which shape education, not just formal rules like not eating in corridors but informal conventions about behaviour and attitudes. Second it enables analysis of the resources used in education, including people, the curriculum, and money. Third it enables us to ask questions about the design and structuring of educational institutions, whether these resemble a pyramid of authority with a boss at the top and students at the bottom or have power more fluidly and equally distributed amongst all members of the organization. Finally an organizational approach focuses on the ways in which educational institutions are managed and run, such as whether women principals run educational institutions differently from men.

### What is an organization?

Organizations can be viewed as containers for ordering activities, people and resources (Reed 1992), or they can be seen as ways of organizing activities. This definition applies whether they are schools, factories or supermarkets. In contemporary societies, organizing is often assumed to be rational, that is ordered and with a clear relationship between ends and means, though we might want to question this assumption. Bureaucracies are one of the most common forms for large modern organizations, and organizations like the civil service epitomize this form, though we might equally well cite a hospital or a university as examples. Bureaucracies are supposed to be impersonal, non-nepotistic (people get appointed on merit, not on the fact that their relatives already work there) and based on hierarchies of office-holding-related authority and tasks; they also place great emphasis on written (increasingly computer held) records of what takes place. This implies that relations and characteristics based on gender and ethnicity are not seen as relevant, in other words as Acker has noted, organizations assume a 'disembodied worker' (Acker 1992). Thus gender or ethnicity or the household responsibilities of workers may be ignored or considered irrelevant to what someone is expected to do when they are at work (for instance working late), although it is clear that these things may sometimes enter into decisions about who is to be employed or promoted and may even be used to determine what clothes people wear to work, with very different conventions for women and men (Adkins 1992).

Some contemporary organizations are not organized bureaucratically but instead rely on networks of contracted out employees working from home rather than a conventional workplace, with just a few people in an organizational headquarters to coordinate the whole organization. The Open University, a UK and European-wide distance teaching institution where students study written course materials at home and keep in touch with part-time tutors is a partial example of this, although it also has a large central bureaucracy. Other organizations are also developing a flatter authority structure than that of the hierarchical bureaucracy, so that all those who work or study in the organization have some chance to influence what goes on (sometimes this is termed empowerment).

Organizational theorists write about flat and networked organizations as though they are commonplace. It is also implied that organizations using new techniques such as Total Quality Management (TQM), which emphasize flat power structures, are much more sensitive to gender and other embodied characteristics of workers (Peters 1989; Morgan and Murgatroyd 1994). In fact TQM may simply exploit women workers by providing them with so-called flexible hours and intensified work tasks. Genuinely 'flat' or networked organizations are not often found in formal educational institutions like schools. They are more often found in informal educational groups which are run for and by their participants, such as women-only discussion groups (Deem 1993). However it may be that the recent introduction of quasi-market conditions to public sector services like education and health may also affect the ways in which those services are organized and provided (Le Grand and Bartlett 1993).

Educational organizations, formal or informal and bureaucratic or not, are both somewhat like and somewhat unlike other organizations. Like other organizations they provide a service, often employ people, have their own rules and resources and require managing and running. However they may also have a range of not very clearly defined purposes and goals. Thus teaching and learning are core activities of educational institutions but they cover a wide range of goals and purposes (social skills, passing exams, etc). How teaching and learning occur isn't always clear either, as is demonstrated by the longstanding controversy over different methods of teaching children to read. Educational institutions are also distinctive in that they are not usually set up with the intention of making a profit and many try to transmit values related to humanism (valuing people for themselves) rather than those of enterprise and business (values based on money and the pursuit of gain).

### What's it got to do with gender?

For the purposes of this chapter we need to ask a key question about how educational organizations articulate gender relations. Obviously, organizations vary in their gender composition as well as in other ways. This has other effects: thus single-sex schools may differ markedly from mixed schools in relation to how gender relations permeate their rules, resources and structure. We can't assume that gender doesn't matter in a single-sex context; indeed there may be heightened awareness of unequal gender relations and power, as is apparent in the continued exclusion of women from some male clubs. There is insufficient space to deal with all the issues concerning gender and educational organizations, so I shall concentrate on four aspects. These are the artefacts, values and taken for granted assumptions (organizational culture) found in formal educational organizations in the UK; power relations, resources and divisions of labour in educational settings; the potential of equal opportunities policies to make for more equal relations between the sexes; and female and male management practices in educational institutions.

## ○ Organizational culture in educational organizations

Most large organizations have more than one culture, although one may dominate over others. For example first-year students in a school or university may have different behaviour, values and beliefs compared with final year students, and male students in each cohort may differ from their female peers in certain respects. Ethnicity, class and age also permeate organizational cultures. The cultural resources available to individual students, from advertising, TV programmes, fashion clothing and the availability of role models, also affect individual student identities. Culture isn't only carried by individuals and groups but also by symbols such as school uniform, logos, wall posters, and rituals such as certificate evenings, farewell parties, social events and sports days. Common institutional practices, who has lunch with whom, who does what for whom without feeling either superior or demeaned, are also useful indices of organizational culture.

Cockburn (1991) argues that many mixed organizations are characterized by male, patriarchal cultures, though conversely in primary and nursery schools predominantly female cultures are more common (Acker 1994). The latter may be characterized by caring, nurturing and concern for the emotions and development of individuals, and the relatively unplanned careers of their women teachers and support staff (Evetts 1990). By contrast, in some mixed secondary schools, male cultures comprising materialism, entrepreneurial spirit, heterosexuality and homophobia, planned careers of male teachers, interest in sport, and evidence of sexism, may be more apparent. Both cultures may prove problematic for those who disagree with, or deviate from them, particularly for people from minority ethnic or social class groupings or with a disability.

Culture also affects other aspects of educational organizations, including what is taught and to whom, and how it is assessed. Historical research shows that women often led the way in developing child centred primary education (Brehony 1987). In the UK at the present time, the school curriculum is not, except in Scotland, something which educational institutions have much determination over since there are national curricula in England, Wales and Northern Ireland. However in higher and adult education and more informal settings there is a greater degree of freedom for teachers and students to make curriculum choices. Curriculum isn't just an arbitrary collection of subjects; the status and location of them is culturally shaped and variable. Thus physics, as a 'hard' physical science, has higher status than English literature so far as governments are concerned but is unpopular with students. However whereas a good proportion of students of English literature in UK higher education are likely to be female, most physics students are male.

A number of researchers have argued that these gender related differences between subjects are partly instilled both by the actual content of each subject and by teaching styles which consciously try to appeal to one gender only (Whyte 1986; Kelly 1987). Some subjects such as maths appear more culturally neutral, though the way they are taught may be organizationally and pedagogically gendered (Girls and Mathematics Unit 1989). This may be reflected in teaching strategies, with boys asked to answer even if girls put their hands up, or in relation to the examples used. Thus '11 boys play in a football team three times a week and always score at least two goals. How many goals would they score in a full season' is not calculated to appeal to those girls uninterested in football. The curriculum may also favour certain ethnic groups, as in the history of white but not African or Hispanic Americans; such ethnic bias may intersect with curricular gender differentiation. Here we can begin to see that exclusion and inclusion, as well as power, are closely linked to what goes on in educational institutions; neither what is taught, nor who studies what, are neutral issues. The cultural rules surrounding curriculum are also closely linked to the organization and resources of teaching itself.

○ **Power, resources and divisions of labour**

Although women are beginning to make an impact in managerial posts in both the public and private sectors, in many educational institutions, caring/domestic jobs like cooking, secretarial and clerical work, cleaning, teaching young children and acting as personal tutors are carried out by women, who may also be more likely to teach humanities, social and life sciences rather than physical sciences or computing. The kind of jobs done by men in educational settings often include those involving physical labour and/or the exercise of power – managing/running big secondary schools, colleges and universities, teaching older students, carrying out grounds and building maintenance, portering and caretaking. In the UK, these latter jobs are often better paid than their nearest female equivalent, so caretakers are better paid than cleaners and male secondary heads better paid than female primary heads.

How the content of a job is perceived is also relevant. Cockburn noted the social construction of skill in the printing industry and showed how for many decades men excluded women, until the onset of new technology meant anyone with typing skills could typeset (Cockburn 1983). This example may seem far removed from education but a glance at the devolved management of school, college and university budgets demonstrates similar examples. Whilst women school secretaries do the housekeeping and bookkeeping, collecting and recording dinner and photocopying money and day-to-day financial transactions, in secondary schools many of those doing more high-profile finance tasks, including whole institution policy decisions and the formal presentation of accounts, are men (Broadbent and Laughlin 1993a; Broadbent and Laughlin 1993b). Yet there is as much technical skill in the bookkeeping as in the more public financial activities. It is possible that organizational housekeeping could prove to be a fertile ground for female resistance, as the male high-profile tasks depend heavily on the more routine tasks carried out by women. This leads us neatly back to the question of power relations in educational organizations.

Primary and nursery schools are often run and staffed by women; the higher up the age group we go, the less likely this is to be so. Furthermore, there are few indications that schools, colleges and universities in the UK have developed flat organizational structures. Indeed Bowe and Ball, looking at schools in England after the radical education reforms of the 1980s, found that as schools got more control over their budgets, power became more centralized and confined to a small group of senior staff (Bowe et al. 1992). Of course power may also flow round organizations in a complex way, and the capacity of women employees and students to resist what is going on may be crucial to ensuring that power does not always benefit men.

However men also exercise power over women in other less formalized ways. Thus Cunnison (1989) talks about gender joking in the staff room, where jokes are told by men but are at the expense of women. Men may also dominate mixed meetings with their frequent interventions, take up more space in staff rooms, and even on occasions engage in sexual harass-ment of female colleagues. Cockburn (1991) suggests that some male employees have difficulty relating to women other than as sex objects or domestic carers and can have particular problems with women who do the same job as they do. Furthermore, Pringle (1989) has argued that female secretaries' jobs are often highly sexualized where they work for male bosses. In addition, black women teachers may be badly treated by colleagues but then asked to 'deal' with black students who are troublesome. All this indicates that changes might be welcome in some educational organizations. Equal opportunities policies are one possibility for achieving such change.

## Equal opportunities policies? Do they make a difference?

Not all equal opportunity policies are about all aspects of social and cultural inequality; some deal only with gender, or only with 'race' or special needs. This is problematic because a policy concentrating on only one aspect of inequality may unintentionally discriminate against those in other social categories (thus a gender policy may ignore the problems of women and girls from minority ethnic groups). Cockburn (1991) suggests that equal opportunities policies don't always prove effective in organizations. This could be because those who are responsible for implementing them are not fully committed to the policies put forward, because the unforeseen effects of particular policies have not been considered and properly monitored, or because the policies are not properly resourced or supported by staff and student training in order to ensure full awareness of the policies.

Can very generalized equal opportunities policies possibly work well, given the differences which exist even between those who share the same gender or ethnicity? This is an important issue which needs addressing. Certainly equal opportunities policies do not always seem to have succeeded in turning hierarchical and male dominated educational organizations into flat 'empowering' structures so beloved of management gurus.

## Do women manage educational organizations differently from men?

For some Women's Studies students different management styles may be seen as a boring issue. However this view is perhaps as much to do with misunderstandings about how educational organizations work as with the intrinsic interest of the topic. Although resistance to change or to male dominated cultures is important for women, there is no doubt that people who run or coordinate educational organizations are central to the way in which organizational culture, power relations, resource use and divisions of labour operate. There's beginning to be a considerable body of literature suggesting that women do manage organizations differently from men (Tanton 1994). Some of this work focuses on managers of educational institutions, arguing that women are more likely to seek cooperation and consensus in decision making, use less hierarchical forms of authority, are more consultative, are kinder and more understanding, are likely to help their employees rather than ignore or bully them, and spend more time on people than paperwork (Shakeshaft 1987; Adler *et al.* 1993); Blackmore and Kenway 1993; Riley 1994). There is also some suggestion that women are more equivocal about holding power over other people than are men (Adler *et al.* 1993).

However there are two problems with the 'women manage differently' thesis. First, the context in which a manager operates makes a great deal of difference to the management styles adopted. Thus a small village school lends itself much more to informal management than does a large college. Second, the attempt to characterize women managers as a group which contrasts sharply with men managers raises awkward questions about 'difference'. This is an area where we still don't know enough about what kinds of management strategies, male or female or both, can actually alter gender power relations and reduce the domination of organizations by male cultures. There are other complexities too. Some women may well have different career profiles when compared with men, as Evetts discovered when studying women primary heads (Evetts 1990). She found many more 'accidental' careers rather than planned ones and those who took breaks for childcaring often reached managerial posts at a later age than men. But not all women have unplanned careers and some men may 'accidentally' find themselves pursuing careers in educational management.

## Conclusion: how is the gendering of educational organizations relevant to the themes of women, power and resistance?

I have tried to show how an understanding of educational institutions as gendered organizations can help us to trace the ways in which gender relations permeate and are articulated by educational organizations, with consequences for both students and staff. Organizations which are strongly male dominated in their cultural orientation may also have other undesirable characteristics including racism, an undue emphasis on heterosexuality, hierarchical power structures, failure to implement equal opportunities policies, and teaching and learning strategies which deny women's capabilities, experience and interests. Although bringing about change is difficult in such circumstances, women who are aware that organizational forms, rules and management techniques are important transmitters of gender power relations have more chance of resisting what is going on. They can also try to find ways of bringing about beneficial changes, whether through single-sex groupings, which can be an important resource for women, curriculum changes like Women's Studies, or the introduction of women managers who share rather than appropriate power. However we also need to take into account how women themselves differ from each other, for example in respect of ethnicity, social class, age and whether they are able-bodied or not, if planned organizational changes are genuinely intended to empower rather than restrict women.

## Acknowledgements

Thanks to Karen Legge and Penny Summerfield for their helpful comments on an earlier draft of this chapter. My students on the 1993/4 'Gender and Educational Organizations' course at Lancaster were also an excellent source of ideas and wisdom about the organizing of educational activities.

○ **Questions and exercises**

> 1 Compare an educational organization you knew in the past with one you are more familiar with now. Make brief notes on them. Pay particular attention to the gender composition of the students and staff and the division of labour amongst the latter, as well as to any gender relevant features of the curriculum.
>
> 2 What, if any, cultural differences or similarities seem to exist between these two organizations with regard to gender? Is either organization one in which unequal gender relations are or were minimized? If so, how do you think this came about?
>
> 3 Try to find out whether a school, college or university near you has an equal opportunities policy and see if you can get hold of a description of it or documents pertaining to it. Does it cover gender? Are ethnicity and 'race' also covered? What effects, if any, do you think the policy might have on the institution's organizational culture, structure and management? Could you suggest any improvements to the policy?
>
> 4 If you know any women in management jobs, whether in an educational institution or not, ask if you may shadow them at work for a couple of hours. Afterwards make notes on what they did and how much if at all it seemed to relate to issues about gender, power and resistance. What did the work-shadow exercise tell you about how easy or difficult it would be to test out the proposition that women manage differently from men?

○ **Further reading**

> If you want to know more about gender and organizations in general, a reader edited by Mills and Tancred (1992) is a useful book though some of the articles are heavy going. On educational organizations a difficult but rewarding edited collection by Blackmore and Kenway (1993) is worth looking out for. If you want to read in some detail about gender issues in schools but not specifically about organizations, a very basic and easy to read book is Measor and Sikes (1992).

Stone's (1994) edited book is a richer source about gender and schools and one which deals with several different countries. On higher education Thomas (1990) is easy to read but deals with physics and English. Weiner's (1994) book has a chapter about a project on higher education management and extensive discussion about gender and the school curriculum, as well as a useful account of what makes research feminist. Myers (1992) and Al Khalifa *et al.* (1993) have put together two excellent resource books on equal opportunities policies; these should be in most university and some school/college libraries. Adler *et al.*'s (1993) account of a collaborative project on women and educational management across different sectors is worth reading but is harder going than the 'tell it how it is' accounts from women managers that Ozga (1993) provides.

## References

Acker, J. (1992) Gendering organisational theory, in A. Mills and P. Tancred (eds) *Gendering Organisational Analysis*. London: Sage.

Acker, S. (1994) *Gendered Education*. Buckingham: Open University Press.

Adkins, L. (1992) Sexual work and the employment of women in the service industries, in M. Savage and A. Witz (eds) *Gender and Bureaucracy*. Oxford: Blackwells.

Adler, S., Laney, J. and Packer, M. (1993) *Managing Women*. Buckingham: Open University Press.

Al Khalifa, E., Hall, V. and McMahon, A. (1993) *Equal Opportunities in School Management*. Bristol, National Development Centre for Educational Management: Bristol University.

Blackmore, J. and Kenway, J. (eds) (1993) *Gender Matters in Educational Administration and Policy*. London: Falmer.

Bowe, R. and Ball, S. with Gold, A. (1992) *Reforming Education and Changing Schools*. London: Routledge.

Brehony, K. J. (1987) 'The Froebel Movement and state schooling 1880–1914: a study in educational ideology'. PhD thesis. Milton Keynes: Open University.

Broadbent, J. and Laughlin, R. (1993a) 'The values of accountancy and education: a question of gender?' Department of Educational Research Open Seminar Series, Lancaster University.

Broadbent, J. and Laughlin, R. (eds) (1993b) 'Financial controls and schools: accounting in "public" and "private" spheres'. Sheffield: Sheffield University Management School Discussion Paper Series.

Cockburn, C. (1983) *Brothers: Male Dominance and Technological Change*. London: Pluto.

Cockburn, C. (1991) *In the Way of Women*. London: Macmillan.

Cunnison, S. (1989) Gender joking in the staffroom, in S. Acker (ed.) *Teachers, Gender and Careers*. London: Falmer.

Deem, R. (1993) Popular education for women: a study of four organisations, in R. Edwards, S. Sieminski and D. Zeldin (eds) *Adult Learners: Education and Training*. London: Routledge.

Evetts, J. (1990) *Women in Primary Teaching*. London: Unwin Hyman.

Girls and Mathematics Unit, Institute of Education (1989) *Counting Girls Out*. London: Virago.

Kelly, A. (ed.) (1987) *Science for Girls*. Milton Keynes: Open University Press.

Le Grand, J. E. M. and Bartlett, W. (eds) (1993) *Quasi-Markets and Social Policy*. London: Macmillan.

Measor, L. and Sikes, P. (1992) *Gender and Schools*. London: Cassell.

Mills, A. J. and Tancred, P. (eds) (1992) *Gendering Organisational Analysis*. London: Sage.

Morgan, C. and Murgatroyd, S. (1994) *Total Quality Management in the Public Sector*. Buckingham: Open University Press.

Myers, K. (1992) *Genderwatch! After the Education Reform Act*. Cambridge: Cambridge University Press.

Ozga, J. (ed.) (1993) *Women in Educational Management*. Milton Keynes: Open University Press.

Peters, T. (1989) *Thriving on Chaos*. London: Pan Books.

Pringle, R. (1989) *Secretaries Talk*. London: Verso.

Reed, M. (1992) *The Sociology of Organisations*. London: Harvester Wheatsheaf.

Riley, K. A. (1994) *Quality and Equality: Promoting Opportunities in Schools*. London: Cassell.

Shakeshaft, C. (1987) *Women in Educational Administration*. Newbury Park, CA: Sage.

Stone, L. (ed.) (1994) *The Education Feminism Reader*. London: Routledge.

Tanton, M. (ed.) (1994) *Women in Management*. London: Routledge.

Thomas, K. (1990) *Gender and Subject in Higher Education*. Milton Keynes: Open University Press.

Weiner, G. (ed.) (1985) *Just A Bunch of Girls*. Milton Keynes: Open University Press.

Weiner, G. (1994) *Feminisms in Education*. Buckingham: Open University Press.

Whyte, J. (1986) *Girls into Science and Technology*. London: Routledge.

Wrigley, J. (ed.) (1992) *Education and Gender Equality*. London: Falmer.

**5** DEBORAH SAWYER

# The Church: egality or patriarchy?

○ **Introduction**

In a posttraditional age that has for many years been recognized as one that is secular, why study the effects on women of such an anachronistic monolith as the Christian church? To answer this question we need to understand the central position and influence of Christianity during the history and development of western society and to realize that what is such a marginal institution today, is an invaluable key to unlocking the workings of western society and culture. Without such keys any critique or reform of western society remains superficial. Even if we abandon 'the master's tools' we still need to understand how his house was built in order to dismantle it effectively and not use the same unsuitable materials when we rebuild.

Christianity as a religious phenomenon manifests a variety of types of institution, but within its central beliefs and practices two basic models of social organization are apparent: egalitarian, where all men and women are regarded as equal; and patriarchal/hierarchical, where certain male individuals are endowed with authority over the majority. The latter has tended to dominate throughout the centuries and is clearly visible today. However, recent movements within Christianity, namely liberation theology and feminist theology have sought to reapply the alternative model, which is evidenced also in the history of Christianity within its scriptures and down the ages, appearing alongside the patriarchal communities.

In what follows we will examine the structures of both models as they have been applied at different times, including contemporary examples. One overriding concern related to this topic is the question of whether the actuality of an egalitarian organization can survive beyond the short term, or whether is it inevitable that the more normative hierarchical organization will supersede it. This question will be explored in the light of contemporary feminist critiques of Christianity, and the phenomenon of women's resistance within the religious institutions.

Although in explaining the models of organization found in Christianity constant reference is made to Christian origins, we have to bear in mind that these models are timeless and have been applied down the centuries and are still authoritative today. Perhaps the greatest authority for Christianity of all types is the Bible which consists of a set of ancient texts that belong to particular historical contexts, but that also exist as scripture, and as such have been, and still are, applied to believers' lives throughout the ages.

## O The Jesus movement and house churches

One popular text in early Christianity which reassured the communities that they were living in the New Age, experienced in their possession of the miraculous Spirit of God, was from the Hebrew prophet Joel 2.28–32:

> And in the last days it shall be, God declares, that I will pour out my Spirit on all flesh, and your sons and your daughters shall prophesy.

Here no gender distinction is made. It would seem that this egalitarian vision of the New Age characterized the earliest manifestation of Christianity. However, another alternative structure characterized by patriarchy was present from early times. It has been argued that this structure can be traced right back to Jesus's own emphasis on the fatherhood of God: 'the Son can do nothing of his own accord, but only what he sees the Father doing' (John 5.19).

Thus in Christianity, we are presented with two structural models: egalitarian and patriarchal/hierarchical. Both these models can be discerned from the earliest evidence we possess. The latter has tended to dominate Christianity throughout the centuries, but since the rise of the feminist movement feminists involved in Christianity have sought to reapply the alternative model. Here we will examine the basis for the egalitarian model.

### The Kingdom of God

The ministry of Jesus gave the early Christian communities many of their characteristics. These can be seen in the house churches described in the Acts of the Apostles, St Paul's letters and in Jesus's preaching on the Kingdom of God. All are invited to join this movement – women as well as men, prostitutes as well as pious people. This is illustrated in the Bible in the parable of a marriage feast where the invitations to the feast are extended to include all types of people (see Luke 14.16–24; Matthew 22.1–14). This theme can be seen also in an early formula that was proclaimed at baptisms which is quoted by St Paul in Galatians 3.28:

> There is neither Jew nor Greek, there is neither slave nor free, there is neither male nor female; for you are all one in Christ Jesus.

The centrality of women in transmitting the gospel is an exceptional feature of Jesus's ministry. According to biblical accounts women accompanied Jesus throughout his ministry; women from Galilee stayed in Jerusalem after Jesus's arrest and were there for his execution and burial; the women are the first witnesses to the resurrection. The central role of women in the early house churches is reflected in those mentioned by name in the Bible as having essential roles in the communities, such as Phoebe, Prisca, Mary, Junias (Romans 16), Chloe (I Corinthians 1.11) and Lydia (Acts 16).

### Family and discipleship

Women's lives in the Roman Empire during the first century AD were contained within the institution of marriage, either in terms of being part of their father's household or of their husband's. When we examine Jesus's teaching and attitudes regarding the family we find something distinctive from the society of his day. Jesus's comments on the family reflect on *a-familial* ethos, for example:

> there is no one who has left house or brothers or sisters or mother or father or children or lands for my sake and for the gospel who will not receive a hundredfold.
>
> (Mark 10.29)

> 'Your mother and your brothers are outside, asking for you.' And he replied, 'Who are my mother and my brothers?' And looking around at those who sat about him, he said, 'Here are my mother and my brothers!'
>
> (Mark 3.32–5)

A similar attitude can be discerned elsewhere in the Bible, for example, in I Corinthians (7.32–4) where St Paul gives advice on marriage:

> The unmarried man is anxious about the affairs of the Lord . . . but the married man is anxious about worldly affairs, how to please his wife, and his interests are divided. And the unmarried woman or girl is anxious about the affairs of the Lord . . . but the married woman is anxious about worldly affairs, how to please her husband.

The new Christian communities would seem to have been offering an alternative lifestyle where familial bonds became redefined in terms of common belief being preferred to blood ties. For women this was a revolutionary option. Instead of having community ties preordained through father, brother, husband or son, they could claim them for themselves by being baptized, that is, born, into a new family of fellow believers. There, rather than managing a household, their energies would be directed first and foremost to the task of spreading the gospel alongside their male colleagues.

For most women their new lives as believers would not be in place of their roles as wives, mothers and daughters, but would run parallel to them. This was the case unless the option of celibacy had been taken. If this choice was made by a woman then her 'family' became the believing community, and, as a non-sexual being, she would be able to work freely with fellow men and women.

From our brief survey of some of the salient issues addressed in Jesus's ministry and practised by early house churches, we can see a distancing between these groups and the standards of a patriarchal/hierarchical society. It could be argued that such an egalitarian model could not sit easily within a society that was essentially patriarchal. This vision of a new order for the new age could only last in the short term, and inevitably would have to concede to pressures of conformity, particularly in the light of persecution.

## ○ Christianity and patriarchy

Patriarchal hierarchy is the second model we need to examine, and is no doubt the one which comes most readily to mind in the context of Christianity.

### Influences on Christianity

When Christianity began to spread from an agrarian setting into the ancient cities of the Greco-Roman world, it encountered more directly the concept of a strictly ordered hierarchically structured society built on solid philosophical foundations. The patriarchal hierarchy, encountered particularly in places where Greek culture had dominated, can be seen to have been underpinned by, for example, the philosophical and political ideas of Aristotle (384–22 BC).

Aristotle believed that the order of the patriarchal family unit formed the foundation of the political state. His ideas became popular in the Roman world some centuries later, and were prevalent in philosophical schools in the first century AD. Furthermore, they have continued to have a lasting influence on western culture down to the present day. His description of the family is characterized by his belief in natural ruler and natural subject:

> as between the sexes, the male is by nature superior and the female inferior, the male ruler and the female subject. And the same must necessarily apply in the case of humankind generally . . . these are by nature slaves for whom to be governed by this kind of authority is advantageous.
>
> (*Politics* I.1254b)

In Aristotle's vision of society the inclusion of slaves into a family unit transforms it into a household, many households form a village, many villages form a city state or *politeia*. The family is the foundation of civilization.

### The Christian household

We can see this Aristotelian model clearly reflected in Christian models of the family as found in biblical texts, for example:

Wives, be subject to your husbands, as is fitting in the Lord. Husbands, love your wives, and do not be harsh with them. Children, obey your parents in everything, for this pleases the Lord. Fathers, do not provoke your children, lest they become discouraged. Slaves, obey in everything those who are your earthly masters, not with eyeservice, as men-pleasers, but in singleness of heart, fearing the Lord . . . Masters, treat your slaves justly and fairly, knowing that you also have a master in heaven.

(Colossians 3.18–4.1; see also Ephesians 5.21–6.9; I Peter 2.11–3.12)

A unit such as this would pose no threat to established society, on the contrary, it would only help to strengthen its foundation.

### Patriarchy in the churches

The concept of patriarchal hierarchy in the household extends in Christianity to the organization of the church as an institution. Women are forbidden to teach men, and they cannot hold authoritative roles in mixed communities:

Let a woman learn in silence with all submissiveness. I permit no woman to teach or to have authority over men; she is to keep silent. For Adam was formed first, then Eve; and Adam was not deceived, but the woman was deceived and became a transgressor. Yet woman will be saved through bearing children, if she continues in faith and love and holiness, with modesty.

(1 Timothy 2.11–15)

Here we see a very clear example of sexual hierarchy, again underlined through theological underpinning. To question this hierarchy is to question the order of creation itself. Furthermore, in the creation story when a woman, Eve, was allowed to exercise authority she was seen to be deliberately disobedient, and this act led to the downfall of the human race. Christianity interprets its foundation myth, its account of how the world and humanity came into existence, in terms of an explanation for sexual hierarchy and the subordination of the female sex.

○   **Women's resistance**

Although we can trace the two models of organization that we have examined to particular historical situations in the ancient world, in application they become ahistorical since they have been in operation throughout the western world and its dominions for 2000 years. Each time a new church is founded, the Bible and the traditions of Christianity are used as the basis for its structure and organization. In this way ancient texts and practices become contemporary for all times and places.

Within Christianity today women perceive their roles in a variety of ways. These differences can be accounted for to some extent by the vast variety of traditions and denominations within Christianity itself. For example, in the Protestant tradition the Bible is understood as the central authority in people's lives as Christians, whereas for Catholics the authority of 2000 years of Church tradition shapes their attitudes, beliefs and practices, and the Bible is mediated to them through the Church's interpretation of it.

Also social and political concerns have always influenced Christianity from its earliest days, as we observed in relation to the influence of the pagan philosophy of Aristotle. Today we can observe how the secular feminist movement has influenced and informed many churches, particularly in North America and Europe.

Women's position within Christianity can be seen in three broad types: those who conform with the traditional roles prescribed for them; those who resist these traditional roles and aim to reform and reinterpret attitudes to women in Christianity; and those whose spiritual journey, once informed by feminist critique, has taken them out of and beyond Christianity.

### Acceptance of prescribed roles

Amongst the evangelical churches the Bible is the central authority. All beliefs, attitudes and practices have to have their source in biblical teaching. We can find examples in this tradition both of women who collude with a patriarchal understanding of society, and those who wish to offer alternative models.

Among the evangelicals we can find examples of aggressive stands against feminism that have been taken by both men and women. In *What's Right With Feminism*, Elaine Storkey (1985) attempts to discover some middle ground for feminism and evangelical Christianity. In doing so she highlights the extreme wings of both ideologies before attempting a workable synthesis. She finds this synthesis comfortable for herself, enabling her to maintain her faith in evangelicalism while not compromising her beliefs on the complementary nature of male and female genders. Although this is considered a radical conclusion amongst evangelicals, to many feminists it is better categorized as Christian apologetics (that is, an argumentative defence) than feminist theology.

In her book she quotes from both extreme conservative evangelical voices and radical feminists in an attempt to show their shortcomings. Her quotations from the former group, dating from the early 1980s when feminism was no longer possible to ignore, divulge the gulf between the reactionary Christian position and secular feminism. For example Storkey quotes the following from a compendium on the Christian family:

> In the name of equal rights for women a whole new life-style is creeping into the family domain, one that is weakening the father's role in the home at the expense of the marriage and the family. Feminine dominated homes are on the increase at an alarming rate, compounding the tragedies of marriage and the home.
>
> (quoted in Storkey 1985: 116)

This extract was written by an evangelical woman:

As a by-product of the women's movement women are increasingly afflicted by ills previously mostly suffered by men. Lung cancer, heart diseases, alcoholism, and a decline in life expectancy . . . Suicide rates are up and women are also involved in crime.

(quoted in Storkey 1985: 117)

Conservative evangelicals argue that feminism not only causes problems for women, but can have dangerous implications for men or masculinity as an institution:

This blurring of mother–father roles can have harmful effects on children. Because many fathers now wash dishes, bath the baby and perform other traditional female tasks, their sons often don't know what it means to be a man.

(quoted in Storkey 1985: 119)

Much of this type of anti-feminist literature is written by women who have accepted for themselves some of the biblical attitudes to women discussed above. Conversely, in her attempt to reconcile her brand of Christianity with feminism, Elaine Storkey moves onto the spectrum of feminist theology. However, she stands at the edge when she is compared to more radical reformers and to those who have moved outside of traditional religion to express and experience their spirituality.

Within the Roman Catholic church, as in the case of the evangelical tradition, contemporary women's resistance can be found both in the form of those who conform to prescribed roles, and in the form of reformists who seek to change the system from within. Roman Catholic anti-feminist women's groups exist. For example, in Britain the Association for Catholic Women has argued against the idea that women should be ordained to the priesthood: 'we accept all the Church's teaching, including her assurance that neither she nor any other body can confer valid priestly orders on a woman' (*The Tablet*, letters, 10 August 1991).

### Feminist reformists

Moving along the spectrum from the position which just begins to accommodate features of feminism with Christianity, we discover theologians who are attempting radical reform of Christianity using the tools of feminist critique. A very early example of this type of reform can be found in Elizabeth Cady Stanton's editorial work, *The Woman's Bible*, published between 1895 and 1898. In realizing the biblical basis for western legal systems, Stanton concluded that any legislative reform for the betterment of women's lives had to begin with a critique of the Bible. This approach has had an enthusiastic renaissance with the advent of the late twentieth-century feminist movement.

The Catholic Women's Network is a British organization of Roman Catholic women which is at the other end of the spectrum from the Association for Catholic Women. Members of the network promote feminism, and see the inclusion of women in the priesthood as a development in harmony with other dramatic developments in church tradition that have happened in recent times.

Feminist Catholic and Protestant theologians exist in many countries, particularly in North America, and include eminent academics such as Elizabeth Schussler Fiorenza, Letty Russell, Phyllis Trible and Rosemary Radford Ruether. Through their research on biblical texts, women's history and theological arguments, they have produced feminist theologies that both challenge the patriarchal structure of the church and encourage women who feel torn between their religious experience and their feminist consciousness.

The results of the research and experiences of the more radical feminist reformists has led many of them to take initiatives in setting up alternative Christian communities with structures that reflect many of the ideals of the feminist movement, as well as applying the concepts of the earliest egalitarian Christian communities which we examined in the first part of this chapter.

When we analyse the contemporary phenomenon of these alternative Christian churches we discover an overlap between radical reformists within Christianity and feminists who have broken out of institutionalized religion but who still claim a Christian identity. The concept of 'Woman-Church' embraces both types of Christian feminist. Elizabeth Schussler Fiorenza, who can be seen both as a reformist of the institutionalized church and as a pioneer in the Woman-Church movement, prefers the term 'ecclesia (Greek for "church") of women' since 'church' reflects too much the patriarchal Christianity of history. She describes her vision of the new phenomenon as follows:

> The image and vision of the people of God, of my people, who are women, theologically sums up my own spiritual feminist experiences and that of my sisters who have celebrated our bonding in sisterhood for empowerment and reclaimed our baptismal call to the discipleship of equals. This image and self-understanding allows us to build a feminist movement not on the fringes of the church but as the central embodiment and incarnation of the vision of church that lives in solidarity with the oppressed and the impoverished, the majority of whom are women and children dependent on women.
> (Fiorenza 1983: 343–4)

According to its adherents, the Woman-Church is the true church embodying the truth of Christianity.

Analysts of religion are tempted to place such theological ideas and practices that belong to Woman-Church outside the spectrum of Christianity. Consequently, the Woman-Church movement is being understood by sociologists of religion as an example of posttraditionalization, although many amongst its adherents would still describe themselves as 'Christian'.

### Post-Christian feminism

Women who overtly reject the Christian religion often use the phrase 'post-Christian' to describe their position. Mary Daly, the North American feminist philosopher, has described her journey out of Christianity most articulately, and, in doing so, hopes to raise the awareness of other women. She calls for women to leave Christianity behind and go beyond it to 'sisterhood as cosmic covenant'. She wrote her book *Beyond God the Father* in 1973 as she was leaving the church and creating a post-Christian stance. A lot of space in this book is taken up with a feminist critique of Christianity, a religion which she sees as being patriarchal to its very core and, therefore, beyond feminist redemption. She describes the Christian trinity of Father, Son and Spirit in terms of rape, genocide and war; she claims that 'when God is male the male is God'. For Daly women can only become themselves outside the patriarchal church in a community of sisterhood and with a spirituality based on women's values and hopes. Some of the imagery and language she uses in *Beyond God the Father* reflects ideas and concepts of ecofeminism today:

> changing our environment from a culture of rapism to a culture of reciprocity with the beauty of the earth, the other planets, the stars. Out of women's becoming in the process of nonbeing can come an ever more conscious participation in the community of being. This means that we look upon the earth and her sister planets as being *with* us, not *for* us. One does not rape a sister.
>
> (Daly 1973: 178)

Daphne Hampson is a British post-Christian feminist, but, unlike Daly, her post-Christian position does not necessarily involve a concept of sisterhood, but instead centres on women discovering their uniqueness and individuality. Her main criticism of sisterhood is focused on Fiorenza's belief that women today can experience a solidarity of sisterhood with women of the earliest Christian communities:

> The difference in life-style between myself (and herself) as white, middle-class women living in the western hemisphere today and that of first century women is such as to make all comparison meaningless.
>
> (Hampson 1990: 34)

A criticism of Hampson is that in stressing her uniqueness, few women feel they can identify with her particular position. Conversely, Daly's position has attracted many admirers and followers because her alternative is built on sisterhood both from her experience within and without Christianity.


## ○ Conclusion

From our brief survey and analysis of Christianity we have seen that a patriarchal hierarchy has been and still is most dominant in the many varieties of Christianity. Christianity has both informed and been informed by its host societies, so that it can reflect, reinforce, and also reform society. Today we can observe an important dialogue taking place between the Roman Catholic church and political situations in many parts of the world:

Haiti, the Philippines, and many countries in Latin America. Here liberation theology is empowering the people to act for themselves and make their own history, and here the organizational model being suggested is the egalitarian one.

Many aspects of feminist theology have provoked discussion about and support for women and their varied situations across the globe through the work of the World Council of Churches. Christianity itself is being reformed by feminist theology, and, by the inclusion of women in the priesthood in many churches, the hierarchy has begun to lose its male identity, and the pyramidal structure is also under question. It would be impossible to identify one single element that has been responsible for recent structural and theological reforms in various churches that relate directly to women's lives. Rather, a convincing explanation would have to include a variety of factors creating pressure for change, for example, on the positive side: the impact on western society of the secular feminist movement, the constant effort of feminist Christian reformers, and sexual equality legislation; and on the negative side: decreasing attendance figures in many churches, lack of available 'manpower', and concern about the widening gap between society's attitudes and those traditionally accepted by Christians.

However, it has to be acknowledged that there are still many prominent examples of where Christianity is a major support of patriarchal society, and where it regards feminism as its enemy. The issues of birth control and abortion are examples where both Roman Catholics and Protestants within conservative Christianity are united in their resistance to women having autonomy over their bodies. On the question of abortion, in particular, together they oppose any legislation that permits it. Likewise, on the question of women's ordination to the priesthood these two brands of Christianity have been closely allied in their opposition to women gaining power and authority in the churches.

Thus the two organizational models we have isolated for discussion can be seen to persist in Christianity today. Historically we can see how one model in particular, the patriarchal hierarchy, was in harmony with politics and society of the ancient world. The fusion of Christian theology with Greco-Roman law and civilization laid the foundation for western culture and society that has persisted through the ages and been reflected in law and government. When we bear in mind the imperialistic nature of western, European civilization, motivated and justified by the Christian religion, we can appreciate its global as well as national influence. Once this basis of our society is fully understood our critique can be rigorous and far reaching.

○ **Questions**

> 1 Think of examples of how Christianity has played a part in developing society's expectations of women.
>
> 2 Could the inclusion of empowered women into a church organization lead to the reform of its structures?

3 Is the option of a 'woman-based' spirituality a more realistic model for inclusive religion in the twenty-first century?

4 Are feminism and Christianity mutually exclusive?

## Further reading

Loades's reader (1990) contains the main types of feminist critique that have been applied to Christianity. Fiorenza (1983) provides a feminist reconstruction of the earliest development of structures for Christianity and provides an excellent historical framework. Ruether (1985) includes foundation texts and symbols for Womanchurch, while King (1994) broadens the issues in her comments on and collection of theology from women living in the third world. King (1989) and Zappone (1991) provide useful introductions to contemporary women's spirituality that has gone beyond Christianity and which has been motivated by the feminist movement. Ruether (1992) is an example of where radical feminist theology has evolved into eco-feminism.

## References

Aristotle (1926) *Aristotle's Politics* (trans. H. Rackham). Cambridge, MA: Harvard University Press.

Daly, M. (1973) *Beyond God the Father: Towards a Philosophy of Women's Liberation*. Boston, MA: Beacon Press.

Fiorenza, E. S. (1983) *In Memory of Her: A Feminist Theological Reconstruction of Christian Origins*. London: SCM Press.

Hampson, D. (1990) *Theology and Feminism*. Oxford: Blackwell.

King, U. (1989) *Women and Spirituality: Voices of Protest and Promise*. London: Macmillan.

King, U. (ed.) (1994) *Feminist Theology from the Third World: A Reader*. London: SPCK.

Loades, A. (ed.) (1990) *Feminist Theology: A Reader*. London: SPCK.

Ruether, R. R. (1985) *Womanguides: Readings Toward a Feminist Theology*. Boston, MA: Beacon Press.

Ruether, R. R. (1992) *Gaia and God. An Ecofeminist Theology of Earth Healing*. San Francisco, CA: HarperSanFrancisco.

Storkey, E. (1985) *What's Right with Feminism*. London: SPCK.

Zappone, K. (1991) *The Hope for Wholeness: A Spirituality for Feminists*. Mystic, CT: Twenty-Third Publications.

## 6

**HIROKO KAWANAMI**

# Women in Buddhism revisited

○ **Introduction**

Buddhism is an ancient religion which is practised in many societies in contemporary southeast, east and central Asia. Its influence extends from Sri Lanka, Burma, Thailand, Cambodia to Tibet, China, Korea and Japan so a vast number of women are affected by it. There are different schools and traditions which represent the historical processes and cultural variations in Buddhism. In this chapter we shall examine how Buddhist women in these societies deal with the understanding of gender and its social organization in these cultural contexts. We shall start by exploring the construction of womanhood and of gender relations in the Buddhist spiritual canon. These texts suggest that women are as capable as men of achieving a high level of spiritual perfection. However Buddhist textual representations and social practices are often at odds. We shall go on to explore the religious status of women in Buddhist societies, and in doing so we shall uncover considerable social discrepancies with woman's representation in the texts as a spiritual equal. Spiritual subordination also applies as we shall see, to lay women in general in Buddhist societies, and to Buddhist nuns in particular. There may, nevertheless, be some advantages to be salvaged for women who renounce the world and follow the path of the Buddha.

○ **The position of women in the Buddhist texts**

'Now Lord, are women, having gone forth from home into homelessness in the *dhamma* and discipline proclaimed by the Truth-finder, able to realise . . . [spiritual] perfection?' The Buddha replied, 'Women, Ānanda, having gone forth . . . are [indeed] able to realise . . . perfection.'

(*Cullavagga* 1952: 354)

The idea that women are spiritually equal in Buddhism is based on an account in the fifth book of the Vinaya-Pitaka (Book of the Discipline). Here an important remark of the Buddha is recorded following an incident led by his stepmother, Pajāpatī Gotamī. She asked him to allow her and her 500 female companions to leave their homes and enter his monastic community. The Buddha was initially reluctant to admit women into his Order and turned them down three times. But when Ānanda, his closest disciple, intervened and questioned him about whether women had the same spiritual potential as men, he admitted that women were just as capable as men, which led him to accept them into his monastic community, the Sangha. These female ascetics were called bhikkhunī, and were accorded a religious status almost equivalent to that of bhikkhu, the male monks.

This account leads us to examine why the Buddha was so hesitant to accept women into his monastic community. Many reasons have been suggested, but first we have to understand his action in its historical context. Buddhism emerged out of a period and society where there was little spiritual leeway for women. Under the influence of Brahmanism, women were oppressed and considered to be spiritually ineligible no less than the untouchables (Altekar 1956: 204). Women were not even allowed to enter holy temples or recite religious scriptures. Matrimony and obedience to male members of their families were the only ways in which women could pursue their religious goals. In this social context, the Buddha's decision to allow women into the Sangha was extremely radical. There are many other reasons why he may have been reluctant. For example, Buddhist mendicants during the Buddha's time led an itinerant lifestyle, which was considered dangerous and inappropriate for women.[1] The celibate lifestyle, which was essential for the disciples to realize his teachings, may have added to practical problems of men and women staying together. Even upon entering a spiritual life, women were looked upon as both threat and temptation for the males, in other words, a major hindrance to their spiritual endeavour. They were, however, reported to have met with unpleasant encounters and harassment that led to the stipulation of more rules in order to protect them.[2] The primary objective of the Buddha was to propagate his religion as widely as possible without losing the support of the general public. So there was a fundamental concern about people's feelings towards these women; would the lay donors appreciate their spiritual guidance and accept them as religious teachers? Would they provide female ascetics with the same amount of donations which were given to male members? Ultimately, the Buddha's concern could have been economic, based on the fear that the acceptance of women would negatively affect the material support of the general public, who would not welcome women leaving their homes.

Even though women were admitted into the Sangha on seemingly equal terms, there were a number of negative constructions of their positions in the Buddhist text. First of all, eight additional rules, called Garudhammā, technically confined them to a subordinate position in the Buddhist community. *Bhikkhunī* were not allowed to live independently of the male members and had to ask for their regular admonition. One of the most problematic rules stipulated that even if a woman had lived as a nun for 100 years, she still had to 'greet respectfully, rise up in the presence of, salute with joined palms, and perform all proper duties towards a monk' even if he had been ordained only for a day (*Cullavagga* 1952: 354). Second, the Buddha is recorded as saying that if women had not received permission to enter the state of 'homelessness' and join the monastic order, the 'true *dhamma*' would have lasted for 1000 years, but since they had gone forth, 'his teaching' would last only for half of that term (ibid.: 356). This suggested that the women's admission was unfavourable for the future of Buddhist religion.

Here the issue is not about whether these rules and reservations were authentic and uttered by the Buddha himself or not. It is about why these rules were in the text at all. There are feminist scholars who denounce the Buddhist texts as 'androcentric' or 'male-centered' (Gross 1993). Other scholars argue that these rules reflect ideas and attitudes towards women customary in the period. For example, Horner argues that 'the rule is the outcome of an age-old and widespread tradition rather than a prudent provision to keep women in their places' (1930: 121). Kabilsingh suggests that this subordination was a 'strategy' to avoid disapproval in the social climate of the time and to ensure women's protection within the monastic community (1991: 29). These rules were probably prescribed to pacify the opposition of the male members by keeping the final authority in their hands. She also shifts the blame for such prejudice onto the male members of the *Sangha* who compiled the official texts 300 years after the Buddha's death. She implies that they may have added to or taken the Buddha's words further by imposing 'their own subjective standards of what was important' (ibid.: 23–4). Or it may be as Dutt mildly puts it, that these rules were introduced to segregate and subordinate women because it was feared that the presence of women might give 'the weaker male members of the Sangha . . . greater chances of moral lapses' (1941: 294). The fact remains, however, that women in the Buddhist community became relegated to a secondary religious status (Barnes 1987: 108).

In spite of the unattractive conditions for female ascetics, it is narrated that women from all walks of life, married or unmarried, widowed or still with family, joined the Buddha's community. People today may question why these women wanted to shave their heads, leave home and give up womanhood in the first place. Songs compiled in the psalms called *Therīgāthā* suggest why such an option was significant for them.

> Home have I left, for I have left my world!
> Child have I left, and all my cherish'd herds!
> Lust have I left, and ill-will, too, is gone,
> And ignorance have I put far from me;
> Craving and root of Craving overpowered,
> Cool am I now, knowing Nibbana's peace.

O woman well set free! How free am I,
How thoroughly free from kitchen drudgery!
Me stained and squalid 'mong my cooking-pots,
My brutal husband ranked as even less,
Than the sunshades he sits and weaves away.

                                          (*Therīgāthā* 1909: 21, 25)

These songs date back to about 80 BC and they are believed to have been written by ancient *bhikkhunī*. They reveal the inner joy of those women who managed to free themselves from endless domestic responsibilities, social burdens and violent men. It was the freed mind, the release from superstition, craving, and the round of rebirth that made them break forth into singing, 'O free, indeed! O gloriously free' (ibid.: 15). The notion of freedom was, as Horner (1930: 165) states,

> either in the more usual 'phenomenal' sense of escape from worldly troubles, cares, responsibilities, temptations, grief, from boredom and from the cloying senses; or in the wider, more 'transcendental' sense of release from the round of existences.

The 'homeless life' was praised and idealized as the ultimate escape from domestic problems and mental miseries. The contents of these verses reveal a striking similarity to the sense of relief and joy expressed by contemporary Buddhist nuns after joining the monastic community. They also provide us with profound insights into their ideals and aspirations. Joining the order for them meant a step forward from being subordinated to fate and caught up in an endless cycle of hopelessness. It presented them with a meaningful way of life, in which they were finally enabled to concentrate on and work for their own spiritual salvation.

Once having renounced the world, *bhikkhunī* in the Buddhist text are reported to have been quite successful in attaining higher spiritual levels. 'Khemā', previously known as King Bimbisāra's consort, received distinction for her wisdom and insight, an honour she shared with 'Uppalavaṇṇā'. 'Nandā' was first in meditation, 'Dhammadinnā' had great ability as a preacher, 'Soṇā' was well known for her diligence in Buddhist practices, 'Paṭācārā' distinguished herself for her knowledge in monastic codes of discipline, 'Uppalavaṇṇā' for her ability in supernatural powers, 'Bhaddā Kāpilani' for remembering past lives. 'Bhaddā Kuṇḍalakesā', developed special intuitive powers and 'Kisā Gotamī', a kinswoman of Buddha, was considered far advanced in her lack of greed and lust. They were said not only to have been successful in their religious practices but in gaining disciples among people of high social standing. *Bhikkhunī* were acknowledged as preachers, teachers and propagators of Buddhism and some of them became Buddhist saints.

In the course of time, however, *Bhikkhunī* Order went through a progressive decline, and it was probably in the late tenth to the mid-eleventh century that *bhikkhunī* disappeared and their lineage became extinct (Gunawardana 1979: 39). It is suspected that the most likely cause was the deterioration in their economic situation spurred by political problems and competition from other religious groups (Falk 1980: 212). Although there were constant attempts to revive the *Bhikkhu* Order of monks which also went through troubled times, there was no attempt to restore the *Bhikkhunī* Order (ibid.: 39).

In Buddhist teaching, gender is ultimately irrelevant in the pursuit of higher spirituality. The Buddhist doctrine takes an 'existential' view and presupposes that nothing in our social reality is permanent since everything changes all the time. That is, all sentient beings, both men and women, are bound to the transient nature of their physical existence; we all get old, become ill and eventually die. Just as we age, the environment surrounding us changes, and our perceptions are fickle and easily influenced. So social categories such as gender, age, status, nationality and so on are perceived as transient, that is, fundamentally irrelevant for the attainment of Buddhist spirituality. At the initiation ceremony of a Buddhist nun in Burma, the initiate is reminded of the transient nature of her physical existence when '32 parts of the physical body and bodily substances' are recited by participant nuns.[3] The parts of the body and bodily substances are listed one by one whilst her hair is cut off and head is shaved. The phrase is chanted repeatedly, 'there is no woman no man, everything is impermanent and nothing stays the same . . . no one escapes the existential cycle of ageing, illness and death'. In this context, gender is described as inconsequential for a woman's ultimate spiritual attainment. To add to that, Buddhism teaches that the 'self' is an illusory entity, in other words, there is no self that is concrete or tangible, therefore the reality that one may grasp as a woman is not concrete nor permanent. Furthermore, since every human existence is conditioned and limited by mortality, the ultimate ideal for Buddhists is to overcome social limitations to which everyone is subject and achieve a higher level of spiritual freedom so that one can eventually liberate oneself from the endless cycle of transmigration (*saṃsāra*). However, this theological ideal is not, as we shall see, borne out in social reality.

## ○ Social implications of being a woman

It is reported that cultural beliefs, taboos and social restrictions in Buddhist societies have often been disadvantageous to women in their quest for higher spirituality (Khin Thitsa 1983). For example, according to the law of karma, one's past action is believed to determine one's present and future positions of wealth, power, intelligence, beauty and gender. Following this, there is a prevalent belief that 'one is reborn as a woman because of one's bad karma'. A woman is openly told that she is in a morally disadvantaged position due to the insufficient amount of spiritual merit accumulated in her previous lives, which has caused her to be reborn as a woman. Kirsch has observed that 'women tend to be specialized in regard to routine merit-making activities, for women "need" more merit than men' (1975: 185).

Whether or not they feel the need for more spiritual merit than men,

Buddhist women, both lay women and nuns, are seen to be far more active than men in helping the monastery, cooking for the monks and offering donations in their role as 'mother-nurturer' (Keyes 1984: 229, Kirsh 1985: 305). The consequence is believed to be the accumulation of spiritual merit, but what ultimately motivates them is the desire to achieve nirvana. A survey in Burma shows that the motivation behind such acts for most women is the desire to be reborn as male, believed to be a prerequisite to achieve the final spiritual goal (Spiro 1970: 81).

In many ways, women compared to men have been viewed as deeply embedded in their worldly attachments. Some local texts imply the impossibility for women to attain the detached level of spirituality advocated in Buddhism without the help of their sons (Keyes 1984: 1228). For example a mother who is compassionate and giving, is seen as an epitome of binding and cohesive attachment. On the other hand, her unfailing 'love' towards her family gives the mother a special place in the heart of every member of the family. Therefore, the image of a mother giving away her beloved son to the monastic community as a Buddhist monk has become a popular ideal for Buddhist women. The overcoming of her exclusive attachment and sacrificing her most valuable possession have become valued as an alternative religious ideal in achieving spiritual freedom.

Yet the belief that a male is superior to a female is conceded in many negative contexts in everyday life. One of them frequently mentioned is that 'a woman is inferior to a man because she is physically weaker'. The physical weakness is also referred to as the major reason for her spiritual inferiority. During my fieldwork in 1986–87 in Burma (Kawanami 1990), when people were asked whether a woman could attain a spiritual stage equivalent to what men were striving for, they said, 'women are weak-minded, easily frightened, dependent on others, prone to illness and vulnerable to spirits'. In addition to all that, they continued, 'women lack the physical stamina to endure the severity of ascetic training and their vessel may break if they tried like a man'. Even intellectually, women are seen as not as capable, because their weaker vessel makes it more difficult for them to learn the Buddhist texts!

Another popular Buddhist belief tells us that women are born with many more causes for hardship and suffering (dukkha) because of their corporeal state of being which is suggested as inferior to men. By being a woman, she is subjected to the 'five hindrances', which are listed as menstruation, pregnancy, childbirth, separation from parents at the time of marriage and having to serve her husband. The ability to reproduce is negatively represented as the beginning of an endless cycle of rebirths, in opposition to men who are capable to aim for the cessation of rebirths. A nun is considered to suffer less than a lay woman since she is celibate and has already left her parents, so she is spared at least four of such female miseries. The only burden she has to carry is the misery of menstruation. Menstruation, however, defines her biological role, and it has also been one of the primary reasons for a woman to be denigrated to an inferior religious position.[4] From a male point of view, female sexual organs and bodily fluids are essentially threatening, and female reproductive power has to be kept under control. In order to do that, the biological aspect of being a woman is stripped of all positive implications, and the ideology that 'women are unclean' is further elaborated to degrade them as impure and even polluting. The whole notion has been used to bar them from participating in special religious occasions and entering sacred sites. In many place, women are kept away from the Buddha image and religious relics.

These descriptions bring out the concept of womanhood in Buddhist societies, how she is represented and how their images are perpetuated. A woman is born with bad karma, and she is at times negative and defiling, and other times weak and clinging. And yet she is innately dangerous and powerful. Therefore, women have to be subordinated and brought under control lest they should infringe on the male sanctity. The distinction between the sexes is ultimately transformed into a symbolic opposition between the sacred and the profane.

## Religious implications of becoming a Buddhist nun

As we have already seen, the original lineage of the *Bhikkhuni*, Sangha has long since become extinct in the Theravada Buddhist tradition. However there has been an ever increasing number of women who shave their heads and follow the lifestyle of religious ascetics, living on alms and observing the Buddhist precepts.[5] These female renouncers, whom I shall call 'Buddhist nuns' for convenience, are not technically imbued with any special religious status. In fact, from an orthodox Buddhist point of view, they are in the same category as 'pious lay women'. But as far as their religious affiliation and mendicant lifestyle are concerned, they are 'Buddhist nuns'.

In spite of the monks playing down their religious status, these female ascetics are seen as challenging the existing order and disrupting the religious and ideological division between carnal women and spiritual men. Nevertheless, looking at female renunciation, from the nun's point of view, suggests a more positive set of possibilities for women. Becoming a nun may not be as advantageous as becoming a monk, but it definitely provides women with an alternative lifestyle. The moment a woman shaves off her hair, it implies that she has rejected worldly expectations and roles as a secular woman, including, as we have seen, a life dominated by domestic burdens. Moreover, in a culture where women have little control over their own sexuality, Buddhist nuns' vow of celibacy has a profound social, as well as a religious significance. Their rejection of sex, rejection of reproduction, rejection of subordination to the biological cycle, and rejection of suffering, is part of an assertion of a religious identity, intended to supersede the common experience of feminine identity, by overcoming what are perceived to be the fundamental limitations of 'womanhood'.

○   **Questions**

1 What does a religious vocation mean to you? Why do you think
   girls opt to become nuns in Buddhist societies?

2 Compare the position in the Buddhist text and the actual social
   reality regarding the spiritual potential of a woman.

3 Why are Buddhist women discriminated against in the religious
   domain?

4 How do Buddhist precepts define the religious standing of a nun?

○   **Further reading**

If you want to know about women in Buddhism in general, Barnes
(1987) is a good start. Gross (1993) provides a feminist view of the
study of Buddhist women. Horner (1930) is an absolute essential for
those who study the history of Buddhist women and ancient
*Bhikkhunī*. Paul (1979) is important if one wants to understand how
women are represented, especially in the Mahāyāna Buddhist texts.
If you are looking for regionally specific material on Buddhist women,
see Mi Mi Khaing (1984) and Kabilsingh (1991). On Buddhist nuns,
see Bloss (1987), Havnevik (1989) and Kawanami (1990).

○   **Notes**

1 There are many stories of women being molested and abused by monk Udāyin
   (*Saṅghadisesa* in *Suttavibhaṅga* 199–228).

2 There were recorded incidents of monks flashing their thighs and private parts
   and throwing dirty water at female members of the monastic community
   (*Cullavagga* 1952: 363–40).

3 The recitation is called *Thonze-hnik-ko-hkanda*, literally meaning, '32 parts of the
   body' in Burmese. It is recited in the Pali language, which starts from *kesa* (hair)
   and ends in *mutta* (urine).

4 In some cultures, Sinhalese culture for example, the degree of abomination and
   fear expressed towards menstruation and menstrual blood seems to be stronger
   than in others. In Burma, social taboos against copulation, menstruation and
   childbirth are more concerned with the imbalance and vulnerability of such
   physical states implied for women than with male fear.

5 Five precepts observed by lay Buddhists:

   1 abstention from killing;
   2 abstention from stealing;
   3 abstention from adultery (sexual misdemeanour);
   4 abstention from telling falsehoods;
   5 abstention from taking intoxicants (alcohol and drugs).

Eight precepts observed by Buddhist nuns and lay people while taking special vows:
Precepts 1, 2, 4, 5, are the same as above.

3 celibacy;
6 abstention from taking solid food after midday;
7 abstention from dancing, singing, music and shows, from garlands, perfumes, cosmetics and adornments;
8 abstention from sleeping on high and luxurious beds.

10 precepts observed by Buddhist nuns:
Precepts 1 to 8 are the same as above:

9 the sending of loving kindness to all sentient beings (strictly speaking, this is not a precept. I have described it elsewhere, 1990: 24);
10 abstention from handling gold and silver (money).

## References

### Buddhist texts

*Cullavagga* (The Book of the Discipline: 5), (1952) (trans. I. B. Horner). London: Luzac & Company.
*Suttavibhaṅga* (The Book of the Discipline: 1), (1938/1992) (trans. I. B. Horner). Oxford: Pali Text Society.
*Therīgāthā* (Psalms of the Early Buddhists: 1. Psalms of the Sisters), (1909) (trans. Rhys Davids). London: Pali Text Society.

### Other works

Altekar, A. (1956) *The Position of Women in Hindu Civilization: From Prehistoric Times to the Present Day*. New Delhi: Motilal Banarsidass.
Barnes, N. (1987) Women in Buddhism, in A. Sharma (ed.) *Women in World Religions*. Albany, NY: State University of New York Press.
Bloss, L. (1987) The female renunciants of Sr Lanka: the Dasasilamattawa, *Journal of International Association of Buddhist Studies*, 10: 7–31.
Dutt, N. (1941) *Early Monastic Buddhism*, vol. 1. Calcutta: Oriental Press.
Falk, N. (1980) The case of the vanishing nuns: the fruits of ambivalence in ancient Indian Buddhism, in N. Falk and R. Gross (eds) *Unspoken Worlds: Women's Religious Lives in Non-Western Cultures*. New York: Harper and Row.
Gross, R. (1993) *Buddhism after Patriarchy: a Feminist History, Analysis, and Reconstruction of Buddhism*. Albany, NY: State University of New York Press.
Gunawardana, R. (1979) *Robe and Plough: Monasticism and Economic Interest in Early Medieval Sri Lanka*. Tucson, AZ: University of Arizona Press.
Havnevik, H. (1989) *Tibetan Buddhist Nuns: History, Cultural Norms and Social Reality*. Oslo: Norwegian University Press.
Horner, I. (1930) *Women under Primitive Buddhism: Laywomen and Almswomen*. London: George Routledge and Sons.
Kabilsingh, C. (1991) *Thai Women in Buddhism*. Berkeley, CA: Parallax Press.
Kawanami, H. (1990) The religious standing of Burmese Buddhist nuns (Thilá-shin): the ten precepts and religious respect words, *Journal of the International Association of Buddhist Studies*, 13: 17–39.
Keyes, C. (1984) Mother or mistress but never a monk: Buddhist notions of female gender in rural Thailand, *American Ethnologist*, 11: 223–41.

Khin Thitsa (1983) Nuns, mediums and prostitutes in Chiengmai: a study of some marginal categories of women, in *Women and Development in South-East Asia*, vol. 1. Canterbury: Centre for South-East Asian Studies, University of Kent.

Kirsh, A. T. (1975) Economy, polity and religion in Thailand, in G. W. Skinner and A. T. Kirsch (eds) *Change and Persistence in Thai Society: Homage to Lauriston Sharp*. Ithaca, NY: Cornell University Press.

Kirsch, A. T. (1985) Text and context: Buddhist sex roles/culture of gender revisited, *American Ethnologist*, 12: 302–20.

Mi Mi Khaing (1984) *The World of Burmese Women*. London: Zed Books.

Paul, D. (1979) *Women in Buddhism: Images of the Feminine in Mahayana Tradition*. Berkeley, CA: University of California Press.

Spiro, M. (1970) *Buddhism and Society: a Great Tradition and its Burmese Vicissitudes*. Berkeley, CA: University of California Press.

# PART II

## The cultural representation of women

The importance of representation has already been suggested in the previous part in Wendy Langford's analysis of romantic fiction and the part it plays in the social organization of gender relations. Here we look more closely at this topic. Tess Cosslett, Lynne Pearce and Gabrielle Russell outline strategies of reclamation and revision in relation to literature, visual art and film. Alison Easton investigates how far autobiography can circumvent oppressive stereotyping. Linda Woodhead concentrates on reclaiming for feminism representations of women in the Christian tradition. Alison Easton and Gabrielle Russell's chapters introduce the question of race as well as gender, a question on which Sara Ahmed expands, relating theories of orientalism and post-colonialism to some magazine images of women.

## 7

**TESS COSSLETT**

# Fairytales: revising the tradition

The literary tradition contains many stereotyped characters and stories that contemporary feminist writers have wanted to revise. In this chapter, I want to use fairytales as an example of this kind of revision. But first I will outline why feminists have found existing well-known fairytales objectionable, concentrating on *Snow White* and *Cinderella*. For instance, the stories assume that beauty is the highest value for women, and that the possession (or not) of this quality sets women against each other as rivals for male approval. So we have a 'beauty contest' between the stepmother and Snow White, and between Cinderella and the 'ugly' sisters, in which it is also assumed that greater beauty means greater virtue. Beauty, in *Snow White*, is also constructed in terms of 'whiteness'; there are race as well as gender biases at work here. This beauty is what gains the love of the handsome, rich Prince; an equation is being set up, in which beauty leads to marriage, which leads to wealth. Wealth is thus the highest goal to be aimed at, and marriage is the end-point of a woman's life.

In order to attain their goals, the heroines are not active, but passive. Snow White in her glass coffin is a particularly extreme example of woman as the passive object of a man's choice; Cinderella too has to wait for the Prince to find her, and her wish to go to the ball is fulfilled by magic, not by her own efforts. In both cases, external agencies function to rescue the heroines. Rescue of a princess who is the object of a quest often appears in stories featuring male heroes, who battle actively to reach their goals. But the passive heroine is not just contrasted with the active hero, but also with the active, evil, older woman. Both have wicked stepmothers, with their own schemes and aims; in *Snow White*, the stepmother is especially active in plotting to get rid of her rival. Female activity, resourcefulness, energy, anger, are equated with evil; female passivity with goodness. The appearance of the Fairy Godmother doesn't really change this – she is not human anyway, not a possible role model for the female reader; and she only puts in a brief appearance. A further, final feature of both stories is that the heroine is associated with the domestic world – Snow White keeping house for the dwarves, Cinderella in the kitchen; Cinderella doesn't want to be there, but she signals her goodness by her passive acceptance of this role.

So it is easy to see these stories as reinforcing the messages of patriarchy to women: women function as passive objects, and as rivals for male attention; marriage is their only goal; a good woman stays in the domestic sphere. Any other kind of female behaviour is demonic, abnormal, monstrous. In this case, then, why bother with fairytales at all? Why not forget all about them and read something else? One argument is that fairytales are an enormously influential part of our culture. In particular, masses of children read them; and fairytale plots reappear in many guises, for instance, in the Mills and Boon romantic novels that huge numbers of women read. The subtitle of Marcia Lieberman's article, ' "Some day my prince will come": female acculturation through the fairy tale' suggests that fairytales actually *cause* women to take on certain beliefs about their cultural role. As she says:

> Millions of women must surely have formed their psycho-social self-concepts, and their ideas of what they could or could not accomplish, what sort of behaviour would be rewarded, and of the nature of reward itself, in part from their favorite fairy tales.
>
> (Zipes 1986: 187)

It is debatable, however, whether fairytales, or *any* representations, actually *cause* children to take on certain cultural roles – though they may *reinforce* what culture is already telling them in other ways. I will return to this question later, when I look at feminist attempts to rewrite fairytales, and at what effect these may have on *changing* attitudes.

So far, I have been concentrating on an interpretation of fairytales as *bad* – reflecting and even reinforcing bad elements of the relationship between men and women in our culture. As such, we can beware of them, learn from them what to avoid, how we might have been brainwashed. Now I want to turn to a different approach, and emphasize what might be *good* about fairytales, how they could be reclaimed for women. This can be done in two ways: rediscovering earlier, more woman-centred versions, and reading against the grain.[1]

Jack Zipes (1979) argues that fairytales were originally part of an *oral* tradition, passed on by word of mouth, not written down. This is why there are so many versions of each tale. They were a popular art, the art of poor people. They were *not* especially for children (this was a later development). Often as not, they were told by women. They began to be written down from the seventeenth century. The two most influential written collections were by Charles Perrault and the Brothers Grimm (Perrault 1982; Grimm 1983). When the tales were written down, a number of changes were made: they were directed at an aristocratic or middle-class audience, and especially addressed to children; consequently, they were 'cleaned up', and made more moralistic and patriarchal. The many oral versions were narrowed down into one or two 'authorized' versions: in fact, the version of *Snow White* I've been talking about is from Grimm, and *Cinderella* from Perrault. This process of narrowing down has continued into this century, greatly helped by Walt Disney and the tales that were chosen to turn into cartoons. These are the ones with passive feminine heroines, and are also the ones endlessly reproduced in storybooks for children. Zipes is very critical of Disney and of the way fairytales have been taken over by what he calls 'the modern culture industry'. They have become the voice of the dominant ideology (Zipes 1979: 2, 97–136).

In contrast, in the past they were tales of the people, expressing their hopes and fears. Zipes locates most of the tales as coming out of a feudal society; the tales don't look forward to any big social changes, but express the hopes of the poor to escape hunger, exploitation and injustice, and get their hands on the power, money and land of the rich. In some tales, Zipes sees evidence of a much earlier, matriarchal society, where women were highly valued, for instance, when he talks about Cinderella. He calls the modern version 'a tale which is an insult to women', and emphasizes that the original story 'revolves around a woman who gets help and gifts from her dead mother, who takes the form of a tree or an animal' (the Fairy Godmother was a very late addition by Perrault). Zipes claims this tale can be traced back to the Ice Age, to a matriarchal society (1979: 6, 9, 29, 172–3). Other critics have disputed this. It is an attractive idea, however, suggesting you could go back and uncover more women-centred tales.

So, prompted by Zipes, I've looked up some of the earlier versions of *Snow White* and *Cinderella*, in *The Virago Book of Fairy Tales*, edited by Angela Carter (1990). In her introduction, Carter doesn't claim these stories show the values of an ancient matriarchal society, but that they show the stratagems, plots, ways of surviving, which women have used under patriarchy. Women in these stories, says Carter, are never just 'passively subordinate'. Carter talks about the nineteenth-century collectors of fairytales, and points out that their aims were often *nationalistic* – for example, to discover authentic German folk culture, as a prelude to the unification of Germany; or to confirm Englishness by collecting specifically Anglo-Saxon folklore; or, a bit later, the movement for Irish independence was accompanied by a great revival of interest in Irish folklore. People look to past popular traditions to give them sense of identity in the present. In the same way, says Carter, as a woman she wants to 'validate my claim to a fair share of the future by staking my claim to my share of the past' (1990: xiv–xviii). She wants to rediscover and create a woman-centred tradition. So she's looking for tales centred on strong, interesting women. Her tales are collected from all over the world; it's notable that once we get beyond a Eurocentric focus, new possibilities for women open up, though there are also woman-friendly tales to be found in the suppressed oral traditions of Europe. This exercise reveals the class and race, as well as gender biases of what we take to be the 'true' versions of these tales.

The versions of *Snow White* in Carter's collection are *Nourie Hadig* and *The Juniper Tree*. The *Cinderella* versions are *The Princess in the Suit of Leather*, *Mossycoat*, *The Little Red Fish and the Clog of Gold*, *Beauty and Pockface*. These all show elements of active plotting and/or anger by the heroine, female choice, female solidarity, or male/female equality, mixed with some of the oppressive features of our present tales. For instance, in *Nourie Hadig* the heroine, instead of living with the dwarves, looks after a sleeping prince for seven years. When she is later cast into a trance, he reciprocates by looking after her. She also forms a bond of friendship with a gypsy girl, who helps her look after the Prince. This friendship is not affected by their being rivals for the Prince, who, by mistake, is at one point going to marry the gypsy. On the other hand, the heroine doesn't assert herself to reveal the truth, but relies on a magical 'stone of patience'. In *Beauty and Pockface*, however, the heroine is more assertive; she gets to go to the theatre (a treat her stepmother has been denying her) with a new dress, new shoes and a white horse to carry her, when she 'was so cross, she smashed everything in the house, including the earthenware pot'. The pot contained the bones of the yellow cow, the protective reincarnation of her mother, killed and cooked by the stepmother. Anger, not passive waiting, together with a powerful maternal bond, gets this heroine what she wants. Moreover, on the way to the theatre, she uses the loss of her shoe to choose her own husband; each man who offers to pick it up if she will marry him, is rejected until the handsome scholar whom she wants offers. This is quite different from the use of the shoe motif in the well-known version. I found it a very liberating experience to read these quite different early versions and realize that our versions are not fixed, not authoritative. Discovering that there are many different versions of these tales can free us to invent our own variations, increasing liberating features and diminishing oppressive ones even more.

Another way of reclaiming these tales, apart from rediscovering old versions, is to read our contemporary popular versions against the grain. A very powerful and interesting example can be found in *The Madwoman in the Attic* (Gilbert and Gubar 1979: 36–44; also in Zipes 1986: 201–8). This book is about the plight of the nineteenth-century woman writer, and the authors use the story of Snow White as a metaphor for the woman writer's position; in doing so, they reinterpret it, so that the stepmother becomes the heroine, a powerful, inventive, active, creative woman, constrained by demands of patriarchy. Her seeming vanity in front of the mirror is explained by their interpretation of the voice of the mirror as the voice of the absent King, representing patriarchy, judging women by their appearance. Her murderous hatred of her stepdaughter is excused by interpreting Snow White as the ideal of the passive, good, angel-in-the-house woman, who would kill the Queen's chance of being an artist. The Queen wants to kill this image in herself. The Queen is defeated because by killing Snow White, she has turned her into just what the patriarchy wants – a beautiful object. But once Snow White is married she too will become the angry, doomed Queen. Gilbert and Gubar see the woman writer caught between two images of woman, the passive, deadly angel, and the active, plotting writer, who is defined as monstrous and evil.

This practice of reading fairytales against the grain is halfway towards rewriting them. There are various degrees of rewriting that can be done. Most simply, you can tell the same tale, keeping the plot intact, but changing the implied values, just as Gilbert and Gubar have made the step-mother the heroine of *Snow White*. You could take this idea further, and perhaps also rewrite the story from *her* point of view. This strategy of keeping the story intact, but changing the values, operates to bring out and emphasize the repressive, patriarchal values of the 'original'. The poet Anne Sexton is especially good at this; in her poems *Transformations*, she takes on the voices of the female victims of these tales (Zipes 1986: 114–18). Tales that do change the basic story more radically still often keep this element of criticizing the values of the parts of the original they do keep; Angela Carter's rewrites of fairytales usually combine a critical retelling of the original, exaggerating and emphasizing certain features, with a changing of the ending (Carter 1979).

The next stage of rewriting would be actually to change the story. The simplest way is by mere reversal; the genders get reversed, princes get to do what princesses usually do, and vice versa. Princesses get to kill dragons, rescue princes; princes are passive, feeble. There are objections to reversal, however. Feminists don't want women just to take over the violent and oppressive values of patriarchy. Reversal also creates a problem with the plot: passive, incompetent princes are not very attractive. The problem is often solved in this type of story by inventing another, more acceptable male character for the princess to marry – for example, the Jester, the Magician; or of course she decides not to marry at all. There are some stories of this type in Zipes's collection (1986: 39–61). The problem of violence is also solved by making the princess defeat the dragon, or whatever other task, by cunning or conciliation, not violence. So it is hard to find straight reversal stories; the strategy usually leads on to something else. However, I don't think we should dismiss reversal entirely as a bad thing; it can be very funny, and provokes readers to think about gender roles, how arbitrary they are, why what is acceptable in one sex isn't in another. What I want to get away from here, is the notion that there's only one correct feminist way to rewrite these stories. There are lots of different ways they can be rewritten, all with different effects, some comic, some tragic.

Apart from simple reversal, tales can be more drastically revised, with new, unexpected incidents; or told as sequels, happening *after* the traditional ending; or introducing new characters. A problem here is, do they then become unrecognizable? Or, a related problem, how far do these rewrites depend on the reader's knowing and recognizing the originals? I don't think there's a problem about straying too far from the originals; those early versions of *Cinderella* and *Snow White* were very far from the versions we know, yet still are recognizable. Some feminist tales don't seem to have one original in mind, but play about with recognizable fairytale plots and conventions – princesses, princes, dragons, castles, happy endings. I also think the question of whether these new tales depend on originals or stand on their own isn't a real problem, either in the sense that they stand on their own, or in the sense that they fail if they get too far from the original. Nearly all literature depends on you recognizing its conventions, or references, hidden or obvious, to previous works. Tales that do refer very closely to original versions give two stories for the price of one: the original story, and the rewritten version, which acts as a kind of commentary or criticism on it.

So how have feminists rewritten *Snow White* and *Cinderella*? There are some examples in Zipes's collection, *Don't Bet on the Prince*. *Snow White* by the Merseyside Fairy Story Collective (Zipes 1986: 74–80) completely recasts the story so that it is about the relations between evil capitalists (the wicked Queen) and noble workers (Snow White and the Dwarves, who work in the Queen's diamond mine). The beauty contest is eliminated: the Queen's mirror answers questions about happiness instead. The all-seeing mirror might be a metaphor for the Queen's secret police. The question of marriage also disappears entirely – the prince is cut out of the story. Marriage is replaced by Snow White's comradeship with her fellow workers, the dwarves, and the ending or goal of the story is freedom, not marriage; a successful, non-violent revolution takes place, and the Queen is deposed. The story thus evades the whole question of gender relationships. The women in the story are certainly not passive; the story dramatizes the conflict between two strong women, representing the oppressed and oppressing classes. The women are still in conflict, but *not* because of rivalry over men, or male approval. I'm never quite sure what I think of this story – it is an imaginative transformation of the usual story into different terms, yet it is curiously gender-blind, and doesn't address the gender issues raised by the original story. There are also some features of the original that are preserved, but seem without much point – why dwarves; why seven; why does Snow White live with them? And then I start wondering about their household arrangements: doesn't Snow White find herself always making the tea, or sweeping up? And when the new revolutionary government takes over, will she find herself banished back to the home, while the dwarves divide power among themselves? Obviously, I want to rewrite *this* story.

*The Moon Ribbon*, a rewrite of *Cinderella*, is by Jane Yolen (Zipes 1986: 81–7), who has written about the earlier versions of *Cinderella*, and obviously has them in mind here. The story restores and reinforces the mother/daughter bond of some of the earlier versions. Once again, this story dispenses entirely with the prince – Sylva, the heroine, does marry, but we don't know to whom, and this isn't part of the story. The chief reason for the marriage seems to be to have a daughter of her own, so she can pass on the magic ribbon of hair that comes from her own mother. The real goal of the story is Sylva's self-discovery, which frees her from her evil stepmother; a magical mother-figure gives her some symbolic jewels, which she finally refuses to give up to the grasping stepmother. Beauty is again not important as Sylva is 'plain but good-hearted'. The story also deals with the question of the heroine's passivity – Sylva is passive to start with, and puts up with suffering. When she begins to act, to discover the strong woman in herself, to assert herself against her stepmother and make choices – she is freed. The story still, however, keeps the evil stepmother and sisters – though they are greedy, rather than envious of the heroine's beauty. But the stepmother and her daughters could be read as created by Sylva's attitudes – the magical mother-figure whom she meets in the story offers to be first her mother, and then her sister, showing her a new way of relating to women as mothers and as sisters. Here, I also want to write a sequel, to see how the new Sylva reacts and relates to other women she meets, and creates bonds of sisterhood.

So these two stories can show you what can be done in feminist rewrites of fairytales, what hasn't been done, and how there are always new possibilities. As further illustration of this last point, here are three different ways *Cinderella* has been rewritten for me by students at Lancaster. One version includes a love affair between the Fairy Godmother and the Queen (the mother of the Prince). This challenges the unquestioning heterosexism of the original. A lesbian relationship for the heroine is also of course a possibility. In another version, the story is kept the same, but Cinderella is the villain, scheming and plotting to get the prince by appearing weak and helpless, and by dramatic gestures like running away from the ball. Her older sisters and mother are the heroines: they have jobs, and lead interesting lives. Cinderella marries the prince, but is seen as getting the boring life she deserves. The last version has a modern setting, Cinderella has a hopeless life with her cruel relatives. Suddenly she realizes there is *no* Prince Charming, *no* Fairy Godmother to rescue her; she goes off on her own and becomes a great actress. All these versions deal in different ways with the problems feminists have with fairytales; there is no one correct version.

Finally I want to take up a different problem – how are these stories read? There is a very interesting study of how children read feminist stories, by Bronwen Davies (1989). Davies spent a long time playing with groups of 4–5 year olds, getting to know them, observing their play, reading feminist stories to them, and talking with them about how they interpret these stories. The main point she makes is that the children often didn't get the point of these stories. They were already so familiar with the old narratives, the traditional gender divisions, and so concerned to acquire correct male or female identities, that they didn't hear what was happening in feminist rewrites; they reinterpreted these rewrites back into versions of traditional narratives. She uses the example of Robert Munsch's story, *The Paper Bag Princess* (1980), in which a princess rescues a prince, defeating a dragon by cunning. She then rejects the prince, because he objects to her dirty appearance (the dragon has burned off all her clothes). From a feminist point of view, this is a very good rewrite. It looks at first like mere reversal, the princess rescuing the prince, but she does it by trickery and cleverness, not violence. The prince fails to appreciate her cleverness in rescuing him, and is concerned only with her appearance. She judges him correctly, refuses to marry him, and dances off into the distance in the last picture. The conventional romance values of the usual fairytales are subverted. But this is how Davies (1989: 60) summarizes what the children thought of the story:

> When the dragon burns Elizabeth's castle and steals Prince Ronald, he also burns her clothes off and makes her very dirty. Most children see her at this point as having magically changed into a bad princess, as if the dragon had cast a spell on her. That badness, because of her

nakedness, has negative sexual overtones. Some of the boys are very switched on to her naked and bereft state . . . Other boys constitute Ronald as hero. Most are unable to see Elizabeth as a genuine hero, and are equally unable to see her choice to go it alone at the end as legitimate or positive. The dragon, for most, is the powerful lascivious male, whose power is untainted by Elizabeth's trickery. In this version of the narrative Elizabeth clearly loses her prince, not because she chooses to leave him, but because she is lacking in virtue. Most children believed Elizabeth should have cleaned herself up and then married the prince.

Depressing, isn't it? As Davies (1989: 69) says,

> The power of the pre-existing structure of the traditional narrative to prevent a new form of narrative from being heard is ever present . . . and there is no single solution to this for the feminist writer or for the adults who are interacting with and reading stories to children.

Clearly books on their own can't have a great effect on children, if they are not reinforced in other ways. But I wonder if interviewing slightly older children might make a difference; this is something you could try out for yourselves.

There is not much at all on how *adult* readers might react to rewritten fairytales. Anne Cranny-Francis's book *Feminist Fiction* (1990) looks at the ways feminist writers have rewritten not just fairytales, but other popular genres such as science fiction and detective fiction.[2] She talks about how these writers construct what she calls 'a feminist reading position' – a reading position is 'the position assumed by a reader from which the text seems to be coherent and intelligible. It is essentially a set of instructions about how to read the text, constructed by the text' (1990: 25). But the children Davies interviewed constructed lots of different readings, all intelligible to them, in different ways. Cranny-Francis also admits that in rewrites 'readers can be irritated by the disruption of their traditional reading practice' (1990: 3). So, not all readers will fit comfortably or willingly into the reading position constructed by the text. And as we saw, it is always possible to read against the grain. I think the attempt to construct or to find just *one* reading position from which the text is intelligible, and gives the correct feminist message, is as misguided as the idea that there is just *one* correct way to rewrite a story. Reading positions will depend on who the reader is, what they already believe. Rewriting fairytales is not therefore a hopeless activity; feminist readers will want to read enjoyable tales that confirm their beliefs, give them heroines to identify with, and help them free themselves from old fairytale patterns; other readers may be provoked into thinking about gender in a new way.

○  **Questions and exercises**

1 Compare Angela Carter's version of *Little Red Riding Hood*, 'The Company of Wolves' in *The Bloody Chamber*, Tanith Lee's version 'Wolfland' in Zipes' *Don't Bet on the Prince*, and the oral version of the story, also in Zipes (1986), with the one you know. What important differences are there? Why have Carter and Lee changed the story in the ways they have? Have they changed it enough? What is wrong with the well-known version of the story?

2 Rewrite a well-known fairytale. Include a short commentary explaining why and how you wanted to change it, and whether you think your version is successful.

3 Can you apply these ideas to other genres, e.g. romance, science fiction, detective fiction, horror stories?

4 Interview a small group of adults or children to discover their reaction to feminist fairytales. Do you think their responses show that revising fairytales works? What does 'working' mean in this context?

○  **Further reading**

There is a *Second Virago Book of Fairy Tales* (Carter 1992), containing more unfamiliar stories and versions. You can find some more versions of Cinderella in Philip (1989). Dundes (1982) and Zipes (1993) provide a variety of interpretations of *Cinderella* and *Red Riding Hood* respectively. Bettelheim (1976) gives psychoanalytic interpretations of all the popular tales, as well as summarizing the Grimm and Perrault versions, but beware of his rather sexist and gender-blind approach. A good feminist article on contemporary rewrites for adults is Rose (1983). The whole of *Transformations* can be found in Sexton (1981). Some more good rewritten fairy tales for children are Cole (1986) and Storr (1980).

○  **Notes**

1 The phrase, 'against the grain' was coined by Walter Benjamin. It is a type of Marxist literary critical practice associated with Terry Eagleton and followers which undermines the 'dominant' reading position offered by a text and offers alternative or oppositional interpretations.

2 Literary and artistic genres are established categories of written work with similar features and common conventions (established stylistic and thematic practices).

○  **References**

Bettelheim, B. (1976) *The Uses of Enchantment*. London: Thames and Hudson.

Carter, A. (1979) *The Bloody Chamber*. Harmondsworth: Penguin.

Carter, A. (ed.) (1990) *The Virago Book of Fairy Tales*. London: Virago.

Carter, A. (ed.) (1992) *The Second Virago Book of Fairy Tales*. London: Virago.

Cole, B.(1986) *Princess Smartypants*. New York: G. P. Putnam's Sons.

Cranny-Francis, A. (1990) *Feminist Fiction*. Cambridge: Polity Press.

Davies, B. (1989) *Frogs and Snails and Feminist Tales*. Sydney: Allen and Unwin.

Dundes, A. (1982) *Cinderella: A Folk Lore Casebook*. New York: Garland Publishing.

Gilbert, S. and Gubar, S. (1979) *The Madwoman in the Attic: The Woman Writer and the Nineteenth Century Literary Imagination*. New Haven, CT: Yale University Press.

Grimm, J. (1983) *The Complete Grimm's Fairy Tales*. London: Routledge and Kegan Paul.

Lieberman, M. (1986) 'Some day my prince will come': female acculturation through the fairy tale, in J. Zipes (ed.) *Don't Bet on the Prince: Contemporary Feminist Fairy Tales in North America and England*. Aldershot: Gower.

Munsch, R. (1980) *The Paper Bag Princess*. Toronto: Annick Press.

Perrault, C. (1982) *Perrault's Complete Fairy Tales*. Middlesex: Kestrel.

Philip, N. (1989) *The Cinderella Story: The Origins and Variations of the Story Known as 'Cinderella'*. Harmondsworth: Penguin.

Rose, E. (1983) Through the looking glass: when women tell fairy tales, in E. Abel, M. Hirsch and E. Langland (eds) *The Voyage In: Fictions of Female Development*. Hanover, NH: University Press of New England.

Sexton, A. (1981) *Complete Poems*. Boston, MA: Houghton Mifflin.

Storr, C. (1980) *Clever Polly and the Stupid Wolf*. London: Puffin.

Zipes, J. (1979) *Breaking the Magic Spell: Radical Theories of Folk and Fairy Tales*. London: Heinemann.

Zipes, J. (ed.) (1986) *Don't Bet on the Prince: Contemporary Feminist Fairy Tales in North America and England*. Aldershot: Gower.

Zipes, J. (1993) *The Trials and Tribulations of Little Red Riding Hood*. London: Routledge.

## 8

**LYNNE PEARCE**

# Reframing resistance: the representation of women in the visual arts

Many contemporary feminist art historians would claim that women have fared worse within the arena of the 'fine arts' (painting and sculpture) than in any other field of cultural representation. Not only have they suffered centuries of exploitation and 'misrepresentation' as the subjects of male-produced art, but they have also been severely frustrated in their attempts to become practising artists in their own right. While on the first point, the issue of (mis)representation, the role of women in art may be directly compared to the experiences of women in other media (literary representation, for example), the exclusion and marginalization of women as *producers* within the art establishment has been far more extreme. Even today, the number of practising women artists remains shockingly small and the efforts of feminist curators and art historians to get their work recognized, both inside and outside the mainstream, seems to be making very little real progress. Yet despite its slow impact in improving the role and status of women within the art establishment, feminism has at least enabled us to understand *why* things are so bad. In her groundbreaking essay from 1973, for example, Linda Nochlin answered the question 'why have there been no great women artists' by drawing attention to their historical exclusion from the institutions of power. Refusing the alternative feminist explanations which argue either that there *are* 'great women artists' but that they are 'hidden from history', or that the art exists but that it has been marginalized by a patriarchally-biased value system, Nochlin (1973: 5–6) identifies the problem as one of politics and economics:

> The fact that there have been no great women artists, so far as we know, although there have been many interesting and good ones . . . is regrettable, but no amount of manipulating the historical or critical evidence will alter the situation . . . The fault is not in our stars, our hormones, our menstrual cycles, or our empty internal spaces, but in our institutions and our education.

What feminist investigations into the history of women's art have shown us is that women have been repeatedly excluded from a proper training on the grounds of their gender. In the nineteenth century they were severely handicapped both by their exclusion from the major European academies and from the prestigious 'life-drawing' classes (see Greer 1981). Meanwhile, in the twentieth century, when the doors of schools and colleges were finally opened to them, they found themselves being taught without being 'taken seriously'.

The fact that the institutional prejudice against female art students can be identified as being one of credibility inevitably suggests that it is their historical role as the (sexual) subjects of art that has prevented them from becoming producers. While such a bald (and depressing) conclusion can in no way be expected to explain the complex of factors that have operated against the professionalization of women artists, many of their autobiographical accounts tell a similar story (see Chicago 1982 and Gerrish Nunn 1986). It is their institutionalization as the 'subjects' of art that has prevented women from entering art's own institutions.

In this chapter I am going to explore some of the ways in which we, as twentieth-century feminist readers and viewers, can enter into this debate by looking at women as both the subjects and producers of visual texts. In my analysis I will be focusing on two examples: *Proserpine* by Dante Gabriel Rossetti (1873–7) and *Reclaim Kate Bunce* by Rose Garrard (1983). One of the ways in which I aim to evaluate the particular matrix of 'power and resistance' surrounding each text is by attending to the way in which it *positions the viewer* as a gendered subject. This is to say, I will be assessing the way in which it either excludes/marginalizes a female viewer or enters into dialogue with her, and also to what extent the viewer is able to *resist* her textual positioning and 'read against the grain' (see Cosslett, Chapter 7, note 1).

○ *Proserpine*

Dante Gabriel Rossetti's *Proserpine* is, in many ways, a typical example of late Pre-Raphaelite art. (The Pre-Raphaelites were a group of mid to late Victorian painters.) In its representation of the mythological figure, Proserpine, this painting is characteristic both of the fashion for 'narrative subjects'[1] in all Victorian art, and also of the move towards classical referents in Rossetti's own late works. Earlier in his career Rossetti had preferred medieval subjects, and his obsession with the story of Dante and Beatrice, in particular, meant that his work from the 1850s featured a somewhat spiritualized version of female beauty. In the 1860s, after the death of Elizabeth Siddal, who was his model for many of the Beatrice drawings, he turned to a more sensual (and sometimes overtly sexual), representation of the female form culminating in his studies based (like this one) of Jane Morris (see Marsh 1984 for details of Morris's own life and work). Such was the extent of Rossetti's output during this period (*Proserpine* itself exists in eight versions including the smaller, Tate Gallery copy reproduced here), the strong jaw, full mouth, columnar neck, and thick, wavy hair of Jane Morris have become, for many people, synonymous with the Pre-Raphaelite female. Indeed, these key characteristics were widely reproduced and stylized in the work of Edward Burne-Jones and many other of Rossetti's *fin-de-siècle* followers.

The question I wish to take us directly onto here, however, is how does a nineteenth-century male-produced text like *Proserpine* position you as a twentieth-century female/feminist reader? What are your immediate impressions when confronted with the image, and how can you begin to explain your feelings of pleasure, identification, desire, alienation or exclusion (many of us will experience a bewildering combination of many of these)? Putting the pleasure and fascination aside to return to later, I suggest that we first deal with the means by which such an image can be excluding of a female audience. What combination of textual and contextual features mean that this representation of a female subject is *not* directed to a female viewer?

The first details to attend to when analysing a text's exclusionary practices are *contextual*. We need to discover who it was painted by, who it was painted for, where it was exhibited, and by whom it has been owned. The 1873 'original' version of *Proserpine* (formerly on loan to Manchester City Art Gallery), like many Pre-Raphaelite paintings, was originally the subject of a commission, but after being severely damaged in the winter of 1877, was reworked and remounted before being sold to another collector, W. A. Taylor. Such patronage, especially from bourgeois industrialists looking to increase their cultural status through the acquisition of contemporary artworks, was common in Pre-Raphaelite circles, and, in feminist terms, points clearly to the patriarchal economy in which such works were produced and consumed. As I have speculated elsewhere, it is hard to guess what the contemporary women who saw such paintings (the wives of the great collectors, for example) made of them. Although some wealthy women *were* collectors in their own right, the majority were positioned strictly outside the market in which they were produced (see Pearce 1994). Thus, if we, as twentieth-century female viewers feel excluded or alienated from such images, there is a good chance that our female predecessors did also.

Another important contextual factor which will have contributed to the nineteenth-century female viewer's exclusion from this painting is its classical subject matter. Although this is another generalization for which there will be significant exceptions, we must assume that the *majority* of nineteenth-century women – including women of the middle classes – did not have the same classical education as their male contemporaries. Very few of them would have been conversant in Greek and Latin and their associated literatures, and this would produce particular problems with artworks like Rossetti's which frequently came with a Latin or Italian text inscribed on the canvas or attached to the frame. The fact that the Italian sonnet (by Rossetti himself) inscribed on this particular version of *Proserpine* is also offered in English translation on the frame will, of course, have helped matters, but its intertextual literary and historical allusions (to the

*Figure 8.1  Proserpine* by Dante Gabriel Rossetti (1874), copyright the Tate Gallery, London.

Tartars, for example) will still have been challenging.[2] This is not to say that it was *only* female viewers who would have suffered an educational disadvantage in dealing with such texts (the fact that Rossetti 'tells the story' of Proserpine to the painting's purchaser, W. A. Turner, in a letter suggests that he, too, may have lacked the necessary 'cultural capital' to appreciate it), but that they were the most obviously disadvantaged in this respect.[3]

In a painting like *Proserpine*, the formal integration of a written text onto the canvas means that it must inevitably play a major role in controlling the viewer's response to the artwork as a whole. Moving on from the contextualizing factor of education which means that any text of this kind (especially one based upon a classical referent or one written in a foreign language) will alienate certain groups of readers, we need also to attend to the *specific conditions of address* associated with the particular text in question. The English translation of the sonnet attached to the frame of the 1873 version of *Proserpine* reads as follows:

Afar away the light that brings cold cheer
Unto this wall, – one instant and no more
Admitted at my distant palace-door.
Afar the flowers of Enna from this drear
Cold fruit, which, tasted once, must thrall me here.
Afar those skies from this Tartarean grey
That chills me: and afar, how far away,
The nights that shall be from the days that were.
Afar from mine own self I seem, and wing
Strange ways in thought, and listen for a sign:
And still some heart unto some soul doth pine,
(Whose sounds my inner sense is fain to bring,
Continually together murmuring) –
'Woe's me for thee, unhappy Proserpine'.

Although the reader's first impression of this text might be a critical indictment of its awkwardness as a poem (!), it nevertheless exercises considerable power over our interpretation of the image it describes. While, from a feminist perspective, it could be said to be a text which enjoins the sympathetic response of a female reader (female 'imprisonment' is a theme traditionally associated with women's oppression), its representation of a woman so overwhelmingly *powerless* (she is 'fated' to be a prisoner of the 'underworld' for the rest of her days) reinforces all the cultural stereotypes of 'woman as victim'. It is precisely this denial of *agency* – the fact that Proserpine is presented here as a mythological female figure who was denied all possibility of *resistance* – that makes this, I feel, a very difficult text for the feminist reader/viewer to 'read against the grain'. While I will presently suggest some ways in which this kind of resistant reading can be performed, it is important to recognize that the text's *dominant* ideological message is the all-too-familiar one of woman as (sexual) slave. The sonnet might well evoke sympathy for Proserpine's plight (especially amongst a female audience), but the male viewer/collector (to whom it was historically addressed) will undoubtedly have been reassured by the connotations of female passivity and availability. It is my opinion that Rossetti's painting does everything to reinforce this myth while allowing few loopholes through which it could be questioned or resisted.

This textual positioning of Proserpine as 'powerless victim' is vividly echoed in the painting's formal qualities. As is the case with many Pre-Raphaelite paintings, the image is very two-dimensional: there is little depth to the composition and virtually no contextualizing 'background' apart from the square of light behind Proserpine's head (referred to in the first line of the poem). Her body fills virtually all of the available picture space; indeed, at points (her right arm, her hair) she even exceeds it, and this undoubtedly contributes to the sense of claustrophobia which is most viewers' first impression of the painting. The long, narrow rectangular space into which she is crammed, arms folded tightly across her chest, may also be likened to a coffin: a framing device which echoes that of other Pre-Raphaelite artists like Arthur Hughes who frequently presented his female subjects in a frame shaped like a tombstone. The two 'background details' included in the composition – the incense-burner and the trailing vine of ivy – are decorative and symbolic rather than contextualizing. Were it not for the poem, indeed, we would have little idea of who this female figure was or where she was located. In order to know her story we need to know the story to which the painting refers.

Apart from the framing and composition of the female form which emphasizes its imprisonment, Proserpine is also denied agency (the possibility of 'resistance') by being rendered so supremely decorative. As I have argued elsewhere, the decorative, two-dimensional quality of much late Pre-Raphaelite art makes its female subjects strikingly lifeless (see Pearce 1991: 137–8). Although many contemporary viewers enjoy Pre-Raphaelite art precisely because it seems, upon first inspection, to be quasi-photographic in its 'truth to nature', the figure of Proserpine is far too 'flat' and stylized to be mistaken for a 'flesh and blood' woman. Indeed, the decorative and symbolic ingredients of the painting strongly militate against such an apprehension. Observe, for example, the way in which the severely limited palette – it is essentially a composition in green, white and red – is articulated both to create a 'rhythm' of colours and to encode the text's narrative symbolically: the green ivy is in counterpoint to Proserpine's green robes; the red pomegranate in counterpart to her red lips; and her ghostly face and hands form part of a graceful cascade down towards the glow of the golden incense-burner. The artful ('artificial') quality of the painting can, indeed, be seen to be replicating Proserpine's exile from the living world and her incarceration in an underworld with 'nothing natural' in it.

This reading of the painting's formal qualities, then, would seem unequivocally to echo and to support the interpretation of the subject inferred from the verbal text. Rossetti would appear to be corroborating the view of Proserpine as a tragic, but helpless, prisoner of circumstance, a woman whose small misdemeanour (the eating of the pomegranate seed) has condemned her to a lifetime of sexual slavery. This is, at least, the 'official' way in which the viewer is positioned to understand the text. What I want to move onto, finally, is the possibility of us – as twentieth-century feminist readers and viewers – making an alternative 'resistant' reading. Can we somehow escape the text's dominant viewing-position and claim a different perspective on this representation of our hapless female subject?

In embarking upon an 'oppositional' feminist reading of this kind, the first thing to observe is that – unlike the majority of middle-class Victorian women – many of us *will* have had the benefit of an education that makes a classical text such as this one less intimidating. Furthermore, as scholars we have access to the information (catalogues featuring Rossetti's work, for example) which will fully contextualize the artist's choice of subject and provide translations of texts (such as the Italian sonnet) written in languages we do not understand. This is to say that we are, ourselves, coming to the text from a position of (educational) power, and this goes some way to mitigating the gender and class exclusions that operated at the time of its production. Having (re)familiarized ourselves with the myth of Proserpine we are able, if we choose, to resist the dominant reading-position offered us and to make an alternative reading.

One of the most attractive aspects of this painting for the feminist viewer will probably be the apparent physical strength and presence of the female figure. Although in my previous description I referred to her as being 'powerless', this was in terms of her lack of narrative agency (Rossetti tells her story in such a way that we are offered no glimpse of her possible anger and resistance). If we temporarily forget the story or, at least, Rossetti's telling of it, and concentrate on the figure *out of context* she may, indeed, be perceived as powerful. Her strong neck and shoulders suggest that the gown is concealing an equally strong body, and her facial expression which, when read in the light of Rossetti's poem might be seen to signal a passive dejection, can alternatively be seen to register pent-up anger. Instead of seeing this as an image of a woman forlornly resigned to her fate, we can see it as one in which the subject is furious with what has happened to her and is actively plotting a means of escape. As feminists, then, we can read it as a painting which denotes women's *resistance* to patriarchal oppression and sexual slavery. Proserpine has been tricked and is threatening revenge.

That the possibility for this sort of alternative reading readily exists is confirmed by the comments of one of the 1873 painting's later owners, L. S. Lowry. Writing about *Proserpine* in 1976, Lowry complains: 'I don't like his [Rossetti's] women at all, but they fascinate me, like a snake' (see *The Pre-Raphaelites* 1984: 232). This recognition of the 'phallic' power of Rossetti's (later) female figures has been taken up by feminist art historian, Griselda Pollock, to explain their double-edged fascination for the masculine Victorian art market in which they were produced and consumed (Pollock 1988: 153). Pollock argues that subjects like Rossetti's 'Astarte Syriaca', conceived as images of sexual potency and invitation, wreak a covert feminist revenge upon their creators and audiences by being *too potent*. This is a sexuality 'in excess' and 'out-of-bounds' which threatens to overwhelm the male viewer even as the figure of Proserpine threatens to burst her frame. Perceiving this, the twentieth-century feminist viewer can quite successfully imagine that the female subject of such a painting is in active conspiracy with herself rather than existing as the passive object of the male gaze.

In conclusion, however, I must confess to having my doubts about the politics of such a reading. While it is undoubtedly true that *Proserpine* is a text which can be 'read on behalf of feminism', I am wary of blindly overriding its dominant reader-positioning in this way. As I have argued elsewhere, most feminist appropriations of Pre-Raphaelite texts depend upon a radical decontextualization of the subject, both in the way in which they must ignore the circumstances of the text's production and consumption (the patriarchal economy in which it was produced, exhibited and sold), and through the necessity of removing the female subject from the narrative in which she is textually embedded (see Pearce 1994: 155–72). While this sort of 'guerilla' activity is most certainly one way of wresting power from the art establishment by making the images a source of feminist pleasure, it is always at the risk of minimizing (and hence forgetting) the textual and contextual factors which have worked to exclude female viewers from such texts. If we do choose to read such texts 'against the grain', it is therefore imperative that we remain self-reflexively aware of what we are doing.

## Reclaim Kate Bunce

Rose Garrard's *Reclaim Kate Bunce* is a feminist 'reworking' of a painting called *Musica* (Birmingham City Art Gallery) by the late nineteenth-century artist Kate Bunce. Like a number of other women artists from this period who were trained in the provincial art schools of the period, Bunce's painting is very much in the tradition of a late Pre-Raphaelite art which developed the more decorative and stylized aspects of artists like Rossetti and Edward Coley Burne-Jones. The 'femininity' implicit in this school of art has been noted by Germaine Greer who observes: 'Voluptuous surface-patterning in a single plane, statuesque posture submerged in detail helped to make painting more like embroidery' (Greer 1981: 129). Such an emphasis on the decorative surface inevitably works against a 'deeper' textual meaning and, indeed, the unkind would probably say that *Musica* is effectively 'subjectless'. Unlike Rossetti's *Proserpine*, there is no dark myth behind the representation of this female subject.

While the image of the female subject remains strikingly similar to the original, however, Garrard has radically transformed its 'meaning' through a number of formal dislocations. The first and most obvious of these is the fact that this 'Musica', instead of being neatly and harmoniously centred within a safe, decorative space, is literally bursting out of her frame. This effect of 'excess', of a subject who is somehow 'uncontainable', is achieved both through 'imaging' her on a canvas which is stretched, torn, and spilled beyond the top of the frame, and through making her figure fill the whole of the available picture space: parts of Garrard's Musica, rather like Rossetti's Proserpine, are very noticeably 'off-frame'. (The figure's largeness is

*Figure 8.2  Window; Reclaim Kate Bunce* by Rose Garrard (1983). Reproduced by kind permission of the artist.

also emphasized through comparison with the silhouette superimposed upon it to which I will refer directly.) The symbolic connotation here is very clearly one of frustration and desire: women's needs and ambitions are way beyond the limits that have been set for them (a statement that is further underlined by reconfiguring the frame as a *window* from which the subject peers, presumably longing for escape).

In addition to the primary dislocations of scale, Garrard has liberated the figure from the claustrophic decorative background of Bunce's painting. Instead of being subsumed in a cascade of hot-house flowers, Garrard's Musica exists in an empty white space (a symbolic *carte blanche*) which, being very obviously a piece of raw canvas, is also the space of artistic production. Thus, while in Bunce's original the female figure is constituted as an essentially 'meaningless' decorative object, here she is reconstituted as a powerful self-portrait of a woman artist. Instead of receiving the original painting as a typical and mediocre example of late Pre-Raphaelitism, Garrard has rendered it part of the hard-fought history of women's artistic production; its subversion lies not in *what* it represents, so much as *how* it came to be represented. A further dimension to this argument is, of course, that by liberating Bunce's figure from her original decorative space Garrard was doing what the original artist would have liked to have done herself but was unable to do; that is, operate within a different artistic genre – portraiture instead of room decoration.

Another striking recontextualizing device enjoined by Garrard in this and other artworks is the imposition of her own image on the composition. In some works this 'intervention' takes the form of an actual self-portrait (in the 'Tumbled Myths' series, for example, she situates herself alongside other famous women/artists from history), while in others, as here, she presents herself as a silhouette that is (literally) *part* of the canvas (see Garrard 1994). For Garrard, the ambiguity of this self-figuration being also an 'empty space' is clearly very important. In a revealing interview with Fiona Byrne-Sutton and Julia James (which focuses directly on the 'feminism' of her work), she observes:

> There is a cleaning, or a retaining of the ground of the image; what is left within the skin of the painted portrait is my own silhouette. There is a determination of a role through the process of copying, or replicating a pre-existing image – the woman from history – but at the same time there is a retaining of the white ground, which is myself, still undetermined.
>
> (Robinson 1987: 51)

What Garrard wishes to emphasize here is the 'newness' of the woman artist's role. In 'reclaiming' figures like Kate Bunce, she is also exploring the *provisionality* of her own status as a female producer within a traditionally masculine realm, a tension which she also highlights through making her silhouette purposefully androgynous:

> I made the silhouette image of myself – holding a book, pointing a gun and so on [note that here it is a paintbrush] – in my studio clothes and the assumption of many viewers has been that these are male figures. There is no contemporary image for a female artist. We only recognise a female if she's wearing a petticoat. Also, I wanted a womb-like

sensation, of being enclosed within a figure from history. There was a comfort in that, a sort of conspiracy – even though some of these images were actually painted by men.

(Robinson 1987: 51)

What the androgyny of Garrard's 'self-portrait' asks, in effect, is: 'Is it possible to be a woman *and* an artist?' Certainly much traditional art history has answered this question in the negative: to proclaim oneself an artist is to deny oneself femininity. The two identities are mutually exclusive. However, 'women' and 'artists' is precisely what Bunce and Garrard are, and *Reclaim Kate Bunce* is a celebration (as well as an interrogation) of female artistic production.

The last quotation from Garrard also refers – rather cryptically – to her 'conspiratorial' relationship to the figures represented in her works. This leads directly into my final observation on the expressly feminist politics of her art, namely, the way it effects a subversive dialogue between herself (as a contemporary woman artist), the women artists from history (such as Kate Bunce), and the contemporary feminist viewer. For where, in a painting like Rossetti's *Proserpine*, the artist is very clearly exercising a repressive 'authority' over both subject and audience (forcing us to interpret the text in a particular way or excluding us altogether), Garrard enters into a reciprocating relationship. The act of putting herself so literally 'in the picture' indicates her desire to connect with these women from the past, to join with them in the (re)construction of a history and tradition which we, as viewers, can also share. Her 'empty' silhouette is, in other words, the cipher through which we (as female viewers) can enter into dialogue with these women 'hidden from history' and 'reclaim' them for our own (transgressive) feminist purposes.

○ **Conclusion**

It should by now be clear that the feminism of Garrard's art lies in her ability to translate transgressive acts of 'reading' visual images (the sort of 'reading against the grain' that I demonstrated in my own analysis of Rossetti's *Proserpine*) into stunning new visual representations which both interrogate and celebrate women's artistic production.

Her role, as it were, has been to provide us – the twentieth-century feminist viewer – with the *recontextualization* necessary to reappropriate artists and images from the past, and to set about establishing an alternative tradition of women's art. In this practice, she is liberating us from the political anxieties which make us uneasy about either 'decontextualizing' a work like *Proserpine* or naively 'celebrating' a ('mediocre') work like Bunce's own *Musica*. Through a work like *Reclaim Kate Bunce* we thus come to a feminist appreciation of the earlier works without being forced to argue that those works are, themselves, 'feminist'. In Garrard's own work, feminist reading and feminist artistic production come together in a newly creative way.

Avoiding the 'essentialist trap' of other feminist artists who have tried to argue that women's art is 'different' from men's on the grounds of women's biological and cultural 'experience' of the world, Garrard has nevertheless set about forging a tradition to which all women's art, past and present, may refer.[4] She has done this by shifting our attention from the 'what' (i.e. 'representation') to the 'how' (i.e. 'production') of women's art, thus uncovering the vital connection between representation and production with which I opened this chapter. The feminist project in the visual arts depends crucially on wresting 'woman' from her historical subjugation as the 'object' of art, and reinstating her as an active and resistant subject. Garrard's work reframes resistance in just this way.

○  **Questions**

1 With reference either to the Pre-Raphaelite painting discussed in this chapter or another piece of male-produced Victorian art consider your 'positioning' as a female/feminist viewer. To what extent is it possible for you to *resist* the dominant reader-positioning?

2 What does Rose Garrard's painting (or the work of another contemporary woman artist) reveal about the obstacles women artists face in representing the female subject in their work?

○  **Further reading**

The issues of reader-power and feminists reading against the grain that are central to my discussions here are dealt with in more depth in my book *Woman/Image/Text* (1991) and in the chapter 'Pre-Raphaelite painting and the female spectator' (Pearce 1994). The work of Griselda Pollock (1988), Marcia Pointon (1989), Whitney Chadwick (1990) and Deborah Cherry (1993) also demonstrates some of the new ways in which feminists are now considering the representation of women in the visual arts.

○  **Notes**

1 During the Victorian period 'narrative subjects', paintings which 'told a story' (often with a strong moral focus) were extremely popular.

2 'Intertextual' is the term used to describe the way in which some literary and other texts make implicit or explicit reference to other texts.

3 'Cultural capital' is a concept invented by the sociological theorist, Pierre Bourdieu, to explain the way in which power is relayed in capitalist societies through the individual's access to or exclusion from the practices of 'high culture'.

4 Essentialism is the view that there are biologically fixed and unchangeable differences between male and female natures, so that all women are seen as identical.
This view has been criticized for reducing women's historical and cultural
differences to an expression of their biological and sexual difference, and for
collapsing the important differences that exist *between* women.

## ○ References

Chadwick, W. (1990) *Women, Art and Society*. London: Thames and Hudson.

Cherry, D. (1993) *Painting Women: Victorian Women Artists*. London: Routledge.

Chicago, J. (1982) *Through the Flower: My Struggle as a Woman Artist*. London: The
Women's Press.

Garrard, R. (1994) *Rose Garrard: Archiving my Own History: Documentation of Works
1969–1994*. Manchester and London: Cornerhouse and South London Gallery.

Gerrish, Nunn, P. (1986) *Canvassing: Recollections by Six Victorian Women Artists*.
London: Camden Press.

Greer, G. (1981) *The Obstacle Race*. London: Picador.

Marsh, J. (1984) *The Pre-Raphaelite Sisterhood*. London: Quartet.

Nochlin, L. (1973) Why have there been no great women artists?, in T. B. Hess and
E. C. Baker (eds) *Art and Sexual Politics*. New York: Macmillan.

Pearce, L. (1991) *Woman/Image/Text: Readings in Pre-Raphaelite Art and Literature*.
Hemel Hempstead: Harvester Wheatsheaf.

Pearce, L. (1994) Pre-Raphaelite painting and the female spectator: sexual/textual
positioning in Dante Gabriel Rossetti's *The Beloved*, in S. Mills (ed.) *Gendering the
Reader*. Hemel Hempstead: Harvester Wheatsheaf.

Pointon, M. (1989) *Pre-Raphaelites Reviewed*. Manchester: Manchester University
Press.

Pollock, G. (1988) *Vision and Difference: Femininity, Feminism and the History of Art*.
London: Routledge.

*The Pre-Raphaelites* (1984) (exhibition catalogue). London: Tate Gallery/Penguin
Books.

Robinson, H. (ed.) (1987) *Visibly Female: Feminism and Art Today*. London: Camden
Press.

## 9

**ALISON EASTON**

# Autobiography, gender and race: Maya Angelou's *I Know Why the Caged Bird Sings*

In this part of *Women, Power and Resistance* we have started to look at how cultures represent women and women's experiences, and at how women have attempted to revise those images, characters and plots. In looking at female self-representation in autobiography, this chapter explores what happens when a woman writes her own life story. Are readers going to see a more 'authentic' picture of women's lives, to what extent are women free to create themselves in opposition to prevailing cultural constructions of female identity, and what special issues confront women of colour writing their lives, faced by the dual oppression of racism and sexism?

To begin to answer these questions we need, first of all, to understand that autobiography does not give the reader a 'real' woman telling her 'actual' story. There is a vital difference between experience as it is lived and the textual representation of that experience. We are well aware of this when reading fiction, but it is also true of autobiographies, though we often forget this because autobiographies appear to give direct access to the author. A quick way to grasp this essential point is to take 10 minutes now to start writing your own autobiography. You won't, of course, get very far, but already you'll begin to make certain choices: where do you start (in the present time, your childhood, at birth, your family history); who is your audience (you, your daughter or friends, the general public); what do you include or leave out (your achievements, your sexual history); what feels new to write about and what seems familiar to the point of cliché; and what is your purpose in writing it? Clearly, This Is *not* Your Life, but a textual representation of experience and a textually constructed self. Now, if you like, take a further five minutes to try writing another version, and consider how different the second autobiographical piece is and why. The word 'autobiography' derives from three Greek words: *auto*, meaning one's own self; *bios*, meaning the course of one's life; and *graphein*, meaning to write. We must concern ourselves with the interrelationship of all three of these equally important elements (see Stanley 1992).

All autobiographies, whether male-authored or female-authored, are textual constructions, but women face gender-specific problems and influences when setting out to write their life. I want to introduce some of these problems by looking at how four female autobiographers (women of different centuries, countries, classes and races, though all writing in English) introduce or conclude their works.

Margaret Cavendish published *A True Relation of My Birth, Breeding and Life by Margaret, Duchess of Newcastle* in England in 1656 at a time when it was unusual to write one's life story and even more unacceptable to publish it. In her closing paragraph Cavendish directly confronts this hostility: 'but I verily believe some censuring readers will scornfully say, why hath this lady writ her own life?' She argues back in a spirited way that, since many men and women have written personal narratives, 'I know no reason I may not do it as well as they'. She goes on to say, 'I write it for my own sake . . . for, my lord having had two wives, I might easily have been mistaken, especially if I should die and my lord marry again' (Graham *et al.* 1989: 98–9). We can note several things here: her fear of being obliterated because of her tenuous social identity; her definition of self in relation to the men in her life (she begins her autobiography with a long account of father and brothers); the focus on her private experience rather than the major public events through which she lived; and the power of autobiography to respond to the crisis of identity she faces here.

Two hundred years later, though in utterly different circumstances, Harriet Jacobs confronts similar problems in her introduction to *Incidents in the Life of a Slave Girl* (1861). An escaped American slave with a desperate sexual history, she cannot trust her white, middle-class, female audience. Her definition of self is bound up with other black people rather than a wider public, she feels inferior, she has to defend her writing. In spite of this she asserts her right to undertake this autobiography:

> Reader, be assured this narrative is no fiction . . . I wish I were more competent to the task I have undertaken . . . But I do earnestly desire to arouse the women of the North to a realizing sense of the condition of two millions of women at the South, still in bondage, suffering what I suffered, and most of them far worse.
>
> (Jacobs 1861/1987: 1)

The introductions to two twentieth-century autobiographies, Maxine Hong Kingston's Chinese-American *The Woman Warrior: Memoirs of a Girlhood Among Ghosts* (1977) and Caroline Steedman's British working-class *Landscape for a Good Woman: A Story of Two Lives* (1986) continue these concerns. Kingston's opening chapter, 'No-Name Woman', begins with instructions which she will go on to disobey: ' "You must not tell anyone," my mother said, "what I am about to tell you. In China your father had a sister who killed herself. She jumped into the family well. We say that your father has all brothers because it is as if she had never been born" ' (Kingston 1981: 11). Here again a woman speaks of being silenced, and draws attention to the taboos broken when women tell secret stories which the dominant culture refuses to acknowledge.

Unlike the more individualistic models of the autobiographical self which patriarchal society expects from its successful men, these women writers conceive of their own story as the story of others who not only share the same sex but also race or class. Being Asian or working-class women greatly complicates their sense of difference and difficulty, since race and class alter the experience of gender, just as gender alters the experience of race and class. They express a sense of being on what Steedman calls the 'borderlines': their lives and sense of self are unrepresented by mainstream culture, none the less they are in part shaped by those dominant structures of meaning. Steedman's (1986: 5) opening section, 'Stories', begins thus:

> This book is about lives lived out on the borderlines, lives for which the central interpretative devices of the culture don't quite work . . . This book, then, is about interpretations, about the places where we rework what has already happened to give current events meaning. It is about the stories we make for ourselves, and the socially specificity of our understanding of these stories.

Although a woman cannot ever be wholly free of the culture she inhabits, neither is she impotent or muzzled. Faced with the gap between how women are constructed socially and their unrepresented experiences, the woman writer can make a self through her writing in opposition to but also in negotiation with the dominant culture. This autobiographical self is not false, but is a positive act of creation and social recognition. From being an object in others' eyes, she becomes the subject of her story.

The way she writes this self will involve three key elements: image and language, plot, audience. She will have to rethink the language used to describe her and her experiences, adapting the discourses of her society. She will have to rewrite the narratives by which patriarchy controls women's lives, perhaps rejecting the love-and-marriage plot in preference for other narratives which emphasize instead work, female friendship and the new turns women's lives can take once past 50 (see Heilbrun 1989). She needs an audience in order to achieve recognition, but how this audience is envisaged will alter what can be said and how it is said.

I want now to explore these issues of representation in relation to a twentieth-century African-American autobiography, Maya Angelou's *I Know Why the Caged Bird Sings* (1970/1984). Even if you don't know this work, you should find this discussion of general relevance, and of course I hope you'll go on to read the book later.

From slavery times onwards autobiography has been a supremely important literary genre for African-Americans, both women and men. It has been the primary means of expressing their experience. There have been many black American women's autobiographies – about 100 of them before Angelou published *Caged Bird* in 1970 (see Braxton 1989), and many more since, including four more volumes by Angelou herself. *I Know Why the Caged Bird Sings* concentrates on Angelou's childhood in a small town in the Deep South of the United States in the 1930s and early 1940s, her upbringing by her grandmother and life in her community, her rape at the age of eight by her mother's black lover, her ensuing speechlessness until adolescence, and finally her becoming a single mother at 16. Angelou is concerned with the shared experience of African-Americans. She did not originally set out to write her own autobiography:

> I wasn't thinking so much about my own life or identity. I was think-ing about a particular time in which I lived and the influences of that time on a number of people . . . I used the central figure – myself – as a focus to show how one person can make it through those times.
>
> (Tate 1985: 6)

The times she speaks of here was the period of publicly sanctioned racism and legally enforced segregation especially in the Southern states which the civil rights movement of the 1950s and 1960s successfully challenged.

In looking at this text we are going to investigate the ways in which Angelou negotiates with the audiences she faces, resists racist and sexist stereotypes of black women, and makes use of the narratives she inherits from her African-American past.

All autobiographies speak of the past from a specific position in the present. In this case, Angelou's work reflects the confidence and increas-ing freedoms born of the campaign for civil rights. But Angelou still has to face problems with her racially mixed readership. Her account of being raped has been attacked by some African-American commentators, not for its sexual content (as would have happened in a nineteenth-century narra-tive), but for giving a white readership a possible cause to attack black men. Even so, despite the appearance of candour, Angelou's book contains its silences, and there are definite gaps in her narrative. It is still dangerous to tell the whole truth, as the young Maya learnt when she identified her rapist in court and he was subsequently murdered. She quotes her secre-tive grandmother: 'If you ask a Negro where he's been, he'll tell you where he's going' (Angelou 1970/1984: 189). It's an odd motto, if you think about it, for an autobiographer, though it is possibly even stranger to draw atten-tion to such a strategy. The effect is to signal the existence of a private black female world which still cannot be wholly shared. It is particularly impor-tant for white readers (such as myself) to remain aware of this. Angelou has stated: 'Some [events], though, were never recorded because they either were so bad or painful, that there was no way to write them hon-estly and artistically without making them melodramatic' (Tate 1985: 7).

In *Caged Bird* Angelou comments: 'The Black female is assaulted in her tender years by all those common forces of nature [puberty] at the same time that she is caught in the tripartite crossfire of masculine prejudice, white illogical hate, and Black lack of power' (1970/1984: 265). This cross-fire took a number of forms. First, for African-Americans until the 1960s the deeply segregated South terrifyingly embodied the persistence of con-ditions and attitudes which the 1865 abolition of slavery had failed to change. By 1900 most southern rural blacks were not measurably better off than they had been in slavery, and the twentieth century continued this situation – lynchings, no voting rights, persistent poverty, little land ownership, and the 'Jim Crow' laws which made segregation legally enforceable and thus ensured such complete separation between whites and blacks that white southerners practically never saw African-Americans except as servants or in other clear caste conditions. This is why there are so few white people in *Caged Bird*, and why confrontation is rare and fear so rampant. It was an exceptionally violent world: 'If growing up is painful for the Southern Black girl, being aware of her displacement is the rust on the razor that threatens the throat' (Angelou 1970/1984: 6).

In addition, African-American women face the effects of sexism from both white and black men. In *Ain't I a Woman: Black Women and Feminism* the cultural theorist bell hooks comments on how African-American women 'did not see "womanhood" as an important aspect of our identity' and were 'afraid to acknowledge that sexism could be just as oppressive as racism' (hooks 1982: 1). She traces the historical roots of this pervasive situation back to the mid-nineteenth century when black men finally received the vote but the same rights were not accorded to women, white or black. hooks argues that as the social status of black men improved, however slowly, they encouraged black women, like white women, to take up a more subservient role (unlike the previous equal burden of slavery). As racism was appalling and overt, black men found some power in being more powerful than black women, so that by the time of the civil rights movement 'sexist role patterning was as much the norm in black communities as in any other American community' (hooks 1982: 4). In fear of being denounced for not supporting their race, only a few black women in the 1970s wished to ally themselves with the women's movement which all but ignored racial issues at that point.

Consequently, part of the oppression African-American women suffer derives from powerful, pervasive and insidiously damaging images of black women which are found in literature, film, advertising, mass media and even sociological studies. The black woman may be depicted as either a matriarch attacked by sociologists for driving men away from the home they should head, a 'strong', masculinized Amazon, a submissive, long-suffering mammy ('Aunt Jemima') or a lascivious, treacherous sexual bitch ('Sapphire', or 'Jezebel') (hooks 1982: 51–86).

It is important to understand that all such figures are creatures of white imagination, invented to satisfy various white needs. However, even African-American writers have fallen into using these culturally powerful stereotypes and projecting them onto black women. As hooks comments, 'All the myths and stereotypes used to characterize black womanhood have their roots in negative anti-woman mythology. . . . [These] make it extremely difficult and oftentimes impossible for the black female to develop a positive self-concept' (1982: 86).

Angelou is able to take these stereotypes and either revise or reject them. No woman in her work resembles the mammy figure lovingly cooking and caring for a white family. We get to see only one black servant. She seems resigned to her subservient position, but even she is roused to contradict her white employer (portrayed as an arrogant and absurd figure) when the rebellious Maya, sent to learn a maid's ways in her house, revenges herself surreptitiously on her employer by 'accidentally' breaking her favourite china. Her beautiful mother who has lovers and works in saloons and gambling halls is not the Sapphire figure of male fascination and hate, but a complex portrait of a woman from the point of view of her loving but frustrated children who have been sent away from her to enable her to live this life but also to protect them from it. Momma, Maya's grandmother, is one of the most powerful figures in her community, but she is careful to respect her son whose name heads her store. Matriarchy does not really exist in America, especially for a black woman faced with the daily dangers of racism. Angelou both celebrates her childhood awe of her grandmother, but also shows her impotence in the face of white men. Angelou describes Maya's grandiose imaginings of Momma defying the white dentist who refuses to treat her toothache in spite of having borrowed money from her, but the reality is that in the face of insults her grandmother has to demand 10 dollars to take Maya to a black dentist in another town. Momma's strictness with Maya and her brother is born of fear for her grandchildren's physical safety if whites perceive them as 'taking liberties'. She has absolutely no practical power against white racism, only moral superiority. Maya grows up in and then beyond her grandmother's ways. As she becomes tall and assertive, she may seem like one of those Amazon figures. However, her story, painful and in turns funny, should make it impossible for readers to speak romantically and too easily of 'strong' black women. Too often the conditions of oppression are not eradicated but merely survived. The woman who introduces Maya to literature and with her beautiful voice persuades her to speak again, Mrs Bertha Flowers, has no resemblance to any of those stereotypes of black women.

Faced with a white mainstream culture in which blacks are misrepresented or simply invisible and forgotten, African-American writers have turned to their own expressive traditions. These help to 'identify the autobiographer in relationship with her community and culture' (Braxton 1989: 191). *I Know Why the Caged Bird Sings* shows the influence of two forms of black expression. Oral folk forms (see Levine 1977), such as the sermon, ghost stories, songs, stories told by older people, children's rhymes, underlie her tale: 'I write because I am a Black woman, listening attentively to her talking people' (Evans 1985: 40). Alice Walker (1984: 240), in her essay, 'In search of our mother's gardens', comments on the same influences:

> so many of the stories that I write, that we all write, are my mother's stories . . . through years of listening to my mother's stories of her life, I have absorbed not only the stories themselves, but something of the manner in which she spoke, something of the urgency that involves the knowledge that her stories – like her life – must be recorded.

The literary genre of the slave narrative also helps shape Angelou's narrative and purpose. Over 100 personal narratives by former slaves were published between 1760 and 1930. Their role was to testify to the conditions in which blacks were forced to live and die, as well as demonstrate the slaves' courage and resourcefulness. These autobiographies are about journeys to freedom. They battle for justice and a place in society. They exercise one clear freedom, the freedom to tell your story.

In many ways Angelou shows that 'slavery' was not dead, and its narratives are still relevant. But Angelou does have to adapt some of its key patterns. Maya's sexual violation by the ironically and tragically named Mr Freeman may recall the central subject of white rape of black women in nineteenth-century slave narratives, but here it indicates instead that one aftermath of slavery is damaged relations between black men and women. Motherhood was a keynote of the female slave narrative, but it is both problematic and triumphant in Angelou's story. The slave mother fought to keep her children, but Maya's parents have to send them to their grandmother whom they call Momma. None the less Angelou herself becomes a mother, and her fight to raise her son is a central theme of the four subsequent volumes of her autobiography. Her struggle for autonomy (an important goal of the male slave narrative) is set in relation to the demands of motherhood.

There is a double perspective throughout *I Know Why the Caged Bird Sings*: the older woman who narrates the story and the younger woman who lives the events. Slowly they converge. The forms of resistance by young Maya and her community are seldom overt, though there is a wonderful moment at her school graduation ceremony when the entire community overturns their public humiliation by singing what Angelou calls the Negro national anthem: 'Lift ev'ry voice and sing/Till earth and heaven ring,/Ring with the harmonies of Liberty' (1970/1984: 178). She learns from her elders what Sandi Russell calls 'survival skills', song, sewing, gardening, cooking, tale telling, humour (Russell 1990), the ways in which, as Alice Walker (1984: 234) argues, 'the creativity of the black woman [was] kept alive, year after year and century after century, when for most of years black people have been in America, it was a punishable crime for a black person to read or write'. However, Angelou also gradually leaves the South and the past mentally as well as physically. Most important of all, as a singer and writer Maya Angelou overcame the silence in which she had once been forced to live.

○   **Questions and exercises**

> 1   Write your own autobiography (or part of it). Make this about 2000 words long. Follow this with a critical afterword (about 1500 words) in which you examine your autobiography in the context of general issues round women's autobiography.
>
> 2   Read *I Know Why the Caged Bird Sings* (or any other appropriate autobiography) and identify events and passages where race, class and sexuality intersect with gender. To what extent does the writer resolve these tensions?

○  **Further reading**

For other autobiographies by African-American women, see Washington (1989), Jacobs (1861/1987), Hurston (1942/1986), the other four volumes of Angelou's series (1974/1985, 1976/1985, 1981/1986, 1986/1987), Lorde (1982). For a wide range of critical discussions of women's autobiography, see Jelinek (1980), Benstock (1988), Brodzki and Schenck (1988), and Stanley (1992). As well as occasional essays in the above, there are discussions of African-American writing in Levine (1977), Walker (1984), Evans (1985), Tate (1985), Braxton (1989), Carby (1989), Russell (1990), Wall (1990), Collins (1991) and Andrews (1993). Further information on Africa-American history and discussion of race issues, see hooks (1982) and Roberts (1994).

○  **References**

Andrews, W. L. (ed.) (1993) *African American Autobiography: A Collection of Critical Essays*. Englewood Cliffs, NJ: Prentice Hall.

Angelou, M. (1970/1984) *I Know Why the Caged Bird Sings*. London: Virago.

Angelou, M. (1974/1985) *Gather Together in My Name*. London: Virago.

Angelou, M. (1976/1985) *Singin' and Swingin' and Gettin' Merry like Christmas*. London: Virago.

Angelou, M. (1981/1986) *The Heart of a Woman*. London: Virago.

Angelou, M. (1986/1987) *All God's Children Need Travelling Shoes*. London: Virago.

Benstock, S. (ed.) (1988) *The Private Self: Theory and Practice of Women's Autobiographical Writings*. London: Routledge.

Braxton, J. M. (1989) *Black Women Writing Autobiography: A Tradition Within a Tradition*. Philadelphia, PA: Temple University Press.

Brodzki, K. and Schenck, C. (eds) (1988) *Life/Lines: Theorizing Women's Autobiography*. Ithaca, NY: Cornell University Press.

Carby, H. V. (1989) *Reconstructing Womanhood: The Emergence of the Afro-American Woman Novelist*. Oxford: Oxford University Press.

Collins, P. A. (1991) *Black Feminist Thought: Knowledge, Consciousness, and the Politics of Empowerment*. New York: Routledge.

Evans, M. (ed.) (1985) *Black Women Writers: Arguments and Interviews*. London: Pluto Press.

Graham, E., Hinds, H., Hobby, E. and Wilcox, H. (1989) *Her Own Life: Autobiographical Writings by Seventeenth-Century Englishwomen*. London: Routledge.

Heilbrun, C. G. (1989) *Writing a Woman's Life*. London: Women's Press.

hooks, b. (1982) *Ain't I a Woman: Black Women and Feminism*. London: Pluto Press.

Hurston, Z. N. (1942/1986) *Dust Tracks on a Road: An Autobiography*. London: Virago.

Jacobs, H. (1861/1987) *Incidents in the Life of a Slave Girl: Written by Herself* (ed. J. F. Yellin). Cambridge, MA: Harvard University Press.

Jelinek, E. C. (ed.) (1980) *Women's Autobiography: Essays in Criticism*. Bloomington, IN: Indiana University Press.

Kingston, M. H. (1981) *The Women Warrior: Memoirs of a Girlhood Among Ghosts*. London: Picador.

Levine, L. (1977) *Black Culture and Black Consciousness: Afro-American Thought from Slavery to Freedom*. Oxford: Oxford University Press.

Lorde, A. (1982) *Zami: A New Spelling of My Name*. London: Sheba.

Roberts, D. (1994) *The Myth of Aunt Jemima: Representations of Race and Region*. London: Routledge.

Russell, S. (1990) *Render Me My Song: African-American Women Writers From Slavery to the Present*. London: Pandora.

Stanley, L. (1992) *The Auto/Biographical I: The Theory and Practice of Feminist Auto/Biography*. Manchester: Manchester University Press.

Steedman, C. (1986) *Landscape for a Good Woman: The Story of Two Lives*. London: Virago.

Tate, C. (ed.) (1985) *Black Women Writers at Work*. Harpenden: Oldcastle Books.

Walker, A. (1984) *In Search of Our Mothers' Gardens: Womanist Prose*. London: Women's Press.

Wall, C. A. (1990) *Changing Our Own Words: Essays on Criticism, Theory, and Writing by Black Women*. London: Routledge.

Washington, M. (ed.) (1989) *Invented Lives: Narratives of Black Women, 1860–1960*. London: Virago.

## 10

GABRIELLE RUSSELL

# Women in film: Scarlett O'Hara and Orlando: 'This Is Your Life!'

This chapter examines how the lives of women have been represented in cinema and the significance of those lives for women cinema goers. It focuses on the lives of Scarlett O'Hara of *Gone with the Wind* (*GWTW*) (directed by David O. Selznick, for MGM Studios in Hollywood in 1939) and Orlando of *Orlando* (directed by independent British film maker Sally Potter in 1993). Both films were adapted from novels written by women in the early twentieth century, *GWTW* by Margaret Mitchell in 1935 and *Orlando* by Virginia Woolf in 1928.

In the first part of the chapter I analyse Scarlett's representation visually and narratively and discuss her significance for women when the film was released and today. These readings will then be contrasted with the representation of black women in the film (via the characters of Mammy and Prissy) and Scarlett's relationship to feminism will be addressed. I will then consider some of the similarities and differences between the lives of Scarlett and Orlando and discuss the extent to which these two powerful women can be perceived as icons of resistance to the status quo.

The role of Scarlett O'Hara is one of the most celebrated ever played by a woman in fiction film. *GWTW* was an instant success (in the wake of the best selling novel) and by 1989 when Helen Taylor published *Scarlett's Women*, the film had been seen by more people than populate the United States (Taylor 1989). This audience will be even greater today due to the marketing of the film on video format in 1994. I have chosen to write about Scarlett because, due to this far reaching and prolonged popularity, she is one of the most significant representations of women in film of all time.

○ **Scarlett O'Hara ... what's in a name?**

'Scarlett O'Hara' holds multiple meanings in our culture. Scarlet is a colour with associations of danger, blood, passion, sexuality, anger, madness, all visual comments on Scarlett's personality. For novelist Margaret Mitchell, 'Scarlett O'Hara' also had other meanings relating to the Irish class struggle: the Scarletts had fought with the Irish volunteers for a free Ireland and been hanged; and the O'Haras had died at the Boyne. So in 1939, when the film was released, 'Scarlett O'Hara' was a name that signified conflict, martyrdom, and a nation that fought for its land – experiences a European audience fighting the second world war would easily identify with (Taylor 1989).

## ○ A closer look . . .

Now we have been introduced, let's take a closer look at Scarlett and consider how the film *GWTW* represents her on screen for us to *look at*. Scarlett appears in 90 per cent of scenes in the film and in all of these she is central to the action (Taylor 1989). One of these scenes is particularly revealing of the ways in which the film visually presents Scarlett. It takes place at Melanie's house after Scarlett has been attacked in her buggy on the way home from town. There are only women at the house as the men have gone out into the night to wreak revenge on the shanty town from which the attackers came. As they sit in suspense and fear, hoping for the safe return of their husbands, they are paid a visit by the Yankee officer in charge of the area who has heard that the men are planning an attack on the shanty town. (It is necessary to point out here the nature of this 'revenge' which is not made entirely clear by the film: Scarlett's attacker was a black man in the book, and the vengeful men are in the Klu Klux Klan.) Whilst watching this scene several observations can be made:

- Each woman's face is shown in big close-up in turn as they sew.
- Melanie and Scarlett are shown more than once each.
- Scarlett is shown more times than any other woman in this scene.
- Scarlett is the only woman to be shown in the most extreme close-up (a single shot when we see only her eyes).

The film encourages spectator identification with Scarlett over every other character. We are shown her face more often, but crucially, we are *physically* brought closer to her, encouraging intimacy. Similarly, in the other 679 scenes in which she appears, Scarlett is the central spectacle of the camera's (and thus the spectator's) gaze. We follow her every move, in fact, she is hardly out of our sight. Thus we see how the cinematic specificities of camera shot and editing operate in *GWTW* in conjunction with Scarlett's character, highlighting her as the most important object of our looking.[1]

## ○ Scarlett O'Hara: a scarlet woman?

Scarlett's personality has been a perennial site of identification to her many female fans. Her intelligence and ambition in business, her singlemindedness and passion in love are all admirable, but she exhibits much less

honourable characteristics which have made her a surprisingly ignomini-
ous heroine. She is selfish, scheming and ruthless. She is a liar, adulteress
and murderess. She is often violent, hitting Prissy, Ashley, Suellen and
Rhett (three times!).

Despite this catalogue of infamy Scarlett somehow manages to maintain
our support. Maybe it is *because of* rather than *despite* her fallibility, that
women identify with Scarlett. She appears so human and believable as a
heroine. Another factor could be that because Scarlett loses so much of
what she loves, this compensates for her misdemeanours. Her mother and
eventually her father die; Ashley leaves her for Melanie; her first husband
dies of pneumonia at war; all her earthly possessions are lost during the
war; she loses her sister-in-law Melanie; her daughter is killed in a pony
accident and eventually even Rhett leaves her. Perhaps she redeems
herself as heroine because all this suffering is perceived as adequate
punishment for the misery she has inflicted on others in the pursuit of her
desires.

Scarlett suffers throughout the film. It could be said that her life is a story
of anguish and pain, but she survives it all and says 'I'll think about that
tomorrow' as she battles on. Scarlett is a survivor – a quality not insignifi-
cant in endearing 1940s wartime women to her plight. Her strength,
determination, optimism and grit were integral to her powerful magnet-
ism as an icon of female resilience and fortitude. As Helen Taylor
(1989: 37–8) writes:

> . . . women have clearly been strengthened through identification
> with Scarlett. Many echo the words of Francesca Sullivan: 'I think as
> a girl I held up Scarlett as a kind of model for myself, especially in
> regard to her "Never give up" sentiments'.

## ○ Scarlett as a prototype feminist

Another explanation for Scarlett's female following is that women find her
transgression of her social role exciting, not entirely iniquitous and enjoy
a vicarious freedom through her actions. Taylor (1989: 103) writes, 'Scarlett is often seen as a progressive figure and model for women because of
her refusal of all that simpering Southern belle-ery involves' and raises the
question of whether Scarlett could be described as a feminist. She highlights the comments of several women in her study who described their
identification with Scarlett's strength and resourcefulness:

> Many women saw her as an early feminist – 'a premature women's
> libber' as one put it. This is expressed in different ways, and often by
> women over the age of fifty in terms of bravery and 'guts'.

Taylor (1989: 104–5) concludes that,

> Scarlett O'Hara becomes the very symbol of the 'New Woman' recog-
> nised as such by 1940's wartime women workers and mothers, 1960's
> liberationalists and careerists and 1980's 'Me' generation post-feminists.

However some women found the emancipated Scarlett disturbing because she maintains a master/slave relationship with her servants even after the liberation of black people from slavery. Taylor only received a handful of responses from black women spectators about the film but all of them were highly critical of the film's representation of the relationship between black and white characters. One of her respondents, Darlene M. Hantzis asked

> Where are the abolitionists? Where are the other Northerners? Where are the angry slaves, thrilled to be free? Where are the average Southerners? Too much romanticisation equals trivialisation.
>
> (Taylor 1989: 194)

This questions the identification of Scarlett as a prototype feminist – if Scarlett is practising women's liberation, which women is she liberating? Let's take a closer look at her relationship to black women in *GWTW*.

## ○ The representation of black women in *Gone with the Wind*

The characters of Mammy and Prissy have been subjects of much controversy. Hattie McDaniel's 'Mammy' role has been identified as *the* most powerful icon in Hollywood's representation of black women. McDaniel played Mammies 12 times before *GWTW* and she became the defining actress of the type. Scarlett's Mammy exhibits all the characteristics of this mythic type. Mature, grinning, huge, turbaned, tray carrying, warm, serving, happy, devoted to her family and children, she is omnipresent, passive, and patient, with no needs of her own. She is loyal to the whites, asexual, very dark skinned (so as not to suggest any racial mixing), nameless, and has no history, or future; she is a constant black woman.

When contrasted with historical fact, Scarlett's Mammy is set into sharp relief. In reality, mammies were mostly young, rarely fed enough and often underweight. They were used to breed more slaves, often sexually abused and raped by white owners and were subject to frequent beatings. So the Mammy of *GWTW* is revealed as being a fantasy, a white fantasy, romanticizing the lives of black women living in slavery.

The character of 'Prissy' the young maid servant played by 28-year-old Butterfly McQueen left even less room for the truth. Irresponsible, lying, foolish, squeaky-voiced, irritating and comical, she is chastised and even slapped by Scarlett (twice). Prissy supports the antebellum white belief that Negroes are stupid, lazy, untrustworthy, unreliable, sly, devious and in need of stern discipline – Scarlett's violent frustration with her only serves to confirm this (Taylor 1989).

## ○ Scarlett O'Hara, This Is Your Life!

Scarlett O'Hara may be a prototype feminist in some respects, an icon of resistance to those factors which would stand in her way. But it is *only with white women's emancipation that she can be aligned.* For black women and feminists who are anti-racist she represents a point of myopia in the development of feminism, a colour blindness that considered the advancement of white women to be the advancement of all women. Since then, there have been many black feminists who have corrected our sight, among them are bell hooks, Audre Lorde, Alice Walker, Julie Dash, Andrea Stuart, Toni Morrison, Maya Angelou and many others. Let it be with a clear and focused vision then, that we say 'Scarlett O'Hara, This Is Your Life'.

Now, I consider how the lives of Orlando and Scarlett are told, how their biographies are structured, where they are similar and also where they differ. I suggest that *Orlando* differs from *GWTW* in the way that it is constructed cinematically, breaking away from the classic realist text and exploring alternative ways of communicating the life story of Orlando.[2] I argue that this textual difference allows Orlando the power to *break through* the boundaries of female existence where Scarlett could only *resist*. Finally, I consider the significance of Orlando's life for female spectators.

○ **Common threads: Scarlett and Orlando**

Orlando is an immortal changeling being, born in 1592 as a male, who on reaching maturity, becomes female, and lives to the present day. Despite some obvious differences between Scarlett and Orlando (immortality and gender mutability not least among them) there are many common threads that connect their lives. Like *GWTW*, *Orlando* is an epic film, following Orlando's life over four centuries. Like Scarlett, Orlando is born into wealth and social standing and holds a powerful position in society as a lord. Both experience mourning and loss (Orlando loses the Queen in his youth and Sasha and Shelmerdine as lovers). As a woman, Orlando, like Scarlett, experiences a massive change of lifestyle, and loses all her worldly possessions. Like Scarlett she falls in love and has a daughter. Like Scarlett, she survives against all odds. These connecting threads are based on a common theme: *the experience of what it is to be a woman in society* and the constraints and restrictions of the female condition are pointed out by both.

There are several scenes in each film that exhibit this commonality between the two women. The *dressing-down* Orlando is subject to when she is informed by the poets of the cultural currency and lack of autonomy accorded women (in the 'Society' section of *Orlando*), echoes the *dressing-up* of Scarlett in the constricting corset by Mammy (in the early scenes of *GWTW*). Both these scenes serve as indicators of the binding confines of their physical and social lives as women. There are other definitive scenes of this type: Scarlett's attack as she rides home alone in her buggy (a woman unescorted by a male); Orlando having to leave his ambassadorship when he changes into a woman; Scarlett's mourning period after the death of her first husband (which she does not want to endure); Orlando's lawyers telling her that as a woman, she has no rights to her estate unless she has a male-child heir and their reasoning that she is legally dead by the fact of her femininity 'which amounts to the same thing'. It is through these scenes that both Orlando and Scarlett *point to the edges of female existence and delineate the possible experience of a woman.*

Yet whereas Scarlett's life is circumscribed by these delineations, Orlando transgresses them. She sheds her estate like an old skin, a cause for celebration rather than mourning, as Sally Potter explains in her introduction to the script:

> Orlando's loss of property and status in the twentieth century takes on a different significance. Whilst Orlando's disinheritance is a symptom of the second class status of women, there is also an aspect which is worthy of celebration: the loss of privilege and status based on an outdated English class system.
>
> (Potter 1994: xi–xii)

Orlando also achieves her lifelong ambition to be a poet and towards the end of the film, she has her script accepted by a publisher.

Whereas Scarlett's survival is the result of stubborn resistance in the light of insurmountable odds (making clear the frustrations experienced by women fighting against an inflexible establishment), Orlando, via her resourceful adaptability and her ability to conquer time, is able to overcome all obstacles in the path of her self-fulfilment, even managing to turn events to her favour. *Orlando*'s narrative optimism relies on the *impermanence* of any status quo or social restriction of existence, made fluid by the vagaries of time. Sally Potter subtitled *Orlando* 'A Celebration of Impermanence'.

In contrast, Scarlett O'Hara exists in a temporally coherent socio-historical context. Her life experience is navigated according to a strict set of social norms, and is circumscribed by the cultural expectations of women of her time. Although she resists many of these and battles on, her victory is hard won and costly, and never secured. This is because her story, *GWTW*, abides by the requirements of 'realism' performing all the functions of a classic realist text. In contrast, *Orlando* breaks with this tradition, and explores the realms of fantasy and possibility.

○ **Realism, film and the classic realist text**

The classic realist text is a combination of filmic tropes which became typical of narrative film in the early Hollywood period, a result of attempts to make films seem as similar to 'real life' as possible (a marketing ploy).[3] There developed patterns in the ways films were made to appear 'real' and a language of realism was developed. Some key components have been identified as follows:

1 Film, like the photograph, has the outward appearance of *'reality'*. This

produces a confidence in the spectator that what is seen projected *was once there*. This effects a slippage of film = reality, investing the photographic image with a credence of being closer to reality than any other type of representation (Barthes 1977).

2 When making films, efforts would be made to enhance this 'realism', for example, by endowing sets with naturalistic qualities, paying close attention to detail, props and appropriate lighting.

3 Film makers attempted to mirror real time in sequencing narrative events chronologically so as to maintain temporal integrity.

4 Visually, the camera's point of view would be as like that of the human character's in the narrative as possible. This gives the spectator the feeling of being in the same space as the action thus sealing the spectator into the film itself, a process called suture. This effect was often heightened by the practice of continuity editing and the development of shot–reverse–shot structures.[4]

Feminist film theorists have argued that these textual elements of the classic realist text have been manipulated to give a particular view of the world. They have argued that camera positioning and editing not only draw the spectator into the space of the film via the process of suture, but that these elements *position* the spectator in relation to the characters in the narrative. Feminists have criticized the ways in which the classic realist text has been employed by Hollywood, to the advantage of a patriarchal hegemony, depicting a patriarchal status quo as natural and real.[5]

Laura Mulvey is one such feminist theorist. In 'Visual pleasure and narrative cinema' she expands on the theory that camera angle and editing situate the spectator of film, and defines the concept of the gaze (Mulvey 1989). Mulvey considers that there are three looks in cinema:

1 the look of the *camera* as it records the pro-filmic event;
2 the look of the *audience* watching the film;
3 the looks of the *characters* at each other in the film.

She argues that the first and second of these 'looks' are subordinated to the third so as to emulate the experience of looking into a private and autonomous 'world'.

The 'camera's look' is political for feminist theorists, because it presents women in films as *passive objects* providing specular enjoyment for the male characters in the film, and by extension, Mulvey argues, men in the audience. She proposes that women in films have been so repeatedly presented in this way, that whereas the function of a man in a film is to forward the action, the function of a woman is to be pleasing to look at. Women in films represent 'to-be-looked-at-ness', subject always to an objectifying and fetishizing male gaze.[6]

The subordination of 'the look of the audience' also effects a *distancing* of the spectator from the ideological premise of film, such that this representation of women would appear *natural*.

○  **Orlando's break with the classic realist text**

In contrast to *GWTW*, Sally Potter's *Orlando* breaks with the classic realist text at many different levels. Casting against gender (Quentin Crisp as Queen Elizabeth and Tilda Swinton as Orlando) prevents the slippage of film=reality, as does the blatant lie about Orlando's gender – '*narrator*: He, for there could be no doubt about his sex . . .' (Potter 1994) – when the person playing Orlando is clearly (even at this stage in the film) a woman. These instances expose the illusory nature of film and alert the spectator to their own complicity with this illusion of reality.

Unearthly, ethereal characters (Jimmy Somerville as an angel floating above Orlando at the end of the film) disrupt the naturalism of the film. Also extraordinary sets and costumes (the plastic wrapped garden, the topiary, the wigs) encourage a recognition of the contrived nature of film making.

Potter also uses *symbolic action* in Orlando's transformation scene where he/she splashes him/herself with water (a symbol of metamorphosis in its capacity to be solid, liquid or vapour). Such evident iconography exposes the symbolically saturated quality of film and again, challenges the reality effect.[7]

*Orlando*'s impossible temporality is another factor in the break from the classic realist text in that the spectator's suspension of disbelief is stretched to the extent that unrealism becomes part of the story.[8] Sally Potter pointed to this effect when she described the film as 'non-realistic and completely believable in its own terms'.

Textual devices which disrupt the realism of the film are also employed. Camera techniques such as slow motion (see Orlando's transformation and later her running through the maze from the seventeenth to the eighteenth century) make the camera's 'look' obvious. Laura Mulvey refers to this as 'freeing the look of the camera', denying the prevalence of the look of the characters within the filmic 'world'. Direct address (Orlando's punctuating addresses to the spectator through the lens of the camera) is another strategy which challenges the objectifying effect of the camera looking at a woman (Mulvey's 'to-be-looked-at-ness'), as Orlando looks back directly at the spectator. This device allows her to transcend the camera's describing function, refuse its control of her image and announce herself as the subject of the film:

> *Narrator*: He . . .
> *Orlando*: That is I . . .
>
>                                              (Potter 1994)

Direct address also has the effect of momentarily destroying the spectator's comfortable position as unseen voyeur of the private film-world. This is simultaneously quite shocking and amusing. Spectator detachment is destroyed and one becomes implicated within the story as the confidant of Orlando, not as her observer, but as her friend. The male gaze is resisted via a personal relationship with the spectator, who can no more objectify Orlando than ignore her. To quote Sally Potter:

I hoped that this direct address would create a golden thread that would connect the audience through the lens, with Orlando, and in this way, the Spectacle and the Spectator would become one through the release of laughter.

(Potter 1994: xiii)

So Sally Potter's *Orlando* breaks with the traditional model for the representation of women in film by *resisting* the classic realist text.

## ○ Orlando, This Is Your Life!

Same person, different sex.

(Orlando)

Finally we come to consider the significance of Orlando's life. What does the tale of Orlando mean? What is the point of changing gender and living for 400 years? Some of the meanings I have found during my research are as follows. Sally Potter suggests that Orlando's change of gender from a man to a woman represents a crisis in masculine identity. Potter writes:

Orlando's change of sex in the film is a result of his having reached a crisis point – a crisis of masculine identity. On the Battlefield he looks death and destruction in the face and confronts the challenge of kill or be killed. It is Orlando's unwillingness to conform to what is expected from him as a man that leads – within the logic of the film – to his change of sex.

(Potter 1994: xi)

She follows this comment, however, with 'Later as a woman, Orlando finds that she cannot conform to what is expected of her as a female either'. So Orlando is unable to conform to any strict gender identity. Not only this, but Orlando actually points to the ridiculousness of gender binaries *per se* and questions what it means to be undoubtedly male or female. Potter writes:

The longer I lived with Orlando and tried to write a character who was both male and female, the more ludicrous maleness and femaleness became, and the more the notion of the essential human being predominated. Here was a character called Orlando: a person, an individual, a being who lived for 400 years, first as a man and then as a woman. At the moment of change, Orlando turns and says to the audience, 'Same person, different sex'. It's as simple as that.

(Potter 1994: xiv–xv)

Aside from the humanist message Potter is representing – an important one for feminism is its acceptance of the basic equanimity and similarity of women and men – other significances of Orlando's life also present themselves.

Orlando's mutability and metamorphosis says something about the nature of identity that is not restricted to a gender paradigm and challenges the conception of the self as fixed, whole and in control. This under-standing of one's identity as a fluid and changing *condition* rather than as a continuous and autonomous *being*, is of momentous importance for con-temporary feminism. Feminist thinkers are often divided as to its helpful-ness. If we take up this view, we must recognize identity as a fragmented, unstable composite of multifarious and often contradictory elements – as in the words of Rachie Evemy-Taylor (1994):

> Identity, as a site about which, and from which, to make strong and safe assertions to truth, is as a rock crumbling to sand, tiny particles slipping through the gaps of conceptual surety.

This condition not only describes us as individuals, but is by extension applicable to our identity as feminists. This can be threatening in that it shat-ters any conception of 'feminism' as a unanimous movement for women's interests (it even questions the possibility of pinpointing what 'women's interests' might be). It also lays down a challenge to our previously estab-lished understanding of '*the* female condition' as a unifying concept, to the extent that 'feminism' must be recognized as an uneasy alliance of multiple and differential standpoints. What were previously political imperatives are no longer authoritative and binding, but are subject to questioning and criti-cism – not only from without, but from within – from other feminists.

More positively, acknowledgement of multiple and differentiated femin-ist identities and standpoints has been encouraged and embraced by some feminists – most notably by black and lesbian feminists whose presence has been traditionally subsumed within, if not ignored by and absent from, feminist politics. By acknowledging and affirming these differences we broaden, mature and arguably strengthen the very foundations of femin-ism. By opening our minds to new ways of seeing ourselves and each other we allow for the development of new strategies as well as creating a richer and more fertile terrain for the growth of the movement. Sally Potter (1994: xiv) is perhaps making a similar point when she writes,

> Through the vehicle of Orlando's apparent immortality we experience the mutability of all things and relationships. This brings with it a sense of loss (of the past) and a feeling of joy (of a possible future).

What more of a preface does the women's movement need for the next 400 years?

## Questions

> 1  Both films are biographies of women's lives – why is this important?
>
> 2  Could the films be described as feminist? In what ways?
>
> 3  How do these representations of women compare with popular representations of women today? Choose examples of both black and white women for discussion.

4 How does *Gone with the Wind* represent black women? How does *Orlando* explore 'Englishness' as an ethnicity in relation to different cultures?

○ **Further reading**

For a comprehensive audience study on Scarlett O'Hara, see Taylor (1989). Particularly relevant are the chapters on Scarlett, and *Gone with the Wind* and race. Donahue's (1993) interview with Sally Potter is very interesting as a document of *Orlando*'s production and Potter's process of adaption from Woolf's novel. Mulvey (1989) will be a difficult but worthwhile read for those wishing to pursue the concept of the male gaze. Gamman and Marshment (1988) further investigate the gendering of the gaze concept and suggest theories for a female gaze. Barthes (1977) will be useful for philosophical debates around the relationship of photography to 'reality', as will Bordwell and Thompson (1990). The latter will also be of much use in identifying shots and explaining shot structures (it also has a good glossary of terms). Kuhn (1982) is an excellent source for the main debates around the representation of women in film and the attempts made by feminist film makers to counter conventions of representation.

○ **Notes**

1 Cinematic specificity refers to elements of signification which operate only in cinematic language and no other (for example, camera shot, angle, framing, lighting, editing, etc.).
2 The classic realist text is a type of film which adheres to a classic narrative structure of disruption and resolution, and mobilizes the styles of realism as a significant narrative device.
3 Tropes are symbolic styles or patterns in films or across film history which have been recognized and made significant through analysis, such that they are heralded as emblematic of a particular type of film or style of film making.
4 Suture (a French surgical word which means to be *sewn into*) is used in film theory to describe the process in which the spectator is constantly being caught up in and made part of the narrative space of a film. This is usually achieved through the effects of continuity editing (a method of joining shots which emphasizes smooth transitions between shots, with ellipses of time and space made as unobtrusive to the spectator as possible) and shot–reverse–shot structures (a type of edited shot sequence within a film, usually showing the point of view of a character looking at a second character, followed by a shot of the second character's point of view looking back at the first character).
5 Hegemony is the way in which dominant social groups exercise their authority via cultural influence, winning popular consent through manipulation of ideological tools (for example, the family, media, education, religion, etc.) rather than by physical force.

6 The act of gazing is played upon in cinema, creating the pleasure of the spectator of looking at another person. In Mulvey's argument, this pleasure in looking is a sexual instinct (scopophilia). In classical Hollywood cinema, the gaze is split along lines of sexual difference. The male characters within the film gaze at the female characters who become the centres of erotic contemplation. Mulvey called this phenomenon 'the male gaze'.

7 Iconography consists of those visual elements of a film which can be analysed as having some symbolic meaning.

8 'Suspension of disbelief' refers to the process of alignment of the spectator to the realism of the world within a film. The spectator suspends the knowledge that what is being seen is a constructed artificial situation, and becomes absorbed within the action of the film.

## ○ References

Barthes, R. (1977) The photographic message, in *Image, Music, Text* (ed. and trans. by Stephen Heath). London: Fontana.

Bordwell, D. and Thompson, K. (1990) *Film Art: an Introduction* (3rd edn). London: McGraw-Hill.

Donahue, W. (1993) Immortal longing (an interview with Sally Potter), in P. Cook and P. Dodd (eds) *Women in Film: A Sight and Sound Reader*. London: Scarlet Press.

Evemy-Taylor, R. (1994) 'A celebration of impermanence. How have feminist film makers investigated sexual and gender identities?', unpublished dissertation in Women's Studies. Lancaster University.

Gamman, L. and Marshment, M. (eds) (1988) *The Female Gaze*. London: The Women's Press.

Kuhn, A. (1982) *Women's Pictures: Feminism and Cinema*. London: Routledge.

Mulvey, L. (1989) Visual pleasure and narrative cinema (1973), in *Visual and Other Pleasures*. London: Macmillan.

Potter, S. (1994) *Orlando*. London: Faber and Faber.

Taylor, H. (1989) *Scarlett's Women: Gone with the Wind and its Female Fans*. London: Virago.

Williams, L. R. (1993) Everything in question: women and film in prospect, in D. Cook and P. Dodd (eds) *Women in Film: A Sight and Sound Reader*. London: Scarlet Press.

**LINDA WOODHEAD**

# Religious representations of women

○ **Religion and feminist theory**

Since religion is a powerful force in human life, the way in which it represents women should be of great interest to Women's Studies. From the first, feminist writers acknowledged the significance of religion for women's lives and social position; one of the best known works to emerge from the first phase of the women's movement was Elizabeth Cady Stanton's *Woman's Bible*, a Bible edited and annotated from a feminist perspective. Second phase feminism has not always taken religion as seriously, perhaps because of the more secular climate in which it has developed. Nevertheless, from the mid-1970s onwards a significant number of feminist works addressing the topic of women and religion have appeared. Much of this literature is classified as 'feminist theology', that is to say theology (talk about God) written from a feminist perspective.

Feminist theologians tend to divide into two groups: liberals who, like Rosemary Radford Ruether, wish to reform traditional religion in order to make it non-sexist, and radicals who, like Mary Daly, wish to abandon traditional religion in favour of new forms of feminist spirituality. During the 1980s feminist theology began to be supplemented by a slightly different genre, studies of women and religion written by academics working within established disciplines like History or Religious Studies, but increasingly influenced by Women's Studies. These scholarly studies differ a little from feminist theology in that they tend to be less concerned with evaluating the worth of religion for women, and more with simply understanding the historical interactions between women and religion.

Both feminist theology and the more recent scholarly studies of women and religion have made some important claims about religious representations of women. Though none of these claims have met with universal acceptance, a number have become particularly prominent and influential. The most common and most widely accepted claim is also the most wide-ranging: that religious representations of women are both quantitatively and qualitatively inferior to those of men. That is to say, not only are women less frequently represented in religion than men, but even when they are represented it is in ways which suggest their inferiority. This general claim about the sexism of religious representations of women is often attached to another: that patriarchy in the religious realm engenders and supports patriarchy in the social realm. As Mary Daly (1986: 19) famously put it in *Beyond God the Father*, 'if God is male, then the male is God'.

Further feminist claims about religious representations of women tend to be refinements and specifications of the wider claim about the inferiority of such representations. Two of the most common such claims are first, that religions are schizophrenic in their attitudes to women, tending either to demonize or to divinize them, and second, that religions show a marked tendency to represent women in terms of their sexuality (Armstrong 1986). One or both of these claims is often tied up with the further claim that religions are characterized by a dualistic mode of thinking which divides the world into opposed principles such as good and evil, spirit and matter, high and low, male and female. Because the female is linked with nature and matter, this dualistic way of thinking ensures that women are seen as sexual and material and are opposed to men who are 'spiritual'. Dualism ranks women with the forces of darkness and evil rather than with those of goodness and light.

## Three religious representations of women: Eve, Mary Magdalene and Mary the mother of Jesus

The best way of investigating feminist claims about religious representations of women is by looking at some actual examples of such representations. Since most of these claims have been made in relation to Christianity, it makes sense to test them against representations of three of the most prominent female figures within that tradition: Eve, Mary the mother of Jesus, and Mary Magdalene. All three women have a significant place in the Bible and in the story it relates, the story of God's gracious dealings with the world. Furthermore, legends about these women have developed and circulated throughout Christian history, sometimes in oral form, sometimes in written. All three women are also common subjects of sculpture, painting, stained glass, music, liturgy, poetry and drama.

### Eve

Eve makes her appearance at the beginning of the Bible, in the book of Genesis. As its title suggests, Genesis is a book about origins. It explains how the world came into being and why it is as it is – on the one hand glorious and good, on the other marred by sin, drudgery and death. Adam and Eve are pivotal in the Genesis story, for they are part of the good creation, indeed the pinnacle of its goodness, but become the cause of its evil.

Genesis tells how Adam and Eve are created by God at the very end of the process of creation, and are both created 'in the image of God' (1.27). Adam is created from dust, Eve from one of Adam's ribs (2.7–25), and the two cleave together and become 'one flesh' (2.24). Soon, however, the partnership between Adam and Eve turns out not to be as blissful as intended. Tempted by the serpent, Eve eats from a forbidden tree and tempts Adam to do the same. Instead of bringing advantage as the serpent had promised, this transgression brings disaster, Adam and Eve are cast out of Paradise into a life of woes, woes which all their descendants are doomed to suffer. For Eve the woes are those surrounding childbirth, and the fact that 'your desire shall be for your husband, and he shall rule over you' – interestingly patriarchy seems here to be pictured as one of the results of the Fall (3.16).

As the feminist biblical scholar Phyllis Trible (1978) has explained in some detail in her book *God and the Rhetoric of Sexuality*, it is not at all clear that the Genesis story in fact represents Eve as inferior to Adam. Nevertheless, subsequent Christian tradition has often interpreted the story in this sexist way, and some Christian writers have developed much more negative representations of Eve than the story warrants. Generally such representations occur when writers are seeking justification for the subordination of women to men; then the story of Eve's creation from Adam is interpreted in terms of her inferiority, and the story of the Fall in terms of her greater culpability. As the New Testament epistle I Timothy puts it, 'Adam was formed first, then Eve; and Adam was not deceived but the woman was deceived and became a transgressor' (2.13–14). A couple of centuries later we find just the same sort of argument being employed by the theologian Tertullian (c.160–c.225) in a treatise 'On the Apparel of Women'. In his attempt to make Christian women shun display in dress and bearing Tertullian (1959: 117–18) exclaims:

> Do you not believe that you are each an Eve? The sentence of God on this sex of yours lives on even in our times and so it is necessary that the guilt should live on also.

Tertullian is here engaged in sexual politics in the most literal sense, for he is trying to make women live chaste and celibate lives. The association of Eve with matters of sexuality which emerges in Tertullian's writing was further reinforced by Augustine (354–430), who suggested that one of the chief woes brought about by the Fall was concupiscence (the loss of control over one's bodily appetites), a disorder particularly manifest in sexual desire. Augustine's ideas gave rise to the view that Eve and the Fall have something to do with sex, an interpretation which has retained its power despite the fact that it gains no support whatsoever from the Genesis story.

### Mary the mother of Jesus

At the Christian Council of Ephesus in 431, Mary the mother of Jesus was given the official title of *Theotokos*, 'Mother of God'. This title gives a clear indication of her importance to Christians, an importance which rests above all on the indispensable part she plays in bringing God's son, Jesus Christ, into the world. As the mother of Jesus Mary is the single human agent without whom the incarnation of God in human form could not have taken place, and for most Christians she is consequently the most exalted of all human beings.

In the New Testament, Mary appears at the very start of the story told by the gospels. Both Luke and Matthew tell of Jesus's conception and birth, and for both Mary is centre-stage in the drama. It is she who sets the whole story in train by joyfully accepting God's promise of a child (Luke 1–2; Matt. 1.18–2.23). Mary is depicted not as a passive recipient of God's grace, but as an active participant in the miraculous events which take place, speaking with her own voice and acknowledging that 'from henceforth all generations will call me blessed' (Luke 1.46–55). Artistic representations of Mary often focus upon the events depicted in Luke and Matthew, and some of the most famous of all images in western art are those of the angel appearing to Mary (the Annunciation), Mary's visit to Elizabeth (the Visitation), the birth of Jesus (the Nativity), and the Holy Family.

For about the first thousand years of Christian history, Mary was often represented in art and iconography as a heavenly figure, exalted and glorious. Though the New Testament said nothing about her birth and her death, legends soon arose which told how both were miraculous, and how when Mary died she was transported instantly to heaven to dwell with God and with her beloved son. The iconography of the churches of both East and West depicted Mary in this way. Such belief in the unique status of Mary, though widely accepted throughout the history of Christianity, was formalized and made official doctrine by the Roman Catholic church when it promulgated the doctrine of the Immaculate Conception in 1854 and the doctrine of the Assumption in 1950. The former speaks of how Mary, alone of all human beings, was born without taint of sin, the latter of how she was 'assumed' into heaven on death.

It is not only in heavenly guise, however, that Mary has been venerated by Christians. From as early as the tenth century there arose a form of popular piety which emphasized and revered the humanity of Christ and his mother as much as their divinity. Mary was increasingly seen as a mother who shared the joys and sorrows of motherhood with her earthly sisters, and it was from this time that the portraits and sculptures of a very human Mary nursing the infant Jesus and weeping over the dead Christ became commonplace. Because Mary was thus represented as a very human mother, as well as a citizen of heaven, she was seen as an ideal intermediary between human beings and God. For many Christians, Mary became a mediatrix between earth and heaven. Sharing their humanity, she could sympathize with their needs; occupying a place in heaven, she could intercede on their behalf with her beloved son.

Whilst it is common for Roman Catholics to pray to Mary and venerate her, most Protestants are reluctant to do so. For Protestants her significance lies in the key role she has in the Christian story, and perhaps in the fact that she is a figure who should be emulated. Catholics too have sometimes held Mary up as an example to be imitated by ordinary men and women.

Different aspects of her character have been singled out for imitation at different times, but her humility, her obedience to God, her trust in His purposes and her acceptance of suffering have been particularly emphasized in the last few centuries. So too, from earliest times, has her virginity, despite the fact that the New Testament clearly mentions Jesus' brothers and sisters (e.g. Mark 6.3).[1] Early Christian leaders often used Mary's virginity as an example to encourage celibacy, particularly amongst women, and it was regarded as such a key characteristic of Mary that 'Virgin Mary' quickly became one of her most common titles.

### Mary Magdalene

Although representations of Mary Magdalene have probably become far less familiar to contemporary men and women than representations of Eve and Mary, her relative obscurity is only recent. Up until the last century Mary Magdalene was one of the most widely represented of all female figures: churches, cathedrals, schools, colleges and streets throughout the world bear her name, innumerable portraits have been painted of her, dramatic re-enactments of her story have been popular; she has even given her name to a word in the English language – 'maudlin'.

Mary Magdalene's importance rests above all on the fact that she was the first witness of Jesus's resurrection; on this all four New Testament gospels agree. Since the entire edifice of Christian belief is built upon belief in Jesus's resurrection, Mary Magdalene consequently has a claim to be the first Christian, even the first apostle.[2] Elsewhere in the gospels she appears only at the crucifixion, and earlier in Jesus's ministry as a follower of Jesus from whom he had cast out seven demons (Luke 8.2). In its desire for a fuller picture of this important woman, however, subsequent Christian tradition took a number of gospel stories about unnamed women, or women named Mary, and maintained that their subject was in fact Mary Magdalene. By this process Mary Magdalene was identified with both the woman caught in adultery whom Jesus forgave (John 8.3–11) and the woman who anointed Jesus's feet, washed them with her tears and wiped them with her hair (e.g. Luke 7.36–50). As legends about Mary Magdalene developed outside the confines of the Bible, she came to be seen as a prostitute who was converted from her life of carnal love by Jesus and who then became the greatest of his spiritual lovers. Legend even supplied an ending to the story of the Magdalene: after Jesus's death she travelled to France as an evangelist, then spent her last years as an ascetic, repenting of her sins and preparing to meet Jesus, her heavenly bridegroom (see Haskins 1993: 98–133).

Representations of Mary Magdalene are many and varied. One of the most common is the 'Noli Me Tangere' ('touch me not'), the picture of Mary stretching out her hand to touch the risen Christ. She also appears kissing Jesus's feet – both at the anointing and at the crucifixion. All these representations emphasize her great love for Christ, a passionate love expressed through physical touch. As she is regarded as a sinner saved by her love for Jesus, the figure of Mary is one which conveys a message of hope to the believer: however sinful you are, if you love Jesus with your whole heart you may be saved. Often her portraits show her holding a scroll bearing a message like the following: 'do not despair, you who are accustomed to sin; following my example ready yourselves again for God'.[3] Mary is also pictured at the end of her life in the guise of an ascetic. From the High Renaissance period on, this image of the former prostitute repenting of her sins in solitude became the subject of some highly erotic works of art, works which by the nineteenth century had developed into the first popular pornographic images. Interestingly, this representation of the Magdalene as a sexual or erotic figure seems to continue to haunt the contemporary imagination, being clearly in evidence in Martin Scorsese's film *The Last Temptation of Christ* based on Kazantzakis's novel (1960), as well as in a number of feminist novels (for example, Roberts 1984).

## ○ Re-evaluating the feminist claims

Even such a cursory examination of religious representations of women as that undertaken above throws interesting light on the feminist claims made about them. The first and most important of these claims was that religions represent women as inferior to men. Yet an examination of the ways in which Eve, Mary Magdalene and Mary the mother of Jesus have been represented in the Christian tradition suggests that there may be some good reasons for being cautious about this claim.

In the first place this examination makes it clear that far from being inferior figures, there are in fact women in absolutely key positions in the Christian story. As we have seen, Mary the mother of Jesus and Mary Magdalene are *the* key figures in the Christian story both at the beginning and the end of the gospel. Without Mary the mother of Jesus there would be no story at all, for the salvation of the human race is seen to depend upon the free assent of a young, unknown, unmarried woman. And without Mary Magdalene the story would have ended with the death of Jesus, it would not have become the 'gospel' (good news) on which the Christian religion rests.

Yet it cannot of course be denied that it is a man, Jesus, who is at the centre of the Christian story. Women are important only in relation to him. Does this validate the feminist claim that women are represented as inferior to men? An adequate answer to this question would require a chapter in itself; here it can only be pointed out that Christians believe it is Jesus's *humanity* which has saving significance, not his maleness.[4] Theologically, there is no reason why Jesus could not have been a woman, just as there is no reason why God the Father cannot be addressed as Mother as well as Father – as indeed He has been at various times in Christian history. In other words, from a Christian point of view the key position in the Christian scheme of things is occupied by God, not man. And the key positions in the story of human response to God are occupied by women just as much as by men. From a secular point of view, however, things will inevitably look rather different; to the eyes of an unbeliever there is just a man at the heart of the story, not God. Interestingly, then, it may be that from the standpoint of a believer Christianity looks rather less sexist than from that of an unbeliever.

Second, this brief study of Christian representations of women makes clear the dangers of pronouncing upon their sexist nature without paying very close attention to their particular contexts and purposes. Take representations of Eve, for example. Clearly many of these are negative, Eve is portrayed as a foolish and wicked woman. But before jumping to the conclusion that these representations are therefore misogynous it is necessary to consider their context and purpose. Is the primary aim of the Genesis stories about Eve to explain woman and woman's nature? No, their primary aim is to explain why there is so much evil and suffering in the world and why a good God allows it; they have a theological rather than misogynous point. But is the latter nevertheless a secondary implication of the story? If Eve alone were blamed for the Fall, then clearly yes, that could be said to be so. But since Adam is blamed just as frequently, or the two together are blamed, it is hard to view the story as sexist. There is of course no doubt that the stories have been used in sexist ways; we have seen how some Christian writers invoke Eve not in order to explain the miseries of the world, but in order to show why women should be subordinate to men. When *this* becomes the context and purpose of the representations of Eve then there clearly are good grounds for regarding them as sexist.

In short, it seems that the claim that religious representations of women are sexist is too blunt an instrument with which to interpret these representations; each must be looked at in its specificity before any such claim can be adjudicated. Representations of women are not *always* about women or women's status; to think that they are is as mistaken as reading 'Baa Baa Black Sheep' as a straightforward comment upon sheep or upon race.

To imagine that representations of women always make a point about women's status is to impose a feminist agenda rather crudely upon the past. To claim that sexist religious representations of women always support a sexist society should be seen as similarly anachronistic. For the way that women are represented in the world's religions does not always have a direct bearing upon the ethos and institutions of those religions. A religion like Hinduism which worships goddesses, for example, is no less likely to be sexist than one which does not. The reason is simple: despite the contrary assumption made by a modern, secular agenda, religious representations are not necessarily role models. In Christianity, for example, relatively few of the most prominent figures are prominent because they are role models. This is true not just of figures like Peter and Paul, it is true of the three women we have considered. Eve is not a role model at all, and the two Marys are so only in a secondary way. For Catholics in particular, Mary the mother of Jesus is not primarily a role model at all, she is a saint. As such she should be venerated and prayed to more than imitated. Again, context must be taken seriously.

Moving on to the further feminist claims about religious representations of women, claims which aim to specify the wider claim about the inferiority of these representations, what of the claim that women are represented in a schizophrenic way by Christianity, as either divine or demonic? If, from the many Christian representations of women, one selects just Eve and Mary and sets them alongside one another, ignoring their proper contexts, a case could possibly be made for this claim. If, however, one considers Christian representations in their wealth and variety, it receives little support. Most representations of women in Christianity, like most male representations, are of forgiven sinners – witnesses to God's grace rather than to human perfection. This suggests also that there is little substance to the claim that Christianity slots women into a dualistic scheme of thought. Indeed it would be surprising if there were, for Christianity has always devoted considerable energy to attacking dualism, as its early struggles against Gnosticism show. Christianity does indeed know of one key dualism, but it is the flesh/spirit dualism, which is quite different from a body/spirit dualism, for it is simply a contrast between that which is for and that which is against God. It is not a dualism which dictates the nature and place of women either, for women, like men, have the potential to be either of the spirit or of the flesh.

Though there is little substance to the claim that Christianity identifies women with nature and matter as opposed to spirit, there seems to be a great deal more substance to the rather different claim that Christianity often represents women in terms of their sexuality. Representations of Eve and the two Marys bear this out. Eve's sin comes to be seen as somehow a sexual one, Mary's virginity is highlighted and venerated, and Mary Magdalene comes to be thought of as a reformed prostitute. Likewise, a glance down a list of female saints venerated by the church will show a high preponderance of virgins, wives and mothers. Why this emphasis on women's sexuality, an emphasis almost absent in representations of men? Is the reason to be sought in the prestige which celibacy enjoyed in some forms of Christianity, and in the overwhelming fear which male celibates felt for women, women whom they naturally viewed as sexual temptresses? This may be a partial explanation, but it cannot account for the fact that even those Christians who reject celibacy, Protestants for example, have often viewed women in terms of their sexuality. In fact, the emphasis on women's sexuality is best understood as part of a wider Christian emphasis, an emphasis upon what might inelegantly be called women's 'relationality'. Christianity tends to represent women in terms of their relationships; as mothers, as wives, as concubines, as prostitutes, as brides, as virgins. This is clearly sexist in the sense that men are rarely represented in this way, but is it sexist in the sense that it denigrates women? The answer to that question will depend on one's view of relationality. If, like some feminists, one sees women's relationality as a strength, then clearly it is not denigrating. If, however, like some other feminists, one values independence as a higher goal for women than relationality, then clearly it is.

Finally, it is worth mentioning a feature of religious representations of women which is rarely mentioned in feminist accounts: their 'transparency'. Not all representations of women demonstrate this feature, but an interesting number do. To speak of the transparency of a representation is to speak of how a viewer's eye tends not to rest upon it but to look through it to something else. The representation becomes important not so much for what is as for what it may symbolize. Thus, as we have seen, Eve becomes a symbol of sin, of greed, of lust, of pride. Mary the mother of Jesus becomes a symbol of humility, of the church, of obedience. And Mary Magdalene becomes a symbol of redemption or penance. An interesting example of this phenomenon appeared in the arguments of some of those opposing the ordination of women in the Church of England where women were frequently spoken of in terms not of what they were, but of what they stood for: for the secularization of the church, for the triumph of liberalism, of permissiveness, even of pantheism (the belief that the natural world is divine). Transparency is not necessarily harmful, for clearly in some human beings certain qualities or virtues or tendencies do come to a focus, but it becomes harmful when human beings become nothing more than ciphers or symbols, when what they stand for obscures rather than reveals what they actually are. Then they cease to be actual people with particular histories and characteristics and become mere signs to be manipulated at will. There is no doubt that this has been the fate of representations of women in Christian history far more than it has of representations of men.

If there is a general conclusion to be drawn concerning feminist claims about religious representations of women it is surely that they are at their weakest when they are at their most general and when they pay least attention to the proper contexts of these representations. Then they cease to illuminate their subject, and are revealed as little more than ideologically motivated attempts to see patriarchy everywhere. But when they respect the context and the particularity of representations of women and try to identify dominant features in these representations, then they can be original and illuminating. Then they help us to see these representations clearly, more clearly than was possible in previous eras of male-dominated scholarship.

○  **Questions**

> 1 Would you think that Christian representations of women have helped or hindered Christian women? western women in general?
>
> 2 Do women still need religion?
>
> 3 Consider whether feminist claims about religious representations of women hold more or less true for religions besides Christianity.
>
> 4 Compare the ways in which Jesus's male and female followers are represented in the New Testament.

○ **Further reading**

> For the first programmatic statement of the radical feminist theo-
> logical position see Daly (1973/1986). Hampson (1990) offers a more
> recent British version. Ruether (1983) is the most influential work of
> liberal feminist theology. Loades (1990) is a well edited reader which
> introduces the several varieties of feminist theology. Two pioneering
> scholarly studies of women and religion are Ruether (1974) and
> Power (1975). Those interested in women in religious traditions
> besides Christianity will find Sharma (1987) a good place to start their
> investigations. Brown (1991) serves as a good general introduction to
> the topic of women's representations in Christianity. Phillips (1984),
> Warner (1985) and Haskins (1993) offer excellent and wide-ranging
> surveys of the ways in which Mary, Mary Magdalene and Eve respec-
> tively have been represented in western culture.

○ **Notes**

1 Mary was given the official title *Aeiparthenos*, virgin at and after conception, in
451 at the Council of Chalcedon. This was declared a dogma of the church in 649
at the First Lateran Council.
2 Mary Magdalene was celebrated as an apostle by some of the early Christian
writers, Hippolytus (c.170–235) referring to her as *apostola apostolorum* (apostle of
the apostles), but Christians have not always acknowledged her apostolic status.
See Haskins 1993: 65.
3 This particular example is from the painting of Mary Magdalene as a hermit by
the Magdalen Master (c.1280). Reproduced in Haskins 1993: 227.
4 The radical feminist theologian Daphne Hampson concedes this point (Hampson
1990: 53–8).

○ **References**

Armstrong, K. (1986) *The Gospel According to Woman: Christianity's Creation of the Sex
War in the West*. London: Pan Books.
Brown, A. (1991) *Apology to Women: Christian Images of the Female Sex*. London: Inter-
Varsity Press.
Daly, M. (1968) *The Church and the Second Sex*. New York: Harper and Row.
Daly, M. (1973/1986) *Beyond God the Father*, republished with a new introduction.
London: The Women's Press.
Hampson, D. (1990) *Christianity and Feminism*. Oxford: Blackwell.
Haskins, S. (1993) *Mary Magdalene: Myth and Metaphor*. London: HarperCollins.
Kazantzakis, N. (1960) *The Last Temptation*. New York: Simon and Schuster.
Loades, A. (ed.) (1990) *Feminist Theology: A Reader*. London: SPCK.
Phillips, J. A. (1984) *Eve: The History of an Idea*. New York: Harper and Row.
Power, E. (1975) *Medieval Women*. Cambridge: Cambridge University Press.
Roberts, M. (1984) *The Wild Girl*. London: Methuen.
Ruether, R. R. (ed.) (1974) *Religion and Sexism: Images of Women in the Jewish and
Christian Traditions*. New York: Simon and Schuster.

Ruether, R. R. (1983) *Sexism and GodTalk*. London: SCM.

Sharma, A. (ed.) (1987) *Women in World Religions*. Albany, NY: State University of New York Press.

Stanton, E. C. (1985) *The Woman's Bible*, new abridged edition. Edinburgh: Polygon.

Tertullian (1959) On the Apparel of Women, in *Fathers of the Church*, Vol. 40. Washington DC: Catholic University of America.

Trible, P. (1978) *God and the Rhetoric of Sexuality*. Philadelphia, PA: Fortress.

Warner, M. (1985) *Alone of All Her Sex: The Myth and Cult of the Virgin Mary*. London: Picador.

## 12 | SARA AHMED

# Constructions of women and/in the Orient

In this chapter I want to consider contemporary media culture in relation to Orientalism and the imaging of 'woman'. How does the media produce myths of 'the East' (the Orient) and 'the West' (the Occident) and to what extent are these myths themselves gendered? How does the representation of the Orient intersect with the representation of 'white women' within the western media? I will attempt to address these questions through a textual analysis of some photographic images from *Marie Claire*: an editorial series entitled 'The Orient' (May 1994).

My concern with examining the way in which the intersection between Orientalism and gender in contemporary media culture reflects some of the recent developments in feminist theory. It has become increasingly important to feminism to recognize that cultural representations of women do not operate in isolation from other regimes of difference, such as race, class and sexuality. Rather than simply focusing on 'images of woman', feminism needs to account for the production of divergent, often contradictory, images of 'woman' in specific cultural formations. Recent developments in Black feminism have suggested that 'images of woman' do not exist independently of racial differences – what we have is conflicting images of white and Black women (hooks 1992). However, racial differences do not themselves operate in isolation from historical processes which produce and reproduce racial relationships. Such racial relationships can be defined in terms of specific forms of colonialism. Colonialism describes the massive economic and political processes involving the territorial domination of whole countries and nations by an imperial power. But, if colonialism is a name for this devasting material process, then what would it mean to understand colonialism in terms of culture? To consider colonialism as cultural would be to examine the way in which colonial situations are maintained through representations that privilege the interests and values of the imperial or colonial centre. Cultural representations participated in the colonial process whereby the colonizing power (for example, the British empire) was seen as the source of civilization and progress. It is important to recognize that the massive effects of colonialism means that there is no homogeneous 'global culture' which supports a singular gender ideology. Rather, the power relations between colonizing and colonized nations means that women from different nations, regions or ethnic groups are represented in relations of power and antagonism. As a result, we need to consider contemporary cultural representations in terms of a complex network of intersections between gender, race and colonialism.

This chapter will examine such intersections in terms of the construction of 'woman and/in the Orient'. I will first address in more detail how an analysis of cultural intersections enables us to rethink previous accounts of patriarchal and colonialist representations. Second, I will discuss Edward Said's influential account of Orientalism. I then consider how contemporary media culture involves the transformation of 'Orientalism'. Finally, I will examine how some 'advertisements' in *Marie Claire* involve the production of the figure of the 'white woman' through the use of Orientalism. In conclusion, I raise the question of how we can resist these patriarchal and colonialist representations.

## ○ The importance of cultural intersections

The term 'cultural intersections' refers to the meeting or collision between different representations and images. A consideration of cultural intersections between gender, race and colonialism is important for two main reasons. First, it demands that feminism reject any approach which isolates the production of gender from race and colonialism (see Cross, Chapter 17, this volume). As a result, it also requires us to consider how certain feminisms may themselves function as part of colonialist culture. For example, Chandra Mohanty discusses how feminist attempts to account for the universality of gender oppression have led to the production of the category of the 'third world woman' within feminist analysis. She writes:

> An analysis of 'sexual difference' in the form of a cross-culturally singular, monolithic notion of patriarchy or male dominance leads to the construction of a similarly reductive or homogeneous notion of what I call the 'third world difference' – that stable, ahistorical something that apparently oppresses most if not all the women in these countries.
>
> (Mohanty 1991: 53)

Here, the 'third world woman' is interpreted in terms of a western understanding of gender oppression: the representation of her as a victim of a universal patriarchy positions the western feminist subject as an authority, while taking the West as a reference point for understanding different forms of power relations. In this way, Mohanty argues that western feminism's universalist models can reinforce a colonial relation.

Second, looking at points of intersection between gender, race and colonialism may help to confirm that an analysis of colonialism which does not consider gender relations is insufficient. Feminists have pointed out that colonialism has been discussed in terms which exclude any consideration of how it affects women differently, both as part of colonizing and colonized peoples (see Chaduri and Strobel 1992: 2–6). And indeed, colonialist culture has been examined without due consideration of how that culture may itself be gendered.

An analysis of cultural intersections also requires that we reject the temptation of seeing 'patriarchy' and 'colonialism' as analogous. One of the most problematic tendencies in some recent theoretical approaches is the use of analogies between different kinds of power relations: how women experience 'patriarchy' is *like* how colonized peoples experience colonialism. Take the following quotation from *The Empire Writes Back*:

> Women in many countries have been relegated to the position of 'Other', marginalized and, in a metaphorical sense, 'colonized'. . . They share with colonized races and peoples an intimate experience of the politics of oppression and repression, and *like* them they have been forced to articulate their experiences in the language of their oppressors. Women, *like* post-colonial peoples, have had to construct a language of their own when their only available 'tools' are those of the 'colonizer'.
>
> (Ashcroft *et al.* 1989: 174–5, emphasis added)

The problem with relying on such analogies is that it excludes an analysis of the contradictions between different power relations (Donaldson 1992: 6). It excludes an analysis of, for example, the power difference between women who are colonizers and those who are colonized. Indeed, by seeing woman as already colonized such an analysis would exclude a consideration of how women may be positioned, however ambivalently, as colonizers as, for example, in the case of white women travel writers (Mills 1993; Blunt 1994). Given this, for feminism and anti-colonialism to translate one set of differences into another (patriarchy to colonialism and back again) would be deeply problematic. We need to consider how relations of power do not simply merge into each other. Rather the intersection of such relations of power involves their *transformation* in historically specific contexts. Thinking of intersections as transformative also requires us to reject an 'additive analysis' (race + gender + colonialism), where different relations of power are understood as simply adding to the other (Brewer 1993: 16–17). Rather, we need to consider the *contradictions* between relations of power; so, for example, Black women's experiences of racism and colonialism are different from white women's experiences, as Black women's experiences of gender and sexism are different from white women's experiences.

## O  Orientalism as colonial discourse

The path-breaking work in the understanding of Orientalism as colonial discourse is Edward Said's *Orientalism*, first published in 1978. He examines the construction of the Orient within European culture. The construction of the Orient through discourses such as history, anthropology, travel writing, philosophy and sociology defines the Orient in relation to a notion of Europe. So while Said discusses 'the Orient', as a category constructed by western culture, he also, more specifically, argues that 'the West' is itself constructed through the representation of the Orient as outside or beyond it. That is, the Orient creates Europe or the Occident as a bounded space by being positioned as outside of, or other than, Europe. The fascination with the Orient within western imperial culture is a fascination which, in Said's terms, creates an idea of Europe, 'a collective notion identifying "us" Europeans as against all "those" non-Europeans' (1978: 7). Orientalism creates *an imaginary geographical divide* based on the binarism of Occident/Orient. As such, the Occident and Orient form a power relation within western culture. As Said (1978: 244) argues:

> the effect of this [Oriental] style is that it brings Asia tantalisingly close to the West, but only for a brief moment. We are left at the end with a sense of the pathetic distance that separates 'us' from an Orient destined to bear its foreignness as a mark of its permanent estrangement from the West.

Said's work has been criticized for being overly-totalizing, that is, for presenting too simple and absolute a picture of the production of Orientalism – so precluding the possibility of local resistances. Other commentators have argued that we need to consider the local encounters between colonizers and colonized without assuming the production of the Orient as a figure for the West (see Thomas 1994: 8). Blunt argues that Said overly totalizes the dichotomy between the colonizing self and the colonized other and, following Lisa Lowe (1992), suggests that we need to account for multiple, contradictory 'orientalist situations' (1994: 24). Furthermore, I think we need to develop a more multiple and contradictory model of the production of Orientalism precisely to account for the complex intersection between Orientalism and gender hierarchies.

At one point Said does consider the style of the Orient in terms of 'its feminine penetrability' (1978: 206). But despite this recognition of how the Orient becomes sexualized in the western imagination, his work tends to exclude a consideration of gender as a set of *power relations*. For example, when Said (1978: 6) considers a scene in Flaubert's novel, *Madame Bovary*, he suggests that:

> Flaubert's encounter with an Egyptian courtesan produced a widely influential model of the Oriental woman; she never spoke of herself, she never represented her emotions, presence, or history. *He* spoke for and represented her. . . It fairly stands for the pattern of the relative strength between East and West, and the discourse about the Orient that it enabled.

Here Said introduces the production of the Oriental woman as spoken for, as without history. But he then reads this as simply standing for the relation between East and West. The specifically gendered nature of this *relation of address* (in which the man speaks and the woman is spoken for) is hence excluded from his interpretation (likewise, a feminist interpretation which would focus on gender without reference to Orientalism would be inadequate). Rather than simply claim that Orientalism is gendered, we need to examine how both Orientalism and gender work as relations of power that intersect with each other in contradictory ways.

## Orientalism and contemporary media culture

The specific concern of this chapter is to consider contemporary media culture in relation to the intersection of Orientalism and the imaging of 'woman'. While the European empires may have been formally dismantled (so-called decolonization) the cultural forms of Orientalism are very much in place; in fact, given the formal dismantling of empire, it could be argued that media and cultural representations function as an even more important means for the strategic protection of western interests (this is not to deny that there remain extensive economic and political structures in place which reproduce neo-colonial relations). Said's *Orientalism* does attempt to consider 'Orientalism' in relation to contemporary culture. He argues as follows:

> One aspect of the electronic, postmodern world is that there has been a reinforcement of the stereotypes by which the Orient is viewed. Television, the films, and all the media's resources have forced information into more and more standardized molds. So far as the Orient is concerned, standardization and cultural stereotyping *have intensified the hold of the nineteenth-century academic and imaginative demonology of 'the mysterious Orient'.*
>
> (1978: 25, emphasis mine)

However, recent shifts in cultural and media studies, which attend to the impact of technologies on global culture and the breakdown of the boundaries of the nation-state, may question this model. Mike Featherstone argues in his introduction to *Global Culture: Nationalism, Globalization and Modernity* that globalization involves not just global cultural interrelatedness but 'persistent cultural interaction and exchange' (1990: 6). This series of global cultural flows involves a repertoire of images and information, that is, a *mediascape* (ibid.: 7). Such a mediascape undermines the boundaries of the nation-state (ibid.: 2). The impact of globalization on culture may suggest that the boundaries between 'East' and 'West' as determined by Orientalism are constantly threatened. However, I think this model of the global mediascape as involving cultural interrelatedness and interaction needs some qualification. In light of *Orientalism*, we can see that the boundaries of nation-states (or even geographic entities such as the 'East' and 'West') have always been imaginary. While the contemporary mediascape may involve a global flow of images and objects, this is not to say that those images and objects do not create and reinforce such imaginative boundaries (and hence relations of power) between, for example, the 'East' and 'West'. William M. O'Barr's work, *Culture and the Ad: Exploring Otherness in the World of Advertising*, may serve to suggest that images of 'otherness' and 'difference' function to sustain rather than simply problematize the imaginary boundaries between different nations, or groups of people. He suggests that the fascination with otherness within advertisements helps define the boundaries of a product's market: that is, to define who is and is not the consumer audience (O'Barr 1994: 2, 12). Hence, the flow of cultural images and objects which play with 'otherness' and 'difference' may serve to reproduce as well as threaten the imaginary boundaries between social or racial groups. Cultural images and objects can be seen as a site of contestation, where distinctions and boundaries between social and racial groups are both secured and threatened. For a feminist anti-colonialist intervention into the mediascape, it becomes necessary to consider how the imaginary boundaries that are contested through representations of 'otherness' and 'difference' affect the imaging of 'woman'.

## ○ Woman and/in the Orient

Feminist analyses of media culture have focused on how 'woman' is presented in terms which involve objectification: she is defined through her body, appearance and sexuality, rather than through what she can do (Root 1984; Myers 1986). Her body and looks are used to sell commodities; in this sense, 'woman' as a sign within advertisements becomes commodified. I will question this focus by examining some 'oriental' images from *Marie Claire* (May 1994) as a part of our contemporary mediascape which thrives on the exploration of racial or 'ethnic' difference. I will consider this difference in relation to the positioning of 'woman' within these advertisements, and suggest that the 'objectification of woman' that feminists have perceived as an aspect of contemporary visual culture relies, in contradictory ways, on Orientalism. However, the texts I will be discussing are not strictly advertisements. I was reminded of this when I asked the editorial team that produces *Marie Claire* to give me copyright to reproduce them as part of this chapter. The reply told me firmly that these photographs were not advertisements, but part of an editorial series. However, given the fact that the written text on the reproduced photographs provides the price of the woman's clothes depicted (and where to buy them), the reader is positioned as potential consumer of the *commodity object*, even if these images were not produced as advertisements. In other words, they function as advertisements at the level of *consumption*, if not production. Given that these advertisements are produced as part of a women's magazine, my analysis will assume that the consumer is positioned as female, which is not to imply that different consumers will not read these images in different ways.

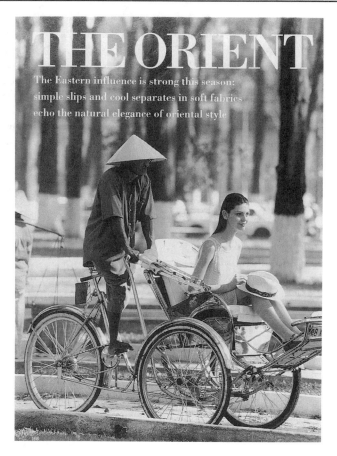

*Figure 12.1* reproduced with kind permission of A. Carrara, Société
Photographique Internationale, Paris.

The series of images begins with a capitalized title, 'THE ORIENT' (see
Figure 12.1), and the caption, 'The Eastern influence is strong this season:
simple slips and cool separates in soft fabrics echo the natural elegance of
oriental style'. The image depicted entails a 'western' construction of the
style of the Orient. A close analysis of the images (and indeed of the small
print at the end of the series) informs the reader that the photographs were
taken in Vietnam. As such, the naming of the series as 'the Orient' involves
a loss of the cultural specificity and difference of Vietnam: the images
become a sign for a homogeneous Orient defined or produced by a western
photographer. So underneath the caption, an 'Oriental man', whose face
is covered by a hat, is pushing a white woman on a bike, who is gazing
beyond the frame of the photograph. She is dressed in white, the 'Oriental man' is dressed in grey. The price of her clothes is listed (on the adjacent
page which is not reproduced here), but not the price of his. What is interesting about the image is the way in which 'the Orient' becomes a context

which the white woman enters into, and a style which she takes on. Given that it is her clothes that are for sale, she becomes the centre of the advertisement, while the grey shadowy and faceless Oriental figure is positioned as a vehicle for her. The reader is invited to glance over his image to hers, which is white, crisp and distinct from the rest of the text. In other words, the Orient as context and style enables her to be the centre of the image; it enables her to be distinguishable as a commodity. The advertisement also implies her agency: she looks ahead brightly to where she is going (he simply pushes) and it is she that is 'wearing' or 'taking on' the Orient, while he simply *is* the Orient, a part of a scene. In this sense, the commodification of the 'white woman' (which feminism has traditionally seen as involving her exploitation and objectification) relies on a form of Orientalism, a positioning of the East as foreign or Other to the value of the commodity: as a simple place in which that commodity circulates.

This distinction of the white woman through the use of contrast with the Oriental background relates to the written text. The title announces the Orient. The reader/consumer is invited to enter the Orient (perhaps like the white woman whose clothes we could buy). The East is positioned as an influence, which defines the consumer audience as 'the West', as that which is being influenced (without reference to 'the East' that definition would not be *explicit* in the text). The West is seen as 'echoing' the East. The Oriental is defined in terms of 'natural' and in terms of 'style'. This implies that the West follows from (echoes, is influenced by) the East; the East is on the side of 'nature', the West on the side of 'culture'. That is, the West provides a copy of the original natural styles of the East. The implicit narrative in the caption is very interesting. It implies that the 'East' provides the 'raw material' (and one could literally think of the production of commodities from 'the third world' for the western consumer) for the cultural values of the West. The white woman who is in the East finds her value through taking on the 'natural style' of the East and enabling it to become culture or commodity. The East is the means through which the West defines (or even makes) itself as culturally valued: a form of distinction and self-definition. The East can only have value when it is transformed from nature into commodity by the West. The ambivalence of the white woman's role as colonizer (perhaps as a white tourist who 'visits' the East as part of her 'leisure time') and as 'colonized' (where, as woman, she becomes a commodity, symbol or a sign for the West) suggests a contradictory gendering of the Oriental style.

In Figure 12.2 the white woman is also at the centre of the text; indeed, she *is* the foreground of the text. Her gaze again is beyond the frame of the image. She is 'light', while the rest of the photograph seems shadowy and dark. Behind her, out of focus, sit an 'Oriental' woman and man. We can only see their faces (the white woman's body takes up most of the image). They are both staring at her. The white woman is the object of their gaze and the centre of the reader's gaze. In this sense, the reader is aligned with the 'Oriental' figures by the shared act of looking at the white woman, whose gaze is unavailable to us. She becomes the object of an Oriental gaze (and again, the 'wearer' of the commodity) through the pushing of the

*Figure 12.2* reproduced with kind permission of A. Carrara, Société Photographique Internationale, Paris.

Oriental figures into the background. Their gaze makes her the centre of attention; it implies her desirability in the form of her difference as 'white woman'. The Oriental context, blurred and dark, enables the white woman to take the centre stage where she is positioned ambivalently. She is at once *desired* (valued) by the Oriental others, and *identified* with by the western female consumer in the form of a shared difference to those racialized others. That difference enables her to take on (wear) value.

In Figure 12.3 the white woman also 'stands out' through contrast, here, to a group of Oriental women. They all wear white, she wears a blue outfit (which the consumer can buy). She stands above them. The female western consumer is invited to identify with her figure which achieves its value (in terms of its difference) by being singular or particular; that is, she wears clothes, they wear uniforms. The conversion of the uniform 'Oriental women' into the singular 'white woman' is central to this Oriental image; the white woman achieves her value by being set against the

*Figure 12.3* reproduced with kind permission of A. Carrara, Société Photographique Internationale, Paris.

perceived indifference of the Oriental women. From the 'raw material' of the Oriental uniform/style, the 'white woman' achieves her value or distinction.

In the final image, Figure 12.4, the white woman poses alone. It would be easy to think of this image as simply representing 'woman'; indeed her recoiled figure suggests passivity rather than action. However, this image remains a part of 'THE ORIENT' series. This suggests that there does not have to be an *explicit* contrast of 'East' and 'West', or 'blackness' and 'whiteness', for the distinction of the 'West' or 'whiteness' to take place. The woman who poses somewhat indifferently for the camera cannot, then, be simply understood in terms of the representation (and, perhaps, objectification) of women in contemporary media culture. That her westernness or whiteness would become invisible if we lost sight of the inclusion of this image in the Oriental series, is a sign of the *cultural dominance* of westernness and whiteness. The single white woman recurs as a theme in

*Figure 12.4* reproduced with kind permission of A. Carrara, Société Photographique Internationale, Paris.

advertisements not simply as part of a gendered ideology (where women's value becomes linked to their appearance, their bodies or their sexuality) but as a part of an Orientalist (both racist and colonialist) history, in which 'she' gains exchange value via her distinction from racial Others. Indeed, this image represents how 'woman' as a commodifiable sign of difference or distinction becomes conflated with 'the white woman' through Orientalism. If we look closely at the image, we can see in the bottom left hand corner a blurred Oriental figure: a trace of the (violent) colonial context which enables 'the white woman' to take on her value. It can be argued that 'the white woman' is placed in a contradictory position: she is both marked by the cultural dominance of the West, and also by her subordination as 'woman', as a commodifiable object which circulates in the mediascape.

○ **Conclusion: possibilities of resistance**

In this chapter I have focused on the relations of power, both gendered and colonial, that are produced and contested in some advertisements from *Marie Claire* as part of our contemporary mediascape. Hence, the question of 'resistance' has not been foregrounded. Given that my analysis of cultural representations has focused on advertisements – part of our media culture which is directly linked to the selling of commodities – it is inappropriate to think of resistance simply in terms of how women can use alternative images. Rather, I want to suggest a feminist and anti-colonialist resistance is enabled as a way of interpreting, and hence intervening in, this mediascape.

I have suggested that the global flow of cultural images and objects does not mean that Orientalism has been transcended; on the contrary I have argued that the availability of images of cultural difference constitutes a new mode of operation for Orientalism which has significant impact on the representation of women. Hence, I discussed how the use of images of difference enables the distinction of the 'white woman' as the valued commodity in advertisements through the recreation of an imaginary divide between East and West. The dominant culture has an investment in keeping 'Occident' and 'Orient' as well as 'white' and 'Black' apart as distinct entities. Political resistance to these Orientalist images that leads to the conflation of 'woman' with 'the white woman' may be enabled precisely by exposing that these categories (Occident, Orient, White, Black) cannot be separated, but are dependent upon each other: that they only make sense in relation to each other, in part through their very intermingling in cultural space. The dependence of the representation of 'the white woman' on Orientalism reminds us that the absolute distinctions between East, West and 'the white woman' are unstable and open to being contested: that those distinctions form a history, and a history that can be rewritten.

○ **Questions and exercises**

1 Look through some recent magazines for advertisements which use images of racial differences or otherness. What kinds of strategies are employed? Consider the relationship between images of white and Black women in the media.

2 Can you think of any parallels between advertisements and other forms of cultural representation in relation to the intersection between Orientalism and gender (for example, tourist brochures, museums, western films)?

3 Interview a small group of people and ask them what kind of image 'the Orient', and 'the Oriental woman' conjures up. Compare your findings with some of the research on Orientalism as a colonial discourse.

4 Why do you think it is important feminism foregrounds questions
of colonialism and race when considering representations of
women in the media?

○  **Further reading**

Said (1984) reconsiders his germinal account of Orientalism and deals
here with the question of multiple Orientalisms and their intersection
with other power relations. For a broad introduction on approaches
to colonialism, which includes a small section on colonialism and
feminism, see Ashcroft *et al.* (1995). An excellent introductory text
that deals with cultural intersections between class, gender and race
is Jordan and Weedon (1995). Mohanty *et al.*'s (1991) edited collection contains some excellent reflections on the importance of feminism dealing with race and colonial issues (see also the further reading
provided by Cross, Chapter 17, this volume). For feminist work that
deals generally with cultural intersections between gender, race and
colonialism see Chaduri and Strobel (1992), Donaldson (1992) and
Blunt and Rose (1994). Spivak (1990) and Emberley (1993) have
written excellent theoretical pieces on the intersections between
gender, race and colonialism, but their work is very abstract and difficult, so end rather than begin with them! Mills (1993) and Blunt
(1994) both provide interesting analyses of white women travel
writers to elaborate some of the contradictions in the relation
between white women and colonialism. Roberts (1994) gives an out-
standing reading of white women's writings on slavery which considers the discursive construction of 'whiteness' and 'blackness' in
relation to colonialism and gender, and also addresses forms of Orientalism in relation to sexuality. hooks (1992) gives an account of
intersections of race, gender and colonialism in popular culture.
McClintock (1994) examines constructions of gender and colonialism
in some nineteenth-century Pear Soap advertisements. O'Barr (1994)
provides a good introductory account of 'otherness' within advertisements, and also provides lots of pictorial examples.

○  **References**

Ashcroft, B., Griffiths, G. and Tiffin, H. (1989) *The Empire Writes Back: Theory and
Practice in Post-Colonial Literatures*. London: Routledge.
Ashcroft, B., Griffiths, G. and Tiffin, H. (eds) (1995) *The Post-Colonial Studies Reader*.
London: Routledge.
Blunt, A. (1994) *Travel, Gender and Imperialism: Mary Kingsley and West Africa*.
London: Guilford Press.

Blunt, A. and Rose, G. (1994) *Writing Women and Space: Colonial and Post-Colonial Geographies*. New York: Guilford Press.

Brewer, R. (1993) Theorizing race, class and gender: the new scholarship of black feminist intellectuals and black women's labour, in S. M. James and A. P. A. Busia (eds) *Theorizing Black Feminisms: The Visionary Pragmatism of Black Women*. London: Routledge.

Chaduri, N. and Strobel, M. (eds) (1992) *Western Women and Imperialism: Complicity and Resistance*. Bloomington, IN: Indiana University Press.

Donaldson, L. E. (1992) *Decolonizing Feminisms: Race, Gender and Empire Building*. London: Routledge.

Emberley, J. V. (1993) *Thresholds of Difference: Feminist Critiques, Native Women's Writing, Postcolonial Theory*. Toronto: University of Toronto Press.

Featherstone, M. (ed.) (1990) *Global Culture: Nationalism, Globalization and Modernity*. London: Sage Publications.

hooks, b. (1992) *Black Looks: Race and Representation*. London: Turnaround.

Jordan, G. and Weedon, C. (1995) *Cultural Politics: Class, Gender, Race and the Postmodern World*. Oxford: Blackwell.

Lowe, L. (1992) *Critical Terrains: French and British Orientalisms*. Ithaca, NY: Cornell University Press.

McClintock, A. (1994) Soft-soaping empire: commodity racism and imperial advertising, in G. Robertson, M. Mash, L. Tickner, J. Bird, B. Curtis and T. Putnam (eds) *Travellers' Tales: Narratives of Home and Displacement*. London: Routledge.

Mills, S. (1993) *Discourses of Difference: An Analysis of Women's Travel Writing and Colonialism*. London: Routledge.

Mohanty, C. (1991) Under western eyes: feminist scholarship and colonial discourses, in C. Mohanty, A. Russo and L. Torres (eds) *Third World Women and the Politics of Feminism*. Bloomington, IN: Indiana University Press.

Mohanty, C., Russo, A. and Torres, L. (eds) (1991) *Third World Women and the Politics of Feminism*. Bloomington, IN: Indiana University Press.

Myers, K. (1986) *Understains: The Sense and Seduction of Advertising*. London: Comedia.

O'Barr, W. M. (1994) *Culture and the Ad: Exploring Otherness in the World of Advertising*. Boulder, CO: Westview Press.

Roberts, D. (1994) *The Myth of Aunt Jemima: Representations of Race and Region*. London: Routledge.

Root, J. (1984) *Pictures of Women: Sexuality*. London: Pandora.

Said, E. (1978) *Orientalism*. London: Routledge and Kegan Paul.

Said, E. (1984) Orientalism reconsidered, in F. Barker, P. Hulme, M. Iverson and D. Loxley (eds) *Europe and Its Others*. Colchester: University of Essex.

Spivak, G. C. (1990) *The Post-Colonial Critic*. London: Routledge.

Thomas, N. (1994) *Colonialism's Culture: Anthropology, Travel, Government*. Cambridge: Polity Press.

# PART III

## Gender and social identity

In this part we explore popular constructions of women's distinctively 'female' identity, and challenges to them. The starting point of Steph Lawler's chapter is the way that women's biological capacity for bearing children is commonly extended into an assumption that women's primary social role is motherhood. She evaluates feminist responses to this elision of 'woman' and 'mother'. Carolyn Stone then explores the philosophical implications of women's supposed maternal qualities. Robbie Smith, discussing lesbianism, traces the history of an identity which has frequently been denied to women or been regarded as a perversion. Sarah Beresford explores the way that English law constructs 'woman' as a legal category in accordance with essentialist understandings of feminine identity based on the notion of women as heterosexual mothers. We then turn to 'racial' identities. Kathleen Cross argues that black feminist critiques of feminism are causing white women to confront the implications of their racialized identities. Finally Santi Rozario explores differences in women's responses to the identities offered them by Islam. Several of the contributors argue that even though gendered identities are 'constructed' they are experienced none the less as 'real'.

STEPH LAWLER

# Motherhood and identity

## ○ Introduction

Women's ability to bear and suckle children has been seen as not only marking out their 'difference' from men, but also as generating within women a distinctively 'female' identity and personality. Within both popular 'commonsense' knowledge and some academic disciplines, women's reproductive capacity is linked with character traits of nurturance, lack of competitiveness, and so on. 'Nature' is frequently invoked to account for women's difference from men, but also to set up a natural (and therefore, by extension, unalterable) link between bearing a child and bringing that child up. Women's reproductive capacity, therefore, is seen to determine their proper social roles.

Nature in this sense is a powerful legitimating tool for maintaining the status quo (Douglas 1966). Since nature is outside of human control, this type of argument suggests, there is nothing that can be done to alter it. One of the achievements of feminism has been to undermine the association between women's social position and a supposed 'natural' world. Feminists have rejected the basis on which this connection is made, pointing out, for example, that there is nothing that exists outside of the social; humans live in societies and there is nothing that is not governed by social rules and social meanings. This insight has been particularly important in discussions of women's mothering, since mothering, like sexuality, is often considered to be an area which belongs to 'nature' rather than to social arrangements.

Clearly, there are physiological processes going on when a woman becomes pregnant and gives birth to a child. But the *meanings* we give to these physiological processes vary from culture to culture and from historical era to historical era. Further, many feminists have questioned the 'natural' link between bearing a child and rearing that child.

This chapter is concerned with the identification of women with motherhood, with the links made between being a 'woman' and being a 'mother';

I will consider some of the ways in which feminists have both conceptualized and subverted this link. I will focus primarily on the work of the North American feminist Adrienne Rich, whose book *Of Woman Born* has become a classic among feminist analyses of mothering.

○  **Maternal identities**

Central to Rich's analysis is the distinction she draws between motherhood as 'experience' and motherhood as 'institution'. Rich argues that the experience of motherhood – 'the *potential relationship* of any women to her powers of reproduction, and to her children' – has been taken from women's control and has become subject to the institution of motherhood, 'which aims at ensuring that that potential – and all women – shall remain under male control' (Rich 1977: 13, emphasis hers).

In drawing this distinction, Rich alerts us, not only to the ways in which mothering exists under current social arrangements, but to alternatives. Further, in naming motherhood as an 'institution', she places it in the realm of the social, rather than the natural. Motherhood, for Rich, is socially organized; moreover, this social organization, although it is subject to historical and cross-cultural variations, is always dominated by men, and is therefore oppressive to women.

According to Rich, the institutionalization of motherhood sets up an equivalence between women's identity and maternity. Mothering, she argues, is seen as the quintessentially 'feminine' act: 'that thing which patriarchy joins with physiology to render into the definition of femaleness' (Rich 1977: 37). But also, engaging in maternal work, which is only one, temporary aspect of a woman's life, has come to be defined as the whole of her identity. This link is particularly insidious, Rich suggests, because it reduces a woman's maternal work to a 'natural' aspect of her identity. Nurturance, patience, and the rest are not valued (or paid) because it is considered 'only natural' that women should care, selflessly and unconditionally, not only for children, but for adult men also. Because this nurturing is considered to be an intrinsic part of women's 'nature', it is not defined as work at all, but as a 'labour of love'. Yet, as Rich asks, 'Why should women, and women only, work for love only?' (1978: 263). As I will go on to argue later, this naturalizing of caring has implications for women's work in the labour market, as well as in the family.

Rich describes and analyses a number of ways in which she sees motherhood as institution working to women's disadvantage. For example, she argues, the medical and scientific takeover of childbirth has placed women's childbearing in the hands of (mainly) male obstetricians, resulting in a loss of control by women over their own bodies. The nuclear household isolates women from one another, militating against the formation of allegiances and networks of cooperation between women. The ideology of the perfect mother, which creates a standard that no human being could attain, induces tremendous guilt in mothers. And, tragically, the oppressive, isolated conditions of motherhood may lead mothers to the most extreme acts of violence, usually self-directed or directed at their children. The tremendous potential which Rich sees in motherhood is thwarted by the patriarchal control of women's motherhood, and of women's reproduction in general.

Even if women do not become mothers, Rich argues, they cannot escape the oppressiveness of the institution of motherhood. For Rich, all women are defined by their relationship to maternity. That is, women are defined either as 'mothers' or as 'not-mothers'. If women do not bear children, then their 'childlessness' is what defines them:

> Historically, cross-culturally, a woman's status as childbearer has been the test of her womanhood. Through motherhood, every woman has been defined from outside herself: mother, matriarch, matron, spinster, barren, old maid – listen to the history of emotional timbre that hangs about each of these words. Even by default motherhood has been an enforced identity for women, while the phrases 'childless man' and 'nonfather' sound absurd and irrelevant to us.
>
> (Rich 1978: 261)

However, although mothering can be seen as a socially approved activity for many women, it is important to note that not all women stand in the same relationship to maternity. That is, childbearing is socially approved only for certain groups of women, often in very narrowly defined circumstances. As Michelle Stanworth (1987) points out in her discussion of the new reproductive technologies, all women are seen as having a biologically and socially impelled desire to bear children; but, for some groups of women, motherhood is constructed as an inappropriate activity:

> According to ideologies of motherhood, all women *want* children, but single women, lesbian women (and disabled women) are often expected to forgo mothering 'in the interests of the child'.
>
> (Stanworth 1987: 15, emphasis hers; see also Lee and Morgan 1990)

Stanworth's argument is well illustrated by the so-called 'virgin births' which preoccupied the British press in March 1991. The focus of the many newspaper articles which covered this story was the pregnancy of a self-described heterosexual woman who had never had sexual intercourse. She had become pregnant after artificial insemination by donor (AID) at the Birmingham clinic of the British Pregnancy Advisory Service. Again and again, newspaper articles focused on this woman's unsuitability to be a mother. She was represented as 'selfish', as putting her own interests before those of the child, and even as mentally ill (Assinder 1991; Golden and Hope 1991; Milhill 1991; Mullin 1991; Sherman 1991). Clearly, it was not the use of AID which provoked this storm of protest, since this technique is in routine clinical use, without much protest at its use for married women. Rather, it was the woman's autonomous motherhood which seems to be behind the widespread condemnation. We should note, however, that the woman's *desire* for a child is not in question in these representations; rather, it is her *acting on* that desire in circumstances deemed 'inappropriate'.

It is not only autonomous motherhood, however, which is socially disapproved; the maternity of other groups of women is also frequently seen as threatening. Gisela Bock (1992) points out that Jewish women, Gypsy women and women deemed mentally deficient were subject to compulsory sterilization in Nazi Germany. But this eugenicism is not something which belongs only in this notorious historical period; in contemporary Britain and North America, Black women have been the targets of coercive sterilization, for example being offered abortions only if they agree to sterilization also (OWAAD 1979; Davis 1981; Bryan *et al.* 1985). The activities of institutions such as the World Bank and groups such as Planned Parenthood in promoting contraception in the so-called 'third world' (even in parts of the world that are under-, rather than over-populated) have also been seen as stemming from a eugenicist desire to keep the population size of non-White races under control (Cutrufelli, 1983).

Yet Black women are also frequently attributed an 'animal-like' nature, and are seen as more *natural* mothers. As Protasia Torkington comments of her own midwifery training in Britain:

> Black women were more or less equated with animals who pause only to drop the baby and carry on their chores as if nothing had happened. They did not need painkillers, they did not need postnatal care.
>
>                                                            (Torkington 1988: 304)

While Black women are attributed a 'natural' maternal identity, this does not mean that their maternity is approved, nor that they are considered 'good mothers'. It is Black women and White working-class women who are most frequently represented, within discourses of social policy, for example, as 'bad mothers', and their maternal practices are seen as lying at the heart of numerous social problems (see Walkerdine and Lucey 1989; Phoenix and Woollett 1991).

Rich explains the restrictions placed on the fertility of some groups of women as being part of the patriarchal control of women's bodies. In some ways, however, the fact that different groups of women are controlled in different ways raises problems for Rich's argument. This argument – that it is patriarchal domination which explains the control of all women's fertility – could explain why lesbian mothers, for example, are stigmatized (since lesbians are not sexually available to men). But it is not clear how it can explain why Black mothers and White working-class mothers are also stigmatized, and have sometimes been coerced into *not* reproducing. Rich is sensitive to issues of class and race within her work, but the absence of a theory of class or race domination weakens her argument.

Nevertheless, Rich's insight that there is an equivalence between feminine identity and maternal identity is an extremely valuable one. Even when women are represented as bad or inappropriate mothers, it is often the case that they are also seen to have an inbuilt capacity for nurturance. This has important implications for the work women do outside the home, as well as in it.

○ **'Mothering' at work**

Rich's conceptualization of motherhood as 'institution' has been taken up by Lisa Adkins and Celia Lury (1992) in their analysis of women's paid work. Adkins and Lury argue that motherhood is institutionalized in the labour market as in the home.

Adkins and Lury argue that nurturing work is a requirement of many of the jobs women do in the paid labour market. To illustrate their argument, they draw on Arlie Hochschild's (1983) study of airline stewardesses. Hochschild found that a large part of the stewardesses' work involved 'caring' for passengers (particularly male passengers); she parallels this caring work with the work of mothering. Adkins and Lury argue that there are processes going on in the labour market by which women workers come to be positioned as naturally caring. The caring work which they do as part of their jobs is thus naturalized, transformed into 'non-work' (as in the home). Hence the skills and the labour which go into caring are not recognized and not rewarded. In this way, women's nurturing work is exploited; women are doing the caring for free in their paid work, as well as in the home.

This insight provides a way of examining the operation of the equation between 'women' and 'mothers' within the labour market itself. In this analysis, women's caring is not a kind of 'false consciousness' carried over by women themselves from the world of home into the world of paid work; rather, the caring which many women do at work is a feature, and indeed a *requirement*, of many jobs themselves (particularly in the service sector). Even when women are employed in the same jobs as men, the requirements of the work may be different for each gender (see also Adkins 1992).

This exploitation of women's caring work can also be seen in Patricia Hill Collins's (1991) discussion of the 'controlling images' which, she argues, are used to define Black women. According to Collins, there are a number of ways in which African-American women are characterized; for example, as 'welfare mothers' – passive, indolent, and living off the state; or as 'matriarchs' – dominating their families and 'emasculating' their sons. But they are also sentimentalized as 'mammies' when caring for the children of White families. Collins shows how each of these images denigrates Black women and perpetuates gender and race oppression. Her analysis also suggests that Black women's supposedly natural maternal devotion and care is harnessed in the interests of White families; a requirement of the paid work of Black domestic workers is nurturance; yet this nurturance is not rewarded. It is seen as a *natural* characteristic of the 'devoted mammy'.

○ **Reclaiming motherhood**

Although Rich sees motherhood under current social arrangements as oppressive to women, her proposed solution is not for women to refuse motherhood, but to reclaim it. She argues that women need to have genuine choices around whether or not to be mothers, around the type and the timing of childbirth, and around the kind of family form within which children are brought up. The work which women do as mothers should also be valued and claimed as work.

More fundamentally, Rich argues that women have to reclaim control over their own bodies: women's powers of reproduction (including, but not only, motherhood) and women's sexuality should be celebrated and valued, and the conventional western split between mind and body, in which the mind is accorded a superior status over the body, should be healed. This reclamation by women of their bodies is an important part of Rich's political agenda, which, she believes, will lead to a revolution in women's lives:

> The repossession by women of our bodies will bring far more essential change to human society than the seizing of the means of production by workers. The female body has been both territory and machine, virgin wilderness to be exploited and assembly-line turning out life. We need to imagine a world in which every woman is the presiding genius of her own body. In such a world, women will truly create new life, bringing forth not only children (when and if we choose) but the visions, and the thinking, necessary to sustain, console, and alter human existence – a new relationship to the universe. Sexuality, politics, intelligence, power, motherhood, work, community, intimacy, will develop new meanings, thinking itself will be transformed.
>
> (Rich 1977: 285–6)

This transformative vision can sound quietist and mystical, but Rich seems here to be making the quantum leap of the imagination for which she argues in her 1978 essay. She is envisaging new potentialities for women in a world in which their reproduction is no longer controlled by men. At the same time that she advocates the imagining of alternative systems, she is clear that we have to attend to the 'contemporary emergency', arguing that women have to organize against the conditions of their own lives, and suggesting that small-scale, localized political movements are one means of achieving this.

Although Rich's celebration of women's bodies and women's reproduction has been taken up with enthusiasm by many feminists, others have viewed this form of politics with disquiet. Lynn Segal (1987) for example, suggests that solutions along these lines are retrogressive because they rest on a fundamental essentialism. She sees analyses which stress women's difference from men as *exaggerating* sexual difference and as asserting that women have a fundamental 'nature' which is different to that of men. This female nature is presented, she argues, as warm, nurturing and empathetic, in contradistinction to an aggressive and combative 'nature' in men. Hence, Segal sees a 'danger of traditional sexist stereotypes being reaffirmed in this literature' (Segal 1987: 145).

However, Segal's criticisms may be overstated in relation to Rich's work (Walby 1990). It is clear that Rich is arguing that mothering is socially constructed and that she is envisaging new forms that this social construction might take.

Collins (1991), in her analysis of Black women's mothering, demonstrates some of the ways in which motherhood can be valued without falling into stereotypical depictions of male and female 'nature'. Collins argues that, for Black women, motherhood can be a source of affirmation and empowerment:

> Motherhood can serve as a site where Black women express and learn the value of self-definition, the importance of valuing and respecting ourselves, the necessity of self-reliance and independence, and a belief in Black women's empowerment.
>
> (Collins 1991: 118)

The family can be both a site of relative escape from racism, and the place within which Black mothers foster an Afrocentric tradition, thus resisting a dominant White culture which has no place for such a tradition (hooks 1982, 1991; Jordan 1985; Collins 1991). Collins also argues that African-American mothers, acutely aware of the realities of racism in their own lives, teach their daughters that strength is needed for survival. Collins's analysis suggests that mothers who live under difficult and oppressive conditions are likely to teach their children what they know about the hardness of the world, and to try to equip them with the tools they need to fight these oppressive conditions. The maternal work of these women consists in a necessary toughness and even authoritarianism over their children, as well as the nurturance which is socially approved in mothers; this is one of the reasons that mothers who are Black and/or working-class are so often labelled 'bad mothers' (Walkerdine and Lucey 1989; Phoenix and Woollett 1991). Mothering, in this kind of analysis, is a form of resistance to racism and classism; however, its potential as a form of resistance to patriarchy is less clear. Nevertheless, in valuing and validating this type of maternity, Black women writers such as Collins, hooks and Jordan are subverting dominant definitions of 'good mothering', as well as uncovering the political potential of the mothering done by Black women.

## ○ Maternal politics

As well as highlighting the political potential of Black women's mothering within the family, Collins (1991: 192) also points to the significance of 'othermothers' – 'women who assist bloodmothers by sharing mothering responsibilities' – in African-American communities (see also Stack 1974). The practice of othermothering relieves bloodmothers of the burden of caring for children in an isolated nuclear family. Further, this practice subverts the notion, embedded within capitalism, that children are 'private property' belonging only to the biological parents:

> By seeing the larger community as responsible for children and by giving othermothers and other nonparents 'rights' in child rearing, African-Americans challenge prevailing property relations. It is in this

sense that traditional bloodmother/othermother relationships in woman-centred networks are 'revolutionary'.

(Collins 1991: 123)

Collins, then, reclaims women's maternal identity, marking it out as a source of empowerment, both to mothers themselves and to their children. But she also reformulates maternal identity, broadening it to include 'othermothers', and reframing dominant definitions of 'good mothering' to include toughness as well as nurturing.

Other groups of women have used an identity as mothers to forge forms of political action. For example, some women peace campaigners have seen mothering as both the impetus for their campaigns, and as the justification for those campaigns (Young 1990). As Alison Young notes, maternity was seen by women peace protesters at the Greenham Common nuclear weapons base as the basis for their political action, such that 'the issue of "peace" [was] not only a valid concern for women, but also . . . a concern *best* dealt with by women' (Young 1990: 32, emphasis hers). This link between motherhood and peace politics is also at the heart of Sara Ruddick's analysis of 'maternal thinking'. Ruddick sees a congruence between the types of work women do in caring for their children, and the work of preserving peace. She does not claim that mothers can save the world, but:

> if the world itself seems under siege, and if that siege holds any community and all children hostage, the effort of world protection can come to seem a 'natural' extension of maternal work.

(Ruddick 1990: 81)

This linking of motherhood with peace politics has the advantage of bringing maternal work, which is usually defined as belonging in the 'private' sphere, into the 'public' realm of politics. It can also be seen as forwarding a revaluation of the work which mothers do. This is also true of the feminist maternal ethics advocated by Simons (1984) and by Rich (1974), both by whom propose the mother–daughter relationship as a model for relations between women.

However, there are dangers in this valorization of motherhood. First, it can idealize motherhood, promoting as a feminist ethic the type of maternal work which is practised only by White middle-class women of the late twentieth century, and thus denigrating the maternal work of other groups of women. Second, this celebration of motherhood and maternal feelings can be essentialist in its assumption that all women share an intrinsic capacity for nurturance. Margaret Simons (1984: 358), for example, argues that all women can 'claim [their] maternal feelings with pride', but it is not clear exactly what 'maternal feelings' are, nor is it clear that all women (including mothers) share them. Third, and as Christine Delphy (1992) points out, a celebration of mothering can marginalize women who are not mothers.

A further problem in positing the mother–daughter relationship as the basis for feminist practice is that one element of the mother–daughter relationship – the mother's nurture – is extracted and set up as a kind of perfect relationship which can exist outside kin relations. But mothering consists not only in nurturing, but also in the mother's regulation and disciplining of the child. The mother–daughter relationship also involves ambivalence and hostility as well as closeness and affection (Steedman 1982, 1986; Walkerdine and Lucey 1989). By setting up an idealized mother–daughter relationship, feminists may denigrate their biological mothers in the search for more suitable, feminist alternatives (Davis 1992). Indeed, Chodorow and Contratto (1982) suggest that this celebration of motherhood can involve the search for a fantasy mother – a mother who will love and care for us unconditionally, and demand nothing in return (see also Sayers 1984).

## ○ Concluding remarks

In this chapter, I have explored some of the ways in which feminists have seen a 'maternal' identity as oppressive to women, both in the home and in the labour market. I have also explored one strand of feminist thought which advocates the reclamation by women of a maternal identity and the use of such an identity as the basis for political action.

One problem for feminism is how women's motherhood can be valued and validated without slipping into an essentialism which proposes that all women have an intrinsic capacity for nurturing, and without giving way to an idealization which divorces motherhood from its social and political context. In other words, how can feminists emphasize the importance of the work which goes into mothering without reinstating the conventional association between women and nurturing which has been challenged by so many feminists?

This is undoubtedly a thorny issue, especially since the characteristics which are considered to be 'natural' in mothers are closely bound up with socially constructed femininity. As Katherine Gieve (1987: 44) comments:

> If childcare was the only area of a woman's life where she was called upon to be responsive, patient and tolerant, the issue would be less troublesome for women. It is because the quality of motherhood mirrors so exactly the role of women and the idea of femininity not only at home but elsewhere that it is so difficult to deal with.

## ○ Questions and exercises

1 How convincing do you find Rich's argument that a reclamation by women of their bodies will bring about change? What effect might such a reclamation have?

2 Rich advocates making a 'quantum leap' of the imagination in

order to envisage the kind of change we want to see. Write a short piece on how motherhood *might be*, so that it will not be an oppressive institution. What kinds of social changes would have to occur to make your imagined motherhood possible?

3 Do you think political activism which is based on motherhood is fruitful, or does it tie women more closely to an idea of innate nurturance?

○  **Further reading**

For analyses which see a maternal identity as oppressive, but which propose radically different solutions to Rich's, see Firestone (1974) and Allen (1983). Firestone advocates the use of reproductive technology to enable pregnancy to take place outside the body, while Allen proposes that women 'evacuate' motherhood. For overviews of feminist writings on motherhood, see Maroney (1986) and Snitow (1992). Oakley (1976, 1980) provides analyses of women's own accounts of being a mother. Ayers (undated) and Ross (1993) provide evidence of practices akin to 'othermothering' among White working-class communities in the early twentieth and late nineteenth centuries.

○  **References**

Adkins, L. (1992) Hors d'oeuvres, *Trouble and Strife*, 24: 6–11.

Adkins, L. and Lury, C. (1992) Gender and the labour market: old theory for new?, in H. Hinds, A. Phoenix and J. Stacey (eds) *Working Out: New Directions in Women's Studies*. London: Falmer Press.

Allen, J. (1983) Motherhood: the annihilation of women, in J. Treblicot (ed.) *Mothering: Essays in Feminist Theory*. Savage, MD: Rowman and Littlefield.

Assinder, N. (1991) MPs demand ban on virgin births, *Daily Express*, 12 March.

Ayers, P. (undated) *The Liverpool Docklands*. Liverpool: Docklands History Books.

Bock, G. (1992) Equality and difference in national socialist racism, in G. Bock and S. James (eds) *Beyond Equality and Difference*. London: Routledge.

Bryan, B., Dadzie, S. and Scafe, S. (1985) *The Heart of the Race: Black Women's Lives in Britain*. London: Virago.

Chodorow, N. and Contratto, S. (1982) The fantasy of the perfect mother, in B. Thorne and M. Yalom (eds) *Rethinking the Family*. New York: Longman.

Collins, P. H. (1991) *Black Feminist Thought: Knowledge, Consciousness and the Politics of Empowerment*. New York: Routledge.

Cutrufelli, M. R. (1983) *Women of Africa: Roots of Oppression*. London: Zed Books.

Davis, A. (1981) *Women, Race and Class*. New York: Random House.

Davis, D. L. (1992) Feminist critics and literary mothers: daughters reading Elizabeth Gaskell, *Signs*, 17(3): 507–32.

Delphy, C. (1992) Mothers' union?, *Trouble and Strife*, 24: 12–19.

Douglas, M. (1966) *Purity and Danger: An Analysis of the Concepts of Pollution and Taboo*. London: Routledge.

Firestone, S. (1974) *The Dialectic of Sex: The Case for Feminist Revolution*. New York: Morrow.

Gieve, K. (1987) Rethinking feminist attitudes towards mothering, *Feminist Review*, 25: 39–45.

Golden, J. and Hope, J. (1991) Storm over virgin births, *Daily Mail*, 11 March.

Hochschild, A. (1983) *The Managed Heart: The Commercialization of Human Feeling*. Berkeley, CA: University of California Press.

hooks, b. (1982) *Ain't I a Woman? Black Women and Feminism*. London: Pluto Press.

hooks, b. (1991) Homeplace: a site of resistance, in *Yearning: Race, Gender, and Cultural Politics*. London: Turnaround.

Jordan, J. (1985) *On Call: Political Essays*. Boston, MA: South End Press.

Lee, R. and Morgan, D. (1990) A lesser sacrifice? sterilization and mentally handicapped women, in R. Lee and D. Morgan (eds) *Birthrights: Law and Ethics at the Beginnings of Life*. London: Routledge.

Maroney, H. J. (1986) Embracing motherhood: new feminist theory, in R. Hamilton and M. Barrett (eds) *The Politics of Diversity: Feminism, Marxism and Nationalism*. London: Verso.

Milhill, C. (1991) Child's needs before mother's desires, *The Guardian*, 12 March.

Mullin, J. (1991) Wish to avoid sex 'may hide neurosis', *The Guardian*, 12 March.

Oakley, A. (1976) *Housewife*. Harmondsworth: Penguin.

Oakley, A. (1980) *Women Confined: Towards a Sociology of Childbirth*. Oxford: Martin Robertson.

OWAAD (Organization of Women of African and Asian Descent) (1979) *Black Women in Britain Speak Out*. London: Women in Print.

Phoenix, A. and Woollett, A. (1991) Motherhood: social construction, politics and psychology, in A. Phoenix, A. Woollett and E. Lloyd (eds) *Motherhood: Meanings, Practices and Ideologies*. London: Sage.

Rich, A. (1974) Toward a woman-centered university, in A. Rich (1980) *On Lies, Secrets, and Silence*. London: Virago.

Rich, A. (1977) *Of Woman Born: Motherhood as Experience and Institution*. London: Virago.

Rich, A. (1978) Motherhood: the contemporary emergency and the quantum leap, in A. Rich (1980) *On Lies, Secrets, and Silence*. London: Virago.

Ross, E. (1993) *Love and Toil: Motherhood in Outcast London 1870–1918*. New York: Oxford University Press.

Ruddick, S. (1990) *Maternal Thinking: Towards a Politics of Peace*. London: The Women's Press.

Sayers, J. (1984) Feminism and mothering: a Kleinian perspective, *Women's Studies International Forum*, 7(4): 237–41.

Segal, L. (1987) *Is the Future Female? Troubled Thoughts on Contemporary Feminism*. London: Virago.

Sherman, J. (1991) Virgin birth prompts heated debate on human sexuality, *The Times*, 12 March.

Simons, M. A. (1984) Motherhood, feminism and identity, *Women's Studies International Forum*, 7(5): 349–59.

Snitow, A. (1992) Feminism and motherhood: an American reading, *Signs*, 40: 32–51.

Stack, C. (1974) *All Our Kin: Strategies for Survival in a Black Community*. New York: Harper and Row.

Stanworth, M. (1987) Reproductive technologies and the deconstruction of motherhood, in M. Stanworth (ed.) *Reproductive Technologies: Gender, Motherhood and Medicine*. Cambridge: Polity Press.

Steedman, C. (1982) *The Tidy House: Little Girls Writing*. London: Virago.

Steedman, C. (1986) *Landscape for a Good Woman: A Story of Two Lives*. London: Virago.

Torkington, P. (1988) Racism in Midwifery, in S. Grewal, J. Kay, L. Lander, G. Lewis and P. Parmar (eds) *Charting the Journey: Writings by Black and Third World Women*. London: Sheba.

Walby, S. (1990) *Theorizing Patriarchy*. Oxford: Blackwell.

Walkerdine, V. and Lucey, H. (1989) *Democracy in the Kitchen: Regulating Mothers and Socializing Daughters*. London: Virago.

Young, A. (1990) *Femininity in Dissent*. London: Routledge.

**CAROLYN STONE**

# Gender values and identity: Carol Gilligan's work on women's moral development

○ **Introduction**

it is a key element in traditional thinking about the sexes that women and men differ not only in familiar physical ways but also psychologically. Theories about psychological sex differences date back at least as far as the third century BC; with industrialization and the intensifying of the sexual division of labour from the eighteenth century onwards, western notions of feminine and masculine characteristics became more sharply polarized, corresponding to the stereotyped roles of the nurturant, emotionally sensitive, domestic female and the rational, independent, economically productive male.

It is common for perceived differences between the sexes to be interpreted in terms of female inferiority (notwithstanding lip-service paid to the importance of women's maternal role). Where women are thought to differ from men their qualities and capacities are generally regarded as of lesser value, or even as in some way deficient. Partly for such reasons an important strand within feminism has challenged the existence of psychological sex differences, whether it be men's alleged greater rationality or women's supposed distinctive maternal qualities. Proving similarity has been seen as a vital ingredient in the fight for sexual equality.

Some feminist theorists, however, have agreed with traditionalists about the existence of psychological differences between the sexes, but have challenged the traditional view of these differences as indicating female inferiority. Such theorists have, in a variety of ways, reinterpreted the significance of a key traditional feminine identity – women as caring, maternal, emotionally expressive, sensitive, cooperative, concerned to foster personal relations and so on. The main focus of this chapter is the 1982 work of the white North American psychologist, Carol Gilligan, concerning women's moral development. In order to set Gilligan's work in a broader context of writing which reinterprets the significance of traditional feminine qualities, I start by referring briefly to the ideas of Jean Baker Miller, Nel Noddings and Sara Ruddick. Like Gilligan, these theorists are all white North Americans: Miller is a psychoanalyst and Noddings and Ruddick are philosophers.

## Jean Baker Miller: a new psychology of women

Miller (1978) argues that women's oppression by men in patriarchal societies can be regarded as a source of potential strength and power for women rather than merely as a source of weakness. According to Miller, in all societies, those in dominant positions take over aspects of life and culture which they regard as the most important and valuable and relegate other aspects to subordinates. In western culture the dominant groups valued and kept for themselves intellectual and managerial functions and powers related to controlling the physical environment. Aspects that were devalued as inferior and assigned to subordinates were those that were seen as uncontrollable or as evidence of weakness or helplessness. These included, for example, sexuality, intense interpersonal relationships and things generally associated with bodily functions.

In Miller's view some of the tasks assigned to subordinates – and specifically to women – involve human capacities vital to the functioning of a healthy society, for example: an ability to express vulnerability, weakness and helplessness; a capacity to experience, express and interpret emotions; a capacity to cultivate cooperativeness and encourage coordination and working together; a capacity to foster human growth and development.

These traditionally feminine capacities and characteristics are often seen as weaknesses and indeed may work against women. However, in a differently organized society, such capacities could become the basic materials of a new, more humane culture, the psychological starting point for a different approach to living. Moreover, Miller sees these capacities, currently 'more highly developed in women as a group' (1978: 29), as potentially normative for *both* sexes: as the basis for a new *human* ideal.

## Nel Noddings: an ethic of care

Noddings's (1984) work also involves an attempt to base an ethic for *both* sexes on qualities and capacities traditionally associated with women. She outlines an ethic in which the caring relation is central. In an ideal caring relation the 'one-caring' is receptive to the 'cared-for' and tries to understand the latter's point of view, needs and expectations. On this basis the one-caring acts to promote the welfare of the cared-for, who, in response, recognizes and receives the concern and help. Noddings argues that ethical caring arises out of the memory of 'natural' caring – the relation in which we respond in a caring way out of love or natural inclination. People's experience of natural caring motivates them to extend caring outside the circle of natural affection and to maintain caring within the circle when natural affection temporarily falters. In this way people develop and nurture the 'ethical ideal' – the ideal of themselves as ones-caring.

## ○  Sara Ruddick: maternal thinking

Sara Ruddick (1980, 1990) starts with a traditional feminine gender identity – that of women as mothers – but she develops the ideas of maternal thinking in ways which challenge western gender related dichotomies such as those between mind and body and between reason and emotion. Ruddick argues that maternal work is not just an emotional, intuitive, bodily based activity but is also disciplined, rational, reflective. Like any other discipline, for example history or science, maternal work establishes criteria for determining success or failure, sets priorities and identifies virtues that the discipline demands. Maternal thinking is governed by three requirements or 'demands': preservation, growth and social acceptability; that is, the child's life must be preserved, its growth must be fostered and it must be brought up in such a way as to be acceptable to its social group.

The virtues identified by maternal thinking as necessary for maternal work include humility, resilient good humour, realism, respect for persons and responsiveness to growth. This is not to say that mothers always achieve in their work the capacities and virtues that they learn to value as they care for others, but they develop *conceptions* of capacities and virtues, according to which they measure themselves and interpret their actions.

Further, just as Noddings argues for an ethic based on caring for both sexes and for public as well as private life, so Ruddick argues that maternal thinking is not only relevant to the private domain of childcare and the family but to anyone concerned with fostering the growth of persons; in fact, maternal work is an activity in which all adults should be engaged. Ruddick also argues that maternal thinking is a source of distinctive values and strategies which can be used as a basis for peacemaking. She describes it as 'an engaged and visionary standpoint from which to criticize the destructiveness of war and begin to invent peace' (Ruddick 1990: 12).

## ○  *Carol Gilligan: women's moral development*

Miller, Noddings and Ruddick all develop ideas associated with a traditional feminine gender identity in ways which go beyond some of the traditional limitations of that identity. Values, capacities and concerns associated with women are not seen as inferior to those of men, for example, or as relevant only to the private domain of child rearing and personal relationships. Carol Gilligan's (1982) work on women's moral development can also be seen as an attempt to reinterpret the significance of traditional feminine qualities and concerns. Gilligan, however, is not arguing for the superiority of a feminine ethic but rather suggesting that values and priorities stereotyped as feminine need to be *integrated* with masculine ones in order to provide an enlarged and more adequate conception of morality and a more adequate developmental ideal for both sexes.

Gilligan initially worked with Lawrence Kohlberg on his studies of moral development. Kohlberg's theory claims that moral thinking proceeds through a series of stages, from the self-centred stance of the young child, through a socially conventional stage concerned with social approval, harmony, law and order, and ending with a stage based on justice and equality in which the individual is able to bring logic to bear on moral issues and to resolve conflicts of moral principle (for example, Kohlberg 1976, 1984). In the 1970s Gilligan became concerned that women appeared not to score as highly as men on Kohlberg's moral development scale. After carrying out some of her own studies on college students and women considering abortions, she concluded that women actually mature through different stages than men do because they reason differently about moral issues and have different moral priorities. Because women's distinctive moral concerns and priorities are omitted from, or submerged in, standard moral theories, psychological accounts of moral development based on these theories often see women as relatively underdeveloped in their moral reasoning and decision making compared with men. But Gilligan claims that these accounts are biased in favour of masculine modes of moral reasoning and priorities.

Specifically, she argues that men tend to see moral issues in terms of justice, fairness, rules, rights and autonomy, whereas women tend to be more concerned with people's wants, needs and interests, with fostering connection and relationship and avoiding violence or hurt. Moreover, while men often abstract a moral choice from its particular context and analyse it as if it represented some universal type of moral choice, women usually interpret a moral choice within the particular situation that produced it. Thus women's mode of thinking about moral problems is 'contextual and narrative rather than formal and abstract' (Gilligan 1982: 19).

Gilligan describes an interview, which was part of one of her studies, with two 11-year-old children, Jake and Amy. These two were presented with the so-called 'Heinz dilemma', originally devised by Kohlberg to measure moral development in adolescence. A man named Heinz considers whether or not to steal a drug, which is overpriced and which he cannot afford, in order to save the life of his wife.

Jake constructs the dilemma as a conflict between the values of property and life, a sort of 'math problem with humans', to be solved by a logical analysis of the priorities to be accorded to different moral rules. Since 'a human life is worth more than money', Jake is clear that Heinz should steal the drug (Gilligan 1982: 26).

In contrast, Amy's response seems evasive and uncertain. She doesn't think Heinz should steal the drug:

> I think there might be other ways besides stealing it, like if he could borrow the money or make a loan or something, but he really shouldn't steal the drug – but his wife shouldn't die either . . . If he stole the drug, he might save his wife then, but if he did, he might have to go

to jail, and then his wife might get sicker again, and he couldn't get more of the drug, and it might not be good.

(Gilligan 1982: 28)

Amy suggests that if those involved (including the pharmacist) talked through the problem for long enough, they could find some solution. According to Gilligan, she sees the actors in the dilemma 'arrayed not as opponents in a contest of rights, but as members of a network of relationships on whose continuation they all depend' (1982: 30). In standard accounts of moral development such as Kohlberg's Jake would be ranked as at a higher moral stage than Amy. However, Amy is more sensitive to the breakdown of relationships that may underlie the Heinz dilemma and the need for any adequate solution to involve improved communication and understanding among all concerned. She is also more aware of the complexity and uncertain outcome of any moral choice. Gilligan does not argue that Amy's response is superior, but that standard accounts of morality and moral development are one-sided and incomplete because of their exclusion of the 'different' moral voice.

On the basis of her study of women considering an abortion, and thus confronting a real life rather than a hypothetical moral dilemma, Gilligan suggests that women's moral thinking typically goes through three stages. Each represents a more complex understanding of the relationship between self and other, and each transition between stages involves a critical reinterpretation of the conflict between selfishness and responsibility. The first stage involves a concern with caring for the self in order to ensure survival. The perception that this is selfish initiates a transition to the second stage which involves a new understanding of the connection between self and other, articulated by the concept of responsibility. The woman's concern is to ensure care for those who are dependent and unequal. In turn the realization that she has considered only her responsibility to others and has overlooked her responsibility to herself activates the transition to the third stage. Here there is a dissipation of the tension between selfishness and responsibility through a new understanding of the interconnection between self and other.

The abortion study demonstrates the centrality of the concepts of responsibility and care in women's constructions of the moral domain, the close tie in women's thinking between conceptions of the self and of morality, and ultimately the need for an expanded developmental theory that includes, rather than rules out from consideration, the differences in the feminine voice.

(Gilligan 1982: 105)

## ○ Responses to Gilligan's work

Gilligan's *In a Different Voice* has attracted considerable popular and academic attention. Many people who refer to her work take it as *established* that she has shown that the two sexes typically approach moral problems in a different way. However there is also an extensive critical literature challenging Gilligan in a variety of ways and subjecting her work to a range of sometimes conflicting interpretations.

The following discussion concentrates on two types of critical issue: problems concerning the empirical claims Gilligan makes about differences between the sexes in respect of moral reasoning, and problems arising from the possible dangers involved in associating women with an ethic of care.

Gilligan is certainly *cautious* about the way in which the different moral orientations – care and justice – link up with women and men. In her introduction she says that she is not making a sex-based generalization to the effect that all and only women espouse an ethic of care and all and only men espouse an ethic of justice:

> The different voice I describe is characterized not by gender but by theme. Its association with women is an empirical observation, and it is primarily through women's voices that I trace its development. But this association is not absolute, and the contrasts between male and female voices are presented here to highlight a distinction between two modes of thought and to focus a problem of interpretation rather than to represent a generalization about either sex.
>
> (Gilligan 1982: 2)

While it may not have been Gilligan's *intention* to make claims about the possibly distinct moralities of the two sexes, critics have argued that her 1982 research data, her literary examples and the gender-linked way she presents the two different moral approaches, constantly associate them with the two sexes. Thus readers feel justified in interpreting Gilligan as offering generalizations about the sexes.

Critics then point out that such generalizations demand *quantitative* as well as qualitative research: 'A claim that the two sexes speak in different moral voices amounts to a claim that there are more women than men who think, feel or behave in a given way' (Greeno and Maccoby 1986: 315). Gilligan's research, involving relatively small studies of groups not representative of the general population, from which she reports evidence in the form of (again) possibly unrepresentative interview excerpts, does not provide an adequate basis for this claim. In fact one critic comments that Gilligan doesn't always clearly differentiate between theoretical speculation and discussion of research data and that 'The structure of her work . . . is built of solid bricks intermixed with some of cardboard' (Luria 1986: 321).

Moreover, a number of critics have argued that Gilligan is incorrect to claim sex differences in moral reasoning and also to claim sex bias in Kohlberg's theory. For example, Walker (1984) reviews 61 studies in which Kohlberg's scale is used to measure levels of moral reasoning in both sexes. These show few significant sex differences in the development of moral reasoning in childhood and adolescence. In the few studies that show sex differences in adulthood, the women were less well educated than the men: thus education, not gender, appears to account for women's apparent lesser maturity. Throughout this large body of research, there is little indication that the two sexes develop differently with respect to moral reasoning about abstract hypothetical problems.

Further, other writers (for example, Greeno and Maccoby 1986) have claimed that while research findings suggest that women have a greater *reputation* for altruism and empathy, there is little proof that they actually *are* more caring in their behaviour. It is also pointed out that women have been constrained for generations by people's unthinking acceptance of the truth of gender stereotypes; there is a danger of work such as Gilligan's perpetuating this situation.

These concerns have given rise to considerable debate about the way in which Gilligan carried out her studies. Critics argue that in her abortion study, for example, Gilligan should have been more attentive to ethnic, class, religious, age and other differences among the women interviewed. The 29 women in the study were from a variety of ethnic backgrounds and social classes, differed in marital status and education, and ranged in age from 15 to 33. All sorts of important questions were left unasked: for example, about the attitudes to abortion of the lovers, husbands, families and friends of the women concerned. Pursuing such questions might have resulted in a more complex analysis of the links between people's moral orientation and their social circumstances.

Indeed, Stack (1986) argues that Gilligan's work fails to take account of cultural and ethnic differences. Stack studied black migrants returning to the American South and claims that both sexes display a contextual morality similar in some respects to, but not identical with, the care orientation Gilligan found in the women she researched (see also Harding 1987 and Tronto 1987). This adds weight to the criticism that, in focusing on gender, Gilligan has omitted other important aspects of social identity and their possible links with moral orientation. Stack's work also raises the possibility, which some other critics have pursued, of there being a plurality of moral voices, 'a rich diversity of good moral personalities' (Flanagan and Jackson 1987: 637).

○ **Gilligan's response to her critics**

Gilligan has responded to these sorts of criticisms, which she claims to represent a 'central confusion' (1986: 324), by reiterating that she has developed a theory about a different *voice*, that is a different way of constituting the self and morality and thus a way of thinking about moral decisions which contrasts with that articulated in Kohlberg's theory. This different way of thinking is not *identified* by gender, even though Gilligan's empirical observations show it as more strongly associated with women than with men.

In order to claim that there is a moral voice different from those represented by psychologists, Gilligan points out she needs only *one* example: 'one voice whose coherence is not recognized within existing interpretive schemes' (1986: 328). To claim that common themes recur in women's conceptions of self and morality she needs a series of illustrations. She also argues that papers such as Walker's (1984), which claim that there are no sex differences in moral development because there are no sex differences on Kohlberg's scale, miss the point: her own work focuses on the differences between two moral orientations – justice and care – rather than on the question of whether the sexes differ as measured by Kohlberg's scale. Gilligan also refers to a range of studies which suggest that while both sexes use both justice and care considerations in their moral reasoning, 'the focus on care in moral reasoning, although not characteristic of all women, is characteristically a female phenomenon in the advantaged populations that have been studied' (1986: 330; see also Gilligan 1987). This focus on care in the moral reasoning of some women draws attention to the limitations of a justice-focused moral theory.

So Gilligan is claiming that though there *is* a link between women and caring, the most important thing about her work is the identification of a distinct moral voice which is omitted from or underplayed in traditional theorizing about morality. In more recent work she and her colleagues have pursued their study of this voice by tracing its development in girls and adolescent women (for example, Gilligan and Mickel Brown 1992).

## The dangers of associating women with an ethic of care

Regardless of the extent to which women's moral reasoning demonstrates a care orientation, a number of critics have argued that a theory which reinforces the traditional association of women with caring is potentially dangerous for women and should be challenged. It is pointed out that women's caring qualities and concerns are, as a matter of social fact, the qualities and concerns of a subordinate group: women's traditional caregiving activities 'have been historically defined not in accordance with women's freely chosen moral commitments, but in response to the needs of patriarchal institutions' and have 'propped up vast inequities in past society' (Cole and Coultrap-McQuin 1992: 5). We must avoid any naive celebration of 'feminine' characteristics which traditionalists have long been happy to attribute to women. One critic refers to Gilligan's work in this context as: 'The same old tune, sung upside down' (quoted in Romain 1992: 35).

In male dominated societies relations between the sexes are frequently unequal; in particular it is difficult for women and men to be genuinely interdependent and for women to find a workable balance between concern for self and concern for others. In such contexts it could be argued that women must, at least temporarily, care less so that men can learn to care more; any ethic for women that overemphasizes relationships and care and underemphasizes justice and rights risks reinforcing women's subordination (see Grimshaw 1986; Tronto 1987; Puka 1990). Thus, as pointed out by Cole (1993), while it may be that Gilligan's care orientation expresses something that many women both recognize and value about their own moral thinking, such an ethic must be supplemented by a politically viable and central conception of justice; and . . . careful thought must be given to the question of precisely *what kind of society* needs to be constructed in order to ensure that the exploitative potential of the disposition to care does not take center stage.

(Cole 1993: 110; italics in original)

Here it is important to reiterate that, while the association of women and caring is a constant theme of her work, Gilligan does call for the integration of care and justice to provide an enhanced and expanded vision of moral maturity for both sexes:

In the representation of maturity, both perspectives converge in the realization that just as inequality adversely affects both parties in an unequal relationship, so too violence is destructive for everyone involved.

(Gilligan 1982: 174)

Gilligan is also well aware that claims about sex differences in moral reasoning (as with other claims about sex differences) can be used to rationalize oppression, but:

I do not see it as empowering to encourage women to put aside their own concerns and perceptions and to rely on a psychology largely defined by men's perceptions in thinking about what is of value and what constitutes human development.

(Gilligan 1986: 333)

## ○ Concluding points

Finally, the very ambiguity of aspects of Gilligan's work has been fruitful because it invites further interpretation and exploration. Whether or not the dimensions of care and justice actually differentiate the sexes, the high-lighting of the care dimension – a dimension often trivialized because it is stereotyped as feminine – is an important step towards a broader and more adequate understanding of morality. Gilligan's work has been highly suc-cessful in stimulating a wide-ranging debate about gender, caring and justice. Together with the work of theorists such as Miller, Noddings and Ruddick, it has helped to further the search for a feminist ethic in which qualities traditionally associated with women can be valued and celebrated without also unwittingly celebrating and reinforcing women's oppression.

## ○ Questions and exercises

1 In your view does Gilligan's work succeed in reinterpreting a tra-ditional feminine identity (women as carers) in a positive way or

does it reassert a traditional stereotype in a potentially damaging way? (Note that Gilligan is not saying that *only* women should care.)

2 If there are *dangers* involved in associating women with an ethic of care, are there any ways in which these dangers can be avoided or lessened?

3 How do *you* view the relationship between Gilligan's different moral voices? Is one or other superior? Are they in conflict or complementary? (Consider situations in which a concern for justice and equality might conflict with a concern to be caring for all involved parties and to avoid hurt.)

4 Try out the Heinz dilemma on several different people (of different ages, backgrounds, occupations, sex, etc.) and consider their responses in relation to those of Jake and Amy.

5 Try to find examples of moral voices *different* from the two identified by Gilligan.

○ **Further reading**

Kittay and Meyers (1987) and Larrabee (1993) are very useful collections of papers pursuing a wide range of issues arising from Gilligan's work; both also contain papers by Gilligan herself. Critical discussion is also to be found in Grimshaw (1986), which also discusses Noddings and Ruddick, and in Porter (1991). Cole and Coultrap-McQuin (1992) and Frazer *et al.* (1992) provide a broad introduction to issues in feminist ethics and both have excellent bibliographies. Trebilcot (1983) covers issues connected with mothering and contains two papers by Ruddick, including a shortened version of Ruddick (1980). Gilligan's more recent work on women and moral development is usefully represented by Gilligan and Mickel Brown (1992).

○ **References**

Cole, E. (1993) *Philosophy and Feminist Criticism*. New York: Paragon House.
Cole, E. and Coultrap-McQuin, S. (eds) (1992) *Explorations in Feminist Ethics: Theory and Practice*. Bloomington, IN: Indiana University Press.
Flanagan, O. and Jackson, K. (1987) Justice, care and gender: The Kohlberg-Gilligan debate revisited, *Ethics*, 97: 622–37. Reprinted in M. J. Larrabee (ed.) (1993).
Frazer, E., Hornsby, J. and Lovibond, S. (eds) (1992) *Ethics: a Feminist Reader*. Oxford: Blackwell.
Gilligan, C. (1982) *In a Different Voice: Psychological Theory and Women's Development*. Cambridge, MA: Harvard University Press.

Gilligan, C. (1986) Reply to critics, *Signs: Journal of Women in Culture and Society*, 11: 324–33. Reprinted in M. J. Larrabee (ed.) (1993).

Gilligan, C. (1987) Moral orientation and moral development, in E. Kittay and D. Meyers (eds) *Women and Moral Theory*. Totowa, NJ: Rowman and Littlefield: 19–33.

Gilligan, C. and Mickel Brown, L. (1992) *Meeting at the Crossroads: Women's Psychology and Girls' Development*. Cambridge, MA: Harvard University Press.

Greeno, C. G. and Maccoby, E. E. (1986) How different is the 'different voice'? *Signs: Journal of Women in Culture and Society*, 11: 310–16. Reprinted in M. J. Larrabee (ed.) (1993).

Grimshaw, J. (1986) *Feminist Philosophers: Women's Perspectives on Philosophical Traditions*. London: Wheatsheaf.

Harding, S. (1987) The curious coincidence of feminine and African moralities, in E. Kittay and D. Meyers (eds) *Women and Moral Theory*. Totowa, NJ: Rowman and Littlefield: 296–315.

Kittay, E. and Meyers, D. (eds) (1987) *Women and Moral Theory*. Totowa, NJ: Rowman and Littlefield.

Kohlberg, L. (1976) Moral stages and moralization, in T. Lickona (ed.) *Moral Development and Behavior*. New York: Holt, Rinehart and Winston.

Kohlberg, L. (1984) *Essays in Moral Development. Vol. 2. The Psychology of Moral Development*. New York: Harper and Row.

Larrabee, M. J. (ed.) (1993) *An Ethic of Care*. New York: Routledge.

Luria, L. (1986) A methodological critique, *Signs: Journal of Women in Culture and Society*, 11: 316–21. Reprinted in M. J. Larrabee (ed.) (1993).

Miller, J. B. (1978) *Towards a New Psychology of Women*. Harmondsworth: Penguin.

Noddings, N. (1984) *Caring: a Feminine Approach to Ethics and Moral Education*. Berkeley, CA: University of California Press.

Porter, E. J. (1991) *Women and Moral Identity*. Sydney: Allen and Unwin.

Puka, B. (1990) The liberation of caring: a different voice for Gilligan's 'different voice', *Hypatia*, 5: 58–82. Reprinted in M. J. Larrabee (ed.) (1993).

Romain, D. (1992) Care and Confusion, in E. Cole and S. Coultrap-McQuin (eds) *Explorations in Feminist Ethics: Theory and Practice*. Bloomington, IN: Indiana University Press: 27–37.

Ruddick, S. (1980) Maternal thinking, *Feminist Studies*, 6(2): 342–69. Reprinted in J. Treblicot (ed.) (1983).

Ruddick, S. (1990) *Maternal Thinking: Towards a Politics of Peace*. London: Women's Press.

Stack, C. B. (1986) The culture of gender: women and men of colour, *Signs: Journal of Women in Culture and Society*, 11: 321–4. Reprinted in M. J. Larrabee (ed.) (1993).

Trebilcot, J. (ed.) (1983) *Mothering: Essays in Feminist Theory*. Totowa, NJ: Rowman and Allanheld.

Tronto, J. C. (1987) Beyond gender difference to a theory of care, *Signs: Journal of Women in Culture and Society*, 12: 644–63. Reprinted in M. J. Larrabee (ed.) (1993).

Walker, L. J. (1984) Sex differences in the development of moral reasoning: a critical review, *Child Development*, 55: 677–91. Reprinted in M. J. Larrabee (ed.) (1993).

## 15

ROBBIE SMITH

# Sexual constructions and lesbian identity

As a feminist historian and a lesbian, my concern to understand the construction of a lesbian identity and its importance for feminist theory and practice is both academic and personal. My current research is attempting to uncover understandings about lesbianism in the historical period before it was defined as a category of pathological sexuality in the nineteenth century. This chapter, however, will trace the construction of lesbian identity from that nineteenth-century point of identification through to the radical feminist analysis of the 1970s to be found in Adrienne Rich's text 'Compulsory Heterosexuality and Lesbian Existence' (first published in 1980), which argues that heterosexuality as an institution, rather than lesbianism, is problematic for women. It goes on to discuss criticisms of Rich's arguments and the implications of developments in the 1980s and 1990s.

Throughout the second half of the nineteenth century and the first half of the twentieth, anthropologists, evolutionary theorists following Darwin, Marxist theorists, 'sexologists' and psychoanalysts all engaged in the debate about the origins of patriarchal society and what was 'natural', especially in relation to sexual relations. One of the leading sexologists of the period was Havelock Ellis.[1] His work was based on the assumption that 'normal' heterosexual relations were analogous to those in the animal kingdom, which he defined as characterized by male pursuit and conquest of the female, male brutality and female submission. Heterosexual relations were, thus, natural and biologically determined. Ellis claimed that women really enjoyed being raped, beaten, sexually humiliated and brutalized and that in women pain and sexual pleasure were virtually indistinguishable (Ellis 1946).

On the other hand, feminists of the period argued that male violence and sexual aggression were not innate but an aspect of male power which could be changed. The later nineteenth and early twentieth centuries were a period of intense feminist activity around issues of sexuality as well as education, employment and suffrage. Campaigns against the whole spectrum of male violence against women and sexual exploitation through rape, organized prostitution, sexual abuse of children and sexual terrorism, made a central challenge to the double standard of sexual morality and to beliefs about male sexuality. In particular, feminists challenged the belief that men were the victims of sexual urges over which they had no control and regarded male sexuality as a weapon of male power used to keep women in a subordinate position (Jackson 1994).

The investigation of lesbianism and homosexuality in this period and within this wider debate, and the construction of lesbian and homosexual identities as pathological categories, necessitated the construction of a *heterosexual* identity for the first time. The concept of heterosexuality as a sexual identity was invented to describe a view of sexual 'normality' within a founding belief in the sharp distinction between the sexes and an assumption that gender identity and sexual identity were both necessarily linked through the naturalness of heterosexual object choice. Thinking about homosexuality and lesbianism mostly followed the theories of Havelock Ellis and other sexologists. They regarded 'inverts', as lesbians and homosexuals were known, as a 'third sex': a pathological category of pseudo-men and pseudo-women who were characterized by unhealthy obsessions and physical, mental and moral degeneracy, unnatural, abnormal freaks and monsters who were suitable subjects for clinical investigation and medical experiment.

The sexologists' view that a member of this 'third sex' had the mind and emotions of one sex in the body of the other, was shared by many homosexual men and lesbians themselves, who called for public sympathy and understanding of their plight. They included Edward Carpenter, a socialist, sexologist, supporter of the women's movement and himself a homosexual. He defined human sexuality and gender identity as a continuum, with exaggerated masculine heterosexual men at one end, extremely feminine heterosexual women at the other, and an infinite range of sexual and gender identities between them. He attributed strongly gendered characteristics to the intermediate 'third' sex, describing effeminate, homosexual men, and masculine women who were sensuous rather than sentimental, low voiced, sporty and active (Carpenter 1908: 13, 16, 20, *passim*). Similarly, in the 1920s, Radclyffe Hall, a lesbian author, wrote *The Well of Loneliness*, in which she called for sympathy and understanding for the third sex of inverts such as herself, trapped in the wrong body, who could not help their condition but were fated to seek pleasure where they could and to encounter unhappiness and loneliness everywhere (Hall 1928/1982). Although the book was essentially a moral tale, with an ending in which the central character, a female 'invert', heroically relinquishes her lover, who is a 'real' woman, to the properly heterosexual arms of a real man, the book was the subject of an obscenity trial and banned in Britain.

Freud regarded 'inversion' as abnormal, but he did not agree with most of his contemporaries that it was degenerate. He pointed out that 'inversion' could be found in individuals and cultures often distinguished by especially high intellectual and ethical development. In contrast to the main current of psychological opinion about homosexuality and lesbianism during this period, Freud's view was that there is no fixed sexual object for human beings, as we are all born with boundless possibilities of sexuality. He divided 'inverts' into three main categories: those who have as sexual objects exclusively their own sex and for whom the opposite sex leave them cold or even arouse sexual aversion; those we would term bisexual; and 'contingent inverts' who could derive sexual satisfaction from their own sex if the 'normal' sexual object (a member of the opposite sex) was inaccessible. Freud also accepted that, whilst some 'inverts' rebelled against their condition and felt it as a pathological compulsion, others regarded it as natural, legitimate and normal. He refuted the idea that an 'invert' was someone trapped in the wrong body (Freud 1977: 52–3). He rejected the notion of a 'feminine brain in a masculine body', stressing that 'we are ignorant of what characterises a feminine brain' (Freud 1977: 54). This is a rare flash of humility and admission of lack of understanding of gender difference by a leader of the medical and scientific profession.

In contrast to these enlightened views, Freud also argued that the trait of inversion could be traced to an early sexual encounter and could be removed by hypnotic suggestion (Freud 1977: 46). He also believed that lesbianism was an expression of unsuccessful or incomplete transference from the mother to the father and thence to other men in a girl's psychological and sexual development and therefore represented an 'infantile' form of sexuality which could be corrected by psychoanalysis. Despite this, Freud's views were progressive in an era when lesbians and homosexuals were more usually regarded as physically, mentally and morally degenerate monsters.

Before we can talk about the way in which lesbians later came to define themselves, we need to understand the constructions of female sexuality and of female sexual pleasure which were dominant during the first half of the twentieth century. During this period the teachings of Havelock Ellis and his followers were more influential than those of Freud in the writings of those who popularized the theories and findings of the sexologists. Both male and female authors of sex advice literature apparently accepted, uncritically, the model of sexuality and heterosexual relations which had been established by the nineteenth-century sexologists, perpetuating the view that the male sexual urge was stronger than that of the female; that it was uncontrollable and demanded gratification; and that the only 'real' sex was heterosexual, penile and penetrative. Sexual maladjustment was seen as the primary cause of marital unhappiness and instability and as a threat to the family and the social order itself. Consequently, the marriage or sexual advice manuals of the interwar years sought to teach women how to enjoy sexual intercourse within marriage. Gender equality was defined solely in sexual terms, with a woman's right to sexual fulfilment as the only right endorsed by the sex manual experts; and the understanding of these rights which they expounded was based on Havelock Ellis's teachings and so comprised a complete denial of female sexual autonomy. Similar assumptions appeared in sex manuals written after World War II and up to the 1960s and, although subsequent research by

Masters and Johnson (1966), based on very different methodologies to those used in earlier studies, led to further refinements of the model, the essential characteristics remained the same. Margaret Jackson, who discusses the model of sexuality created by late nineteenth and twentieth-century sexologists in some detail, argues that they constructed a model which purported to be objective and scientific but in fact reflected and promoted the interests of men (Jackson, in Caplan 1989: 52; Jackson 1994).

This model not only reflects and legitimates the male supremacist myth that the male sexual urge must be satisfied, at whatever cost; it also defines the very nature of sex in male terms. Although women are now regarded as sexual beings in our own right, male sexuality conventionally serves as the model of human sexuality. Further, by equating human sexual desire with a biological drive to copulate, sex is reduced to a reproductive function. Unlike Masters and Johnson, who maintained that the penis was the primary organ of sexual pleasure for both sexes, many feminists have pointed out that, whether or not penetration is essential to male sexual pleasure, it is not at all essential to female sexual arousal and gratification and often can be not only irrelevant but even a block to female sexual pleasure. In fact, because women's sexual pleasure is not linked to reproduction in the way that men's is (male orgasm and ejaculation releases sperm but female orgasm is entirely independent of ovulation and conception), men are far more in the grip of 'biological destiny' than women are. Hanscombe and Forster (1981: 14) also point out that the idea that sex is only natural when it results in making babies is one which would make all sorts of sexual acts 'unnatural', for example masturbation, oral sex, heterosexual penetrative sex with contraception or when the woman is already pregnant or past menopause, as well as homosexual and lesbian sexual acts.

In the 1950s and 1960s attitudes to many aspects of sexuality slowly began to change. First male homosexuality and then lesbianism became more visible. Male homosexuality was decriminalized in Great Britain in 1967. Theories about the social construction of gender identity and sexuality began to challenge the insistence of biological determinist arguments upon the essential nature of gender identity and the fixity of sexuality. During the later 1960s and throughout the 1970s feminist movements emerged in Britain and the United States and feminists began to apply feminist theories to sexuality and social relations.

One of the most influential texts to come out of this debate was Adrienne Rich's essay, *Compulsory Heterosexuality and Lesbian Existence* (Rich 1981). In this, Rich argues that heterosexuality was not natural but forced upon women to legitimate and reinforce male power (Rich 1981: 5, *passim*). She discusses the bias of compulsory heterosexuality through which lesbian experience is perceived on a scale ranging from the deviant to abhorrent, or is simply rendered invisible. She argues that this is expressed in assumptions, which were widely current in literature and the social sciences, that women are 'innately sexually oriented' toward men, or in views that the lesbian choice is simply an acting out of bitterness toward men. She is also concerned to understand how and why women's choice of women as

passionate comrades, life partners, co-workers, lovers, tribe, has been
crushed, invalidated, forced into hiding and disguise; and the virtual
or total neglect of lesbian existence in a wide range of writings, including feminist scholarship.

(Rich 1981: 4)

Rich believes that there is a connection between these three issues and
that much feminist theory and criticism was limited because of a lack of
attention to these concerns. She says that feminist theory could no longer
afford merely to voice a toleration of lesbianism as an alternative lifestyle
or to make token allusion to lesbians; and that a feminist critique of compulsory heterosexual orientation for women was long overdue. Further,
Rich criticizes the liberal assumption that in a world of genuine equality
everyone would be bisexual. She writes that this 'blurs and sentimental-
izes the actualities within which women have expressed sexuality' and
assumes that women who have chosen women do so simply because men
are oppressive and emotionally lacking. Rich suggests that heterosexuality,
like motherhood, needs to be recognized and studied as a *political institution*
(Rich 1981: 9).

Rich's starting point for such a study is to ask some important questions:
if women are the earliest sources of emotional caring and physical nurture
of both female and male children, why does the search for love in both
sexes not lead toward women? Why have species survival, the means of
impregnation and emotional/erotic relationships become so rigidly identified with each other? Why, if heterosexuality is innate and natural, should
such violent strictures be found necessary to enforce women's total
emotional, erotic loyalty and subservience to men? Her answer is in the
concept of *compulsory* heterosexuality, in which society and men enforce
female compliance. She lists and elaborates eight characteristics of male
power by which men ensure female compliance and says that each of them
adds to the cluster of forces within which women have been convinced
that marriage and sexual orientation toward men are inevitable, even if
unsatisfying or oppressive components of their lives (Rich 1981: 12).

Rich recognizes that to question heterosexuality is an immense step to
take if you consider yourself freely and innately heterosexual and one
requiring great courage, but that not to examine heterosexuality as an
institution would be like failing to admit that the economic system called
capitalism, or the caste system of racism, are maintained by a variety of
forces including both physical violence and ideology (Rich 1981: 20).

Adrienne Rich uses two terms when discussing relationships between
women. She uses the term 'lesbian continuum' to include a range of
woman-identified experience through each woman's life and throughout
history, including the sharing of a rich emotional life, bonding against male
tyranny and the giving and receiving of practical and political support
between women. The second term Rich uses, 'lesbian existence', describes
both the fact of the historic presence of lesbians and our continuing creation of the meaning of that existence. Rich says that the task of examining the institution of compulsory heterosexuality itself will allow us to

perceive a history of female resistance which has until now never fully understood itself (Rich 1981: 20–2, 31, 32).

Adrienne Rich's work has been of immense value to subsequent feminist understanding of the construction of sexual identities. Many feminists have built upon what she has said. However her larger statements need careful consideration. There have been three main criticisms of Rich's arguments. The first is that they are based on a romantic naturalization of female bonds. Jeffrey Weeks (1985: 204) comments that

> it is not always clear whether Rich sees the 'lesbian continuum' as a powerful solidarity that is there but constantly suppressed, or as a potentiality that could be realised in a mythical future, but in either case it stretches toward an essentialism about femininity which can distort the complexities of the construction of women and obscure the necessary politics.

Weeks (1985: 205) has pointed out that, in Rich's scenario, political lesbianism is a return to nature and nature is now 'benign, female and lesbian'. In this way we have come full circle from the nineteenth-century medical and sexological understanding of female sexuality as biologically determined and sexuality, or at least lesbian sexuality, is seen as universal, natural and our destiny.

The second major criticism is centred particularly upon Rich's explanation of compulsory heterosexuality. The view that all women's oppression is due to compulsory heterosexuality suggests, Rich's critics argue, that somehow women are always socially controlled by men as perpetual sufferers and victims beyond the possibility of resistance. They suggest that this results in a narrowing of political focus (Ferguson 1982: 159–60; Weeks 1985: 205–6). In Rich's defence, she introduces the possible points of resistance quite clearly in her discussion of both the lesbian continuum and the lesbian existence, and, when discussing the methods by which men enforce heterosexuality upon women, argues that the range and scale of these forces suggest that 'an enormous potential counterforce is having to be restrained' (Rich 1981: 12).

The third criticism is that the concept of a lesbian 'continuum' along which all women exist, and of the lesbian existence as a political position, denies the specifics of lesbian sexuality. Ann Ferguson says that Rich 'undermines the important historical development of an explicit identity connected to genital sexuality' (Ferguson 1982: 149). Ferguson (1982: 160) also accuses feminists such as Rich of the

> elevation of female sexuality in general into a semi-mystical bonding, where bodily contact and genital pleasure are secondary or even nonexistent, [and which] denies the possibilities of female eroticism, including the real potentiality of lesbianism.

Others argue, however, that Rich does allow for the potentiality of specific lesbian eroticism and sexuality within her understanding of the 'lesbian existence'. The criticisms outlined, however, represent an appraisal not only of Rich, but of trends in the radical feminism and political lesbianism of the 1980s.

Working-class and black feminists also criticized Rich and other radical and lesbian feminists for failing to acknowledge that cultural differences affect notions of sexuality and gender identity, and that working-class and black women might identify their interests more closely with working-class and black men, in struggles around issues of class and racism, than with middle-class white feminists. Lesbianism is sometimes seen as an extension of white, middle-class privilege, and black women and working-class women have, rightly, criticized 'privileged feminists' who have

> been unable to speak to, with, and for diverse groups of women because they either do not understand fully the inter-relatedness of sex, race, and class oppression or refuse to take this inter-relatedness seriously.
>
> (hooks 1984: 14)

In her forward to the 1993 republication of her essay, Adrienne Rich responds to some of the criticisms from other feminists. She says that her essay was written, in part, to challenge the erasure of lesbian existence from so much of scholarly feminist literature, an erasure 'which felt and continues to feel, to be not just anti-lesbian but anti-feminist in its consequences' (Rich 1993: 227). She writes that she did not intend to widen divisions between women but to encourage heterosexual feminists to examine heterosexuality as a political institution, and she goes on to say that she continues to think that

> heterosexual feminists will draw political strength for change from taking a critical stance toward the ideology which *demands* heterosexuality and that lesbians cannot assume that we are untouched by that ideology and the institutions founded upon it.
>
> (Rich 1993: 227–8)

So, where does this leave us now? The understanding of lesbian identity is at the centre of the debate between those who regard sexuality and gender as biologically determined and those who argue that they are socially constructed. It has important implications for society's attitudes toward and treatment of those whose gender identification or sexuality is designated as outside the norm and for our own self-identification and the possibilities of resistance. More recently the debate about sexual and gender identity has been reopened with renewed vigour as a result of the challenges of postmodernist theory to lesbian feminism, and the assumption of shared understandings and objectives of lesbians and homosexual men in the form of 'lesbianandgay' theories, or 'queer' politics. Postmodernists have suggested that all categories and identifications are socially constructed, not by those who control the institutions and processes of power in society or by people in conscious political resistance to those institutions and processes, but by the processes themselves of continual re-creation of self in which we all participate, which contain myriad layers of meanings and not necessarily shared understandings about identities (see, for example, Fuss 1989, 1991; Butler 1990: 30; Wittig 1992).

The explanations given by postmodernist theorists have been criticized. For example, Sheila Jeffreys accuses postmodernist feminists of dropping men out of the analysis of power relations in their theoretical framework. She characterizes the postmodernist view as one in which power 'just floats about constantly reconstituting itself for no real purpose and with no real connection with real human beings' (Jeffreys 1994: 99). Further, she charges postmodernist theory with 'consistently deriding' lesbian feminism and radical feminism generally, arguing that postmodern sexual theory reinvents the notion that lesbianism is simply a reflection of male homosexuality, and that it returns to the explanations of lesbianism put forward in the late nineteenth and early twentieth centuries, that lesbians and male homosexuals constitute a 'third sex' (Jeffreys 1994: 115). Jeffreys argues that postmodernist feminism rejects the notion of lesbianism as a political choice within a feminist consciousness, taking us a long way from the political lesbianism of the 1970s and of Adrienne Rich's notions of a universalistic woman-centred 'lesbian continuum' and the specific political, social and sexual identity of the 'lesbian existence'.

Finally, interest in the possibility that there is a 'gay gene' has renewed the debate about whether homosexuality (and, by implication, lesbianism) is inherent and biologically determined or socially constructed, a lifestyle or political choice. The important difference between the nineteenth century and now, is that then the belief that sexuality was innate meant it was unchangeable. Now, with advances in genetic engineering, science has the power to alter 'nature'. This has enormous political and personal implications for us all.

To sum up, all these different positions and debates suggest that there can be political as well as social implications to lesbianism and that there is no necessary relationship between sexual practice and sexual identity. They indicate that identity is not destiny but a choice. In a culture where male homosexual or female lesbian desires are denied and execrated, the adoption of such an identity constitutes a political choice – self-created but within the constraint of the confines of culture. Our understanding that sexual identity, as with any social identity, is historically and culturally contingent and exists always and only in relation to other potential identities does not make it any the less real.

## Acknowledgements

Thanks to all the women (students and staff) in the Centre for Women's Studies who read and commented upon early drafts of this chapter and who gave me a space and support to develop my ideas. Especial thanks to Alison Easton for giving me the courage to try again.

## Questions

1 Do you think Adrienne Rich's notion of the 'lesbian continuum' and the 'lesbian existence' and the definitions and distinctions she

makes between them are valid? How far do they explain lesbian identity in the late twentieth century?

2 What are the implications of Rich's presentation of 'compulsory heterosexuality' for our understanding of sexuality and gender?

3 What are the understandings of lesbian sexual and political identity in postmodernist feminist theory?

○  **Further reading**

If you want more information on the construction of gender and sexual identity, see de Beauvoir (1949/1972); Rosaldo and Lamphere (1974); Sharp (1976); Jackson (1978); Foucault (1981); Evans (1982); *Feminist Review* (1982); Sayers (1982); Coveney *et al.* (1984); Vance (1984); Birke (1986); Weeks (1986); Kitzinger (1987); Caplan (1989); Lorber and Farrell (1991); Thompson and Scott (1991); Jackson *et al.* (1993). Oakley's book (1972) is old but still a good overview. Gilder (1973) poses the essentialist, biological determinist viewpoint in very male supremicist terms. (I needed a stout cushion to throw at the wall at frequent intervals whilst reading this book.)

For information on the sexologists and feminists of the late nineteenth and early twentieth centuries, see Carpenter (1908); Ellis (1946); Freud (1977) whose defence of the 'third sex' of 'uranians' or 'urnings' is poignant and gives useful insights into the social and intellectual environment of the period; Jackson (1994 and in Caplan 1989); Jeffreys (1994). Weeks (1985) gives a very detailed account of the history of sexology from the last quarter of the nineteenth century, the notion of the 'third sex' – and a whole lot more.

For postmodernist feminist theories about gender and sexuality, see Fuss (1989, 1991); Butler (1990); Wittig (1992).

If you want general reading on lesbianism and works by lesbians, there are many. These are just a few: *Signs* (1979); Hanscombe and Forster (1981); Freedman *et al.* (1985); Franklin and Stacey (1986); *Feminist Review* (1990); Jay and Glasgow (1992); Abelove (1993) on lesbian issues.

For more specific discussion of lesbian history, see Hall (1928/1982); Rosenberg (1975); Ettore (1980); Faderman (1985); Duberman *et al.* (1989); Lesbian History Group (1989); Jeffreys (1994).

For Adrienne Rich's theories, critiques and further discussion, see Rich (originally in *Signs* 1980, reprinted in Rich 1981, and reprinted with foreword and afterword 1993); Davies (1982); Ferguson *et al.* (1982); hooks (1984); Snitow *et al.* (1984); Collins (1990); Jackson *et al.* (1993).

○ **Note**

1 Sexology is the study of sexual behaviour as a science.

○ **References**

Abelove, H., Barale, M. A. and Halperin, D. M. (eds) (1993) *The Lesbian and Gay Studies Reader*. London: Routledge.

Beauvoir, S. de (1949/1972) *The Second Sex*. London: Penguin.

Birk, L. (1986) *Women, Feminism and Biology: The Feminist Challenge*. Brighton: Harvester.

Butler, J. (1990) *Gender Trouble: Feminism and the Subversion of Identity*. London: Routledge.

Caplan, P. (1989) *The Cultural Construction of Sexuality*. London: Routledge.

Carpenter, E. (1908) *The Intermediate Sex: A Study of Some Transitional Types of Men and Women*. London: George Allen and Unwin.

Collins, P. H. (1990) *Black Feminist Thought*. London: Unwin Hyman.

Coveney, L., Jackson, M., Jeffreys, S., Kay, L. and Mahoney, P. (1984) *The Sexuality Papers*. London: Hutchinson.

Davies, A. (1982) *Women, Race and Class*. London: Women's Press.

Duberman, M. B., Vicinus, M. and Chancey, G. (eds) (1989) *Hidden from History: Reclaiming the Gay and Lesbian Past*. New York: NAL.

Ellis, H. (1946) *Studies in the Psychology of Sex*. London: William Heinemann.

Ettore, E. M. (1980) *Lesbians, Women and Society*. London: Routledge and Kegan Paul.

Evans, M. (1982) *The Woman Question*. London: Fontana.

Faderman, L. (1985) *Surpassing the Love of Men*. London: The Women's Press.

*Feminist Review* (1982) Issue on sexuality, 11.

*Feminist Review* (1990) Lesbian issues, 34.

Ferguson, A. (1982) On compulsory heterosexuality and lesbian existence, in N. O. Keohane, M. Z. Rosaldo, B. C. Gelpi (eds) *Feminist Theory: A Critique of Ideology*. Brighton: Harvester.

Foucault, M. (1981) *The History of Sexuality*. London: Allen Lane.

Franklin, S. and Stacey, J. (1986) *Lesbian Perspectives on Women's Studies*. University of Kent Women's Studies Occasional Paper, No. 11.

Freedman, E., Gelp, B., Johnson, S. and Weston, K. (eds) (1985) *The Lesbian Issue: Essays from Signs*. Chicago, IL: University of Chicago Press.

Freud, S. (1977) *On Sexuality: Three Essays on the Theory of Sexuality*. London: Penguin.

Fuss, D. (1989) *Essentially Speaking: Feminism, Nature and Difference*. London: Routledge.

Fuss, D. (ed.) (1991) *Inside Out: Lesbian Theories, Gay Theories*. London: Routledge.

Gilder, G. (1973) *Sexual Suicide*. New York: Quadrangle.

Hall, R. (1928/1982) *The Well of Loneliness*. London: Virago.

Hanscombe, G. and Forster, J. (1981) *Rocking the Cradle: Lesbian Mothers, a Challenge in Family Living*. London: Peter Owen.

hooks, b. (1984) *Feminist Theory from Margin to Center*. Boston, MA: South End Press.

Jackson, M. (1994) *The Real Facts of Life: Feminism and the Politics of Sexuality c1850–1940*. London: Taylor and Francis.

Jackson, S. (1978) *On the Social Construction of Female Sexuality*. London: Women's Research and Resources Centre Publications.

Jackson, S., Atkinson, K., Beddoe, D., Pearson, R., Power, H., Prince, J., Ryan, M.

and Young, P. (eds) (1993) *Women's Studies A Reader*. Hemel Hempstead: Harvester Wheatsheaf.

Jay, K. and Glasgow, J. (eds) (1992) *Lesbian Texts and Contexts: Radical Revisions*. London: Onlywoman Press.

Jeffreys, S. (1994) *The Lesbian Heresy*. London: The Women's Press.

Kitzinger, C. (1987) *The Social Construction of Lesbianism*. London: Sage.

Lesbian History Group (eds) (1989) *Not a Passing Phase: Reclaiming Lesbians in History 1840–1985*. London: The Women's Press.

Lorber, J. and Farrell, S. (eds) (1991) *The Social Construction of Gender*. London: Sage.

Masters, W. H. and Johnson, V. E. (1966) *Human Sexual Response*. Boston, MA: Little Brown and Co.

Oakley, A. (1972) *Sex, Gender and Society*. London: Temple Smith.

Rich, A. (1981) *Compulsory Heterosexuality and the Lesbian Existence*. London: Onlywoman Press. (The essay was originally published in *Signs* (1980), 5: 4.

Rich, A. (1993) Compulsory heterosexuality and lesbian existence, in H. Abelove, M. A. Barale and D. M. Halperin (eds) *The Lesbian and Gay Studies Reader*. London: Routledge.

Rosaldo, M. Z. and Lamphere, L. (eds) (1974) *Women, Culture and Society*. Stanford, CA: Stanford University Press.

Rosenberg, C. S. (1975) The female world of love and ritual, *Signs*, 1: 1–29.

Sayers, J. (1982) *Biological Politics, Feminist and Anti-Feminist Perspectives*. London: Tavistock.

Sharp, S. (1976) *Just Like a Girl*. London: Penguin.

*Signs* (1979) Lesbian issues, 9(4).

Snitow, A., Stansell, C. and Thompson, S. (eds) (1984) *Desire: The Politics of Sexuality*. London: Virago.

Thompson, R. and Scott, S. (1991) *Learning About Sex: Young Women and the Social Construction of Sexual Identity*. London: Tufnell Press.

Vance, C. (ed.) (1984) *Pleasure and Danger: Exploring Female Sexuality*. London: Pandora.

Weeks, J. (1985) *Sexuality and Its Discontents*. London: Routledge and Kegan Paul.

Weeks, J. (1986) *Sexuality*. London: Tavistock.

Wittig, M. (1992) *The Straight Mind and Other Essays*. London: The Beacon Press.

## 16

SARAH BERESFORD

# Femininity, sexuality and identity in law

This chapter will introduce some of the legal issues affecting women as subjects of law and the legal process. It will explore how 'femininity', 'gender' and 'sexuality' are constructed by law. These concepts are both social and legal constructs. There are two consequences of this; the first is that as constructs, they are not fixed and immutable. Social and legal concepts of what is feminine for example, are not static; they differ from generation to generation, from culture to culture, and within these confines they change and evolve. The second consequence is that, despite these rather obvious statements, English legal culture[1] appears insistent in its belief that there is something fixed and immutable about these concepts. In this respect, legal culture is essentialist in its approach to women as legal subjects. In other words, law seeks the fundamental 'essence' of woman, the 'perfect' woman against whom all other women must be compared to and measured.

'Law' is divided into distinct areas, 'criminal law', 'family law', 'property law' and so forth, and it therefore sets itself up as a series of categories. Law finds no problem therefore, with creating subcategories, one of which is 'woman'. This, in turn, also has subcategories.

Women can be many things; they can be mothers, criminals, victims, lesbians, heterosexuals and so forth. Sometimes they can be all of these things at the same time. But if a woman does not 'fit' the predetermined identity constructed for her by law, her existence can become legally 'invisible'. In practical terms, this means that in order to obtain the legal remedy she requires, she has to attempt to fulfil the legal criteria of 'perfect' woman. Once she has become a legal subject, she has, in many instances, to abandon her identity and 'conform' to the predetermined construct(s) awaiting her in the courtroom. In other words, she must assume an identity which is not of her own making and construction.

How does legal discourse seek to define the fundamental 'essence' of womanhood? At least since the eighteenth century, 'motherhood' has been defined as a women's chief vocation in life, and the terms 'mothers' and

'women' have been regarded as synonymous. 'Motherhood' has traditionally been established through pregnancy and childbirth. However, modern
developments in what is termed 'artificial reproduction' and the treatment
of infertility mean that the definition of mother must now be rethough.

There is no single legal definition of 'mother' or 'motherhood'. Indeed,
until recently, it was assumed that there was no need to define it. Pregnancy and childbirth were seen as more than adequate 'proof' of motherhood. Now, it is entirely possible for a woman to give birth to a child who
has been produced from another woman's egg. In this instance, who is the
mother? Is it the woman who donates the egg (the 'genetic' mother), or
is it the woman who gives birth('birth' mother)? The Warnock Committee on Human Fertilization and Embryology recommended that the law
should always regard the carrying mother as the child's 'real' mother; the
egg donor should have no rights or duties with respect to the child.[2] Hence
the Human Fertilization and Embryology Act 1990 (S. 27(1)) states that:

> the woman who is carrying or has carried a child as a result of the
> placing in her of an embryo or of sperm and eggs, and no other
> woman, is to be treated as the mother of the child.

Warnock's recommendations were accepted by the government. Therefore, if a woman provides genetic material for implantation in a surrogate
and a child is born, that woman must obtain an adoption order if she is to
acquire the legal status of mother. This effectively means that in these situations at least, the genetic link is now irrelevant to the question of legal
recognition of motherhood, which raises an interesting question. If it is
possible to conclude that genetics has nothing to do with 'motherhood',
why in other areas of law is it seen as such a significant consideration in
relation to the concept of 'motherhood' generally, such as in relation to
the co-parent in a lesbian partnership. If this is so, then the logical conclusion of this argument is that legal culture is now capable of deciding
matters of parenthood in terms other than pure genetics.

So regardless of the varying merits of this approach to the legal definition
of 'mother', law has provided a definition that is certain. It is probably safe
to say that it will only remain so for a limited period of time. However, it
is obvious that the concept of 'motherhood' extends well beyond pregnancy and childbirth. It extends to childrearing. This can be illustrated
by looking further at the Parliamentary debates surrounding the passage
of the Human Fertilization and Embryology Act (1990). During these
debates, Anne Winterton stated that:

> I should prefer if those coming forward for this treatment were married
> couples in a long standing relationship . . . single women who present
> themselves for AID should not be allowed to be inseminated unless they
> are prepared to being forward a man who will stand as the social father.
>                                                              (Hansard 1990)

This amendment was narrowly defeated in the House of Lords by one vote,
but the Act did make concessions to this lobbying, and restriction to what
was termed 'deserving couples' who fitted the stereotype of the nuclear

family gained Parliamentary support. A clinic offering such services can only do so provided that it complies with the statutory requirement that:

> A woman shall not be provided with treatment unless account has been taken of the welfare of the child who may be born as a result of the treatment, including the need of that child for a father.
> (Human Fertilization and Embryology Act 1990: S13(1))

This provision is meaningless. It specifically states that consideration has to be given to the child's need for a father. However, every child has a genetic father or else it would not exist. It is a simple biological fact that it takes a sperm and an egg to create a child. What the provision means therefore, is that consideration should be given to the need of that child for father *figure*. This is obviously something quite different.

The message coming through from this piece of legislation is that children should have and should need father figures. This assumption by law has never been proved or established conslusively, and is based on personal belief. It is also implied that mothers should need husbands, or at least longstanding male partners. The third and perhaps not so obvious conclusion to be drawn is that women should be heterosexual, or at least live a heterosexual lifestyle. These conclusions are confirmed by the Warnock Committee's statement that:

> As a general rule it is better for children to be born into a two-parent family, with both father and mother, although we recognise that it is impossible to predict with any certainty how lasting such a relationship will be.
> (Report of the Committee of Inquiry into Fertilization and Embryology, 1984, para 2.11, and see paras. 4.16 and 5.10)

So we can see that law perceives motherhood as not only about the relationship between a woman and her child, but also as about the woman's relationship with husbands and male partners.

Law is therefore unable to perceive mothers as being separate legal beings from the husband or male partner. In other words, if a mother doesn't have a husband or male partner, she cannot be perceived as a 'real' mother. It also illustrates how prescriptive this is of marriage and families. For if law insists that there should be such things as husbands and wives, it also prescribes rigid rules as to how to become a husband or a wife. Marriage is a highly controlled legal arrangement, and a woman's identity and sexuality is further defined by this institution.

In English law, marriage is defined as being 'the voluntary union for life of one man and one woman to the exclusion of all others' (*Hyde* v. *Hyde* (1866) L.R. 1 P. & D. 130). We can see that this definition requires four elements; marriage must be:

- voluntary;
- for life;
- between one man and one woman, i.e. it must be heterosexual;
- monogamous.

The woman's sexual behaviour is strictly prescribed if there is to be a valid legal marriage. After the marriage ceremony has taken place, the marriage must be consummated. Law dictates exactly how this consummation of marriage should take place, however. Therefore, to be a legally valid marriage, law dictates the consummation requires what is termed 'ordinary' sexual intercourse. Sexual intercourse is defined as 'ordinary and complete' penetration of the woman by the man. The importance placed by judges on this particular element of what constitutes a valid marriage shows a continuing dependence on notions of 'proper' sexuality and its function within marriage. This reliance and dependence upon male penetration of the female demonstrates the narrow judicial understandings of the expression of sexual identity. Furthermore, a definition of sexuality is implied. The judicially unquestioned assumption is that it is the male who consummates a marriage, since the phraseology used describes male sexual activity, not female. Legal culture prescribes precisely how a woman's sexual identity should be expressed within marriage and it does this by sole reference to the male.

Furthermore, historically a wife and husband were treated as the same legal person. Blackstone (1765) said this of marriage:

> By marriage, the husband and wife are one person in law; that is, the very being or legal existence of the woman is suspended during the marriage, or at least is incorporated and consolidated into that of her husband; under whose wing, protection and cover she performs everything.

Thus, as wives had no legal independent existence, it was legally impossible for the husband to rape her, because consent to marriage meant unconditional consent to sexual intercourse which she could not withdraw. In addition, if a wife was raped by a man other than her husband, it was only the husband who could take legal action against the other man. This was because it was only the husband who was considered to have suffered a loss.

The legal definitions discussed above indicate the ways in which the law dictates how each of the parties should behave in marriage, and hence constructs women's identity in a narrow and limiting way. Part of the problem is that the law often confuses the terms gender identity and sexual identity. Why is this important? Its importance lies in the commonly held view that gender identity is integrally linked with masculinity and femininity, with personality traits and behaviour patterns. Sexual identity must therefore mean something different. We could say that sex denotes physical characteristics, hormones, chromosomes and so forth. English legal culture insists that sex is biologically intractable – it is fixed and immutable. It also insists that the expression of gender identity automatically follows sexual identity. This is misleading, for we should assume no such thing. If we accept that gender identity is a social and legal construct, then it follows that gender identity is *not* an automatic continuation of sexual identity. The logical conclusion of this line of argument is that assuming there are only two sexes does not necessarily mean that 'female' will accrue exclusively to the bodies of women.

This line of argument can be taken further. Even if the sexes appear to be unproblematically binary, there is no reason to assume that gender is also binary, that is either masculine or feminine. The presumption of a binary gender system implicitly retains the belief that gender mimics sex. When we think of gender constructs as being totally separate and independent from sex, then gender itself becomes a free-floating artifice, with the consequence that female and feminine might just as easily signify a male body as well as a female one, and of course, vice versa.

But, law proceeds on the assumption that gender identity naturally follows from sexual identity, and as we have seen, this produces legal problems and barriers for women in marriage and relationships with men and for women as mothers.

It was mentioned earlier that law creates and then places women in distinct legal categories, such as wife and mother, both of which are constructs themselves. We have seen that implicit in the construction of the concepts of 'mother' and 'motherhood', is the presumption that all mothers are heterosexual. How, therefore, does law construct identity for mothers who are not heterosexual?

## The legal identity of the lesbian mother

Lesbian mothers challenge another piece of ideology within conventional sociolegal thought: the assumption that 'motherhood' is automatically linked to heterosexuality. Looked at from this perspective, 'lesbian mother' is an oxymoron, a contradiction in terms, as a result of which the legal identity of the lesbian and especially the lesbian mother, has for many years been invisible. In recent legal cases involving lesbian mothers, the traditional perception of a woman as a maternal being is overshadowed by the court's unnecessary preoccupation with perceiving her as a lesbian. This preoccupation with the sexual lifestyle of the lesbian mother can be seen as ironic, in the sense that it contradicts the traditional view that women are not, or shouldn't be, sexual beings unless there is a man present. Despite this however, we are seeing more judicial recognition of the existence of lesbian mothers, but this recognition is not entirely positive. In general terms, the emergence of this different legal identity for the lesbian has produced a legal identity which is as false as the legal construct of wife, mother, husband, father and so forth.

Part of the reason for this false legal identity is that law insists on considering sexual orientation as important only when that particular sexual orientation is not a heterosexual one. The legal identity of the lesbian mother is constructed in several ways. Since 1983 (the year when a lesbian mother first won custody of her child; see Re P (A Minor)(Custody)(1983) FLR 401.), the identity of lesbian mothers is directed by other constructs, namely those of women generally, and less specifically, men. Because part of a woman's constructed identity is her sexuality, which is presumed to be heterosexual, legal culture has difficulty in recognizing the lesbian as a legal subject because her sexual identity is obviously not heterosexual.

Therefore, the concept of legal 'lesbian' had to be treated as distinct from the concept of legal 'woman'.

However, at the same time, the more a lesbian conforms to the pre-existing legal construction of 'woman', the more likely she is to be successful in any parental responsibility case.[3] This pressure to conform to the pre-existing constructed identity may take several guises. Before the case ever reaches the courtroom, this pressure can take the form of the woman's solicitor advising her to wear a skirt, or to put on make-up and so forth. It is painfully obvious that the kind of clothes a person wears has nothing to do with their parenting abilities, but a lesbian mother who conforms to the court's idea of what woman means (the 'perfect' mother), appears to stand a greater chance of success. The no-win situation for the lesbian mother is that she can never fully conform to the particular identity which has been constructed for her, as part of a woman's constructed identity is her sexual identity, which according to sociolegal constructs, is meant to be heterosexual. The main reason for this, is that the court will usually consider the mother's lesbianism as a legally relevant factor in a manner opposite to the case of a heterosexual mother making the same application. If and when the case ends up in court, enquiries as to the mother's lifestyle are not uncommon. In particular questions are asked regarding shows of physical affection in front of the child(ren). The implication is that a lesbian's expression of her sexual identity does not 'conform' to legal culture's expectation of how a woman's sexual identity should be expressed.

How does law construct sexual and gender identity in other areas? One controversial area is that of transsexualism. By way of example, let us assume that we are dealing with a male to female transsexual. This individual will always have considered themselves to be female. In the vast majority of cases, the individual will identify themselves as being heterosexual, that is a woman attracted to men. To the individual themselves, this will provide no difficulty, no confusion, no conflict. To legal culture, however, it presents confusion of massive proportions. As law only recognizes two binary opposite sexes, every person born must therefore be either female or male, and law is firmly rooted in the belief that once biological sex has been assigned at birth, it *can*, and *must* never be changed, regardless of any subsequent surgical treatment. Thus, for the transsexual, factual identity is not matched with legal identity. Obviously, if law insists on perceiving the transsexual as being male, it will further perceive that individual as being homosexual. Arguments given against legal recognition of transsexuals state that to allow people to change the sex assigned on their birth certificate would be administratively too expensive and would not provide accurate historical records. We can question what is meant by 'accurate': Once the gender reassignment is complete, it is the birth certificate which is inaccurate, not the person.

One of the most famous of these cases was *Corbett* v. *Corbett* (1970). Corbett was a post-operative male to female transsexual who had undergone a ceremony of marriage with a man. This case decided first that a person who is considered to be male when born, shall always remain male, regardless of medical and surgical intervention to alter external sexual characteristics. In other words, gender identity is ignored by law. Second, the court held that marriage as an institution is by definition the association of someone of the male sex with someone of the female sex; again, gender has no relevance. Therefore, there was no marriage between the two parties. It was held to be impossible to change one's biological sex, the marriage was held to be void because it purported to take place between two individuals who the law regarded as both being male.

One of the obvious questions here is why there should be legal obstacles to the recognition of the transsexual's wishes? What business is it of law that someone now wishes to be known as a woman where previously she was considered a man? Restricting the legal definition of male and female allows restriction of who can, and who cannot, marry. According to the judge in *Corbett*:

> Since marriage is essentially a relationship between man and woman, the validity of the marriage depends . . . on whether the person is a man or a woman . . . the question then becomes what is meant by the word 'woman'.

Since the law assumes that marriage is 'essentially heterosexual', the criteria used to assess 'womanhood' must, according to the judge, be biological. This is because 'Only a biological female is naturally capable of performing the essential role of a woman in marriage' (Per Ormrod, J. in *Corbett* v. *Corbett* [1970] 2 All ER 33).

The 'essential' role being talked about here is the ability to have 'natural heterosexual intercourse'. This must mean that there is such a thing as 'unnatural heterosexual intercourse'. How would the judge's definition apply to a situation where two 80-year-olds wanted to get married purely for companionship reasons? Is it crucial that they have the capacity for 'natural heterosexual intercourse'?

Even in the area of criminal law, lesbianism has been rendered invisible in contrast to heterosexuality and male homosexuality. For example, the Sexual Offences Act 1967, which partially decriminalized male homosexuality, made no mention of lesbianism. Lesbianism was not considered as important as male homosexuality. In one of the early cases in which the lesbianism of a wife was cited as grounds for divorce, in 1954, the judge refused to acknowledge the very existence of the lesbian relationship. He stated:

> [They] were seen hand in hand, used to call each other darling, kissed on the lips, spent a good number of holidays together, were constantly alone in the wife's bedroom at the vicarage and on two or three occasions, occupied the same bedroom at night. . . It was a very odd business, two grown women spending all this time together often in the same room and often in bed together, but the court is satisfied that that is perfectly innocent.
>
> (Kennedy 1993: 155)

It is extremely rare that lesbians are the subject of the criminal law, and subject to criminal charges as lesbians. Helena Kennedy argues that the reason for this is the historical legal preoccupation with vaginal penetration, based on male concerns about virginity, pregnancy and paternity. Although this means that 'there is little male interest in the punishment of female homosexuality' as such (Kennedy 1993: 156), cases of, for example, domestic violence in which lesbians are involved can become occasions for the public condemnation of lesbianism. As Kennedy argues: 'women who have rejected heterosexuality and their prescribed role are perceived as threatening' (ibid.).

However, even though lesbians experience the criminal justice system as hostile, lesbianism is largely invisible in the law. For example, there are no discriminatory laws for lesbians on the age of consent. Kennedy argues that the law purports to protect women from men, but places even greater emphasis on 'protecting young men from homosexual sex' (1993: 158). Thus men who commit consensual offences with male partners over 16 are five times more likely to be prosecuted than men who have consenting sex with girls under 16, and 'men who commit homosexual offences are four times more likely to be convicted than men who commit heterosexual and violent sex offences' (ibid.). At the same time as indicating fear of men's desertion of a heterosexual masculine identity, Kennedy's evidence indicates the perpetuation of a double standard concerning the protection of women. As Kennedy points out, hardly a woman exists who has not had to deal with unwelcome sexual attention, yet the subject is met with collective denial by men (ibid.).

In conclusion, the law creates the legal category of 'woman' which it constructs within narrow and limited parameters. Women have little say in this construction, which is based on a view of women as mothers within heterosexual marriages in which males are sexually dominant. The law manufactures an essentialist definition of 'woman'. This is particularly evident in lesbian custody cases, and also in the legal treatment of transsexuals, and is an expression of the legal assumption that social gender must follow biological sex. Although the law acts punitively towards lesbians and gay men, however, a major part of the construction of 'normal' heterosexuality is the legal oblivion into which the male sexual coercion of women is cast.

○ **Questions**

> 1 How much reliance do you think law places upon gender? In what ways do you think that law should revise its opinion as to what gender and sexuality mean?
>
> 2 Do you think it's possible for law to describe an individual without reference to sex, sexuality or gender? Try doing this for yourself. What questions does this raise for you?
>
> 3 In the light of your reading, what particular areas of law do you think are particularly suited to law reform?

4 If law constructs a particular identity for women who appear in the courtroom, to what extent do you think that this construction affects women generally?

## Further reading

If you want more information you might find the following books useful. Hoggett and Pearl (1991), explores 'the family' within contemporary society and draws upon other disciplines such as history, sociology and anthropology. It has a lot of useful and interesting materials – not all of them legal. Perhaps a more 'readable' introductory textbook is Dewar (1992); it is easy to understand and is written in a not very legalistic manner. However, the downside to these books and others like them is that they deal mainly with the law surrounding the nuclear family and alternative families are examined only briefly. A very interesting, short and readable book is O'Donovan (1993). If you don't read anything else, read this.

Aside from these three books, the following articles may be of interest; Bradley (1987); Tasker and Golumbok (1991) and Boyd (1992).

## Notes

1 The phrase 'legal culture' relates to the body of legal discourse. It encompasses statutes (Acts of Parliament), judge-made law (common law), and academic writing.
2 A Royal Commission was set up in 1984. Their recommendations eventually became the Human Fertilization and Embryology Act 1990. The Warnock Committee's approach was in conflict with the approach of the Family Law Reform Act 1987, which had provided for parentage to be determined by scientific tests, and that it was the genetic material which should determine parenthood.
3 Since the Children Act 1989, the terms 'custody' and 'access' have been replaced by 'parental responsibility' and 'residence'.

## References

Blackstone, W. (1765) *Commentaries on the Laws of England*, 17th edn, by Edward Christian and others (1830). London: Tegg.

Boyd, S. (1992) What is a normal family? C v C (A Minor)(Custody Appeal), *Modern Law Review*, 55 (March): 269.

Bradley, D. (1987) Homosexuality and child custody cases in English Law, *International Journal of Law and Family*, 1: 155–205.

Dewar, J. (1992) *Law and the Family*, 2nd edn. London: Butterworth.

Kennedy, H. (1993) *Eve Was Framed*. London: Vintage.

*Hansard* (1990) House of Commons, vol. 192, March. London: HMSO.

Hoggart, B. and Pearl, D. (1991) *The Family, Law and Society. Cases and Materials,* 3rd edn. London: Butterworth.

O'Donovan, C. (1993) *Family Law Matters.* London: Pluto Press.

*Report of the Committee of Inquiry into Fertilization and Embryology* (1984) Cmnd 9314, (Warnock Report).

Tasker, F. and Golumbok, S. (1991) Children raised by lesbian mothers: the empirical evidence, *Family Law,* 21 (May): 1847.

### Acts of parliament

Human Fertilization and Embryology Act 1990 (Section 13(1)).

### Cases cited

*Hyde* v. *Hyde* (1866) L.R. 1 P. & D. 130.
*Re P* (A Minor)(Custody)(1983) FLR 401.
*Corbett* v. *Corbett* (1970) 2 All ER 33.

It will be rare that you will need to read the case in its original form, but if you wish to read some of these cases, do not be intimidated by the confusing letters and numbers which appear after the names. They refer to the 'type' of law report in which the case appears. For example, 'All ER' stands for *The All England Law Reports.* Most of the cases are talked about in plenty of detail by the further reading indicated above – just look in the front of the book.

**KATHLEEN CROSS**

# Racism and feminism: white women, power and resistance

## ○ Introduction

Of all the areas of debate and conflict within feminism, the issue of racism has proven to be one of the most persistent and damaging. As Hazel Carby (1982: 232) remarked in her well-known essay entitled 'White woman listen! Black feminism and the boundaries of sisterhood': 'This [racism amongst white women] more than any other factor disrupts the recognition of common interests of sisterhood'. The main aim of this chapter is to illustrate why and how the issue of 'race' is one that has not only to do with the experiences of Black women and other Women of Colour, but also – and arguably in the first instance – with White women (these terms will be explained presently). As the second part of the chapter title above is intended to imply, White women are caught up in complex ways within different webs of power and resistance in society, not least by virtue of their racialized positions. I shall begin by considering the concepts of 'race' and racism and their relation to feminism. This will be followed by a discussion of some Black feminist critiques of White feminist theory. Finally, I shall outline in brief some important challenges to White feminists that emerge from these critiques.

## ○ 'Race', racism and feminism

The word 'racism' derives linguistically from 'race', a word which arose within European scientific thinking in the late 1700s as a way of categorizing human beings supposedly into biologically distinct population groups. Stepan (1982: x) notes that a number of factors contributed to the European preoccupation with 'racial' differences at this time: 'Of these factors, the two most important were the existence of black slavery in the colonies of Europe in the New World and the emergence of the modern, biological and human sciences'. The idea of there being biologically distinct groups of humans has since been widely discredited due to its spurious scientific and historical credentials (see Stepan 1982 and Nederveen Pieterse 1992, especially Chapter 2). In spite of the absence of biological evidence to support the division of the world's population into distinct racial groups, the term 'race' remains a powerful social construction, used to position groups of people as dominant or dominated globally and within individual societies. Its political importance means that any critiques of social relations (including feminisms) which ignore 'race' risk reproducing the hierarchies founded upon the concept.

The problem of racism is, of course, by no means confined solely to feminism. Racism is a complex phenomenon; it takes many different forms, and implicates many different groups of people. It is perhaps more accurate to speak of racisms in the plural. One aspect of the complexity of racisms is that it is possible for a person to be situated simultaneously as dominant *and* dominated within different racialized hierarchies. However, the focus in this chapter is on forms of anti-Black racism in White supremacist societies such as Britain and the United States. The word 'Black' has different meanings in Britain and the USA. In the latter, 'Black' refers specifically to (and is often replaced by the term) African-American people. In addition to this, the term 'People of Colour' is used to refer to non-White people of other than African descent living in the United States. In the British context, the term 'Black' has been adopted widely in the course of anti-racist struggles as a collective term which includes many different people's histories and experiences in Britain. These include

> [those] descended (through one or both parents) from Africa, Asia (i.e. the Middle East to China, including the Pacific nations) and Latin America, and . . . descended from the original inhabitants of Australasia, North America and the islands of the Atlantic and Indian Ocean'.
> (Black Lesbian and Gay Project, quoted by (charles) 1992: 35)

The term 'White' refers to those people of European origin who benefit from and/or help to perpetuate the structural disadvantage of Black people in economic, political and social spheres. It is generally recognized that contemporary anti-Black racism is in large part the extended legacy of relations forged during and after the enactment of slavery and imperial colonialism by White Europeans. 'White' appears here with an upper case W in order to highlight it as both a concept and a social force which requires theoretical and practical attention (not least by White people themselves) as part of anti-racist struggles (see (charles) 1992: 32). Political naming is a complex issue which I shall not pursue here. But it should be noted that neither 'Black' nor 'White' are straightforward descriptive words.

The most blatant form of racism is physical attack, carried out by openly racist White people (most often men) on Black people. Racism also takes rather more subtle forms, however. These range from institutional practices of discrimination, to advertising campaigns based on stereotypical representations of perceived differences between White and Black people.

These less overt forms of racist practice operate not only to conceal (mostly from White people) the systematic nature of racism's effects, but also to obscure the fact that White people's experiences are lived out within racist frameworks of meaning and 'commonsense', everyday practice. Thus, racism is as much about White people's perception of themselves and of their place in the world as it is about Black people's experiences in racist societies.

Feminist campaigns in Europe and North America in the nineteenth and twentieth centuries developed within the broad context of racism sketched here, and White feminists frequently reproduced racist thinking uncritically. As Angela Davis shows in her groundbreaking book *Women, Race and Class* (1982), this was true of the women's suffrage movement in the United States, in spite of the fact that many of the women involved were also active anti-slavery campaigners (Abolitionists). White women's desire to play a role equal to their male counterparts in the Abolitionist movement led to their demands for the vote, but not all of them acknowledged the logical link between struggles for women's suffrage and anti-slavery, that is, the freedom and political participation of Black women who either were or had been slaves. At a women's rights convention held in New York City in 1867, shortly after the American Civil War, delegates proposed the establishment of an Equal Rights Association which would campaign simultaneously for Black men's and for (White) women's suffrage. Davis quotes part of a speech made by White campaigner Elizabeth Cady Stanton at the Association's meeting the following year, illustrating the degree to which racism was embedded in dominant White feminist rhetoric at that time:

> With the black man, we have no new element in government, but with the education and elevation of women, we have a power that is to develop the Saxon race into a higher and nobler life and thus, by the law of attraction, to lift all races to a more even platform than can ever be reached in the political isolation of the sexes.
>
> (Stanton, quoted in Davis 1982: 72)

Black women are completely absent from this statement. The context is debate about Black *men's* voting rights. Black women were effectively excluded from Stanton's reference to the 'education and elevation of women' by her identification of 'women' specifically with the 'Saxon race'. Already 15 years prior to this event, however, a Black woman named Sojourner Truth had argued eloquently for the right of *all* women to vote by challenging the male provocateurs at a women's convention in Akron, Ohio:

> The leader of the provocateurs had argued that it was ridiculous for women to desire the vote, since they could not even walk over a puddle or get into a carriage without the help of a man. Sojourner Truth pointed out with compelling simplicity that she herself had never been helped over mud puddles or into carriages. 'And ain't I a woman?'
>
> (Davis 1982: 61)

As we shall see, the tendency for White women to render Black women invisible in their thinking about sexism and racism has continued into the present day. The title of a book by three African-American feminists highlights this issue: *All the Women Are White, All the Blacks Are Men, But Some of Us Are Brave* (Hull *et al.* 1982).

Davis notes that there *were* White women who saw the connections between the issue of slavery and the oppression of both working-class and middle-class women. She recounts in some detail the activities of the Grimke sisters as an example (Davis 1982: 40 ff.). However, the women's suffrage movement as a whole did not heed their insights; the interests of White educated middle-class women predominated. The particular concerns and needs of Black women were rendered invisible.

Roughly 100 years later, and after Black and White women on both sides of the Atlantic had won the right to vote, there came a renewed movement towards what was now called 'women's liberation'. The late 1950s, the 1960s and early 1970s saw a period of intense political activity in a variety of arenas. The Black civil rights movement in the United States was one of the major forces for change at this time. Women (mostly Black, though some White as well) played a fundamental role in this movement. In Britain, Black women campaigning for improvements in living and working conditions drew inspiration from the activities and slogans of the civil rights movement across the water (see Bryan *et al.* 1985: 140 ff.). By the mid-1970s, when the women's liberation movement had gained momentum, many Black women were experienced in political struggle.

The motivations that inspired many White women's involvement in politics were rather different from those of Black women. This is clear from many of the early 'new wave' feminist writings by White women in both Europe and the United States. Whether from a liberal middle-class or from a socialist perspective, these analyses emphasized patriarchy (male dominance) as the fundamental obstacle to all women's liberation. Thus, some White feminists drew attention to men's sexual dominance of women – most obviously through rape – and to the need for women's sexual and reproductive self-determination (see Daly 1978: 11, for more on this); others were more concerned with the struggle for equality of job opportunities and for equal pay; others still analysed women's oppression within the framework of the exploitative capitalist system (see, for example, Firestone 1971; Mitchell 1971; Rowbotham 1973; Daly 1978; amongst many others).

However, in failing to recognize the significant and damaging effects of racism – including of course White women's racism – on Black women's lives, many White feminists at this time contributed to the propagation of a dominant feminist perspective that emphasized 'patriarchy' as the primary cause of *all* women's oppression. For example, in agreeing with Shulamith Firestone's argument concerning the relation of racism to sexism, Juliet Mitchell stated at the beginning of her book, *Woman's Estate*, 'Racism . . . is *only* an offshoot of sexism' (1971: 19, my emphasis). Thus was established the notion of a global sisterhood which obscured the fact of some women's participation in structures that facilitated other women's oppression.

○ **Black feminist critiques**

It should be emphasized at the outset of this section that work by Black feminists by no means consists solely of critiques of White feminism – the further reading section at the end of the chapter gives a broader selection of Black feminist work. None the less, the critiques are relevant here, and indeed have provided the main source of inspiration for White feminists' reappraisal of their own perspectives and assumptions, where this has occurred.

Many British feminist writers trace the beginnings of a rigorous theoretical critique of White women's analyses to an article that appeared in the anthology *The Empire Strikes Back* (CCCS, Birmingham 1982; see also Amos and Parmar 1984). Hazel Carby's 'White woman listen! Black feminism and the boundaries of sisterhood' identified many of the trends in White feminist work which serve(d) to perpetuate Black women's invisibility and the marginalization of their struggles and political agendas. I shall focus here on two major aspects of Carby's critique of White feminist theory, illustrating them with examples drawn from other Black feminists' work.

First, Carby (1982: 212) refers to Black women's critiques of the negative ways in which '*history*' has portrayed them, and then focuses on 'herstory' in order to 'address questions to the feminist theories which have been developed during the last decade'. In this context she notes that she cannot do justice to all the varied experiences of different Black women in Britain, for 'our herstories are too numerous and too varied' (ibid.). She criticizes the tendency of White feminist work to make sweeping generalizations about 'Third World women' and their countries of origin: 'The level of generality applied to the "Third World" would be dismissed as too vague to be informative if applied to Western industrialized nations' (ibid.: 217). This theme is addressed also by Chandra Mohanty in her article 'Under western eyes – feminist scholarship and colonial discourses' (Mohanty 1988). Here, Mohanty analyses 'the production of the "third world woman" as a singular monolithic subject in some recent (western) feminist texts' (ibid.: 61). A part of Mohanty's argument is that such texts serve to reproduce colonial-based understandings of the relations between White and Black women as members of 'developed' and 'underdeveloped' countries respectively:

> Universal images of 'the third-world woman' (the veiled woman, chaste virgin, etc.), images constructed from adding the 'third-world difference' to 'sexual difference', are predicated on . . . assumptions about western women as secular, liberated, and having control over their own lives. . . Without the 'third-world woman', the particular self-presentation of western women mentioned above would be problematical. I am suggesting, in effect, that the one enables and sustains the other.
>
> (Mohanty 1988: 81–2)

Closely related to this is Carby's observation about the frequent inclusion of Black or 'Third World women' in White feminist work in merely negative ways:

Feminist theory in Britain is almost wholly Eurocentric, and when it is not ignoring the experience of black women 'at home', it is trundling 'Third World women' onto the stage only to perform as victims of 'barbarous', 'primitive' practices in 'barbarous', 'primitive' societies.

(Carby 1982: 222)

This is a subject which Audre Lorde addressed in her 'Open letter to Mary Daly' (Lorde 1984). In this open letter, Lorde's primary concern is the treatment of African traditions in Daly's widely influential book *Gyn/Ecology* (Daly 1978). Lorde asks, referring to the book's 'First Passage' on patriarchal religion and the suppression of the Goddess, 'Why are [Daly's] goddess images only white, western european, judeo-christian?' (Lorde 1984: 67). She asks further why it is that none of the Goddess figures of African religious myths appear in Daly's account. This erasure is compounded by Lorde's second observation, regarding the 'Second Passage' in *Gyn/Ecology*. This part of the book deals with the negative treatment of women in a variety of religious and social contexts, and Lorde notes that it is only here that non-European women are included, namely in the role of 'victims and preyers-upon each other' as, for example, in the case of African genital mutilation (ibid.).

Lorde (1984: 69) points out further how distortions such as those she identifies in Daly's work serve

the destructive forces of racism and separation between women – the assumption that the herstory and myth of white women is the legitimate and sole herstory and myth of all women to call upon for power and background, and that nonwhite women and our herstories are noteworthy only as decorations, or examples of female victimization.

The dual processes of erasure and idiosyncratic exemplification can be identified in much other White feminist work (for a discussion of these and related processes in mainstream Women's Studies, see Bhavnani 1993).

The second major point of Carby's critique concerns the misfit between White feminist analyses of social relations and Black women's 'herstories':

The herstory of black women is interwoven with that of white women but this does not mean that they are the same. Nor do we need white feminists to write our herstory for us, we can and are doing that for ourselves. However, when they write their herstory and call it the story of women but ignore our lives *and deny their relation to us*, that is the moment in which they are acting within the relations of racism and writing *history*.

(Carby 1982: 223, my emphasis)

This denial of historical relationship is a key source of the tension between Black and White feminist analyses. This becomes clear in Carby's discussion of three concepts which she identifies as crucial to feminist theory but problematic in their application to Black women's lives, namely: the family, patriarchy, and reproduction. For example, many White feminist analyses of women's oppression have taken 'the family' as their starting point, since this is seen to be the most immediate site for the perpetuation of patriarchal social relations. Women are seen to be dependent upon men both financially and in terms of deriving their feminine identity from their role as (house)wives and mothers. Carby (1982: 214) explains why such analyses fail to address Black women's experiences of the place of the family in struggle and survival:

> We would not wish to deny that the family can be a source of oppression for us but we also wish to examine how the black family has functioned as a prime source of resistance to oppression. We need to recognize that during slavery, periods of colonialism, and under the present authoritarian state, the black family has been a site of political and cultural resistance to racism.

Carby exposes the hidden connections and contradictions between White and Black women's experiences of the family; while many White middle-class women sought to escape from the narrow confines of domestic existence and enter the paid workforce, it was often Black and/or working-class women whom they employed to take over the domestic tasks they wished to leave behind. Similar arguments apply with regard to the concepts of 'patriarchy' and 'reproduction', where these terms carry different, but interrelated, meanings and implications for Black and White women respectively (Carby 1982: 214–19).

A further example of the significance of different herstories on the way in which feminist theories and campaigns are built is the issue of rape. Davis (1982, Chapter 11) details the way in which the 'myth of the Black rapist' was promulgated by White men after the formal abolition of slavery in the southern United States

> whenever recurrent waves of violence and terror against the Black community [frequently in the form of lynchings] have required convincing justifications. . . The historical knot binding Black women – systematically abused and violated by white men – to Black men – maimed and murdered because of the racist manipulation of the rape charge – has just begun to be acknowledged to any significant extent.
> (Davis 1982: 173)

Davis suggests that one reason why few Black women have participated in the anti-rape movement in the United States is the indifferent attitude that movement has show toward the framing of Black men on rape charges as an incitement to racist aggression by Whites (ibid.). A similar dynamic applied during British colonial domination of non-European countries: 'Protecting the virtue of white women was the pretext for instituting draconian measures against indigenous populations in several parts of the Empire' (Callaway 1987; Ware 1992: 38). The legacy of these racist actions persists today in the White popular imagination (Ware 1992: 3–4).

○  **Conclusions**

In the previous section I highlighted two aspects of Hazel Carby's critique of much White feminist work. These concerned, first, the frequently negative and undifferentiated representation of Black women's lives by White feminists and, second, the building of theory based only on some White women's experiences. This final section will address three issues which arise directly from these critiques. These issues, moreover, point to the importance of considering 'power' and 'resistance' in the context of relations between women and feminists.

The first issue concerns the interconnection between different women's histories, and the crucial relevance of that interconnectedness for contemporary understandings of women's experiences in diverse social locations. It is a commonplace to remark that unless one seeks to understand the past, one cannot adequately understand the present. This is particularly true with regard to women's interconnected histories. For White women, this means gaining knowledge and understanding of the events and ideologies through which slavery and colonialism were constituted, in order to understand the ways in which these continue to play a role in the popular imagination and collective memory of White and Black people respectively. However, as Carby (1982: 212) points out concerning the making and remaking of such connections, this will not be a straightforward process of information-gathering, for the legacy of past events itself plays a role in how we are able to perceive that past. In other words, there is a need for White women to struggle to overcome racist – and masculinist – perspectives on slavery and colonialism, as well as on the often taken for granted treatment of White and Black women and men in our society today. This is necessary if their theoretical and practical feminist work is not to perpetuate such perspectives and practices.

The significance of the interconnections between our different histories/herstories is such that their study should not be considered a topic appropriate only, say, for feminist historians, but should rather become 'common knowledge' amongst all feminists. These interconnections have played a fundamental role in shaping both White and Black women's lives today. As Vron Ware shows in her history of White English women's involvement in British colonial rule in India, the experiences of neither White nor Black women can be adequately accounted for outside this frame of reference (Ware 1992).

The second issue concerns the use of categories in White feminist analyses of oppression, which requires greater care and precision. The categories I am referring to are those of 'race', gender, class, sexual identification, and so on. The early new wave (White) feminist tendency to prioritize gender as the prime factor in (all) women's oppression has left its mark on most subsequent White feminist theory. We saw above why this is a problematic approach from a Black feminist perspective. What needs to be made explicit here is the fact that it is also a problematic approach for theorizing White women's experiences. The inattention to White women's structural position of dominance over Black women in society has, in effect, allowed the implicit assumption to flourish in most White feminists' work that gender is a discrete concept in itself – even if, when pressed, most would accept that this is not the case (for White feminist critiques of this tendency, see Stacey 1985; Spelman 1988). The point that is missed by such an assumption is that *all* women's lives, including White women's, involve the complex intersection of all sorts of factors, not just gender. It does not follow from this that it becomes impossible to talk of women at all, but rather that it matters *which* women's experiences are under analysis; as Spelman points out, there is no such thing as a 'generic woman' (Spelman 1988: 186; see Ramazanoglu 1989 for the contradictory implications of different women's positions in society).

The third and final issue concerns the political significance of Whiteness as an element in White women's experiences and self-identification. In the course of her 'Whiteness' workshop at the 1991 conference of the Women's Studies Network Association (UK), Helen (charles) established that the question '[d]o "white women" exist?' is by no means an idle or frivolous one ((charles) 1992: 31); on it turns the whole issue of exclusion and marginalization in feminist theory and practice, both within and outside the academic field of Women's Studies. 'The problem lies in the fact that many "white women", in appearing to *in*clude women of Colour and the issues arising from race-oppression, create oppositional and dual registers that ignore or displace the position of "white women" on the racism agenda' (ibid.).

A similar point is made by Frankenberg (1993: 293):

a dualistic framework is retained, for example, in new curricular programs that include attention to nondominant cultures but do not simultaneously reconceptualize or reexamine the status, content, and formation of whiteness. Similarly, references to women of color, but not white women, as 'racial-ethnic women', implicitly suggest that race does not shape white identities or experience.

On the basis of a set of interviews with White women in California and her own careful analysis of these, Frankenberg is able to demonstrate in what diverse and specific ways 'race' does indeed shape White women's lives, both in their lived materiality and in the discursive repertoires upon which the women draw to describe their experiences. Her account shows very clearly the possibility – and, arguably, the necessity – of '[recovering] the histories embedded in each narrative' (ibid.: 238). So, for example

a history of dramatically unequal Black-white relations, a US economy structured by race, and resistance to racism during the civil rights movement underlay the existence of Beth Ellison's [one of the interviewee's] all-white residential neighborhood, the possibility of a Black family moving into it in the late 1960s, and white neighbors' hostility when they did so.

(ibid.)

Frankenberg's work points toward the possibilities that exist for White feminists to engage, alongside feminists of Colour and Womanists, in strategies for resisting and destabilizing the dominance of White power.

○ **Acknowledgements**

For their comments at various stages of writing of this chapter, I should like to thank: Helen (charles), Anne Cronin, Ruth McElroy, Consuelo Rivera, Penny Summerfield and Rosie White.

○ **Questions**

> 1 Do you remember the first time you became aware of being cate-gorized as a member of a particular 'racial' group? In what context did this occur? Was it a positive or a negative experience for you?
>
> 2 Do you think it is helpful or unhelpful to highlight issues around Whiteness and being White – what do you think are the possibilities and the dangers of focusing on these issues?
>
> 3 Read Pratt (1984) and note in particular her use of geographical settings as a way of illustrating the workings of 'race', class, gender and sexuality in her life. What other aspects of everyday life could be used to highlight the often hidden ways in which each of us is connected to others along different lines of inequality?

○ **Further reading**

> If you wish to read further on racism generally, you may find the follow-ing texts useful: Miles and Phizacklea (1984); Gilroy (1987); Donald and Rattansi (1992); Miles (1993). Two pieces dealing with racism in Women's Studies are Bhavnani (1993) and Watt and Cook (1991). For an introductory discussion of the interlocking forms of racism, see the video film *Being White* (1987; available on hire from Albany Video Distri-bution, The Albany, Douglas Way, London SE8 4AG).
>
> There is a growing body of literature on Whiteness, from different perspectives. Dyer (1988) deals with images of Whiteness in film; Pratt (1984), Jeater (1992) and Frankenberg (1993) are feminist accounts which approach the issue of Whiteness and being White from an (auto)biographical starting point, and are thus reasonably accessible. See also hooks (1992) which discusses representations of Whiteness in the Black imagination. Roediger (1994) is a collection of essays focus-ing on Whiteness and working-class issues in a US context.
>
> For Black women's political activities around these issues, read Davis (1982) in full. Some examples of work by Black feminists and femin-ists of Colour are Moraga and Anzaldua (1981); Hull *et al.* (1982); Collins (1991). These are anthologies and contain many more refer-ences to others' work – certainly writers such as bell hooks (1981), Audre Lorde (1984) and Michele Wallace (1990) should not be missed!

## ○ **References**

Albany Video Distribution (1987) *Being White*. Video interviews with white people.

Amos, V. and Parmar, P. (1984) Challenging imperial feminism, *Feminist Review*, 17: 3–19.

Bhavnani, K. (1993) Talking racism and the editing of women's studies, in D. Richardson and V. Robinson (eds) *Introducing Women's Studies*. London: Macmillan.

Bryan, B., Dadzie, S. and Scafe, S. (1985) *The Heart of the Race – Black Women's Lives in Britain*. London: Virago.

Callaway, H. (1987) *Gender, Culture and Empire: European Women in Colonial Nigeria*. London: Macmillan.

Carby, H. (1982) White woman listen! Black feminism and the boundaries of sisterhood, Centre for Contemporary Cultural Studies, University of Birmingham. *The Empire Strikes Back*. London: Hutchinson.

Centre for Contemporary Cultural Studies (CCCS), University of Birmingham (1982) *The Empire Strikes Back*. London: Hutchinson.

(charles), H. (1992) Whiteness – the relevance of politically colouring the 'Non', in H. Hinds, A. Phoenix and J. Stacey (eds) *Working Out – New Directions for Women's Studies*. London: Falmer.

Collins, P. H. (1991) *Black Feminist Thought – Knowledge, Consciousness, and the Politics of Empowerment*. London: Routledge.

Daly, M. (1978) *Gyn/Ecology – The Metaethics of Radical Feminism*. London: Women's Press.

Davis, A. (1982) *Women, Race and Class*. London: Women's Press.

Donald, J. and Rattansi, A. (eds) (1992) *'Race', Culture and Difference*. London: Sage.

Dyer, R. (1988) Being white, *Screen*, 29(4): 44–64.

Firestone, S. (1971) *The Dialectic of Sex – The Case for Feminist Revolution*. London: Cape.

Frankenberg, R. (1993) *White Women, Race Matters: The Social Construction of Whiteness*. London: Routledge.

Gilroy, P. (1987) *There Ain't No Black in the Union Jack: The Cultural Politics of Race and Nation*. London: Hutchinson.

hooks, b. (1981) *Ain't I a Woman: Black Women and Feminism*. London: Pluto Press.

hooks, b. (1992) Representing whiteness in the black imagination, in L. Grossberg, C. Nelson and P. Treichler (eds) *Cultural Studies*. London: Routledge.

Hull, G., Scott, P. B. and Smith, B. (1982) *All the Women are White, All the Blacks are Men, But Some of Us Are Brave*. New York: Feminist Press.

Jeater, D. (1992) Roast beef and reggae music: the passing of whiteness, *New Formations*, 18: 107–21.

Lorde, A. (1984) An open letter to Mary Daly, in *Sister Outsider*. Freedom, CA: Crossing Press.

Miles, R. (1993) *Racism After 'Race Relations'*. London: Routledge.

Miles, R. and Phizacklea, A. (1984) *White Man's Country: Racism in British Politics*. London: Pluto.

Mitchell, J. (1971) *Woman's Estate*. Harmondsworth: Penguin.

Mohanty, C. (1988) Under western eyes: feminist scholarship and colonial discourses, *Feminist Review*, 30: 61–88.

Moraga, C. and Anzaldua, G. (1981) *This Bridge Called My Back: Writings by Radical Women of Color*. New York: Kitchen Table.

Nederveen Pieterse, J. (1992) *White on Black – Images of Africa and Blacks in Western Popular Culture*. London: Yale University Press.

Pratt, M. (1984) Identity: skin blood heart, in E. Bulkin, M. B. Pratt and B. Smith

*Yours in Struggle: Three Feminist Perspectives on Anti-Semitism and Racism*. New York: Long Haul Press.

Ramazanoglu, C. (1989) *Feminism and the Contradictions of Oppression*. London: Routledge.

Roediger, D. (1994) *Towards the Abolition of Whiteness: Essays on Race, Politics and Working Class History*. London: Verso.

Rowbotham, S. (1973) *Woman's Consciousness, Man's World*. Harmondsworth: Penguin.

Spelman, E. V. (1988) *Inessential Woman: Problems of Exclusion in Feminist Thought*. London: Women's Press.

Stacey, J. (1985) *Big White Sister*. University of Kent at Canterbury: Women's Studies Occasional Paper No. 7.

Stepan, N. (1982) *The Idea of Race in Science: Great Britain 1880–1960*. London: Macmillan.

Wallace, M. (1990) *Invisibility Blues: From Pop to Theory*. London: Verso.

Ware, V. (1992) *Beyond the Pale: White Women, Racism and History*. London: Verso.

Watt, S. and Cook, J. (1991) Racism: whose liberation?: implications for women's studies, in J. Aaron and S. Walby (eds) *Out of the Margins: Women's Studies in the Nineties*. London: Falmer.

## 18

**SANTI ROZARIO**

# Community and resistance: Muslim women in contemporary societies

○ **Introduction**

The purpose of this chapter is to examine the situation of Muslim women today, both in Islamic societies and in western countries, and particularly to look at how they have responded to the Islamic revival and to feminist critiques of Islam. To make sense of these responses, we need to examine the specific cultural and political situations in which Muslim women find themselves and to understand the dilemmas they are confronted with. These dilemmas centre on the conflict between loyalty to the Islamic *umma* (community, local or worldwide) on the one hand and desire for sexual equality on the other. This conflict takes different forms in Islamic societies and in western countries. If Islam and feminism are difficult to reconcile, we need to recall that, as the Muslim feminist Leila Ahmed (1982: 162) pointed out, 'feminism is irreconcilably in conflict with all or nearly all currently entrenched ideologies. It is in conflict with the dominant ideologies in the West to more or less the same extent that it is with the Islamic.'

The different responses of Muslim women to Islam are integrally linked to the politics of communal identity. In Muslim communities, women and their proper conduct are routinely used as 'symbols of communal identity and markers of "tradition" and culture' (Chhachhi 1991: 162; see also Anthias and Yuval-Davis 1992; Sahgal and Yuval-Davis 1992; Moghadam 1994, Tohidi 1994). Muslim communities everywhere are consequently preoccupied with the position of women, and with women's role in the family and community. This preoccupation in turn is related to a concern with preserving the integrity and purity of Islamic culture, which is seen as linked more to gender roles and to the family than to affairs of the public world.

Thus for Muslim women, whether they live in a Muslim country or belong to a minority community elsewhere (in the third world or in the West), there is a continual pressure not to be seen to be disloyal to Islam, Islamic heritage, Islamic culture. Muslim women (unlike Muslim men, who do not face similar problems) can be disloyal by showing signs of 'western' values in their personal decor, dress, associations with 'western feminism'. Such women are described by terms such as the Farsi word *gharbzadegi* ('western-struck', 'westoxicated'), in other words as corrupted by western values (Najmabadi 1991; Tohidi 1994). Muslim women in a minority situation (as in the UK) find themselves with the extra burden of having to be the carriers of the minority culture. In either case, women are expected to suppress their own needs and rights in favour of the interests of their nation, of Islamic culture or of the local Muslim community. The cost of outright rejection of Islam can be high, and inevitably most women compromise to a greater or lesser degree.

The growth of 'Islamist' movements has added a further important element to the overall situation. These movements, which I deliberately avoid referring to by the loaded term 'fundamentalist', call for a return to true Islamic principles and an explicit rejection of western values, and can thus in some ways be seen as adding to women's oppression. However, the principles enshrined in the Quran (the holy book of Islam) and in the *hadith* (the traditional sayings of Muhammad), despite their generally patriarchal orientation, are by no means entirely anti-women. They offer real possibilities for an improvement in women's situation, particularly for those living in many contemporary Islamic societies. They also offer ways of dealing with what is seen as the degraded and exploited status of women in the contemporary West. Thus Islamist movements provide for women both a threat and an opportunity.

Before looking directly at some of the complex processes of acceptance and contestation of community norms among Muslim women today, it is worth reflecting a little on the historical relationship between the Islamic world and the West and on the way in which the growth of Islamist movements has transformed this relationship. I do this through a discussion of what has become the central symbol of the status of Muslim women: the veil. Following this, the two main sections of the chapter will look at women in Islamic countries, and at Muslim women in the West.

## The veil in western and Muslim discourse

The terms 'veil' and 'veiling' are here used to refer to the whole complex of normative principles associated with the physical veil (*hijab*) – in other words, the norm of veiling refers to women's modesty and restrictions on their interactions with males who do not fall in the specified categories with whom contact is permitted (Jahan 1975; Papanek 1982; Rozario 1992).[1] It can be argued that veiling has always been a political issue, but both within the internal politics of Muslim countries and within international politics it has gained an overwhelming significance with the rise of Islamist movements. Much has been said and written about the political, economic, religious and cultural significance of veiling. Non-veiled, veiled and re-veiled Muslim women have all been involved in the debate, with differing views on the reasons for, the advantages and the disadvantages of veiling.

Muslim women's reasons for veiling are very complex and vary according to their specific class, regional, national, and cultural background (Tohidi 1991, 1994; Ahmed 1992; MacLeod 1992; Milani 1992; Moghadam 1993, 1994; Odeh 1993; Brooks 1995). Veiling can be seen as a status symbol, and as a claim to high social class (Jeffery 1979). It can be seen as a form of ideology parallel to the ideologies of honour, shame, purity and pollution, which appear in many societies, Muslim and non-Muslim, and are used to maintain gender as well as other forms of social hierarchy (El Saadawi 1980; Rozario 1992). Alternatively, it can be seen as a source of female power (Stivens 1994). Historically, many Muslim women have not worn veils. However, more recently in the context of widespread international migration, socioeconomic changes, Islamist revivalism as well as the ever tense political divide between the Islamic world and the West, most Muslim women around the world have had to confront the issue of veiling and take a position in relation to it.

In most countries, whether a woman veils or does not, at least in principle, is an individual decision. Yet in present-day Algeria, Iran, Palestine and Afghanistan women are intimidated into veiling in the name of religious and national values (Moghadam 1994). Meanwhile in western countries, many young, educated and vocal women, as members of minority Muslim communities, have taken to veiling out of free choice. Many argue that it helps them avoid being used as sex objects and enables them to participate in the public world more freely (Kabbani 1989). Admittedly, some form of community pressure is often present in the West as well.[2] However, Islamic women in the West have much more freedom of choice in this issue than their counterparts in the Islamic nations mentioned above.

In their effort to legitimize the veil and women's proper role in the family, Islamist movements routinely use the West and western feminism as examples of corruption and decadence, something the Islamic world must resist at all costs. For instance, when Ayatollah Khomeini took power after the 1979 revolution, the constitution of the Islamic Republic of Iran 'constructed the ideal Islamic woman in opposition to Western values of womanhood' (Yeganeh 1993: 8). It should be noted, however, that Islamist movements and the push for Islamization of women's position do not necessarily prevent women from participation in extra-domestic activities.[3]

As Leila Ahmed has pointed out, the significance of the veil as a symbolic counter today derives from the history of colonial relationships between the Islamic East and Christian West. The British colonialists

> developed their theories of races and cultures . . . according to which middle-class Victorian England, and its beliefs and practices, stood at the culminating point of the evolutionary process and represented the model of ultimate civilization. In this scheme Victorian womanhood and mores with respect to women, along with other aspects of society at the colonial centre, were regarded as the ideal and measure of civilization.
>
> (Ahmed 1992: 150–1)

Although colonialist males were contesting feminist claims on their own home front, this did not stop them from appropriating the 'language of feminism' in the service of their assault on the indigenous religions and cultures of colonial societies (ibid.: 151–2). Ahmed argues that it is by 'combining of the languages of colonialism and feminism that the fusion between the issues of women and culture was created' (ibid.: 151). The idea that men in the societies the colonialists now ruled had traditionally oppressed women

> was used . . . to render morally justifiable the project of undermining or eradicating the cultures of colonized peoples . . . Veiling – to *Western* eyes, the most visible marker of the differentness and inferiority of Islamic societies – became the symbol now of both the oppression of women . . . and the backwardness of Islam.
>
> (ibid.: 151–2)

Thus the veil and the segregation of women became symbolic in colonialist discourse of an Islam that was intrinsically oppressive of women.

During the colonial period, modernizing and westernizing writers and politicians in Islamic societies, such as Qasem Amin in Egypt or Kemal Ataturk in Turkey, often accepted and internalized this discourse of veiling and Islamic backwardness, and set out to eradicate veiling and other 'backward' customs. Others, however, the forerunners and originators of today's Islamist movements, chose to reject the discourse outright and explicitly endorse the veil as a symbol of resistance:

> The veil came to symbolize in the resistance narrative, not the inferiority of the culture and the need to cast aside its customs in favor of those of the West, but, on the contrary, the dignity and validity of all native customs, and in particular those customs coming under fiercest colonial attack – the customs relating to women – and the need to tenaciously affirm them as a means of resistance to Western domination.
>
> (ibid.: 164)

Thus both Western colonial discourse and the Islamist resistant position established a connection between the issues of culture and women, becoming in this way what Ahmed refers to as 'mirror images of each other' (ibid.: 166).[4] In this way culture and women have become inextricably interlinked in the politics of identity of the Islamic world today. The detrimental effects of this connection are evident in the politics of Islamic communities throughout the world, including those of minority Muslim communities in western countries (cf. Kandiyoti 1991; Shaheed 1994; Winter 1994).[5]

It is against this background of the use of women and the veil as central symbols of Muslim identity that contemporary Muslim women have had to construct a meaningful role and identity for themselves. In the next section, I look at some aspects of this process within the Islamic world.

○    **Women's responses in the Islamic world**

To begin with, we may be struck by the variety of Muslim women's responses to Islam. To the western observer, the question of veiling or not veiling may appear as central, and to be more or less equivalent to acceptance or rejection of the Islamist position. In practice, the situation is more complex. Thus, Valentine Moghadam (1993: 250–1) writes that women's responses

> range from participating in the Islamist movement, to working for reform within the framework of Islam, to fighting for a secular state and secular laws. In spite of this wide range of tendencies and strategies, most Muslim women have internalized some of the concepts developed and used by Islamists.

It is nevertheless useful to contrast an older generation of Muslim feminists who are explicitly working for reform, though within the framework of Islam, with the younger women active in the Islamist movements. I discuss two well-known Muslim feminists here as examples: Fatima Mernissi from Morocco and Nawal El Saadawi from Egypt. One could also include the Egyptian feminist writer Leila Ahmed, whose work I have already cited, in this group. Although she has lived and worked mostly in the USA, her writings are directed more towards Islamic societies than to Muslim communities in the West.

Fatima Mernissi (b. 1940), who teaches at Mohammad V University in Morocco, argues that 'our liberation will come through a rereading of our past and a reappropriation of the Muslim heritage as a necessary ingredient of our modernity' (1993: 160). In her writings Mernissi has been concerned with the way sacred texts are manipulated for power by the Muslim elite. Thus, a recent study (*The Veil and the Male Elite*, also known as *Women and Islam*, 1991) discusses the role of the veil in Islam and how it has been misrepresented as an Islamic ideal even in the collection of *hadith* (that by al-Bukhari) which is widely considered the most authentic.

Mernissi, like some other Muslim feminists, argues that women should take advantage of the Islamic tradition of *ijtihad* (individual reasoning by legal authorities on the basis of analogy from Quran and *hadith*), which 'represents intellectual freedom in Islam' and allows individual reasoning in the context of changed social environment (Lippman 1990: 81). This has led to conflict with the male-dominated Islamic establishment, who argue that *ijtihad* is no longer permissible or appropriate. As Mernissi 'does not veil or otherwise flaunt her piety' (Brooks 1995: 232), her findings can be easily rejected.

The Egyptian medical doctor, novelist and Marxist feminist Nawal El Saadawi (b. 1931) takes a more radical position. For her, oppression of women and patriarchy prevails in all religion, and Christianity may even be more oppressive than Islam. El Saadawi has been critical both of the oppressive features within Islamic texts and of the way in which Islam is used to legitimize various 'un-Islamic' practices like female circumcision and virginity tests. These, she argues, operate to maintain both the Islamic patriarchal family and also the wider social hierarchy.

El Saadawi's uncompromising political stance, and her steadfast refusal to endorse Islam, led to her losing her position as director of education in Egypt's Ministry of Health, being arrested on several occasions, and having to spend much of her life in exile in other Middle Eastern countries or in the West. Her books, beginning with her first non-fiction work, *Women and Sex* (published in 1972), and her journal *Nun* have been banned, as was the association she organized (Solidarity of Arab Women). In 1992 El Saadawi was put on the death list of Islamic Jihad (Brooks 1995).

By contrast with women such as Mernissi or El Saadawi, the women most actively participating in Islamist movements belong to a younger generation. They are usually students, educated and vocal, or young working women of lower middle and middle-class background (Ahmed 1992; MacLeod 1992; Odeh 1993; Brooks 1995). They take to veiling as a way of showing their loyalty to Islamic causes, and in turn they may enjoy various benefits, for example grants for education or free medical care, offered by Islamist groups (Moghadam 1993).

It would be wrong to assume that Islamist women are not concerned about sexual inequality in their societies. However, their strategy is not to confront the ideologues directly, but to gain recognition from within the existing constraints. Such indirect resistance involves accepting what Kandiyoti calls the 'patriarchal bargain': women may use the pro-women arguments from the Quran and *hadith* in order to get Muslim men to live up to their obligations, but they

> will not, except under the most extreme pressure, compromise the basis for their claims by stepping out of line and losing their respectability. Their passive resistance takes the form of claiming their half of this particular patriarchal bargain – protection in exchange for submissiveness and propriety.
>
> (Kandiyoti 1988: 282–3)

Given that many of the problems Muslim women face cannot really be traced back to the Quran but rather to the political situation of their particular society, it is not difficult to appreciate the stand taken by the Islamist women. If Muslim men behaved according to 'true' Islam, many of the difficulties faced by Muslim women would disappear. This, at least, is the argument of women working within Islamist movements (see also MacLeod 1992).

Nevertheless, the differences between the older generation of Islamist feminists, few of whom wore the veil, and the younger generation of women, many of whom have adopted the veil as symbol of adherence to the Islamist movement, may be less than appears on the surface. Leila Ahmed suggests that a differentiation between the 'establishment Islam' rejected by the older feminists and the 'lay Islam' adopted by the younger Islamists may help clarify the situation. 'Establishment Islam', the 'Islam of the politically powerful' is 'authoritarian, implacably androcentric, and hostile to women' (Ahmed 1992: 225–6). This, however, is not the Islam with which veiled Islamist women sympathize and to which they are expressing their adherence by wearing the veil. For them, the Quran and

Islam are the source of an ethical teaching which affirms and supports the position of women. These different meanings of Islam 'are at the root of the profoundly different views of Islam held by the preceding generation of feminists and the current generation of women adopting Islamic dress. They are seeing and arguing about two different Islams' (ibid.: 226).

It is difficult to evaluate the longer-term impact of this 'lay Islamic' style of Muslim feminism. Ahmed suggests that while it has a real and 'perhaps unprecedented' potential for the advancement of Muslim women, it also runs the risk of being coopted by those who wish to create and enforce 'authoritarian theocratic states' and so have an ultimately destructive impact on women's condition (Ahmed 1992: 230–1). The point is arguable, but in the meantime one can recognize both the pragmatic logic of Muslim women working within Islamist movements, and the extent to which these movements can also provide women with a positive identity in a complex and changing world.

○  **Muslim women in western countries**

With this background in mind, I now turn to look at Muslim women in western countries today. Here I shall be looking primarily at women who are migrants (or children of migrants) from Muslim societies, rather than the much smaller number of western women who have converted to Islam, who perhaps understandably are usually strong supporters of ortho-dox Islamic values and opponents of 'western feminism'.[6]

Women in the West of Muslim migrant origins tend to be more aware of the problems with traditional Islamic social systems. Nevertheless, most such women choose, in public at least, to identify as traditional Muslims, while adopting elements from Islamist movements, such as the veil (i.e. *hijab*) and the critique of some traditional customs as 'cultural' rather than 'Islamic'. Others, particularly in the younger generation, may reject Islam altogether. The kinds of reformist position taken by Muslim feminists such as Leila Ahmed or Fatima Mernissi seem to be relatively unrepresented in the general community. In the remainder of this chapter, I look at two major positions adopted by Muslim women in western societies: accept-ance, with incorporation of 'Islamist' elements; and outright rejection.

Acceptance of traditional Islam was very evident in some research I carried out in Melbourne in 1990–91. This research was originally intended to be on health issues among Muslim women. In practice, it was dominated by questions of Islamic identity and relations with the host community. My respondents were young, well-educated, most having grown up in Australia, and they were very vocal and politicized. All wore either headscarves or a complete veil, and all those who veiled had started to use the veil fairly recently. A common response of my interviewees were that 'if the Australian [i.e. Anglo-Celtic] population changed their nega-tive attitudes about the Muslims we would have no problem, in the health system or anywhere else'. For these Muslim women, their main problem was one of misperception of Muslims by the non-Muslim Australians. They

were conscious of the media's role in generating various misperceptions
about them, and they were anxious to present me with a true picture of
Islam, as a religion which gives Muslim women rights to property, rights
of divorce, and the right to be maintained by husbands.

Such arguments and sentiments are typical also of the official self-
presentation of Muslim women in western countries. To give some further
Australian examples, Maha Abdo, the current President of the Muslim
Women's Association, at a seminar in Newcastle (Australia), talked of the
need to 'improv[e] people's understanding of the world's most misunder-
stood religion, i.e. Islam' (1993: 1). She argued that

> Islam placed both men and women on the same footing in economic
> independence, property rights, right to contract and legal processes.
> There is only one situation in which men are a degree over women.
> And that is because they are required to provide financially for the
> family and to protect them.
>
> (1993: 3)

Likewise, Nada Roude, the previous (and first) president of the association, described herself at a seminar in Sydney as hoping 'to correct just
some of the misconceptions held by the West about Islam and Muslim
women' (1992: 1). Her paper used Quranic quotations to argue that Islam
is all about equality and justice. In these and many other similar presen-
tations I have attended in Australia and the UK, problems experienced by
women in traditional Muslim societies are seen as cultural rather than
Islamic in origin. To quote Nada Roude again, here in an interview in a
popular Australian magazine:

> it is important for people to distinguish between what is essentially
> Islamic and what is traditional and culture specific. A lot of things are
> blamed on Islam that have their roots in specific ethnic cultures and
> this is unfortunate.
>
> (Musgrave 1989: 15)

Perhaps the most articulate spokeswoman for such positions has been the
Lebanese writer Rana Kabbani (now resident in the UK), whose *Letter to
Christendom* (1989), a sustained defence of Islam against western criticism,
I return to later.

In Australia, there are few publicly dissenting voices among Muslim
women, and attempts to express reformist positions are clearly unwelcome. Thus in 1992, when Imrana Jalal, a Fijian Muslim feminist, gave a
lecture in Sydney which argued for a moderate reformist position and
endorsed the principle of *ijtihad*, a violent argument ensued between Jalal
and a group of Muslim men whose wives and sisters had been attending
the talk. It was evident that male community leaders were unwilling to
tolerate any kind of overt critique of the position of women in Islamic
societies.

Traditional Islamic norms for women are particularly problematic for
young women growing up in western societies, who are caught between
the values of western societies and the demands of their parents that they

conform to strict Islamic norms in their behaviour (see Begic 1993). Such conflicts have led to intervention by government agencies such as the NSW Child Protection Council. The Australian Muslim Women's Association has taken an active role in attacking such interventions, justifying sexual segregation and the 'stringent control' of adolescent Muslim girls (for example, Maha Abdo in *The Australian Magazine*, 3–4 September 1994: 27).

The situation in the UK, with its larger and older migrant community, is somewhat different. Here oppositional positions, including radical rejection of Islam, have established themselves, if with considerable difficulty. Organizations such as Southall Black Sisters and Women Against Fundamentalism openly contest religious practices and cultural values, mounting an active struggle against what they see as oppression of women by their own communities.

Southall Black Sisters (SBS), an organization of Asian and Afro-Caribbean women, was set up in 1979. They defined themselves as 'black' in a political sense in order to unite 'on a common front against racism' (Siddiqui 1994: 20). SBS membership and its clients have mainly been Asians, though by no means exclusively Muslims, because Southall is an area heavily populated by Asians. Siddiqui pointed out that while the Asian community as a whole was ready to protest against racism in the UK, they were silent when it came to the oppression of women in their own communities. She cites cases such as that of a woman and her five daughters who had been killed by her husband simply because the woman had failed to give birth to sons. 'There was a need for us to organise as women, as Black women, within the community to address some of these issues which the community did not want to take up' (Siddiqui 1994: 20). In the area of domestic violence against women, SBS, the Organization of Women of African and Asian Descent, Birmingham Black Sisters and other similar women's associations have organized to confront sexual inequality within their own communities, and helped set up separate refuges for Asian women facing domestic violence (Trivedi 1984: 48).

SBS and its sister organizations were not only concerned with oppression of women within Asian and African communities. They have also been active in the unionization of women in the workplace; they protested against the virginity tests on Indian women at Heathrow airport, and they have been involved in providing information and counselling to women in relation to immigration problems, homelessness and childcare needs (Trivedi 1984: 48; Anthias and Yuval-Davis 1992: 103). However, as one might expect, they have met resistance from within the Asian community. The established male leadership of the Asian community, whether from the right or the left, saw them as a threat and tried to prevent their activities. In Southall, they tried to influence the local authority to cease funding the SBS's centre through threats and other means, and they have been successful in several cases in closing down hostels for young women. SBS have been labelled as homewreckers, as alien and westernized, with the implication that what they had to say was not an authentic expression of community attitudes.

Others advised SBS 'to maintain a silence on domestic violence because if we talked about the issue within the Asian communities we would create a racist backlash' (Siddiqui 1994: 23). These concerns are real; an analysis of women's oppression which links it to cultural, religious and communal factors can easily be taken up by racist ideologues, in whose hands any problem faced by members of minority communities simply becomes another stick with which to beat the minority community. SBS members were not blind to this possibility for they themselves had been involved in fighting against racist ideologues and had been involved in debates with white middle-class feminists on related themes (Davis 1981; Amos and Parmar 1984; Bryan *et al.* 1985; Bhavnani and Coulson 1986; Nain 1991), but they nevertheless felt that women's oppression within Asian and other minority communities could not be ignored.

In understanding why the (mostly male) leadership within minority communities is unwilling to address the oppression of women, we have to return to the wider context of communal and national politics. The rhetorics of multiculturalism and anti-racism continue to prioritize culture (which often becomes conflated with religious identity) at the expense of the class interests of 'ethnic' communities. Thus many 'ethnic' associations formed on the basis of caste, religion and cultural basis are dominated by elite men of particular communities. It is these leaders, who claim to speak for their community, to whom the state turns when seeking 'ethnic' opinion (Trivedi 1984: 48).

While the politics of SBS and similar organizations did not necessarily involve an attack on Islamist organizations as such, in practice their activities led them increasingly into confrontation with such movements. This confrontation came to a head at the time of the agitation about Salman Rushdie's *Satanic Verses*, and led to the creation of an explicitly anti-fundamentalist women's network, Women Against Fundamentalism (WAF) (Connolly 1991: 68). Women Against Fundamentalism's members came from different religious backgrounds. While 'not an antireligious organization' they claimed to be equally opposed to all religious 'fundamentalisms' (ibid.: 70). Thus WAF did not merely target Islamic fundamentalists, but also attacked the double standard of the British state in relation to Christianity and other non-Christian religions. Their founding statement called for 'the separation of state and religion in Britain as a precondition for defeating "fundamentalism"' (Connolly 1991: 69; see also Sahgal and Yuval-Davis 1992).

Thus WAF questioned the existence of 'an established church, closely connected to parliamentary institutions; a set of blasphemy laws which protect only the Christian denominations; and a state education system profoundly influenced by Christianity' (Connolly 1991: 69). They argued that this situation not only discriminated against non-Christians but also gave scope to other religious orthodoxies to demand similar provisions for their religion. In this way the Muslim fundamentalists' demand for the death of Salman Rushdie could come to seem reasonable and legitimate. Similarly, the established principle of state support for Christian denominational schools helped to legitimate demands for state-subsidized Muslim schools in which girls' sexuality could be policed while reinforcing 'their religiously defined roles as future wives and mothers' (Connolly 1991: 72; see also Khanum 1992).

WAF met considerable opposition within the Muslim community, both from male community leaders and from 'Islamist' women. A paradigmatic case was that of the 'Islamic feminist' author Rana Kabbani, who attacked WAF as 'the political equivalent of *The Satanic Verses*' and as contributing to the racist backlash against Islam. In a review of Kabbani's *Letter to Christendom* (1989), Hannana Siddiqui, a member of both SBS and WAF, pointed to the privileged class position from which Kabbani makes her criticisms. As a woman with a Cambridge education and an elite background in Syria, Kabbani could exploit the advantages of an Islamic identity in the West without falling a victim to patriarchal authority (Siddiqui 1991: 82). The working-class Muslim women whose problems Siddiqui encountered at the SBS centre did not have such freedom.

The conflict here is worth noting, because it points to the important class component underlying the identity and religious politics of Muslim communities in the UK. Women such as Kabbani could identify with what they see as the liberating potential of Leila Ahmed's 'lay Islam' in their own lives. The reality for Siddiqui's working-class clients is the 'establishment Islam' of the migrant community, with its traditionally oppressive attitudes towards women. It may well be true that most of the problems with 'establishment Islam' are cultural or political rather than 'Islamic' in origin, but this is little help to its working-class victims.[7]

## ○  Acknowledgements

I would like to acknowledge the facilities and resources made available to me by the Department of Religious Studies at Lancaster University while I was writing this chapter, and Geoffrey Samuel's editorial assistance. My research in Melbourne was supported by a grant from the University of Newcastle, New South Wales.

## ○  Questions

1  To western eyes veiling symbolizes the oppression of Muslim women and backwardness of Islamic culture in general. Yet today many Muslim women who were traditionally unveiled are adopting the veil in one form or another. Discuss the politics of veiling and re-veiling.

2  In communal politics women often become 'crucial symbols of communal identity and markers of "tradition" and culture', with adverse implications for women. Discuss.

3  Can we talk about Muslim feminisms? Discuss the different strategies adopted by different sections of Muslim women to deal with women's oppression in Islamic societies and in Islamic communities within western societies.

## Further reading

Ahmed (1992) does a meticulous job of analysing the developments in Islamic discourses on women and gender from the time of Muhammad to the present. Mernissi's book (1991) examines whether Islam is opposed to women's rights and argues that Islam is much more egalitarian than it has been interpreted to be by the Muslim male elite or portrayed to be in the *hadith*. The collections of articles in Moghadam (1994) and Kandiyoti (1991) illustrate well how women's status is integrally linked to communal, national and international politics, and how women come to symbolize the numerous 'boundaries'. The articles by Kandiyoti (1988), MacLeod (1992) and Moghadam (1993) are useful for understanding the different strategies adopted by modern day Muslim women. Several articles in Sahgal and Yuval-Davis (1992) deal with the situation of Muslim women in the West caught up in the politics of 'fundamentalism'.

## Notes

1 *Hijab* is the appropriate mode of clothing for a Muslim woman, often used to refer specifically to the head-covering. *Hijab* does not necessarily include covering the face, though 'all of the hair, the neck and arms must be covered' (Khattab 1994: 17).
2. Thus Yasmin Ali argues that 'few women in the non-metropolitan North of England are in any position to withstand the pressure to conform' (1992: 120).
3 Thus the constitution of the Islamic Republic of Iran 'advocated a set of patriarchal relations which strengthened male control over women in the family while granting women the right to be active participants in society' (Yeganeh 1993: 8–9). This is in line with Baykan's (1990) argument that 'fundamentalism' is not opposed to modernization but to 'modernism'. A similar point is made by Shaheed (1994) in relation to selective implementation of *shari'ah* (the Islamic law code).
4 See also Moghadam (1993: 250) and compare Laura Nader's argument that Said's 'orientalism' – the West's distorted construction of the East – needs to be complemented by 'occidentalism', the East's distorted construction of the West (Nader 1989). Nader argues that both eastern and western women go along, to a large extent, with the existing patriarchal structure because they are convinced that at least they are better off than the 'other' women.
5 Of course, this is not an exclusively Islamic phenomenon. The use of women as communal/national or other social group boundary markers is common across different cultural and religious groups as demonstrated by numerous studies on South Asia, the Middle East and the West. See, for example, Anthias and Yuval-Davis (1992).
6 Thus the Australian woman convert, Shifa Mustapha, a regular contributor to the *Australian Muslim Times*, sees feminism as a destructive force within Australia and as a dangerous influence on Muslim women:

Feminism has been a major tool of division in this country [Australia]. It has brought with it a great increase in divorce, sexual promiscuity, homosexuality, abortions, alcohol and drug abuse, as well as juvenile crime . . . Feminist, anti-Muslim texts are being taught to student teachers for use in the classrooms. The Muslim, particularly the Muslim woman, who sincerely lives her Islam, is the greatest threat to feminism in all countries.

*(Australian Muslim Times,* No. 58, 21 August 1992)

The British Muslim convert Huda Khattab, author of *The Muslim Woman's Handbook* (Khattab 1994) and editor of a monthly newsletter, *Usra – The Muslim Family Magazine,* is equally dismissive of the 'so-called liberation movement [which] has succeeded only in placing a double burden on women's shoulders' (1994: 30).

7 WAF and SBS work closely with the international network of Women Living Under Muslim Laws (WLUML), whose aims and objectives include 'the creation of international links between women from Muslim countries and communities and between Muslim women and other progressive feminists around the world' (Bard 1991: 89; see also Shaheed 1994: 1004).

## ○ References

Abdo, M. (1993) Women in Islamic faith. Paper presented at a seminar organized by the Migrant Resource Centre of Newcastle, Australia on 'Muslim Women in the Hunter', 27 July.

Ahmed, L. (1982) Feminism and feminist movements in the Middle East, a preliminary exploration: Turkey, Egypt, Algeria, People's Democratic Republic of Yemen, in A. Al-Hibri (ed.) *Women and Islam.* Oxford: Pergamon Press.

Ahmed, L. (1992) *Women and Gender in Islam: Historical Roots of a Modern Debate.* New Haven, CT: Yale University Press.

Ali, Y. (1992) Muslim women and the politics of ethnicity and culture in northern England, in G. Sahgal and N. Yuval-Davis (eds) *Refusing Holy Orders: Women and Fundamentalism in Britain.* London: Virago Press.

Amos, V. and Parmar, P. (1984) Challenging imperialist feminism, *Feminist Review,* 17: 3–20.

Anthias, F. and Yuval-Davis, N. (1992) *Radicalized Boundaries: Race, Nation, Gender, Colour and Class and the Anti-racist Struggle.* London: Routledge.

Bard, J. (1991) Review essay: generations of memories, *Feminist Review,* 37 (Spring): 85–94.

Baykan, A. (1990) Women between fundamentalism and modernity, in B. Turner (ed.) *Theories of Modernity and Postmodernity.* London: Sage.

Begic, A. (1993) 'Young Muslim women'. Paper presented at a seminar organized by the Migrant Resource Centre of Newcastle, Australia on 'Muslim Women in the Hunter', 27 July.

Bhavnani, K. and Coulson, M. (1986) Transforming socialist-feminism: the challenge of racism, *Feminist Review,* 23: 81–92.

Brooks, G. (1995) *Nine Parts of Desire: The Hidden World of Islamic Women.* New York: Doubleday.

Bryan, B., Dadzie, S. and Scafe, S. (1985) *The Heart of the Race: Black Women's Lives in Britain.* London: Virago Press.

Chhachhi, A. (1991) Forced identities: the state, communalism, fundamentalism and women in India, in D. Kandiyoti (ed.) *Women, Islam and the State.* Philadelphia, PA: Temple University Press.

Connolly, C. (1991) Washing our linen: one year of Women Against Fundamentalism, *Feminist Review,* 37 (Spring): 68–77.

El Saadawi, N. (1980) *The Hidden Face of Eve: Women in the Arab World*. London: Zed Books.

Jahan, R. (1975) Women in Bangladesh, in Women for Women's Research Group (eds) *Women for Women: Bangladesh 1975*. Dhaka: University Press.

Jeffery, P. (1979) *Frogs in a Well: Indian Women in Purdah*. London: Zed Press.

Kabbani, R. (1989) *Letter to Christendom*. London: Virago Press.

Kandiyoti, D. (1988) Bargaining with patriarchy, *Gender and Society*, 2(3): 274–90.

Kandiyoti, D. (ed.) (1991) *Women, Islam and the State*. Philadelphia, PA: Temple University Press.

Khanum, S. (1992) Education and the Muslim girl, in G. Sahgal and N. Yuval-Davis (eds) *Refusing Holy Orders: Women and Fundamentalism in Britain*. London: Virago Press.

Khattab, H. (1994) *The Muslim Woman's Handbook*, 2nd rev edn. London: Ta-Ha Publishers.

Lippman, T. W. (1990) *Understanding Islam: An Introduction to the Muslim World*. London: Penguin Books.

MacLeod, A. E. (1992) Hegemonic relations and gender resistance: the new veiling as accommodating protest in Cairo, *Signs*, 17: 533–57.

Mernissi, F. (1991) *The Veil and the Male Elite: A Feminist Interpretation of Women's Rights in Islam*. Reading, MA: Addison-Wesley [Also published by Blackwell's in Oxford in 1991 under the title of *Women and Islam: An Historical and Theological Enquiry*].

Mernissi, F. (1993) *Islam and Democracy: Fear of the Modern World*. London: Virago Press.

Milani, F. (1992) *Veils and Words: The Emerging Voices of Iranian Women Writers*. London: I. B. Tauris & Co.

Moghadam, V. (1993) Rhetoric and rights of identity in Islamist movements, *Journal of World History*, 4: 243–64.

Moghadam, V. (1994) *Gender and National Identity: Women and Politics in Muslim Societies*. London: Zed Books.

Musgrave, A. (1989) Islam: Come and get to know us, *ITA* December.

Nader, L. (1989) Orientalism, occidentalism and the control of women, *Cultural Dynamics*, 2(3): 323–55.

Nain, G. T. (1991) Black women, sexism and racism: black or antiracist feminism?, *Feminist Review*, 37: 1–21.

Najmabadi, A. (1991) Hazards of modernity and morality: women, state and ideology in contemporary Iran, in D. Kandiyoti (ed.) *Women, Islam and the State*. Philadelphia, PA: Temple University Press.

Odeh, L. (1993) Post-colonial feminism and the veil: thinking the difference, *Feminist Review*, 43: 26–37.

Papanek, H. (1982) Purdah: separate worlds and symbolic shelter, in H. Papanek and G. Minault (eds) *Separate Worlds: Studies of Purdah in South Asia*. New Delhi: Chanakya Publications.

Roude, N. (1992) 'Muslim women's perspective on justice and empowerment'. Paper presented at the National Muslim Women's Conference, Sydney 'Bridging the Gap', 9–12 October.

Rozario, S. (1992) *Purity and Communal Boundaries: Women and Social Change in a Bangladeshi Village*. London: Zed Books.

Sahgal, G. and Yuval-Davis, N. (1992) Introduction: fundamentalism, multiculturalism and women in Britain, in G. Sahgal and N. Yuval-Davis (eds) *Refusing Holy Orders: Women and Fundamentalism in Britain*. London: Virago Press.

Said, E. (1978) *Orientalism: Western Conceptions of the Orient*, London: Penguin Books.

Shaheed, F. (1994) Controlled or autonomous identity and the experience of the network, women living under Muslim laws, *Signs*, 19(4): 997–1019.

Siddiqui, H. (1991) Review essay: winning freedoms, *Feminist Review*, 37 (Spring): 78–84.

Siddiqui, H. (1994) Southall Black Sisters: Hannana Siddiqui speaks to Rasna Warah, *Manushi: A Journal About Women and Society*, 80: 20–7.

Stivens, M. (1994) Gender and modernity in Malaysia, in A. Gomes (ed.) *Modernity and Identity: Asian Illustrations*. Bundoora, Victoria: La Trobe University Press.

Tohidi, N. (1991) Gender and Islamic fundamentalism: feminist politics in Iran, in C. T. Mohanty, A. Russo and L. Torres (eds) *Third World Women and the Politics of Feminism*. Bloomington, IN: Indiana University Press.

Tohidi, N. (1994) Modernity, Islamization, and women in Iran, in V. Moghadam (ed.) *Gender and National Identity: Women and Politics in Muslim Societies*. London: Zed Books.

Trivedi, P. (1984) To deny our fullness: Asian women in the making of history, *Feminist Review*, 17 (Autumn): 37–50.

Winter, B. (1994) Women, the law, and cultural relativism in France: the case of Excision, *Signs*, 19(4): 939–74.

Yeganeh, N. (1993) Women, nationalism and Islam in contemporary political discourse in Iran, *Feminist Review*, 44 (Summer): 3–18.

# PART IV

## Women and political change

In this final part, we look at some ways you can act to change the situation of women. First, Penny Summerfield charts three powerful tendencies in the British women's movement in the nineteenth and twentieth centuries; then Sue Wise's chapter finds encouraging signs of where feminism is now. Next we change to a more international focus, and Consuelo Rivera Fuentes describes the women's movements in Latin America, and her involvement as an activist. Finally, the chapters by Ruth Henig and Kathleen Sullivan illustrate the contrast between women's resistance within and outside existing power structures: Ruth, herself an active politician, evaluates women's participation in government in Britain, and Kathleen outlines the 'alternative' world of ecofeminism in which she is involved.

## 19

**PENNY SUMMERFIELD**

# The women's movement in Britain from the 1860s to the 1980s

The history of the women's movement is commonly thought of as dividing into two waves. 'First wave feminism' is seen as starting around 1860 and subsiding after the parliamentary vote was won for women over 30 in 1918. The 'second wave' is thought of as springing up in 1968, reaching its peak in the 1970s and continuing to have effects into the 1990s. The simplicity of this chronology is compelling, but it has the disadvantage of ignoring the arguments against the unjust treatment of women that were made before 1860, and which indicate a longer history of resistance to male power. Further, the idea of two distinct waves creates the impression that there was no women's movement between 1918 and 1968.

In this chapter we shall focus on the relatively recent history of the women's movement, from 1860 to 1990. However, instead of dividing this period into waves and troughs, we shall discuss three tendencies in the women's movement, towards moral, welfare and equal rights goals, across the entire time span. Nancy Cott (1986) draws our attention to two tensions within feminism which we shall also explore: between arguments based on gender difference and equality, and between unity and diversity among women.

What did women find oppressive in 1860? A simple answer would be, 'their confinement in the "separate sphere" of femininity'. Nineteenth-century society was dominated by a highly polarized construction of masculinity and femininity. According to this view, men belonged in the public world of money-making, politics, military activity and intellectual life, where they protected and provided materially for women. Women were located in the private world of home and family where, through domestic and caring skills and the exercise of moral judgement, they provided for the needs both of their children and of their economically, physically and intellectually dominant husbands.

Even though poets and politicians saw the division of the spheres as natural and even divinely ordained, it was not always an accomplished

reality in the nineteenth century. The constraints of poverty, the absence
of opportunities for marriage because there were fewer men than women
in the population, as well as individual determination to live differently,
precipitated some women into the public sphere. But in spite of the exceptions, the separate spheres ideology exerted enormous pressure as a set of
prescriptive ideas. Nancy Cott sees it as 'both the point of oppression and
the point of departure for nineteenth century feminists' (Cott 1986: 51)
and Jane Rendall notes that even when women were campaigning for
equality 'all in some way used the language of difference, of separate
spheres' (Rendall 1987: 27). Much of that language was drawn from
religion, particularly evangelical Christianity, and it enabled women to
claim moral power, based on ideas of women's natural purity and moral
restraint.

## Moral feminism

A cluster of late nineteenth-century campaigns was addressed to issues of
morality and the body. The most famous is the campaign against the Contagious Diseases (CD) Acts led by Josephine Butler. The CD Acts were
passed between 1864 and 1869 and meant that women living in areas
where soldiers and sailors were stationed could be forced to undergo
medical examination for venereal disease on the grounds that the police
suspected them of being prostitutes. If a woman refused she could be
imprisoned, but if she acquiesced she was virtually admitting that she was
a prostitute. Women found to have VD were sent to special hospitals for a
repressive regime of correction and treatment.

The moral feminist argument against the Acts was that they were 'a plan
for providing healthy women for profligate men' (quoted Levine 1990:
91). They embodied the double standard of morality under which men
demanded morality and purity from their wives, while exercising their
own right to indulge in immorality and impurity with other women.
Josephine Butler and the Ladies National Association campaigned for the
repeal of the CD Acts on three specific grounds: women were held responsible for the consequences of a 'vice' for which men were really responsible; there were no checks on men's capacity for spreading disease (men
were not forced to undergo medical examinations in the same way); and
any woman who ventured out of her home into the public sphere of the
streets could be apprehended as a suspected prostitute (Walkowitz 1982).

The CD Acts were repealed in 1884, the age of consent was raised from
12 to 14 years of age, and official steps were taken against seduction and
child abuse. But the campaign to 'banish the brute' of male selfish and
violent sexual behaviour was by no means over. It continued in campaigns
for social purity from 1885 to 1914, which aimed to censor lewd enter-
tainment, to close brothels and to control prostitution (Bland 1995). It was
also present in demands for marriage reform made by the women of the
Men and Women's Club of the 1880s (Bland 1986) and in the pages of the
feminist journal *The Freewoman* between 1911 and 1914 (Jackson 1994).

These demands included the idea that men could subjugate their so-called uncontrollable urges, and that women had a right to sexual autonomy in marriage, that is to refuse sex and maternity. The idea of sexual freedom for women, so defined, was an element in the suffrage campaign of the 1910s, particularly under the guiding hand of Christabel Pankhurst who demanded 'Votes for Women, Chastity for Men' because she thought that women's political freedom would be meaningless if women remained subject sexually. Moral feminists wanted the vote to pursue the goal of an equal moral standard for men and women, and legislation did follow enfranchisement. It included raising the age of consent to 16 in 1922, and divorce reform in 1923, which made it possible for women, rather than men alone, to sue for divorce on the grounds of adultery.

Change occurred in the language in which the objectives of moral feminism were expressed, which was maligned as prudish and repressive in the 1920s and 30s. Later campaigns were based on the same principle, however, namely that male sexual and physical aggression must not be accepted as inevitable, but could be contained and controlled. These campaigns included the battle against pornography, the fight against male violence against women, such as the 'reclaim in the night' marches and the insistence upon women's refuges in the 1970s and 80s, and attempts to challenge sexual coercion and harassment at work in the 1980s and 90s. At stake were the issues of space and safety that moral feminists 100 years earlier had been wrestling with: could women in and out of their homes be 'free from all uninvited touch of man' (Jeffreys 1982)?

There were, however, problems of universality and diversity in the campaigns of the nineteenth-century moral feminists. They assumed that they were working on behalf of all women, but the universalisms of their claims trampled on the diverse needs of women. For example moral feminists found it difficult to see prostitutes as working women with rights and liberties, rather than victims who had been driven by seduction and poverty into vice from which they could be saved. In the tradition of middle-class philanthropy, which was often patronizing towards its working-class targets, they worked to 'rescue' and reform prostitutes through religion and training for respectable employment (Walkowitz 1982). In a similar way, middle-class women involved in the anti-slavery movement of the 1830s to the 1860s worked to free black women from slavery, but saw as the only alternative for the women they wrote of as 'sisters', a different type of subordination, that of obedient servants or domestic wives (Midgley 1992).

Did moral feminists' campaigns challenge the separate spheres ideology? Moral feminism was based on the view that women were fundamentally different from men, but its aim was equality, that is that the same moral code should apply to men and women. Unlike campaigns concerned with economic, political and educational matters, however, it did not demand that women should be allowed to behave as men did, but sought to bring men up to women's supposed moral standards. There are at least three respects in which it did challenge the separate spheres. It was opposed to the idea that it was natural and right for men to use and abuse women; it demanded for women the right to leave their homes and go out in public without fear of male violence; and it claimed a place for women in the public political sphere, where moral feminists staged their protest (Levine 1990).

However there were also two ways in which moral feminism was conformist. First, it was predicated on ideas of difference between male and female sexuality that were central to the notion of the separate spheres: masculinity involved an active, lustful sexuality, and femininity was passive and chaste, unless corrupted. Later feminists such as Stella Browne, Marie Stopes and Dora Russell challenged these ideas, demanding for women the right to express their sexuality actively and with enjoyment, and (through the use of birth control) without fear of pregnancy. This 1920s vision, however, was universalist in its view of heterosexuality as 'normal', and denied lesbians the right to the same freedom of expression (Jackson 1994). Second, moral feminism deployed separate spheres values, namely the sanctity of the home, men's responsibility as breadwinners towards it, and the vulnerability of women and children. This way of thinking was also central to the development of welfare feminism.

O **Welfare feminism**

It is often mistakenly thought that the suffrage movement was devoted to obtaining the vote as a symbol of equal rights and an end in itself. On the contrary, for many of the groups involved the vote was the means to the end of obtaining legislation that would promote social change. Working-class suffragists, such as the group of Lancashire textile workers organized by Selina Cooper, and the East London women led by Sylvia Pankhurst, argued for programmes which included better maternity and childcare facilities and family allowances (Liddington and Norris 1978). So too did members of working-class women's organizations linked to the labour movement, like the Women's Cooperative Guild founded in 1883 to promote the interests of the housewife. From 1870, working and middle-class suffragists involved themselves in local political work on school boards, Boards of Guardians, and, later, town and county councils. They were particularly involved with issues relating to health, food supply, education and morals, bringing into the public arena concerns that had traditionally resided in the private sphere, and seeing their work as a form of 'social motherhood' or 'public housekeeping' (Lewis 1984). The term 'welfare feminism' is used to describe such political activities relating to the role of women as wives and mothers.

Welfare feminism in the early twentieth century focused on the needs of poor women. For example the Women's Cooperative Guild (WCG) published a moving collection of accounts of pregnancy and childbirth in 1915, in the middle of a war in which there was much concern about the appalling loss of young male lives on the battlefield (Llewelyn Davies 1915/1977). The WCG's purpose was to put pressure on the government to pass a law giving all women the right to free ante- and postnatal care, adequate attention in childbirth, and maternity benefit. The campaign achieved partial success in 1918, when the Maternity and Child Welfare Act was passed, enabling local authorities to set up clinics for mothers and children. Other campaigns, for example for widows' pensions, for better maintenance allowances for women after separations, and for women's equal rights to the guardianship of children after divorce, also led to legislation in the 1920s, following the enfranchisement of women over 30. However, historians have pointed out that the new laws were passed relatively easily because governments wanted to appeal to the new female electorate and they often appeared more radical than they really were; their purpose was to strengthen the family, not to give women more independence (Banks 1981: 164; Smith 1990b: 52, 54).

It is not clear, however, that independence was welfare feminists' goal. Their central campaign from the First to the Second World War was for the 'endowment of motherhood'. The proposal, developed by Eleanor Rathbone and the Family Endowment Society, was originally for mothers to receive state payments in recognition of the importance to the state of motherhood. Rathbone argued that the scheme would raise the status of women in marriage by making them less dependent on their husbands, and remove the need for wives to add the burden of paid work to their primary task of homemaking (Smith 1990b: 57). Rathbone campaigned for family endowment from 1917 until 1945, but the scheme gradually altered. The payments for the support of mothers as well as children were whittled down to family allowances to alleviate child poverty and boost the falling birthrate. During the Second World War women's voluntary groups helped to implement the government policy of evacuating children from cities, and publicized the poverty and deprivation that evacuation revealed, contributing to mounting pressure for new forms of family support. But they did not keep alive the arguments for a mothers' wage. The eventual legislation, in 1945, introduced family allowances for second and subsequent children as a safety net against poverty. Only at Rathbone's insistence were the allowances paid to mothers, rather than being included in fathers' pay packets.

The 1945 family allowances did not approximate Rathbone's original ideas, but later feminists campaigned to enlarge and preserve them. During the 1970s feminists argued that women, especially the growing number of single mothers, rarely benefited from the tax relief for wives and children given to men. In 1979 the allowances paid to mothers and tax relief for fathers were replaced by Child Benefit, payable with respect to all children to whoever had day-to-day responsibility for them. These direct payments were welcomed by feminists, who continued to work with child poverty activists to defend child benefit in 1987–88, when the idea that it should be replaced by a means-tested tax benefit was mooted (Meehan 1990). Also in the 1970s the idea that wives should be paid was revived in the 'wages for housework' campaign. This differed from the 'endowment of motherhood' proposals, in that it was based on the idea of the vital part that unpaid domestic labour played in the maintenance of both male power and the capitalist economy, rather than on the idea of the dependence of the state on motherhood (Rowbotham 1989).

Where did welfare feminism stand in terms of gender difference and equality? Olive Banks (1981: 167) argues that it accepted as unchangeable the social differences arising from the different reproductive functions of men and women, and 'sought to recognize and enhance women's function as wives and mothers' on the assumption that maternity was central to women's lives. Welfare feminism focused on improving life for women within the separate sphere rather than facilitating new roles, and was suspect in the eyes of some equal rights feminists in the 1920s because of this. For example, Lady Rhondda, an ex-suffragette who established the feminist weekly *Time and Tide* in 1920, argued that the focus on maternity meant accepting men's view of women's role, as a result of which, even if much-needed reforms were obtained, they would do little to alter women's lives (Smith 1990b: 50–1). A number of feminists left the main feminist organization of the 1920s, the National Union of Societies for Equal Citizenship, of which Rathbone was president, in 1927. They did so not because they disagreed with the endowment of motherhood and other welfare proposals as such, but because they did not like the way these goals were being prioritized over equal rights proposals (Banks 1981: 170).

The universalism of the welfare feminists' claims was also resented by some women. Family endowment apparently had little to offer women who did not see maternity as their exclusive role. They included women who wanted support against the marriage bars which prevented women who married continuing to work, and single women who were committed to long-term careers and whose main interest was in equal pay. Rathbone's original proposal, however, was intended to recognize spinsters' needs. Family endowment would open the door to equal pay, since there would no longer be any need for a 'breadwinner element' in men's wages. This appealed to some labour movement women's organizations, which supported both family endowment and equal pay, while others, including some members of the Women's Cooperative Guild were lukewarm; family endowment might undermine the independence married women derived from earning a wage (Smith 1990b: 58).

The plight of women in poverty was a real one, however, as a survey published by a women's health enquiry group, under the title *Working-Class Wives*, indicated in 1939 (Spring Rice 1939/1980). The appeal of welfare feminism was that it addressed real problems affecting ordinary women, such as health, housing, pregnancy and childbirth, in a concrete way. Just as moral feminism was made to appear outdated, narrow and prudish in the 1920s, so welfare feminism made demands for equal rights for women seem old fashioned and selfish.

## ○ Equal rights feminism

The exclusion of women from political citizenship was an insult that mobilized vast numbers of women. The suffrage campaign gave the women's movement a powerful focus from 1866 to 1928, in which year women were finally granted the vote on the same terms as men. But the demand for the vote was one among a number of campaigns geared, in Harriet Taylor Mill's words, to 'equal rights, equal admission to all social privileges' (Mill 1851/1983: 42). Another was the struggle to change the law under which a husband took possession of his wife's property, including her earnings, when he married her. Following a campaign which began in the 1850s, the Married Woman's Property Act was passed in 1882. It established that a wife could legally possess separate property from her husband. However it was only a beginning; feminists were still fighting for married women's right to their savings as well as their earnings in 1943 (Banks 1981: 175), and for wives to be taxed separately from their husbands in 1988 (Meehan 1990: 199). There were also major nineteenth-century campaigns for women's rights to the same education as men, conducted by figures such as Emily Davies and Elizabeth Garrett-Anderson. They demanded academic schooling, professional training in medicine and law, and university degrees for girls and women (Purvis 1991). The challenge to male privileges implied by all these campaigns provoked considerable opposition. Perhaps less well known, but equally significant for women, are the struggles over women's employment rights.

One way in which the nineteenth-century ideology of the separate spheres was expressed was through regulations banning women from certain types of work, in the name of the protection of womanhood. For example the 1842 Mines Act prohibited women from working underground in mines, and trade union agreements banned women from various industrial processes, such as compositing and some types of cotton spinning. The justifications were threefold: women were not competent to do work that was heavy or skilled; the work involved indecent dress and contact with men; and women's proper place was at home. In 1874 Emma Paterson formed the Women's Protective and Provident League (WPPL) to campaign against such regulations. Her argument was simple: rather than genuinely protecting women, the regulations imposed restrictions on their opportunities for work and should be removed (Bradley 1989; Rose 1992).

The demand was controversial. Much nineteenth-century employment was exploitative, with deadly consequences for the men and women who did it. Protection of women from excessive hours in mills and public houses, and from heavy work in foundries and at the pit-head, seemed humane to middle-class trade unionists and suffragists. From the 1880s to the 1900s, however, women workers in the trades just mentioned rejected protection, preferring to keep their jobs. The WPPL was superseded in 1889, and women's trade unionism moved away from Paterson's uncompromising stand, accepting protection and working for women to join men's unions, and for an end to the super-exploitation of women as 'sweated labour'. Women workers were divided on the issue of industrial protection. Some argued that women needed it as a ring-fence round a vulnerable workforce. Others wanted legislation that would protect *both* sexes from adverse conditions of work, rather than exclude women (Strachey 1928/1978; Smith 1990b).

The issue of barriers to women's employment affected middle as well as working-class women. Equal rights feminists campaigned for the Sex Disqualification (Removal) Act of 1919, which allowed women entry to previously forbidden professions like law and accounting. Hopes that it would outlaw marriage bars, too, were dashed by a hairsplitting legal judgement in 1923; while sex and marriage did not disqualify a woman, neither did they entitle her to a job. Marriage bars were imposed by statute in 1922 on women in public service, and were the practice in many other types of employment. In 1927 the National Union of Societies for Equal Citizenship (NUSEC) sponsored a bill to remove them, but it failed, in part because the labour movement was not keen to add to competition for jobs and in part because of fears for the birthrate if more married women worked. Meanwhile more bills proposing further protective legislation exclusively for women were introduced. In 1926 Lady Rhondda formed the Open Door Council to oppose them, and to demand equal pay, equal status and equal opportunities for all women workers. But she did not get the support of welfare feminists in the NUSEC, who voted in favour of protective legislation in the name of the vulnerability of women. Labour women's organizations portrayed the claim for 'a fair field and no favour' as a middle-class ideal which bore no relation to the realities of working-class life (Graves 1994).

Protective legislation, establishing different conditions of work for women and men, was seen as contributing to the segregation of women in the workforce, and hence to the difficulty of achieving equal pay. During the Second World War equal rights feminists tried to take advantage of the dependence of the government on the increasing numbers of women in the workforce, by insisting on equal pay and the removal of restrictions on women's employment. They were not successful. Equal pay was limited to those few women directly replacing men on a temporary basis, and an attempt to build equal pay for teachers into an Education Bill in 1944 was defeated by the intervention of the Prime Minister himself (Summerfield 1989: 174). The issue of equal pay was deflected to a Royal Commission. Its cautious recommendations in 1946 led to another decade of campaigning, culminating in 1955 in agreements that equal pay would be introduced for female civil servants and teachers in identical jobs to men. During the 1960s women in trade unions and professional organizations worked for the extension of equal pay and against the restriction of women's employment opportunities, achieving the Equal Pay and Sex Discrimination Acts of 1970 and 1975. But the segregation of women in the workforce, a product in part of the regulations against which Emma Paterson had campaigned 100 years earlier, continues to plague the achievement of equal pay and equal opportunities at work.

In conclusion, the concept of two waves in the British women's movement encourages the view that rights for women became 'a dead issue' between 1918 and 1968 (Pugh 1990: 160). This, as we have seen, was far from the case. The three strands of feminism discussed here separated at some points in the period 1860–1990, particularly in the 1920s, when long-term tensions came to a head, caused by opposed universalisms based on constructions of social class, and manifest in divergent emphases on gender difference and equality. Even these tensions did not prevent women with different feminist principles working together, however, and the strands became intertwined at other times, particularly in the 1960s and 70s. What is often underestimated in assessments of the women's movement is both its own resilience, and the formidable opposition to women who dared to challenge the gendered social hierarchy.

○ **Questions and exercises**

> 1 Pretend it is 1900. Divide yourselves into three groups: moral, welfare and equal rights feminists. Each group should draw up a programme designed to improve women's position, and then present it to and discuss it with the other groups.
>
> 2 Did nineteenth-century feminists' starting point within constructions of feminine difference make it difficult for them to challenge the concepts of masculine dominance and feminine subordination inherent in the ideology of the separate spheres?
>
> 3 In what ways does the history of the women's movement illuminate Nancy Cott's statement 'it is too easy and mistaken to expect that women's interests are "normally" a unity' (Colt 1986: 58)?

○ **Further reading**

> There are now a number of histories of the women's movement in the nineteenth and early twentieth centuries, though Strachey (1928/1978) remains unsurpassed as a gripping account. The collection edited by Rendall (1987) (and her introduction) are particularly useful on feminism before 1860. Levine (1990) offers thoughtful interpretations of the period 1850 to 1900, particularly of moral feminism, and Caine (1992) provides fascinating biographical sketches of some leading Victorian feminists. There is a short account of the suffrage movement, which sets it in a European context, in Anderson and Zinsser (1988). Harrison (1978), Liddington and Norris (1978), Vicinus (1985), Holton (1986) and Kent (1987) contribute perspectives which must not be overlooked. For a discussion of women in the trade union movement readers should consult the chapters by Thom and by Bornat in John (1986) as well as the comprehensive account provided by Lewenhak (1977). Cott (1986) provides a useful conceptual framework. Banks (1981) compares the British and American women's movements over the period 1840 to 1970. The collection edited by Smith (1990a) offers some thought-

provoking alternative interpretations, particularly of the interwar years, to which Alberti (1989) adds valuable biographical sketches. Pugh (1992) focuses on the 40 years following enfranchisement, arguing that the cult of domesticity displaced feminism in women's lives. Stacey and Price (1981) are useful on the 1960s, and accounts of more recent developments can be found in Coote and Campbell (1987) and Rowbotham (1989).

○ **References**

Anderson, B. S. and Zinsser, J. P. (1988) *A History of their Own. Women in Europe from Prehistory to the Present*. London: Penguin Books.

Alberti, J. (1989) *Beyond Suffrage. Feminists in War and Peace 1914–28*. London: Macmillan.

Banks, O. (1981) *Faces of Feminism: A Study of Feminism as a Social Movement*. Oxford: Martin Robertson.

Bland, L. (1986) Marriage laid bare: middle-class women and marital sex, c.1880–1914, in J. Lewis (ed.) *Labour and Love. Women's Experience of Home and Family 1850–1940*. Oxford: Blackwell.

Bland, L. (1995) *Banishing the Beast: English Feminism and Sexual Morality 1885–1914*. London: Penguin.

Bradley, H. (1989) *Men's Work, Women's Work. A Sociological History of the Sexual Division of Labour in Employment*. Cambridge: Polity.

Caine, B. (1992) *Victorian Feminists*. Oxford: Oxford University Press.

Coote, A. and Campbell, B. (1987) *Sweet Freedom, The Struggle for Women's Liberation*. Oxford: Blackwell.

Cott, N. (1986) Feminist theory and feminist movements: the past before us, in J. Mitchell and A. Oakley (eds) *What Is Feminism?* Oxford: Blackwell.

Graves, P. (1994) *Labour Women. Women in British Working-class Politics 1818–1939*. Cambridge: Cambridge University Press.

Harrison, B. (1978) *Separate Spheres: The Opposition to Women's Suffrage in Britain*. London: Croom.

Holton, S. S. (1986) *Feminism and Democracy: Women's Suffrage and Reform Politics in Britain, 1900–1918*. Cambridge: Cambridge University Press.

Jackson, M. (1994) *The Real Facts of Life: Feminism and the Politics of Sexuality c.1850–1940*. London: Taylor and Francis.

Jeffreys, S. (1982) 'Free from all uninvited touch of man': women's campaigns around sexuality 1880–1914, *Women's Studies International Forum*, 5(6): 629–45.

John, A. V. (ed.) (1986) *Unequal Opportunities*. Oxford: Blackwell.

Kent, S. K. (1987) *Sex and Suffrage in Britain 1860–1914*. Princeton, NJ: Princeton University Press.

Levine, P. (1990) *Feminist Lives in Victorian England. Private Roles and Public Commitment*. Oxford: Blackwell.

Lewenhak, S. T. (1977) *Women and Trade Unions*. London: Benn.

Lewis, J. (1984) *Women in England 1870–1950. Sexual Divisions and Social Change*. Brighton: Harvester.

Liddington, J. and Norris, J. (1978) *One Hand Tied Behind Us: The Rise of the Women's Suffrage Movement*. London: Virago.

Llewelyn Davies, M. (ed.) (1915/1977) *Maternity: Letters from Working Women*. London: Virago.

Meehan, E. (1990) British feminism from the 1960s to the 1980s, in H. Smith (ed.) *British Feminism in the Twentieth Century*. Aldershot: Edward Elgar.

Midgley, C. (1992) *Women against Slavery. The British Campaigns 1780–1870*. London: Routledge.

Mill, H. T. (1851/1983) *Enfranchisement of Women*. London: Virago.

Pugh, M. (1990) Domesticity and the decline of feminism 1930–1950, in H. L. Smith (ed.) *British Feminism in the Twentieth Century*. Aldershot: Edward Elgar.

Pugh, M. (1992) *Women and the Women's Movement in Britain 1914–1959*. London: Macmillan.

Purvis, J. (1991) *A History of Women's Education in England*. Milton Keynes: Open University Press.

Rendall, J. (ed.) (1987) *Equal or Different. Women's Politics 1800–1914*. Oxford: Blackwell.

Rose, S. O. (1992) *Limited Livelihoods. Gender and Class in Nineteenth-Century England*. London: Routledge.

Rowbotham, S. (1989) *The Past is Before Us: Feminism in Action Since the 1960s*. London: Penguin.

Smith, H. L. (ed.) (1990a) *British Feminism in the Twentieth Century*. Aldershot: Edward Elgar.

Smith, H. L. (1990b) British feminism in the 1920s, in H. L. Smith (ed.) *British Feminism in the Twentieth Century*. Aldershot: Edward Elgar.

Spring Rice, M. (1939/1980) *Working-class Wives, their Health and Conditions*. London: Virago.

Stacey, M. and Price, M. (1981) *Women, Power and Politics*. London: Tavistock.

Strachey, R. (1928/1978) *The Cause: A Short History of the Women's Movement in Great Britain*. London: Virago.

Summerfield, P. (1989) *Women Workers in the Second World War. Production and Patriarchy in Conflict*. London: Routledge.

Vicinus, M. (1985) *Independent Women*. London: Virago.

Walkowitz, J. (1982) Male vice and feminist virtue: feminism and the politics of prostitution in nineteenth-century Britain, *History Workshop*, 13: 79–93.

# Feminist activism: continuity and change

I myself have never been able to find out precisely what feminism is:
I only know that people call me a feminist whenever I express sentiments
that differentiate me from a doormat.

Rebecca West

○ **Introduction**

Anti-feminist commentators have argued that the feminist movement of
the late twentieth century, rather than promoting the interests of women,
is instead the source of our current problems (Lyndon 1992; Quest 1994).
Feminist writers have suggested, in a slightly more sophisticated argument,
that the feminist movement may have become counter-productive by producing a 'victim' mentality in women which prevents us from getting 'in
touch' with our real 'power' (Paglia in Benn 1994; Wolf 1994). Alongside
the expression of such views, usually seen as part of the anti-feminist
'backlash' (Faludi 1992), other feminists have suggested that feminist
activism is in terminal decline; younger women do not see its relevance,
while older activists, politicized in the 1960s and 1970s, are either 'burned
out' or have become incorporated into the 'establishment', or else are plain
tired of the painful splits and divisions that the recognition of 'difference'
has brought (Coward 1994).[1] So, has feminist activism outlived its useful-
ness, or not?

Feminist activism in Britain is supposed to have died on a number of
occasions before, perhaps most famously in the period between the so-
called 'first wave' and 'second wave' of feminism. But, as I shall go on to
argue, now as well as then, it may be that reports of the demise of feminism are both premature and exaggerated. In spite of the glee with which
the media has exploited 'backlash' arguments I shall argue that feminist
activism is not only alive but positively flourishing. Many of the issues that
concerned both first wave (Victorian and Edwardian feminism, including
the suffragettes, up to the first world war) and second wave (the women's
liberation movement [WLM], beginning in the late 1960s and petering out
in this particular form in the 1980s) feminist movements are still relevant
to the majority of women today. Moreover, there are interesting continuities between the two 'waves', both in the *kinds* of issues addressed and

the *ways* in which they were addressed, as well as crucial differences. I shall use this chapter to explore some of these continuities and changes.

## ○ What is feminist activism?

We need to define what we mean by 'feminist activism' in order to determine how it has changed or remained the same, and if it still exists today. Our first step therefore is to ask what is 'feminist activism'? Does feminist activism consist only in organized campaigns collectively undertaken, or can it be undertaken by individuals? For example, can activities such as raising children in a non-sexist way be seen as feminist activism, or does it, by definition, have to involve organized campaigning around a public policy issue? What about feminists producing art and writing and performing poetry – is this purely individual activity or is it a political response to collective issues and analyses? Are students taking a Women's Studies course engaged in feminist activism?

In fact all these activities have been considered feminist activism, both by feminists of the last century and also of this. Feminism has always been concerned, not only with the more conventional forms of political activism such as single issue campaigning and pressure group politics, but also with producing its own cultural artefacts, with education, with self-help, and with what has come to be called lifestyle politics. 'The personal is the political' has been a defining feature of British feminism because it has always been concerned with changing women's – and men's – everyday lives in the here and now, and not just for future generations.[2] Feminist theorizing does not exist for its own sake, but is part of a complex process of making a revolution for change. In order to successfully change the world we must first understand how it operates; theorizing and then acting on the basis of feminist experience – what is called 'feminist praxis' – is crucial. Feminist theory is completely intertwined with practice – it both informs it and is derived from it, and its relationship to activism is crucial – otherwise theory becomes empty rhetoric.

## ○ Types of feminist activism

Feminist activism has taken a wide variety of forms, from very high profile law breaking and civil disobedience, through to what can seem utterly mundane, like departing from convention in styles of dress or hair length, or simply refusing, as West suggests, to be treated like a doormat. However, when most people think about feminist activism, it is the more public and visible activities that come to mind because of the way in which the media focuses upon these. Indeed, this portrayal of 'popular knowledge' about feminism by the mass media is in itself one of the continuities between first wave and second wave feminisms in Britain. Direct action and civil disobedience, in the form of Edwardian suffragettes chaining themselves to railings, burning down buildings, slashing paintings in the National

Gallery, and WLM feminists in the 1960s and 1970s disrupting the Miss World contest, camping out at, and encircling Greenham Common, attacking sex shops, and marching to 'reclaim the night', have come to popular attention via the media. They are therefore accessible to being reclaimed as feminist history, yet, as I have already suggested, activism can take a number of different forms – some of them perhaps less newsworthy, yet each of them equally valid and effective.

The model or typology below sketches types of feminist activism, moving from the most public and therefore, in conventional terms, most political, through to the apparently more private and conventionally not thought of as political at all. It concentrates on specifically feminist/women's activism, rather than mixed campaigning, where feminists may have had an input. However, it is important to note that within some mixed campaigns, such as the Victorian anti-vivisection and animal rights campaigns, feminists played a leading role.

### Direct action

Direct action consists of activities which ignore or deliberately flout what is lawful, to engage in action which falls short of riot or revolt but which does engage publicly with the forces of law and order, often with the intention of being arrested and brought to trial. First wave feminist forms of direct action have included suffragettes mass-stoning shop windows in the West End of London, burning down buildings and firing post boxes, while second wave WLM feminists have tended to be more law-abiding, but have been involved in attacking sex shops, and in causing criminal damage and trespass at places such as Greenham Common.

### Civil disobedience

Civil disobedience is another form of direct action, but consists of activities which may or may not be unlawful in themselves but which, undertaken *en masse* and in public, add up to a major flouting of civil codes of behaviour and conventions. First wave examples of civil disobedience involved suffragettes chaining themselves to railings and gathering in large numbers in public places, or refusing to pay taxes on the principle of 'no taxation without representation'. Examples of second wave civil disobedience are considerably harder to find, with the exception of the non-law breaking events at Greenham, which is perhaps indicative of an interesting difference between the first wave and the second wave.

### Pressure group politics

Pressure group politics consist of activities engaged in by organized groups for some specific political end, usually of a 'single issue' kind. The aim here is to engage with mainstream structures and institutions, such as the parliamentary process, in order to try and make changes through existing 'democratic' processes. Examples of feminist forms of pressure group politics include mid-nineteenth-century campaigns concerned with presenting petitions in support of women's suffrage to Parliament, married women's property rights and financial assistance for separated women and their children, and demanding the repeal of the Contagious Diseases Acts, while, later, there were campaigns in support of 'tactical voting' at elections. In the WLM era pressure group campaigns included the successful defence against many attacks on the 1967 Abortion Act, which gave women the right to free and safe abortion within the NHS. In addition, WLM feminists lobbied for the provision of nurseries, and for the introduction of legislation for equal pay and against sex and marital status discrimination.

### Self-help groups and organizations

Self-help involves women producing autonomous resources, so that they are not dependent on mainstream institutions which may discriminate against them, or simply be oblivious to their needs. Self-help has been a tremendously important aspect of feminist activism, not only in providing much-needed practical services for women that would otherwise not have existed, but also in the way in which self-help eschews the 'expert' and authority status of male-dominated institutions by saying, 'we will do it for ourselves'. Mid-nineteenth century feminist self-help organizations included half-way houses for 'delinquent' children, and suffragette activities included the establishment of feminist presses, newspapers, shops and other kinds of services. In the WLM era, self-help is perhaps best known through its establishment of refuges for women and children on the receiving end of male violence and rape crisis centres dealing with all kinds of sexual assaults. The establishment of well-women groups were also crucial in challenging the medical profession's indifference to women's health problems.

### Cultural activities

Cultural activities may seem non-political, even antithetical to politics, because they are concerned with 'culture', with literature, poetry, the theatre, music. However, feminism, along with other radical movements, has pointed out that what is seen as 'culture' is a product of who has the power to define it thus. Feminist interventions into the cultural sphere have insisted upon 'cultural politics', overturning canonical ideas about culture and those who produce it. Thus suffragette cultural politics included the establishment of suffragette studios, and the use of art within political signs and symbols such as Sylvia Pankhurst's designs for suffragette flags, badges and banners. The written word, in prose and poetry, has also made a feminist impact: in the interwar period, writers such as Virginia Woolf rewrote the modernist form and overturned its canon in explicitly feminist ways; and in the WLM period poets such as Adrienne Rich, June Jordan and Audre Lorde used poetry as a medium to develop language which women could use to articulate experiences for which there had been previously no common idiom.

## Education

Education is a form of feminist activism concerned with the radical potential of learning to transcend oppressive or limiting conditions (the film *Educating Rita* depicts a good example of this). Indeed, 'knowledge is power' was a sentiment shared by many British radical movements during the last century and this. More recently the feminist potential of education has come to be associated primarily with 'women's studies' within the formal confines of further and higher education, although it is important to remember that earlier feminists emphasized self-help and provided a radical critique of education in all its formal varieties.[3] In mid-nineteenth century feminism, there were important and successful campaigns to open up both school and university education to women, even though feminists fervently disagreed with the forms of education provided in these establishments; in the suffragette period, these campaigns continued, but also groups of feminists were involved in non-incorporationist forms of education – within the Worker's Education Association (WEA) and trades unions, for example. Later, in the WLM period there was much support for the free school movement, informally arranged reading and study groups, as well as other forms of education outside of formal structures.

## Lifestyle politics

To call this form of feminist activism by the term 'lifestyle *politics*' immediately places a feminist value upon activities conventionally seen as the antithesis of politics because they occur within the private and domestic domain. Thus for feminism, the conduct of relationships, vegetarianism as a moral code for mediating the relationship between people and animals, what clothes are worn, how children are raised, the choice between celibacy and sexual relationships, and a host of other 'everyday' activities and behaviours are seen as part of the complex nexus of 'the political'. Mid-nineteenth-century feminists were concerned with the abolition of slavery, animal rights, the regulation of relationships between married partners, rights over – and the rights of – children, and 'rational dress'; suffragette politics encompassed English 'rural revivalism', including morris dancing, quilt-making and crocheting, as well as vegetarianism and animal rights; and WLM lifestyle politics included questioning the 'naturalness' of heterosexuality, forms of communal living and attempts to subvert capitalist forms of market production.

The above 'model' or 'typology', by definition, is a simplistic representation of a reality that is considerably more complex. Elsewhere (in Stanley and Wise 1993) I have cautioned that typologies should always be used carefully, since they paint a static and rigid picture of something which is always in a state of flux and change, and where overlaps between 'types' are common. Thus while this typology enables a present-day commentator to sketch out 'types of feminist activism', readers need to keep in mind that these activities flow into each other; that at one point in time an activity can be 'more private' and concerned with lifestyle politics, at others 'more public' and concerned with formal and conventional political engagements. And, perhaps most importantly of all, it needs to be remembered that there were not, and are not, separate groups of women who engage in these different kinds of feminist activism, but rather the same women can be engaged in some or all of them, and this can change over time.

## ○ The in-between years?

For a long time researchers argued that, following the extension of the parliamentary franchise to women in 1918 (property holders) and 1928 (complete adult suffrage), feminism disappeared until its rebirth in the 1960s. This view was largely based on the misconception that virtually all feminist activism up until that time was focused on winning the vote, and that once this was achieved, the victory had been won. From this viewpoint, 1960s second wave feminism owed its origins to social movements in the US for black civil rights, against the Vietnam war, and anti-psychiatry, and from thence to British Marxist feminism, and the Ruskin College conference in which socialist women formulated an analysis of sexism and accompanying demands for change (see Coote and Campbell 1987, and Rowbotham 1989 for their accounts of this).

More recent work on the post-suffrage period (Alberti 1989) challenges the idea that feminist activism stopped after the Edwardian period and points out that the nature of politics changed in all manner of ways over this time. Thus there was an active feminism between the wars, albeit with a different emphasis, analytically and practically, from the earlier period. Post-1945, although in dwindling numbers, these now ageing feminists continued their campaigns. Similarly, Spender (1983, 1984) was also able to find ample evidence to support the existence of a continuous feminist activist presence in Britain, leading her to assert that 'there's always been a women's movement this century'.

Yet for younger women, the events of the 1960s certainly felt like inventing (rather than reinventing) the wheel, and there was perceived to be no recent history of feminist activism to draw on and feel a continuity with. There are numerous possible reasons for this, but a major factor was the simple lack of information in the public domain about the existence and activities of the vast army of feminists who had gone before. With the exception of the suffrage campaigns (and even these were then sparsely documented), little existed in the way of feminist literature or feminist history. For young women of today, used to seeing shelves of feminist textbooks, periodicals and fiction in bookshops and in libraries, and to hearing and seeing (albeit usually in negative terms) depictions of feminists issues and feminists in the mass media, it is almost impossible to imagine a time less than 30 years ago, when there was virtually nothing. Whether we conclude that the 'disappearing' of feminism was accidental or a conspiracy of silencing, the fact remains that emergent feminists of the 1960s and 1970s had very little history to draw on.

○ **Continuities and changes**

There were similarities in the ways in which first wave and second wave feminists enacted their political agenda, but also in the very agenda itself, involving issues such as: work and health; sex and desire; culture and education; violence and peace; human and animal rights; and family and children. There were also clear differences between the two periods, most clearly in forms of organization and in the personal cost of involvement in feminist activity.

Victorian and Edwardian feminist activism has two striking features. First, a very large number of independent single issue campaigning bodies existed without there being any one central coordinating group or organization. Perhaps the nearest to such a thing was the National Union of Women's Suffrage Societies; however, this was concerned with suffrage groups only, and a large number, perhaps even the majority, of feminist groups and organizations across this period were concerned with other, although related, issues. The second feature is the complex way in which these activities and groups, apparently fragmented, achieved overall coherence through the medium of 'feminist networks', through links of friendship and comradeship across apparently different political agendas. Thus across the formal organizational fragmentations existed an informal organizational network linked by powerful ties of comradeship.

In contrast, the WLM attempted to produce an umbrella organization which could appeal to all women through its 'manifesto' of seven demands. These demands were thought to be a comprehensive expression of the needs of all women at the time, and graphically illustrate the problems of exclusion felt so bitterly by women of colour and later by disabled and older women. The demands were for:

1 equal pay;
2 equal education and job opportunities;
3 free contraception and abortion on demand;
4 free 24-hour nurseries, under community control;
5 legal and financial independence;
6 an end to discrimination against lesbians;
7 freedom from intimidation by the threat or use of violence or sexual coercion, regardless of marital status.

In short the WLM wanted an end to the laws, assumptions and institutions that perpetuate male dominance and men's aggression towards women.

These demands formed the basis of many of the campaigns of the WLM. The WLM was based around a perceived anti-structure of a multiplicity of local consciousness-raising groups meeting together at annual conferences which formulated 'policy for activism'. Nevertheless, women did talk about being a 'member' of the WLM, and it did produce a feel of being a national movement with a coherent programme of activism. Ostensibly the key feature of the WLM was its lack of leaders and its informal anti-organization; there was no formal organization to join, no leaders and no followers. However, standing back from the rhetoric something rather different can be observed: what emerged was a clear organizational structure which produced its own distributions of status, power and control and its own anti-leaders. It is this which is the prime difference from the earlier period: a relatively formalized single organizational structure characterized 'the movement', rather than the organizational fragmentation coupled with informal networking of the earlier period.

Another key area of difference is that the risks involved in being a feminist activist changed markedly between the two periods, especially in relation to the more public forms of activism. In the Victorian and Edwardian period, feminists frequently – literally – took their lives into their hands by acting independently and taking up public space. Thus Josephine Butler spoke in public about the sexual exploitation of children, an 'unspeakable' topic, and experienced serious attempts on her life as a direct result. Perhaps an even more dramatic example was the events of so-called 'Black Friday', when publicly protesting feminists were subject to all manner of physical and sexual assaults, from the police as well as from outraged 'men in the street', while the forced feeding of suffragette prisoners was a state-enacted form of punishment on women who dared to redefine their public, as well as political, role. So many women of this period paid with their lives or their liberty for 'the cause', something that was almost unthinkable for the second wave. While inevitably some women were arrested at demonstrations, and many were arrested time and again during the Greenham Common campaign, the risks attached to second wave public feminist activism were considerably smaller because earlier feminists had created the right for women to occupy public space.[4]

## ○ The 1990s: post-feminism – again?

'The decline of feminism' thesis, beloved of the popular media, works only in relation to the WLM 'over-arching model' of feminist activism. What exists now in the 1990s, stripped of interpretive tags such as 'post-feminism', is a situation characterized by fragmentations, relatively few single issue campaigns, no central formal organizational structure, and an emphasis upon cultural, self-help, educational and 'lifestyle' forms of activism.[5] We can read this as feminism in decline, or we can read it, as I do, as a return to many of the defining attributes of first wave feminism.

The return to a more diffuse form of feminism in Britain resulted from a number of factors. First among these was the development of a more sophisticated feminist agenda through an understanding and acceptance of differences between women, most powerfully through feminist debates concerning 'race' and racism. A corollary of this is the acknowledgement that there is no single feminist position on issues where there used to be a clear 'feminist line'. For example, disabled feminists have challenged the uncritical support of abortion on demand as being 'disablist', while feminists against censorship have challenged as misguided the campaign against pornography.

Feminist activism is certainly less visible than before, mainly because overt feminist direct action and civil disobedience have virtually disappeared. Pressure group single-issue campaigns occur occasionally, for example in the Clare Short campaign against 'page 3 girls', but there are few single issues on which feminists now agree. Self-help is probably the greatest success and women's refuges, rape crisis centres and lesbian lines are still going strong. Some feminist publishing outlets survive, and although *Spare Rib* is no longer with us, *Everywoman* celebrated its tenth birthday in 1995. Cultural politics blooms, and we now take for granted bookshops filled with feminist novels and poems, and the growing presence of women in films and broadcast media. The huge growth in Women's Studies, both in higher education and elsewhere, is evidence of the continued importance of education as a form of activism and this is probably now a major way in which women access feminist ideas. As far as lifestyle politics are concerned, feminists continue to be concerned with the implications of their feminist politics for how they lead their daily lives, as the amount of writing about straight and lesbian relationships testifies.

If further evidence is needed that feminism is flourishing, then it is provided by the backlash against it, both in Britain and abroad. It is now more dangerous than at any time since the first wave to be identified as a feminist or feminist sympathizer. This is exemplified by the massacre of 14 female engineering students in Montreal in 1989 by a man screaming 'fucking feminists'; by the murders at American abortion clinics; and by the *fatwa* declared against Bangladeshi feminist writer Taslima Nasrin for daring to challenge fundamentalism. So far in Britain the backlash has taken less dramatic form, but its existence is real and consequential – no longer is it accepted that groups of women are disadvantaged and discriminated against, and we are meant to have 'never had it so good'.

It is difficult to provide a 'conclusion' to this outline discussion of themes of continuity and change in patterns of feminist activism – after all, howsoever commentators may argue about it, they are united in suggesting that feminism is still moving and changing. While the high profile campaigning work that hits the media will only occur from time to time – as it always has – meanwhile, there is a constant drip, drip of ongoing work, wherever there are women who will not be treated as doormats.

○  **Questions**

1 What do you think of Rebecca West's 'definition' of feminism? How would you define feminism?

2 Is the age of feminist activism over, so that all we have to do is 'claim our power', as Wolf, Paglia and others seem to suggest?

3 Have we fulfilled the dreams of our Victorian sisters? Think of a first wave issue and evaluate how far we have come – domestic violence is a good example, but there are lots of others.

4 Are you a 'feminist activist' and, if so, in what ways?

○ **Further reading**

The period preceding first wave feminism remains underresearched, although Rendall (1985) provides an overview of 'origins' and Taylor (1983) an in-depth look at the links between socialism and feminism in the early nineteenth century. First wave feminism sees increasing amounts of in-depth research, although it tends to focus on the Edwardian period. Rubenstein (1986) provides an interesting discussion of mid- and late-Victorian feminism. Some of the more accessible accounts of Edwardian feminism are Raeburn (1974), Rosen (1974), Mackenzie (1975/1988), Forster (1984), Stanley (1988), and Bolt (1993), while an interesting but drier account of its links with mainstream politics is provided by Holton (1986). Highly readable discussions of feminism between and after the wars will be found in Spender (1983, 1984) while more detailed accounts, based on the interlinked biographies of particular women will be found in Harrison (1987) and Alberti (1989).

Accounts of second wave feminist activism are surprisingly few. Perhaps the most evocative discussions will be found in the three readers which collect together contemporary articles from the mass-circulation feminist magazine *Spare Rib* (Allen *et al.* 1974: Feminist Anthology Collective 1981; Kanter *et al.* 1984). In addition, there are two useful, although highly partisan, accounts of feminist politics in Britain from the late 1960s to the mid-1980s by Coote and Campbell (1987) and by Rowbotham (1989). Each of the books deals reasonably well with the separate critiques and struggles of black women and lesbians, offering helpful further reading, while the two years between their publication dates was clearly the crucial point at which disability issues began to be taken seriously, and Rowbotham deals with them, but Coote and Campbell do not. You can supplement this gap with Lonsdale (1990). An excellent more recent account, based on interviews with feminist activists of the 1970s and 1980s, can be found in Lovenduski and Randall (1993).

Popular debates about the current state of feminist activism in the UK are most likely to be found in the feminist current affairs monthly magazine *Everywoman*. Late 1980s and 1990s discussions tend to focus on the backlash against the gains of second wave feminism as well as the perceived reluctance of younger women to associate themselves with feminism. Lyndon (1992), Quest (1994) and Paglia (interviewed in Benn 1994) are examples of the backlash, while Faludi (1992), Roberts (1992), French (1993), Figes (1994) and Wolf (1994) attempt to understand and explain it.

○ **Notes**

1 Every social movement which agitates for change will experience, at regular intervals, a reaction against it. It is most likely that this will occur when the revolutionary social movement is at its strongest and making most impact. The

current anti-feminist backlash takes two forms: on the one hand feminist politics is portrayed as redundant because women have now achieved all the 'equality' that they ever wanted, while on the other hand feminism is blamed for creating new problems and disadvantages in women's lives (see Faludi 1992).

2 Mary Wollstonecraft, for example, lived her private life unconventionally as well as publishing the most remarkable feminist treatise ever written, *A Vindication of the Rights of Women*.

3 Virginia Woolf's *Three Guineas* contains a particularly powerful feminist critique of the seductions and dangers of incorporation into educational elites, something Woolf always resolutely avoided. Her beautifully written analysis is an archetypal example of the interrelationship of theory and practice.

4 This may be changing again in the backlash era, as I go on to argue.

5 There are numerous definitions of postfeminism. It can refer to an era where feminism is no longer necessary, because women have gained equality with men, or else it can refer to an era simply where new generations have been exposed to feminist thinking so that feminism becomes part of the collective consciousness. Many feminists define the notion of postfeminism as yet another manifestation of the backlash.

## References

Alberti, J. (1989) *Beyond Suffrage: Feminists in War and Peace 1914–28*. London: Macmillan.

Allen, S., Sanders, L. and Wallis, J. (eds) (1974) *Conditions of Illusion: Papers from the Women's Movement*. Leeds: Feminist Books.

Benn, M. (1994) Sex, power and rock 'n' roll (interview with Camille Paglia), *Everywoman*, March: 16–18.

Bolt, C. (1993) *The Women's Movements in the United States and Britain from the 1790s to the 1920s*. Hemel Hempstead: Harvester Wheatsheaf.

Coote, A. and Campbell, B. (1987) *Sweet Freedom: The Struggle for Women's Liberation* (2nd edn). Oxford: Blackwell.

Coward, R. (1994) Is it time for a reawakening?, *Everywoman*, March: 12–13.

Faludi, S. (1992) *Backlash: The Undeclared War Against Women*. London: Vintage.

Feminist Anthology Collective (eds) (1981) *No Turning Back: Writings from the Women's Liberation Movement 1975–1980*. London: The Women's Press.

Figes, K. (1994) *Because of Her Sex: The Myth of Equality for Women in Britain*. London: Macmillan.

Forster, M. (1984) *Significant Sisters: The Grassroots of Active Feminism 1839–1939*. Harmondsworth: Penguin.

French, M. (1993) *The War Against Women*. London: Penguin.

Harrison, B. (1987) *Prudent Revolutionaries: Portraits of British Feminists Between the Wars*. Oxford: Clarendon Press.

Holton, S. S. (1986) *Feminism and Democracy: Women's Suffrage and Reform Politics in Britain, 1900–1918*. Cambridge: Cambridge University Press.

Kanter, H., Lefanu, S., Shah, S. and Spedding, G. (eds) (1984) *Sweeping Statements: Writings from the Women's Liberation Movement 1981–83*. London: The Women's Press.

Lonsdale, S. (1990) *Women and Disability*. London: Macmillan.

Lovenduski, J. and Randall, V. (1993) *Contemporary Feminist Politics: Women and Power in Britain*. Oxford: Oxford University Press.

Lyndon, N. (1992) *No More Sex War: The Failures of Feminism*. London: Sinclair-Stevenson.

Mackenzie, M. (1975/1988) *Shoulder to Shoulder*. New York: Random House.

Quest, C. (ed.) (1994) *Liberating Women . . . From Modern Feminism*. London: IEA Health and Welfare Unit.

Raeburn, A. (1974) *Militant Suffragettes*. London: New English Library.

Rendall, J. (1985) *The Origins of Modern Feminism: Women in Britain, France and the United States, 1780–1860*. London: Macmillan.

Roberts, Y. (1992) *Mad About Women*. London: Virago.

Rosen, A. (1974) *Rise Up Women!: The Militant Campaign of the Women's Social and Political Union 1903–1914*. London: Routledge and Kegan Paul.

Rowbotham, S. (1989) *The Past Is Before Us: Feminism in Action Since the 1960s*. London: Penguin.

Rubenstein, D. (1986) *Before the Suffragettes: Women's Emancipation in the 1890s*. Brighton: The Harvester Press.

Spender, D. (1983) *There's Always Been a Women's Movement This Century*. London: Pandora Press.

Spender, D. (1984) *Time and Tide Wait for No Man*. London: Pandora Press.

Stanley, L. (1988) *The Life and Death of Emily Wilding Davison*. London: The Women's Press.

Stanley, L. and Wise, S. (1993) *Breaking Out Again: Feminist Ontology and Epistemology*. London: Routledge.

Taylor, B. (1983) *Eve and the New Jerusalem: Socialism and Feminism in the Nineteenth Century*. London: Virago.

Wolf, N. (1994) *Fire with Fire: The New Female Power and How It Will Change the 21st Century*. London: Vintage.

Wollstonecraft, M. (1792/1975) *A Vindication of the Rights of Woman*. Harmondsworth: Penguin.

Woolf, V. (1938/1977) *Three Guineas*. Harmondsworth: Penguin.

**CONSUELO RIVERA FUENTES**

# They do not dance alone: the women's movements in Latin America

○ **Introduction**

The title of this chapter arises from my strong belief that women who re/act together can never be alone. At the same time it attempts to subvert British singer Sting's song 'They Dance Alone' which refers to Chilean women performing a dance of mourning for their missing relatives.

The chapter concentrates mainly on the women's movements in Uruguay, Argentina and Chile because of my nearness in time and space to the two former ones and due to my active participation in the Chilean ones. I start by giving a brief description of why and how some Latin American women trespassed the boundaries of the private–public dichotomy as well as the evident and not so visible consequences of our transgression.

Next, I attempt to highlight some of the contradictions that arise from the interaction between the feminist and non-feminist women's organizations and the role of two powerful ideologies, namely *machismo* and *marianismo*, in the construction of our social identities.

I end up with only a brief account of what is happening at present in the Chilean women's movements because having been away from Chile for three years at the moment of writing this, I do not feel qualified enough to go into further details. Apologies to my Chilean 'sisters' for that.

Although we share the Spanish language (except for Brazil) and a common history of oppression, first at the hands of the Spanish *conquistadores* and then at the hands of puppet governments controlled by different capitalist economic interests, Latin America is a complex patchwork of cultures, languages, races and peoples. This characteristic makes it hard to write about the women's movement and about Latin American feminism in the singular. That is why I refer to the women's movements and feminisms in the plural. This same plurality makes it difficult to establish the exact date when these movements started, as well as to distinguish between the aims of different ones in that part of the world nowadays. What is clear for me is that women have been active and resistant in many ways, only 'invisible' in traditional accounts of history.

It could be argued (see Fisher 1993a; Villavicencio 1994) that the feminist movements stemmed out of the women's movements once the women who participated in the social and economic upheavals of the 1970s started to have an awareness of their condition as women, although as early as 1913 the first feminist campaigns for the enfranchisement of women started in Chile and other countries of the area. If I go further back in history, I discover that Chilean women in the 1870s took to the streets and campaigned politically to get access to higher education, which they finally achieved in 1877. Julieta Kirkwood (1987) in *Recuperando La Historia Invisible* (*Recovering the Invisible History*) makes an analysis of the Chilean feminist movements and distinguishes three main periods, namely: the suffragist feminist period (1913–53), a second period constituted by what she calls '*silencio feminista*' and a third one which starts, according to her, in 1978. It is important to unveil Latin American feminist pasts in order to realize that our struggles to achieve equality and gender awareness have had continuity in history and that they are not movements that have developed *after* the European ones. Rather, I would say that both Latin American and European women's movements have co-existed and influenced each other, in different political, cultural and economic contexts and periods in world history.[1] However, my concern in this chapter is not with how old these movements are but with *why* Latin American women, especially those in the Southern Cone, began to step out of the boundaries of our homes, *how* we did it and the *consequences* that this trespassing of boundaries had in our private and public lives.[2]

## ○ Why

Different groups and women's organizations began as a reaction to the military dictatorships which violently gained control in Chile (1973), Uruguay (1973) and Argentina (1976). The role of women as mothers of the nation, keepers of the faith and devoted wives was extremely idealized by the military apparatuses and used in their campaigns to get women's support (Boyle 1993; Fisher 1993a). However, it was precisely this idealized notion of motherhood that gave women the courage and authority to protest publicly about the mass murders that were taking place and to walk into military headquarters demanding the immediate release of their children and *compañeros* jailed for opposing and resisting the military systems.[3] It was also this reinforced tradition that encouraged many women, mainly mothers in the poor neighbourhoods, to organize and fight against the legacy of the economic crisis of the late 1970s which the military economic experiments had brought about and which affected state spending on health, education and food welfare (Figueroa and Anderson 1990; Fisher 1993b; Andradi 1994). In other words, the 'personal' (grief, poverty) became 'political' (publicly denounced).[4] Yet this process of politicization was seen, even by the women involved, as the women's 'natural' obligation as good mothers and wives, and not as a 'political' one (Fisher 1993b).

Gradually, however, private matters such as abortion and the need for birth control, childcare, and violence against women at home jumped into the public arena, mixed with discussions on how to raise money for a communal kitchen or how best to gather forces for a public demonstration, within working-class women's groups. This gradual process of change marks, in my opinion, the beginning of a growing awareness about issues of gender.

○ **How**

One of the characteristics of South American women's movements has been the recognition that our identity as transforming subjects of society is something we have to achieve by ourselves. Once we realized that our creative and transforming energy could not be given by others, particularly not by those who were high up in the male political structures of power, women began to be the protagonists of our own history. How we did it depended on our cultural, political, economic and sociological differences; however, the common thread was the recognition of our inner and shared strength. Solidarity was what connected our differences.

In Uruguay, for example, women helped in the reconstruction of the labour movement which had been violently destroyed by the military regime by entering the workforce in higher numbers and by participating actively in trade union matters. The rise in the percentage of women entering the labour market did not mean better conditions of work or pay for them. Numbers grew mainly because poverty (which was the immediate result of the economic policies enforced by the military regime) hit approximately 68 per cent of homes and women were forced to contribute to the survival of their families (see Fisher 1993a; Radcliffe and Westwood 1993). In many cases, they were the only heads of the household because a relatively high quantity of men had been jailed, murdered or sacked for political reasons. This not only happened in Uruguay but also in all the other countries of the area and bears, some would argue, a certain resemblance to the situation of British women in World War II.

Women's participation in the trade unions was not as easy as it seems because men gave little space for female workers to become leaders of their organizations and mainly resorted to their female counterparts to help them fight and win industrial conflicts but not to deal with specific women's issues and demands in the place of work. After years of struggling to be acknowledged as capable and active leaders in the trade unions, some women workers decided (not without strong criticisms from men – and women!) to create women-only spaces in the form of women's commissions inside unions. Women's commissions have, since 1986, campaigned over a number of women's issues such as equal pay for equal work, women's health education with, for example, the implementation of special clinics in the unions set up for breast cancer screening and free smear testing, workshops on domestic violence, sexuality, abortion, etc. (Fisher 1993a). These commissions have established links with feminist and non-feminist women's groups which have resulted in a raising of consciousness concerning issues of gender not only for female participants of the labour movement but also for some men.

Another example of female collective resistance to tyranny has been the spontaneous creation of a group set up to protest against the violation of human rights in Argentina. This organization, known as *Madres de Plaza de Mayo* (Plaza de Mayo Mothers), started with a handful of women silently demanding information about their missing children. Soon they were to be joined by hundreds of women whose children had been taken away and who shared the same pain. Every Thursday afternoon, women wearing white headscarves silently yelled their public accusation, thus challenging one of the most barbaric military regimes we have had in Latin America.[5] Their spontaneous gathering in 1977 quickly gave rise to new ways of organization in an atmosphere of suspicion, brutal repression and dismissiveness on the part of the authorities – who considered them, at first, as 'mad women' and later labelled them 'the mothers of terrorists'. These innovative forms of politics and activism varied, some examples being the writing of messages on banknotes and inside prayer books, the handing out of documents in public places such as local markets and post offices, the organization of fake 'fashion shows' and 'birthday parties' where they could meet safely, the walking of 100 or more of them into political meetings with or without an invitation in order to demand an explanation and information on their disappeared children, and so on. The list is endless and the Mothers' struggle has been an inspiration for human rights organizations and for those women who have refused to come to terms with the disappearance of their children, relatives and friends not only in times of military dictatorships but also during civilian governments.[6] As for Latin American women's movements in general, the Mothers represent a symbol and example of what women can achieve for themselves when we act together.

Chilean women have also been actively involved, for long and painful periods of time, in the struggle to have our personal and political identity defined for and from ourselves. Examples of the methods we have used to achieve this are many and similar to those mentioned above. For reasons of space I will only mention some of them which belong to the period I happened to witness and participate in. We created, for instance, alternative *Centros de Madres* (mothers' centres) to counteract the action of the official one (CEMA Chile) run by the dictator's wife – whose sole purpose was the subduing of women into domestic roles and passivity; created the *ollas comunes* (common pots), set up to share food in poor neighbourhoods, which quickly became sites of political activities; commissioned women inside conventional political parties which opposed the military government; organized groups of *campesinas* (country women) whose political work, in my opinion, was more successful than the work, for example, of the women organized in syndicates, because the *campesinado* (peasant community) was less penetrated by political ideologies. These and many other women's organizations opened a period of mobilization which threatened the apparent stability of the repressive system enforced by the dictatorship.

We resorted to hunger strikes, to massive silent demonstrations of women dressed in black and carrying big notices with photographs of their missing relatives, or to the making of thousands of natural size black card-board human figures to be put in various public places while women read proclamations on different corners in the capital, Santiago. The 'funny' side of this action was that the police forces not only reacted violently against these women but also against the dark figures, silent witnesses of the aggression! Other instances of Chilean women's creativity were campaigns such as the one initiated by *Mujeres por la Vida* (Women for Life) in which they advertised an enlarged fingerprint with the reading: 'Where do the exiled, the political prisoners, the disappeared, the murdered vote? They cannot vote. Don't forget this in your NO'.[7] Or the proliferation of 'activist art', as I call it, such as performing plays in the streets to show what was happening and what we were feeling, or the visiting of political prisoners to take *arpilleras*, which denounced human rights violations through pic-tures and short poems, out of the prisons in order to sell them in and out of the country.[8] Some books, such as *Mi Rebeldía es Vivir*, written by poet Arinda Ojeda (1988) while she was a political prisoner, were smuggled out of the jails bit by bit, scribbled on bus tickets, on chewing-gum papers, etc. to be published by clandestine and/or foreign publishers.

Also, I cannot but mention the dancing of the *cueca* (our national dance and normally performed by a man and woman) on our own and dressed in black to denounce the enforced 'disappearance' of a man. As mentioned in my introduction, the title of this chapter borrows from the song 'They Dance Alone' which refers to this particular type of dance known as *la cueca sola*. Dancing for me signifies creativity, activism and participation. In this dancing we played our own music and created our own steps. Although women mourned the killing of our male and female relatives and danced on our own on stage, we never danced *alone*, we were all dancing together, with or without men.

Last but not least, getting official 'permission' to celebrate certain events was another tactic used by women's organizations to get other women to 'dance' with us. In this context, I clearly remember that on the 8th of March 1978, the military government gave permission for a women's meeting in one of the most popular theatres in Santiago to celebrate Inter-national Women's Day.[9] It might look strange that the *Dictadura* (dictator-ship) had authorized such an event when the gathering of more than three people in public or private places was considered subversive. The expla-nation given at the time by dictator Pinochet was that there was nothing to worry about because only 10 'female cats' would attend the celebration and thus the political parties of opposition would realize that they had nothing to do with women.

His projection was short by 10,000 'cats'! I was lucky to attend the act as one of the thousands of women organized around political parties, syn-dicates, human rights and popular groups, as well as feminist groups. I saw the whole act, cheered, danced and shared the emotion, anger and determination of all those women united by the same wish: that of achieving freedom from an oppressive regime as well as learning to recognize ourselves, collectively and individually.

○ **Consequences**

There are some consequences derived from the transgressions of boundaries sketched above which are more obvious than others. The obvious ones are for example, death at the hands of military men, the 'disappearance' of thousands of women, imprisonment, constant fear, rape, torture and exile. Those of us who survived these punishments for daring to speak, denounce, love and have sex with other women and organize ourselves, will have to live for ever with the scars that no plastic surgery can erase.[10]

Some of the less obvious results are: first, the sometimes ferocious antagonism between women who were on either side of the struggle, that is, between those who defended the military regimes and the role of women as passive daughters, mothers and wives whose place was the privacy of their homes, and those who wanted to subvert the 'this-is-the-way-it-has-always-been' type of ideology; second, the disintegration of their families with the separation from their husbands due to the resistance on the part of men to accepting 'their' women's activism and public participation in the social changes that were taking place; third, the realization that the fall of military dictatorships did *not* mean the end of patriarchal structures. This awareness led to conflictive relationships between men and women, and between women and women, both within conventional political parties and in their homes.

An example of these conflicts is illustrated by Gaviola *et al.* (1994: 198–9) when they describe a sketch created by a Chilean popular women's organization. The collective creation consisted of three acts, without words. In the first act, some women dressed in black go from one part of the dark stage to the other, searching, trying to hide, weeping. One woman enters one of the small houses represented by fake doors and the audience can hear a man telling her off, yelling at her. In the distance, the sound of shots. In the second act, the stage is brightly illuminated and there is the sound of cheerful music. Women carry banners, throw pamphlets, shout the names and demands of their organizations. The final and third act depicts an empty stage. In the background, several silent files of women observe the audience. Some of them bring a table to the centre of the stage and cover it with the national flag, others bring some chairs and put some glasses on the table. They then go back to joint the silent women in the background while some men dressed in elegant suits sit at the table. The sketch finishes with the men raising their glasses and listening to the national anthem being played loudly.

The most important consequence of the processes mentioned has been, in my opinion, the growing recognition of gender issues in Latin American society and the visibility, at all levels, of women questioning the power relationships established between men and women, creating new ways of becoming autonomous as social beings, participating in conventional political parties, writing our own herstories, and so on.

## ○ Do feminist and women's movements dance together?

In this section I try to illustrate the relationship between Latin American women's movements, feminist and non-feminist, as it is my belief that it is this relation which provides the music to keep us in movement, always dancing together but with our own particular rhythms. Despite their mutual influence and a shared history of repression, feminists and women's groups who emphasize more general social aspects and party politics have had and continue to have many differences and conflicts.

On the one hand, very few working-class women saw or see themselves as feminists. This reaction can be due to various reasons: to media campaigns which labelled feminists as lesbians, man-haters, anti-family, and as witches who protested against beauty contests only because they were ugly!; to the generalized assumption that being a feminist is the same as being a *machista* (a chauvinist) and that feminists only wanted to *dar vuelta la tortilla* (turn the tables); to the middle-class nature of the women (academics, university students and professionals) who identified themselves as feminist women organized around gender-based demands; and to the well-aired criticism that feminists contribute to divide the class struggle by emphasizing issues of gender instead of those of class. In other words, the feminist gender-based orientation of some groups who regarded themselves as being independent from political parties was seen as being in direct opposition to the women's popular groups.

Feminists, moreover, were and are often accused of essentializing and universalizing accounts of the concept 'woman'. Leila Gonzáles, cited in Radcliffe and Westwood (1993: 5), for example, argues that this universalization ignores (by making it abstract) the 'pluricultural and multiracial' nature of the people in the region. She has accused Latin American feminisms of being 'racist by ommission' and of generalizing the oppression of black and indigenous women, thus hiding 'the hard reality' lived by the latter. Despite these difficulties, feminists have been trying to redefine their position by adding other political issues to those of gender (Andradi 1994).

Feminists, on the other hand, accuse the women's movements of disconnecting themselves from the 'necessary analysis of gender power relations which is the basis of all other social relationships characterized by inequality' (Gaviola *et al.* 1994: 206, my translation). They also argue that party militants are 'impure in their feminism and inherently subordinate to men in their political-party activities' (Stoltz Chinchilla 1993: 19) and that feminist participation in human rights development has not been acknowledged.

However, and although some of the above arguments could be true, feminisms in Latin America are more complex than this and nowadays there are people who speak about grassroots feminists or *políticas* (who work from inside traditional political parties, unions and communities) and middle-class feminists or *feministas* (who theorize and campaign specifically around issues such as divorce, domestic violence and abortion, without getting involved in any political party), possibly because gender issues have been integrated into social and economic demands, and vice versa.

Some activists and/or theorists, based on the above arguments and contradictions, deny the existence of a harmonious relationship between these organizations. However, and paraphrasing Lorde (1983), differences, when acknowledged, can be 'forces for change' rather than for separation. Personal experience in the movements has taught me that what matters in the end is that popular women's organizations and feminist ones have grown both in form and content, albeit in an automous way and/or collaborating with each other but *never alone*. Both popular women's organizations and feminists continue to fight for their rights and for the right to be a visible and active force in Latin American history, thus influencing the political processes in a continent characterized and, in a sense, ruled by two predominant and powerful ideological concepts: *marianismo* and *machismo*.

## ○ *Marianismo* and *Machismo*

Women in Spanish colonial legal codes were considered 'imbeciles by nature' (Fisher 1993a: 3). This incredibly offensive colonialist Spanish commonsense assumption and other images about women added to Roman Catholic ideas of male predominance gave rise to a system of gender relations known as *machismo*. This form of sexism, swept away the 'egalitarian ideology of the complementarity of the sexes and the essential role of each in agricultural production' (Figueroa and Anderson 1990: 3) which existed among the indigenous people of pre-Columbian times. *Machismo* is an ideology that exaggerates the differences between men and women, putting men in a superior moral, economic and social position over women (Figueroa and Anderson 1990; Fisher 1993a). 'Even in rural areas', write Figueroa and Anderson, 'where a greater equality between the sexes is [still] detectable, a midwife is paid more if the baby she delivers is a boy' (1990: 16).

The indirect consequence of the European Christian teachings, brought to the continent by the Spanish, is that of women being socialized into believing that their natural place is within the home. It is precisely this idea of motherhood which gives women in Latin America a powerful role in the family place and in the construction of the female equivalent of *machismo*, i.e., *marianismo*, the European version of which is called mariology.

*Marianismo* is an ideology of religious origin in which women are thought of as pure, spiritual, self-sacrificing and submissive. The wife and mother figure symbolizes this *spiritual* character of Latin American women. Because we are the symbol for the Virgin Mary, we share Mary's virtue and responsibility for the protection of the (Catholic) faith. This model, however, is unrealistic because it sublimates women's roles, that is it diverts the attention of society from the devalued position of women into social and more acceptable and useful concepts to patriarchal structures, thus depicting us as superior spiritual beings in contrast to the more down-to-earth *macho* men. They are 'ugly, smelly and hairy', that is, socially acceptable as virile, non-monogamous and active. Women, within this ideology, are reinforced in a sexless image; we are unreal and do not possess our own personality. Women's identity is tied up to this *supermadre image*, a supermother who protects her family against all adversities.[11] We are, in other words, the 'mothers of the nation', a phrase used, more often than not, by military men in general.

Mary is the feminine ideal, therefore it is not surprising that the Chilean dictator said: 'the more a woman is feminine, the more she is admirable' (Fisher 1993a: 11), a typical example of the deliberate attempts on the part of military tyrants to eliminate the public role of women alongside their achievements with respect to childcare, labour rights, maternity provision and to leave the total control of public and political space to men. Pinochet went even further by asking women to 'show the strength that [they] submit to the person who at [that] moment [was] responsible' (Boyle 1993: 160), which is precisely the kind of *macho* discourse and attitudes that permeate Chilean culture. In this example, Pinochet assumed a collective *macho* image and compared himself to God ('not a single leaf moves without me knowing about it', he used to say) and commanded women to 'submit' to him, the 'father (the saviour) of the nation', therefore he was as all the women's husband. Similar statements were made by Argentinian, Uruguayan and Paraguayan dictators.

This 'ideological offensive' (Fisher 1993a: 11) had in fact a boomerang effect; it bounced back on the dictatorships and '[t]he military fell victims to the misconception of its own machismo' (Fisher 1993b: 30). Andradi (1994: 5), when talking about the Argentinian Mothers of the Plaza de Mayo asserts: 'The mothers turned the most patriarchal[ly defined] role in patriarchal society into a subversive one'.

*Machismo* and *marianismo*, although present in many parts of South America, are no longer the only defining features of our social identities and transformations. They might still be part of *history* but do not have a place in *herstory*. We have developed a politics of difference in diversity which is gradually intermingling with and influencing other women's movements in the world, a world with *no preceding ordinal* number (the hierarchical division of our earth into 'first', 'second' and 'third' worlds is part of his-torical language and does not help the women's movements). I will assert my right to 'deviate' here by inviting other women not to perpetuate and create more alienation because we are different. I ask women from all cultures, lesbian, bisexual, heterosexual, young and old, with and without disabilities, feminist and non-feminist, theorist and activist women to listen to ourselves and dance to the music that comes from our diversity. Let's listen to the different shades of our skins and use our differences *creatively and with respect for ourselves and each other*.

○ **Chilean women and democracy today**

What are Chilean women doing now that the military rule has ended?[12] My friends write to me saying that some women's organizations have become increasingly swept under the carpet of conventional party politics. Remember the play described earlier which describes precisely this situation. Women are no longer needed in the process of 'democratization'. Women are needed to set the table, put the glasses on it and then disappear into the background while men take 'important' decisions and are being served by 'their' women. Women's previous apparent autonomy from political parties seems to be in conflict with their real integration in them.

The return to civilian power was possible because both men and women struggled together to end oppression, yet this did not mean that women had representation in the government, at least in the initial period of the composition of the cabinet. Does this mean that all the things we achieved with respect to our demands as women were useless? I do not think so. Women's issues are part of the political agenda, not because men want these topics to be in their public programme but because women have pressed to be visible, women have put pressure not to 'disappear' as many others have in the past dictatorship. This pressure, for example, gave rise to the creation of a national service for women (SERNAM) which coordinates and promotes the participation of women in the nation. This sounds nice but there are many conflicts with the role being played by this institution because of conventional political reasons I cannot analyse here. Waylen (1992) and Boyle (1993) give fairly good accounts of these conflicts, if you are interested. These conflicts, however, have not prevented the setting up of a Women's Studies Diploma in the Universidad de Concepción; the beginning of one of the first feminist radio stations in South America – if not the first in the world as Boyle (1993: 171) claims – called *Radio Tierra* (Radio Earth, 'because the earth is feminine', used to be their slogan); and women's newspapers and magazines, such as *Fempress* which is part of a Latin American network, etc. The feminist radio initiative has been taken up by feminist groups in Peru and other countries in the area. The opening of women's issues to the public has also had an impact at the level of issues of sexuality that resulted in the 'coming out' in Concepción of a second lesbian organization called LEA (Rivera 1996). The number of feminist organizations is high and their influence can be felt throughout Chile. There is still a lot to do but what we cannot forget is that in order to transform ourselves and achieve a society of equality in and between the sexes we must continue to dance together.

○ **Questions and exercises**

1 What strategies can you suggest to prevent the 'sweeping of women and women's issues under the carpet' of conventional political parties?

2 Feminism is the same as *machismo*, only reversed. Discuss.

3 Compare *marianismo* and *mariology*. What are their similarities and/or differences? Is *marianismo* a black ideology and *mariology* a white one? Do you think that the former stemmed out of the latter or was it the other way round?

4 Write a short essay on feminist radio stations in Europe, specifically in England. When did they start? What were their initial purposes and are these aims the same nowadays? How many are there? Where are they? What types of programmes do they do? Are non-European women included in the organizational teams?

○ **Further reading**

Peters and Wolper (1995) is a new book on the influence of feminisms on the development of human rights worldwide. You can refer to Jaquette (1989), Jelin (1990), MacDonald (1991), Radcliffe and Westwood (1993) and Kuppers (1994) for information about other Latin American women's movements not covered in this paper. The concepts of *marianismo* and *mariology* are covered, among others, by Daly (1985), Warner (1985), Brown (1991) and Ranke-Heinemann (1991).

○ **Notes**

1 Although most of the literature on the women's movements and feminism in Latin America is in Spanish, more and more scholars are writing about it. Refer to the further reading section.

2 The so-called Southern Cone comprises Chile, Argentina and Uruguay (some authors include Paraguay). In all three countries, women led the struggle against the military rules which were destroying their nations.

3 *Compañero/a* is a political term which used to mean something like comrade but which soon turned to mean *partner*, both in a political and a personal sense. Men and women were more than comrades, the relationships established went beyond the political sense.

4 Villavicencio (1994) argues that although Latin American feminisms adopted 'the personal is political' principle from the European and North American feminists, we somehow moved through different stages. For a detailed account of these stages refer to her article: 'The Feminist Movement and the Social Movement: Willing Partners?' (Villavicencio 1994).

5 The Mothers, mainly housewives, were between 40 and 50 years of age, but later, as the movement grew, older women grouped themselves as the Grandmothers of the Plaza de Mayo.

6 Similar 'motherist' groups, as Schirmer (1989) labels them, were created in Guatemala (The Mutual Support Group), in Chile (Group of Relatives of the Detained–Disappeared) and in Uruguay (The Mothers and Relatives of Those Tried by Military Justice).

7 This was in the framework of a call for referendum (with the options Yes or No) made in 1988 by Pinochet to decide whether he stayed in power for eight more years. The campaigns carried out by the joint popular and political opposition groups was successful and the NO option won, giving way to a period of democratic transition in 1990.

8 Boyle (1993) gives a fairly good explanation of the term *arpilleras*. However, I want to add to her description the fact that this cultural and political 'weapon' or 'activist art', as I understand it, was used by men and women who were in jail to shout our truth to the world. It was transmitted from one political prisoner to the other, from one 'generation' of political prisoner to the next.

9 This experience and a similar account of it by Gaviola *et al.* (1994) makes me strongly disagree with Fisher's (1993a: 176) assertion that Chile's first International Women's Day celebration happened in 1980.

10 The lesbian group *Ayuquelén* was created after a lesbian woman was murdered in 1984 by a man who kicked her to death (Gaviola *et al.* 1994). In my experience, being a lesbian in 'democratic' times is painful but desiring a woman (and acting on that desire) in dictatorship is dangerous to our health as we can be killed with total impunity.

11 The Cornell-Peru project used the term *supermadre* to suggest how women in high government positions in Peru perceive their role (Figueroa and Anderson 1990: 18).

12 Although, at present, there is a 'democratic' government led by a Christian Democrat president, former dictator Pinochet is still the general in chief of the armed forces, hovering like a sinister shadow over the process of institutional change.

○  **References**

Andradi, E. (1994) Foreword to G. Kuppers (ed.) *Compañeras: Voices from the Latin American Women's Movement*. London: Latin American Bureau.

Boyle, C. (1993) Touching the air: The cultural force of women in Chile, in S. A. Radcliffe and S. Westwood (eds) *'Viva': Women and Popular Protest in Latin America*. London: Routlege.

Brown, A. (1991) *Apology to Women: Christian Images of the Female Sex*. Leicester: Inter-Varsity Press.

Daly, M. (1985) *The Church and the Second Sex* (new edn). Boston, MA: Beacon Press.

Figueroa, B. and Anderson, J. (1990) Women in Peru, *Change: International Reports*, Report No. 5, New Edition. London: Calverts Press.

Fisher, J. (1993a) *Out of the Shadows: Women, Resistance and Politics in South America*. London: Latin American Bureau.

Fisher, J. (1993b) Women and democracy: for home and country, in *Latin American Women: The Gendering of Politics and Culture*. NACLA: Report on the Americas, 27(1) July/August.

Gaviola, E., Largo, E. and Palestro, S. (1994) *Una Historia Necesaria: Mujeres en Chile: 1973–1990*. Santiago, Chile: Akí & Aora Ltda.

Kuppers, G. (ed.) (1994) *Compañeras: Voices from the Latin American Women's Movement*. London: Latin American Bureau.

Jaquette, J. (ed.) (1989) *The Women's Movement in Latin America: Feminism and the Transition to Democracy*. Boston, MA: Unwin.

Jelin, E. (ed.) (1990) *Women and Social Change in Latin America*. London: Zed Books.

Kirkwood, J. (1987) Recuperando la historia invisible, in P. Crispi (ed.) *Tejiendo Rebeldías: Escritos Feministas de Julieta Kirkwood*. Santiago, Chile: CEM, La Morada.

Lorde, A. (1983) The master's tools will never dismantle the master's house, in C. Moraga and G. Anzaldúa (eds) *This Bridge Called my Back: Writings By Radical Women of Color* (2nd edn). New York: Kitchen Table: Women of Color Press.

MacDonald, N. (1991) *Brazil: A Mask Called Progress*. Oxford: OXFAM.

Ojeda, A. (1988) *Mi Rebeldía es Vivir*. Santiago, Chile: Ediciones Literatura Alternativa.

Peters, J. and Wolper, A. (eds) (1995) *Women's, Rights, Human Rights: International Feminist Perspectives*. London: Routledge.

Radcliffe, S. A. and Westwood, S. (eds) (1993) *'Viva': Women and Popular Protest in Latin America*. London: Routledge.

Ranke-Heinemann, U. (1991) *Eunuchs for the Kingdom of Heaven: Women, Sexuality and the Catholic Church*. Harmondsworth: Penguin.

Rivera, C. (1996) 'Todas Locas, Todas Vivas, Todas Libres': Chilean Lesbians 1980–1995, in M. Reinfelder (ed.) *Amazon to Zami: Towards a Global Lesbian Feminism*. London: Cassell.

Schirmer, J. (1989) 'Those who die for life cannot be called dead': Women and human rights protest in Latin America, *Feminist Review*, 32: 3–29.

Stoltz Chinchilla, N. (1993) Women's movements in the Americas: feminism's second wave, in *Latin American Women: The Gendering of Politics and Culture*. NACLA: Report on the Americas, 27(1) July/August.

Villavicencio, M. (1994) The feminist movement and the social movement: willing partners?, in G. Kuppers (ed.) *Compañeras: Voices from the Latin American Women's Movement*. London: Latin American Bureau.

Warner, M. (1985) *Alone of All Her Sex: The Myth and the Cult of the Virgin Mary*. London: Picador.

Waylen, G. (1992) Women's movements and democratization in Chile, in Occasional Papers in Politics and Contemporary History No. 31. University of Salford, Department of Politics and Contemporary History.

# (22) RUTH HENIG

# Women and political power in Britain in the 1990s

## ○ Introduction

This chapter aims to explore the ways in which women exercise political power in Britain in the 1990s. It will suggest that while women find it diffi-cult to make a significant impact on the political process at the national level, they are much more successful at a local level. A study of gender and party politics noted that information about women as local councillors was 'surprisingly scarce' (Lovenduski and Norris 1993). Using data collected from Lancashire County Council covering the period 1981–93, this chapter will discuss the growing impact of women councillors in local government, and explore the reasons why they find local political structures so much more accessible than national ones. It is interesting to note that a study of the activities of women in British working-class politics in the interwar period concluded that 'women made their most significant political contri-bution to the political labour movement of the 1920s at the local, not the national, level' (Graves 1994). The continuation of this pattern into the 1990s, of women playing an important political role at a local but not at the national level, raises significant questions about the slow pace of political change in Britain, and about the nature of the political structure. It suggests that there are still considerable hurdles to be overcome before women are able to exercise substantial political power at the national level.

The 1991 census has revealed that 51.58 per cent of the United Kingdom population is female, and the figure rises to 52.41 per cent if we consider only those of voting age, i.e. the over 18s. Yet in the current House of Commons only 9.2 per cent of members of parliament (MPs) are women. While this percentage has trebled since 1979, when it was an abysmal 3 per cent, the proportion of women members of parliament in the United Kingdom is one of the lowest in Europe. While most male MPs would claim to represent the interests of all their constituents, and while many have been willing on occasion to highlight issues of concern to women, their ability and willingness to bring about any substantial and practical changes to benefit women has been very limited. Therefore, with only 41 women in the 1987–92 House of Commons, and 60 since 1992, we should not be surprised that the legislation that is passed does not in any significant way reflect women's interests or seek to change social and economic structures to benefit women.

The position in Lancashire County Council, however, is somewhat different. Women comprised 16 per cent of the council in 1981, and a sizeable 27 per cent in 1993 – still not a true reflection of their majority position in the population, but clearly a significant move in that direction. Despite the attempts of the government to restrict local government spending, county councils continue to provide important local services in the fields of education, social services, libraries and the arts, welfare rights, highways and transport, and fire and public protection. The choice of policy options in many of these fields will have a considerable impact on women's everyday lives and on the work and leisure opportunities open to them. We can therefore examine some of the initiatives introduced in Lancashire over the past few years to assess whether the growing numbers of women councillors have resulted in changes of policy specifically benefiting women.

However, the presence of a significant minority of women will not in itself be enough to bring about change. Women also need to occupy leadership positions in order to be able to exercise political power and to influence political agendas. In the present cabinet, there are two women, who represent about 9 per cent of that crucial policymaking body, hardly a significant proportion. That figure roughly corresponds to the percentage of women in the House of Commons, though it may also be a result of the outcry which resulted when John Major appointed no women at all to his first cabinet. In contrast, in Lancashire, three of the 10 major committees since 1993 have been chaired by women, and four have female vice-chairs. Again, this is roughly proportionate to the percentage of women in the council as a whole. While it is true that Britain had a woman prime minister throughout the 1980s, she showed little interest in prioritizing women's issues, and came under no pressure from her own party to do so. In Lancashire, however, each of the three major parties on Lancashire County Council has been led by a woman since 1983, and women have constituted a significant and vocal minority within each party. Women have been encouraged to play an active role in their local political processes, as well as in the council chamber itself, unlike the situation at Westminster, where the party machinery of all groups is almost totally dominated by men. This has enabled them to influence the political agenda and to give priority to issues of concern to them.

An important factor assisting women at the local level to exercise political influence is the relative openness of the council structure as compared to the adversarial parliamentary structure. Though the priorities for action are drawn up by the party in political control, individual council committees have considerable power in framing policies and in determining how they are implemented. Cross-party cooperation on many issues is a frequent occurrence, and there is also considerable scope for individual local representatives to make a decisive imput into decisions affecting their own areas. In striking contrast, decisionmaking at the national level, though it is also initiated by the ruling party, comes under much tighter government control. Parliamentary bills are framed by a male-dominated and still largely Oxbridge-educated higher civil service, and are carefully guarded by male party whips as they proceed through parliament. There is virtually no chance for an individual member of parliament to bring about any significant amendments, and the highly-charged political atmosphere in the House of Commons, characterized by tactics of political confrontation and personal attack, not only makes cross-party agreement difficult but also reduces the influence of women members who seek to achieve change through cooperation rather than through confrontation.

## The role of women in local government

It is difficult to assess how typical Lancashire is of county councils or of local government as a whole. It has been under Labour control since 1981, except for the period 1985–9 when there was no overall majority and Labour exercised power as a minority administration. It is not within the scope of this chapter to analyse the role and significance of women in different political parties, though research along these lines would undoubtedly reveal interesting findings. It is conceivable that Labour controlled authorities may well pursue policies more beneficial to women than Conservative councils, but there is hardly any published data available at this point in time which could substantiate or disprove this hypothesis. What we do know is that research suggests that since the early 1990s, 25 per cent of local councillors have been women (Lovenduski and Norris 1993). If this is the case, why are there three times as many women on local councils as in the House of Commons? A number of possibilities might help to explain this situation.

In the first place, there is considerable evidence that women are not selected for winnable or safe parliamentary seats. In 1992, there were only five women out of the 57 candidates who inherited safe Conservative seats, and three women out of 24 who inherited safe Labour seats. Statistics show that women tend to be selected for less winnable parliamentary seats, but there is little evidence that this happens at council level. It is therefore much easier for women at local level than at national level to be selected for seats they can win. The Labour party is currently trying to address this problem by laying down a quota of seats in all categories – safe, marginal and unwinnable – which must be contested by women. While this move has guaranteed that significantly greater numbers of Labour women will become MPs after the next election, it has aroused considerable controversy at constituency level and amongst male candidates and has recently been declared unlawful. Finding a winnable seat, of course, is not the only obstacle women face when they consider a parliamentary career. There are also the additional problems of the unsocial hours of parliamentary sittings, the total lack of facilities for families and for childcare in the House of Commons, and the prospect of having to uproot the family unit, especially if young children are involved, which act as a major deterrent for many women.

Local government is much more accessible to women; they can combine it with family responsibilities and with other work and it is not too distant from home. This fact, plus the greater possibility of finding a winnable seat, must go a long way to explain why there are three times as many women on Lancashire County Council as in the House of Commons. Furthermore, increasing numbers of women in more recent years have made a full-time career out of their work as local councillors, exploiting to the full the opportunities offered by local government to develop skills and widen their experience, and this has encouraged other women to enter the political fray. In this sense, local councils serve the needs of women in a very practical sense, and growing numbers of women have used local government as an important stepping stone to national politics – Emily Blatch from Cambridgeshire, Patricia Hollis from Norwich City Council and Josephine Farrington from Lancashire being three examples of women now in the House of Lords as a direct result of their local government experience, and Margaret Hodge, the former leader of Islington Council elected to the House of Commons in 1994. Large numbers of women gain their first taste of chairmanship and of decisionmaking at the local level, and develop skills which increase their confidence and their employment prospects.

It could be argued that this is no new phenomenon, and that throughout history women have played important roles in their own localities. It is undoubtedly the case that in Victorian times, women played leading roles in the prison reform movement and as hospital and workhouse visitors. But until well into the twentieth century women were assumed to have particular characteristics and skills and to be best fitted to operate in their 'separate spheres'. Now at local level women are competing directly with men for power in all policy areas, not just in social services but in the traditionally more male-dominated areas of finance, police and fire.

Let us now turn to consider the impact women have made on the policies formulated by Lancashire County Council. Have they used their numbers to push for particular measures? Have they brought about changes in emphasis or in direction which have been of benefit to women in the county? Of particular interest are policies relating to nursery education and childcare provision, especially after school hours, equal opportunities initiatives, continuing education provision and job-training facilities, and welfare rights policies.

○  **Nursery provision**

The low level of nursery provision in most parts of Lancashire was a major issue in the county council elections of 1981. It motivated a number of women to participate in the elections and to stand as candidates. I made a speech at the Labour party conference of 1977 pointing out that it was easier to get a child into Eton or Harrow than into one of Lancaster's two nursery schools, and that to stand any chance of success, parents had to put down their child's name within a few days of birth. Women across the political spectrum pushed for an expansion of nursery education throughout Lancashire in the 1980s, despite the problems that this caused for the education budget. Education funding is provided to county councils to cover the education facilities which have to be provided by law, which is to say largely for 5–16 provision and for sixth-form education. Therefore, running costs for nursery facilities had to come out of this overall budget, and building works had to compete for priority with new and replacement primary and secondary schools. This is an interesting example of differences of approach at national and local level. If there were more women in Parliament, it is highly likely they would press for nursery education to be available for all children, and for the appropriate funds to be provided. Indeed, the Labour party has adopted this as one of its policy objectives for its next term of office, in part due to the pressure from women's groups. However, up to the present time, the provision of nursery education is discretionary, and councils may provide it if they wish, but they do not get extra government finance for it.

Nevertheless, despite the difficulties, the number of nursery places in purpose-built schools and in nursery classes has increased considerably in Lancashire. In 1981 there were 2743 places available. Now there is capacity for 3808 3- and 4-year-olds, and this is utilized to provide 3448 part-time and 87 full-time places in nursery schools, and 4294 part-time places in nursery classes. In addition, for most of the 1980s and early 1990s, the county has operated a 'rising fives' admissions policy for primary schools, whereby children are admitted to schools at the beginning of the school year in which their fifth birthday falls. There are still not sufficient nursery places available in Lancashire for all who want them for their children, and facilities in rural parts of the county and outside the major towns lag behind those in Burnley, Blackburn and Preston. Increasingly strict curbs on local government spending have severely restricted the nursery programme in recent years, and political action urgently needs to take place at national rather than local level to bring about a significant improvement in the current situation.

Women on Lancashire county council have also used their power to increase the provision of childcare facilities offered by the social services department, and to launch some afterschool child-minding initiatives in different parts of the county. In addition, a creche/nursery facility was provided in the mid-1980s near County Hall for the use of council staff and councillors. These measures have gone some way to help women who have child-minding responsibilities, but again they need to be reinforced by changes in social security and taxation legislation at the national level.

## ○ Equal opportunities initiatives

In the early 1980s, Lancashire County Council adopted a new code of practice spelling out its intention to operate as an equal opportunities employer. Two new committees were set up in 1983, one to formulate equal opportunities policies in the education service, and the second to cover the county's other areas of policy. I chaired the Education Equal Opportunities subcommittee for six years, during which time it pursued a number of initiatives and lines of enquiry. About a third of the membership of the committee consisted of women, as councillors or coopted teacher representatives, and it is significant that they chose to give priority to issues of sex discrimination over race discrimination, though in more recent years the latter has also been the focus for considerable activity.

By 1983, many women councillors had taken part in headship and deputy headship appointments across the county, and had become aware of the fact that one of the reasons why so few women were being appointed to senior posts in schools was because there were so few female applicants. Furthermore, the criteria being used to evaluate the suitability of candidates for posts included aspects such as a range of experience in different schools, some demonstration of leadership skills in a senior position, and evidence of preparation for a senior post, including attendance on relevant courses, all of which favoured male rather than female applicants.

One of the first things the committee did was to ask for an up-to-date report on the numbers of women on the different points of the scale in both primary and secondary schools in Lancashire. This showed the extent of the discrimination faced by women very clearly. Whereas over 70 per cent of primary school teachers were women, they were to be found predominantly in the most junior positions in their schools, and well over half the senior positions were filled by men. In secondary schools, the numbers of male and female teachers recruited at the bottom end of the scale were more equal, but men were much more likely to be promoted to senior positions than women, and men held most of the headship and deputy headship positions.

Given that, in the 1980s, appointments within schools and even headship appointments were to a considerable extent the responsibility of governing bodies – and exclusively so in the case of aided schools of which Lancashire has the highest number in the country – the Education Equal Opportunities Committee recognized that a range of new approaches and policies would need to be implemented to begin to change the situation. Governing bodies of all schools were circulated with the county's equal opportunities code of practice and asked to look at the situation in their own schools with a view to ensuring that promotion policies were fair and non-discriminatory. Interview procedures and criteria for selection were reviewed to ensure that female applicants were not disadvantaged by the types of questions asked, the forms to be filled in or criteria used to make the final decisions. In-service training needs were assessed, and courses provided at times and in places accessible to women. One of the biggest problems facing women teachers in Lancashire arose when they left their jobs to start a family, and then had to start their teaching careers all over again some years later. A scheme was devised to enable teachers to leave their jobs for a year or two to have children, while at the same time keeping in touch with their schools, and being assured of a return to work at the same level of seniority at the end of the period.

At the same time, the committee looked at the type of curriculum provided in schools and the ways in which gender issues were handled. It sent a regular stream of material through to governing bodies, and kept a strong focus on examples of sex discrimination and sexist attitudes in schools. Slowly but surely the numbers of women in senior positions in both primary and secondary schools increased, though it has to be recognized that in more recent years national legislation to devolve power to individual schools, under the local management of schools initiative, has lessened the ability of county councillors and officers to influence school appointments. Statistics drawn from the period 1993–4 covering primary school appointments to headships and deputy headships in Lancashire maintained schools show that 56 female and 128 male candidates applied for seven headteachers posts, emphasizing the point that women are still not reaching middle-rank and senior positions in anything like their proportion of the overall primary teaching force. None the less, three female candidates were successful. Fifty-five females and 31 males applied for three deputy headships, and all three posts went to female candidates. Considerable obstacles still face women seeking promotion at work in the 1990s, and many can only be removed by action at national level, but Lancashire County Council has made considerable efforts in the past 10 years to bring about equal opportunities for council employees, and to promote non-sexist attitudes and policies in council establishments.

○  ## Continuing education

In the early 1980s, across the county, the provision of continuing education was 'rationalized' by the merger of adult education centres and colleges of further education. Just before the 1981 county council elections, the merger of Lancaster Adult College and Lancaster and Morecambe College of Further Education was proposed. This was strenuously opposed by Lancaster county councillors, largely on two grounds. The first was that the Adult College was readily accessible to students in Lancaster, a large number of them women with family responsibilities, whereas Lancaster and Morecambe college was at least one if not two bus rides away. The second was that a college of further education, largely dominated by 16–19-year-old students, would not provide as conducive a learning environment for adults as the Adult College. The proposal to merge the two colleges was rejected, and since the 1980s the Lancaster Adult College has flourished and expanded, from its converted workshop premises to a purpose-built education centre in a renovated stone mill. It provides a wide range of educational opportunities, a great many aimed at women returners to study and to the job market, and at ethnic minorities, and has helped many women to find employment locally. Its access courses have also encouraged women to take degree courses at universities in the northwest, even in cases where women enrolled initially out of interest or to boost their confidence, never thinking that they would be successful in qualifying for higher education. Many of the full and part-time teaching and administrative posts at the college are held by women, who use their own experience and the problems they have encountered to counsel and advise their students, and to encourage them to continue in education. As with nursery education, most of the funding for adult and continuing education has to be found from the general education budget, and also out of fees, but the county council has so far managed to safeguard its adult and continuing education provision, especially at the Lancaster Adult College.

## Training and economic regeneration

Since 1981, the county council has identified as one of its central concerns economic regeneration and development. A company, Lancashire Enterprises Limited (LEL), was established to raise investment finance, both public and private, and to provide a range of employment initiatives. In recent years, LEL has utilized large amounts of European Community finance in a variety of projects, many of them of particular benefit to women. Members of the LEL board and women councillors have successfully pressed for the adoption of a number of schemes directly aimed at women workers and at women wishing to return to the labour market. Despite the government's attempts to distance LEL from the county council, and to discourage the funding of regional economic initiatives by councils, large numbers of training and employment opportunities of particular benefit to women have been provided across Lancashire in the past few years.

## Welfare rights

One of the most successful initiatives of Lancashire County Council in the mid-1980s was the establishment of a welfare rights service, offering expert advice and guidance on the maze of benefits and allowances available to people across the county. Given that responsibility for looking after elderly relatives and children falls predominantly on women, the availability of this service has been of tremendous benefit to women in the county, and various poster and press advertising campaigns have been launched to ensure that mothers and carers are aware of the benefits available to them and know how to apply for them.

## Conclusion

There is no doubt at all that the women on Lancashire County Council, sometimes acting in unity across party lines in opposition to many male colleagues, have brought about significant changes of policy which have been of particular benefit to women. Could this also be achieved at national level? Could a House of Commons with an equivalent proportion of women members at last begin to address women's issues in a positive and systematic way? Or would the parliamentary political structure prevent significant change from being achieved? Clearly, numbers alone would not be sufficient. Women would also have to occupy significant positions both at cabinet level and within their different parties. But just to bring the proportion of women in the House of Commons up to the Lancashire level will require at least a trebling of the numbers of women elected at the next general election. There are a number of current initiatives aimed at increasing the numbers of women members of parliament. We have already referred to the quota scheme adopted by the Labour party's national executive to ensure that more than a third of all seats, including safe seats, are contested by Labour women candidates. There is also the 300 Club scheme, sponsored by women of all parties, which aims to secure the election of 300 women members of parliament, and Emily's List, an idea imported from the United States of America, to give financial help and practical assistance to women candidates. Will these measures prove successful in trebling the numbers of women in the House of Commons, or are our parliamentary structures so antagonistic to women that their numbers and influence will remain low?

If we look at the political systems and practices of other countries, a number of differences are immediately apparent. Many European countries have election by proportional representation rather than by a system of 'first past the post'. There is some evidence that this favours the election of greater numbers of women, particularly if parties draw up lists of candidates drawn from different regions and representing different sections of the party. Some parliaments have different seating arrangements, and their parliamentary procedures are not so rowdy and antagonistic as those displayed regularly on television from the House of Commons. Some enjoy better arrangements for families and more normal working hours and routines than their British equivalent. Further research needs to be done to identify countries with significant numbers of women in parliament, and to see the extent to which parliamentary structures, the national political system, or other social and economic factors, help them to exercise political influence at a national level. Meanwhile, until the British parliamentary system is significantly changed, women will continue to find it easier to exercise significant political influence at a local rather than national level.

○ **Questions**

1 What changes at national level would make it easier for women to become members of parliament?

2 Would an emphasis on women's issues make it easier or more difficult for women to win marginal seats in a general election?

3 Have countries with a large number of women in their national
  parliaments passed a significant amount of legislation benefiting
  women?

4 Which measures of benefit to women would you most like to see
  passed successfully through the House of Commons? What can you
  do to help to bring them about?

○  **Further reading**

Very few books have been written about women and the political
process in Britain. A very useful publication is *Gender and Party Politics* (Lovenduski and Norris 1993) which has some interesting statistics and material relating to gender and party politics in contemporary
Britain. *Gender and Trade Unions* (Lawrence 1994) casts light on the
range of problems faced by women in the trade union movement.
*Defining Women: Social Institutions and Gender Divisions* (McDowell and
Pringle 1992) contains a useful Part 4 devoted to women and politics.
There is a growing list of studies of women who have played active
political roles in the last 100 years, including a biography of the Victorian crusader for women's rights, Annie Besant (Taylor 1992), a
study of four Victorian feminists (Caine 1992) and a volume of essays
on Sylvia Pankhurst (Bullock 1992). *Labour Women: Women in British
Working Class Politics, 1918–39* (Graves 1994) gives an interesting
account of the political activities of working-class women in the
interwar period. Useful historical insights are also provided in *Women
in England, 1870–1950* and *Women in Britain since 1945* (Lewis 1984,
1992).

Material from other European countries is not easy to come by, but
both *Gender and Party Politics* (Lovenduski and Norris 1993) and
*Women and Social Policies in Europe: Work, Family and the State* (Lewis
1993) provide useful material relating to the position and political role
of women in other European countries. The evolution of equal opportunities policies is covered in *Sex, Race and the Law: Legislating for Equality* (Gregory 1987), and wider issues of social provision and welfare
legislation are discussed in *Democracy and the Welfare State* (Gutman
1988) and *Women and the Welfare State* (Wilson 1977).

○  **References**

Bullock, I. (ed.) (1992) *Sylvia Pankhurst: From Artist to Anti-Fascist*. London: Mac-
    millan.
Caine, B. (1992) *Victorian Feminists*. Oxford: Oxford University Press.
Graves, P. M. (1994) *Labour Women: Women in British Working Class Politics, 1918–39*.
    Cambridge: Cambridge University Press.

Gregory, J. (1987) *Sex, Race and the Law: Legislating for Equality*. London: Sage Press.

Gutman, A. (ed.) (1988) *Democracy and the Welfare State*. Princeton, NJ; Princeton University Press.

Lawrence, E. (1994) *Gender and Trade Unions*. London: Taylor and Francis.

Lewis, J. (1984) *Women in England, 1870–1950*. Brighton: Wheatsheaf Press.

Lewis, J. (1992) *Women in Britain Since 1945*. Oxford: Blackwell.

Lewis, J. (ed.) (1993) *Women and Social Policies in Europe: Work, Family and the State*. Aldershot: Elgar.

Lovenduski, J. and Norris, P. (eds) (1993) *Gender and Party Politics*. London: Sage Press.

McDowell, L. and Pringle, R. (eds) (1992) *Defining Women: Social Institutions and Gender Divisions*. London: Polity Press/Open University.

Taylor, A. (1992) *Annie Besant: A Biography*. Oxford: Oxford University Press.

Wilson, E. (1977) *Women and the Welfare State*. London: Tavistock.

**KATHLEEN SULLIVAN**

# Ecofeminism and the invaluable tool of despair-and-empowerment work

Ecofeminism is an emerging philosophical and action oriented framework that offers hope and constructive change in this present time: a time of crisis. It is an undisputed fact that life on earth is in danger. The ozone layer is being depleted; rainforests, the lungs of the earth, are being destroyed; human suffering in private and public sectors continues unabated. At times I feel it is too late. Sometimes I feel we've gone too far. But from this place of despair there still sprouts hope, a seed germinating new alternatives, or growing from the grassroots. Yes, we are in a time of crisis, but crisis can be countered with creative change. Indeed, that is what the word itself calls for. The Chinese characters for crisis are 'danger' and 'opportunity' (Walsh 1995). Therein lies our challenge: to name and face the danger then work towards suitable alternatives. My work as an activist aims to do just that. Ecofeminism fuels this work.

The voice of ecofeminism, like feminism, is both personal and political. My experience as an activist, the gateway to my experience of feminism, is the key to my own understanding of ecofeminism. In this chapter I will explore what ecofeminism is and why as an activist I have found 'despair-and-empowerment work' invaluable in bringing together the movement's philosophy and action initiatives.

○ **What is ecofeminism anyway?**

So what exactly is ecofeminism? Many attribute the early 'rumblings of an avalanche' (Carson 1962: 262) to Rachel Carson and her pioneering work, *Silent Spring*. In it she chronicles the literal silencing of the countryside due to pesticide poisoning under the guise of 'agricultural control programs' (Carson 1962: 8–9). Carson was a marine biologist by profession and an author under the authority of the US Fish and Wildlife Service. She began writing *Silent Spring* in 1958 in a scientific field populated mostly by men.

Perhaps, more than 'a woman before her time', Carson was a woman of the times with the privilege of a voice in a majority male-only club, the public sector of society at large.

Thirty years later in 1988, Andree Collard's posthumous work, *Rape of the Wild*, became a cornerstone for early ecofeminist philosophy. Collard (and later Joyce Contrucci who saw the book to publication after the primary author's death in 1986) provides a solidly grounded critique of western patriarchal culture and that culture's rape of the natural world and animals. She describes the exploitation of what is wild, while at the same time exposing the inherent exploitation of women. Collard asserts that we have been continually taught to '[see] the world . . . through the eyes of man' and have thus 'been taught his version of the past and have been indoctrinated with his values' (Collard 1988: 40). She makes a powerful plea for new values, new ways of thinking and relating to one another, and urges us to protect and respect the earth. With great respect for the works of both Carson and Collard, many would argue that it is no coincidence that two women invoke such impassioned pleas. The sentiment and will underlying written works like *Silent Spring* and *Rape of the Wild* sets the tone for the emerging philosophy of ecofeminism.

The term ecofeminism was first coined by French author Francoise d'Eaubonne in 1974 (Merchant 1992: 184). In 1976 the idea was further developed by Ynestra King at the Institute for Social Ecology in Vermont (the irony here is that the Institute is now hugely critical of ecofeminism, see Biehl 1991). Ecofeminism was then formally launched as a movement in 1980 with the conference 'Women and Life on Earth: Ecofeminism in the 80s' (Merchant 1992: 184).

From the very start, ecofeminism has focused on the similarities in the oppression of women and of nature in a patriarchal society, as well as the liberation of the two simultaneously, and thus began the partnership of feminism and ecology. As ecofeminist philosopher, Karen Warren, puts it, 'the quilt of ecological feminism' is a veritable tapestry of women's words and deeds. There are many ways in which women and men are called to the work of ecofeminism. Karen Warren states, I don't think there will be, nor should there be, only one future for ecofeminism. Ecofeminism promises to have a rich and varied future much like a multi-textured quilt made by lots of different quilters (*woman of power* 1991). The various works, ideas and indeed textures of an ecofeminist quilt are informing and inspiring. They reach in breadth and depth from critiques of modern science, to a move towards ecological selfhood, to the envisioning of women-centred, earth-honouring spirituality. Furthermore, this accumulating wisdom is not left to hang in women's mouths becoming dead air, for always included in an ecofeminist framework is action for creative change.

Much critical work on modern science and philosophy has been accomplished by women such as Susan Griffin in her book *Women and Nature* (1978) and Carolyn Merchant's *The Death of Nature* (1980). Both seek to disentangle the connections made during the so-called Age of Enlightenment between women and non-human nature. The Enlightenment was the time of a shift in western thinking about the earth, a shift from nature as alive and immanent to nature as dead and mechanical, and thus, had many untold consequences for women and nature. Griffin and Merchant both cite the European witch-hunts as 'Reason's' attack on nature. Women healers and midwives were likely targets as they were outcasts in a society whose sights were set on 'scientific progress' and the rise of modern medicine. Surely, these 'witches' and their age-old herb lore needed to be ousted in order to make way for the big fixes of a medical practice that only men of 'high culture' and 'worth' were suited to carry out. Merchant describes how, during the 1600s, nature, like the wild witches, was slated for taming and torturing. The practice of mining ensued, as did the practice of clear-cutting and the 'scientific pursuit' of draining wetlands and attempting to straighten rivers (Merchant 1980). Nature and women became enslaved during this period of 'scientific achievement', as did other human beings stolen from their homelands in Africa and elsewhere. For these people it was skin colour that denoted a closeness to what is wild in nature and therefore, what needed to be harnessed and tamed for the good of the 'enlightened white man'. Merchant (1980: 169) describes, using the words of sixteenth-century philosopher, Francis Bacon, the sentiment of this time of shifting paradigms:

> The new man of science must not think that the 'inquisition of nature is in any part interdicted or forbidden'. Nature must be 'bound into service' and made a 'slave', put 'in constraint' and 'molded' by the mechanical arts. The 'searchers and spies of nature' are to discover her plots and secrets.

It is not only the voices of western women of European descent that colour the quilt of ecofeminism. Vandana Shiva provides an excellent critique of reductionism, born of modern science, in her book *Staying Alive: Women, Ecology and Development* (1989). As an Asian woman and physicist, she deconstructs the western promise of development in her native country, India, and cites the development project as one of western patriarchy where land is parcelled for monocrop use, feeding no sustainable future. She, like Griffin and Merchant, calls for the recovery of the feminine principle:

> Recovering the feminine principle as respect for life in nature and society appears to be the only way forward, for men as well as women, in the North as well as in the South. The metaphors and concepts of minds deprived of the feminine principle have been based on seeing nature and women as worthless and passive, and finally as dispensable. These ethnocentric categorizations have been universalized, and with their universalization has been associated the destruction of nature and the subjugation of women. But this dominant mode of organizing the world is today being challenged by the very voices it had silenced.
>
> (Shiva 1989: 223)

Of course defining a 'feminine principle' is problematic in so much as it assumes that women can be defined as a whole, or as a cohesive group. Many questions arise from this assumption such as, are women closer to nature and does biological determinism have a role to play in this presupposed closeness? Could a feminine principle be constructed as the reverse of Francis Bacon's claim where he proposes separateness from nature? Is it necessarily essentialist to state that a feminine principle in particular needs to be reintroduced in our ailing societies? The questions are many and some of them have been addressed in other chapters of this book. I do believe, like many ecofeminists, that both women and men have a great affinity with nature and what is wild. How could we not, if we are a part of the earth and the earth is a part of us? Nevertheless, the contemporary patriarchal worldview sees feminine values as being more closely associated with nature/nurture and connectedness and masculine values associated with science/culture and separateness. I believe that ecofeminism, by naming and reclaiming these feminine values as something positive, is attempting to reappropriate a sense of real responsibility in our culture, not only for women but for all of humanity.

As well as a critique of modern science and the recovery of a feminine principle, ecofeminism aims to reintroduce the notion of an alive earth. The concept of the earth as a living being is re/emerging in our time (for it is not a new idea) and is inspiring ecology movements in the West today. Ecofeminism is, therefore, a philosophy and movement which claims that we are a part of this living earth, and so are called to act on a personal and political level. In protecting and sustaining the earth, we are able to do the same with our own lives. If the earth in part is being destroyed (i.e. felled forests, poisoned water and air) then it is part of our own wider, ecological self that dies. Joanna Macy (cited in Plant 1989: 202) writes thus:

> [Ecological selfhood] combines the mystical and the pragmatic. Transcending separateness and fragmentation, it generates an experience of profound interconnectedness with all life. This has in the past been largely relegated to the domain of mystics and poets. Now it is, at the same time, a motivation to action. The shift in identity serves as ground for effective engagement with the forces and pathologies that imperil us.

As well as the ideas of a living earth and the ecological self, ecofeminism has also brought with it an awakening/reawakening of women's spirituality. The ancient traditions of earth-honouring spiritual practice are re-emerging, as well as new forms coming into being. Ecofeminists like Starhawk, Rianne Eisler, Ursula King and Elizabeth Dodson-Gray have both uncovered stories of an unwritten past and created new tales for a future where humans, earth and all being are seen as sacred. Starhawk (Plant 1989: 184) takes this view of women's spirituality:

> Feminist spirituality, earth-based spirituality, is not just an intellectual exercise, it's a practice. For those of us called to this way, our rituals let us enact our visions, create islands of free space in which we can each be affirmed, valued for our inherent being. In ritual we can feel

our interconnections with all levels of being, and mobilize our emotional energy and passion toward transformation and empowerment.

## ○ The ecofeminist ethic? The personal/political is ecological

As I have just reviewed, there are many strands or 'ways in' to ecofeminism. Perhaps an important query to pose now is whether or not there is an ecofeminist ethic. I would argue that even with all of the varieties of style and approaches to ecofeminism, there can be and needs to be the development of an ecofeminist ethic. I see it as a shift in an overarching ethic within second wave feminism, namely, 'the personal is political'. I would put it simply: where in the feminism of the 1970s the personal is political, in the 1990s – with all the challenges of living on a sore planet with an ailing social and economic system – the personal/political is ecological.

Let's unpack this statement. I will begin the process by looking at the development of that wonderful rallying cry. Catharine MacKinnon (1989: 119–20), in *Toward a Feminist Theory of the State* gives a concise account:

> The personal is political is not a simile, not a metaphor and not an analogy . . . It means that women's distinctive experience as women occurs within that sphere that has been socially lived as the personal – private, emotional, interiorized, particular, individuated, intimate – so that to know the politics of woman's situation, is to know women's personal lives, particularly women's sexual lives.

Kate Millett's monumental work of 1969, *Sexual Politics*, lays the groundwork for what has now become cliché in feminist circles. Her question – what is political? – moves towards a feminist/sexual politics. She writes that

> sex is a status category with political implications . . . The word 'politics' is enlisted here when speaking of the sexes primarily because such a word is eminently useful in outlining the real nature of their relative status, historically and at the present.
>
> (Millett 1969: 24)

Millett brings the lofty idea of politics, which typically existed in a category outside the subject, down to a *personal* level. A true politics depends on a person's experience and location. As one result of this shift in thinking, feminists began organizing and participating in 'consciousness raising' groups. These intimate, trust-building gatherings have enabled feminists to share their personal experiences of oppression. They have also proved a valuable form of group organizing and a means of empowering women.

After a wealth of feminist consciousness raising in the 1960s and 70s there came stirrings of the need to move 'beyond the personal' (Stanley and Wise 1983: 59). Liz Stanley and Sue Wise (1983: 60) in *Breaking Out:*

*Feminist Consciousness and Feminist Research* take up the criticism around 'the personal is political' levelled by feminists who assert that dwelling in personal experience can lead to stagnation or an inability to step fully into the political realm. Others argue that personal awareness and the changes in lifestyle that follow are often superfluous to real political change. Stanley and Wise refute these claims and argue for a continued and mindful consciousness raising within a building up of feminist theory. This is a feminist theory where the 're-appearance of "objectivity" and "subjectivity" must not be seen as "dichotomous"' (Stanley and Wise 1983: 61). 'If "subjectivity" is seen as limited, a stepping off point only; and "objectivity" as the *"proper substance* of theorizing", we are in danger of *not learning* from "a personal is political" process of *real politics'* (Stanley and Wise 1983: 61, emphasis mine). Their argument opens up many questions for academic feminists, such as, how can I, as a woman, write about oppression in an objective way only, in accordance with 'the proper substance of theorizing'? Objectivity serves to remove us from the subject. Academia, in espousing objectivity, equally removes us from any notion of responsibility to act, to change. The advocation of objectivity within the institution of academia is a negative downward trend which requires women to continue to give away power.

Cynthia Enloe in *Bananas, Beaches and Bases: Making Feminist Sense of International Politics* takes the personal/political one step further in introducing 'the personal is international'. Enloe aims to broaden our idea of the political out beyond the self and the self's surrounds and the self's society into the wider realm of the world. She writes:

> Accepting that the personal is international multiplies the spectators, it especially adds women to the audience, but it fails to transform what is going on on stage. The implications of a feminist understanding are thrown into sharp relief when one reads 'the personal is international' the other way round: *the international is personal* . . . [This] implies that governments depend upon certain kinds of allegedly private relationships in order to conduct their foreign affairs . . . [They] depend on ideas about masculinized dignity and feminized sacrifice to sustain that sense of autonomous nationhood.
>
> (Enloe 1989: 196–7)

In asserting that 'the international is personal', Enloe is directing our attention to global issues, whereas the personal/political in its original sense could be constructed closer to home. Indeed, the very operation of industrialized nation-states largely depends on a patriarchal style of 'business as usual'. That is, the system perpetuates itself through the subjugation of women. The 'feminized sacrifice' of which Enloe writes includes (among countless other things) unpaid women's work: the cooking, the cleaning, caring for and reproducing the next generation.

So what would happen if we continued to expand on this notion? I believe that it is not only sexual politics in the international arena, but an expansion that broadens beyond nation-state to an earth-scale. The development of 'the personal is political' has shown that women's personal lives are political through the historical subjugation of women. It has also been shown that industrialized nation-states depend on the subjugation of women. Ecofeminism goes on to show us that the subjugation of women necessarily presupposes the subjugation and domination of nature. Thus, for an emerging ecofeminist ethic, I would argue that the personal/political is ecological. By this, I am intending to surmise a 'life cycle' of responsibility in both politics and ecology. My personal life informs my politics. As my politics is informed by being a woman, my personal/political life is equally informed by the international, the global. Furthermore as a feminist, I am aware that the personal life I am living as a woman of white European descent affects and is affected by politics on a global scale. For instance, my relative privilege and the gross consumption of the West deprives others of a decent quality of life. My participation in western capitalism fuels the international arms trade. As a US taxpayer, I enable the continued development of nuclear technology, and so on.

To take 'the personal is political' further down a contemporary path is to introduce ecology. Ecofeminism bridges feminism and ecology and in so doing, has set free a truth. This truth, now very much at home in our personal/political consciousness, points to the fact that women and nature have been systematically invaded, dominated and rendered soul-less. Far from being a nay-saying philosophical framework, ecofeminism also highlights the many ways in which *all of life* on earth is interdependent. Collard (1988: 137) writes:

> Feminist values and principles directed towards ending the oppression of women are inextricably linked to ecological values and principles directed towards ending the oppression of nature. These values and principles are distilled from women's everyday experiences everywhere of all times. Their realization for women and the earth is predicated on women and men refusing to endorse the destructive values that drive sexism, racism, classism, and speciesism. It is ultimately the affirmation of our kinship with nature, of our common life with her, which will prove the source of our mutual wellbeing.

'The personal/political is ecological' not only means that ecology informs personal/political life, but likewise the converse, my personal/political life informs ecology. I have therefore a responsibility to take care, to walk lightly, and to act in accordance with principles of interdependence. Initiating and taking action is the next necessary and obvious step.

## ○ Why activism? Get out of your head and into your body!

As ecofeminism has asserted from the start, theory alone is not enough. We need a balance between developing good, well-grounded theory within ecofeminism and action initiatives that speak to the problems highlighted. Yenstra King calls the bridge of action and theory ecofeminist praxis, and defines it as 'the unity of thought and action, or theory and practice' (Plant 1989: 25). Furthermore, Lee Quimby in 'Ecofeminism and the politics of resistance' claims that '[s]truggling against specific sites of power not only weakens the junctures of power's networks, but also empowers those who do the struggling' (Diamond and Orenstein 1990: 124). Isn't the 'secret to the stew' that taking action, making a move on something you believe in, can be effective, empowering and also enjoyable? Starhawk reminds us that,

> [t]he actual unsung truth about a lot of organizing is that it feels really good, and that's why people do it, again and again and again. It feels good because when we're actually organizing and taking action to stop the destruction of the earth, we're doing an act of healing and we are free. There are few times when we are free in this culture and this is one of them. We need to speak about the joy and wildness and sense of liberation that comes when we step beyond the bounds of the authorities to resist control and create change.
>
> (Diamond and Orenstein 1990: 79)

There are countless examples of women the world over taking action to curb the destruction of the earth and the subjugation of their sisters. The Chipko 'tree hugging' movement in India put clear-cutting to the test when women refused to allow tress to be felled, a source of richness and diversity only when left to stand, to live. Similar concerns prompted the women's Green Belt movement in Kenya, founded in 1977. Here women plant trees as a sign of solidarity with one another and their interconnectedness with the forests which provide habitat, food and shelter. The Pacific women's movement, Nuclear-Free Pacific, has long acted as a solidarity movement aiming to expose the extreme damage of nuclear testing, conducted in the 1950s by countries such as the US, Britain and most recently France. These women also work on behalf of their communities which have been dislocated and suffer the effects of radiation poisoning. They will have new cases on their hands now, as the French government in the latter part of 1995 and early in 1996, conducted six nuclear tests in the South Pacific, to the surprise and chagrin of many nations and peoples. An international boycott of French goods was launched and bowing to international pressure, President Jacques Chirac stopped the testing program two bombs early. A statement from Greenpeace claimed that the decision came 'six nuclear bombs too late' and criticized a US plan to resume underground testing in Nevada later this year (*Colorado Daily*, 30 January 1996: 1).

Women all over the world resist the global military industrial complex in a variety of creative and effective ways. The US Women's Pentagon Action encircled the Pentagon and sang songs for earth healing in the early 1980s. Women at Greenham Common lived outside the site which housed US nuclear warheads for over 10 years. Greenham women, although the targets of police violence and 'white noise', resisted in such a creative and effective way that their example led to other peace camps in England, Scotland, the US and elsewhere. All of these are but a few examples of women campaigning on behalf of earth and self-healing, while creating effective and engaged communities for change.

There exists a need for a warning sign, however. Once we commit to involving ourselves in the struggle, there is a danger of burning out. Many activists know the sensation of burn-out. This occurs when the campaigner has worked tirelessly at an often thankless job and sees no end in sight, or perhaps there has been little sleep or sustenance for this person. In any case, burn-out, or a profound sense of 'I can't do a thing', may begin to set in. It seems a cycle for activists: doing the thankless job, burning out and then jump-starting the whole process again. I too have been on this tread-mill, but in the last few years, I have been looking at burn-out through a different lens. I now see burn-out not as the inevitable and cyclical process I have just described, but rather as a potent sign of despair. In the last few years I have found working with despair-and-empowerment an invaluable tool for the transformation of the self and society. I would like to describe that work here.

## Dealing with pain for our world: the importance of despair-and-empowerment work

The practice of 'despair work' has emerged in many cultures throughout time from Native American vision quests to the practice of 'speaking bit-terness' in post-revolutionary China (Macy 1983: 110). The notion of using despair to transform and create change is not a new one. In its modern form it has been developed by American scholar and activist, Joanna Macy. She writes:

> What is it that allows us to feel pain for our world? And what do we discover as we move through it? What awaits us there 'on the other side of despair'? To all these questions there is one answer: It is inter-connectedness with life and all other beings. It is the living web out of which our individual, separate existences have risen, and in which we are interwoven. Our lives extend beyond our skins, in radical interdependence with the rest of the world.
>
> (Macy 1983: 24)

Despair-and-empowerment work is informed by twentieth-century science in so far as it takes its theory of radical interdependence from general systems theory. Modern science and philosophy led humanity to believe that in order to know something it must be reduced to its smallest particle. Systems theory makes a departure from this cognitive model by looking at the whole, not smaller and smaller parts of the whole. This has made possible the discovery that

> these wholes – be they cells, bodies, ecosystems, and even the planet itself – are not just a heap of disjunct parts, but dynamic, intricately organized and balanced systems, interrelated and interdependent in every moment, every function, every exchange of energy.
>
> (Macy 1983: 25)

The practice of despair work, or feeling pain for our world, takes place within a supportive environment. Here participants are offered experiential exercises, meditation practices and cognitive models. These structures aim to enable a person to feel their pain, their despair and then take a quantum leap back into empowerment. There are five principles or guidelines for despair-and-empowerment work. The principles, developed by Macy and her colleagues, have proved successful in empowering activists all over the world during the 1980s and 90s. The principles are as follows:

- Feelings of pain for our world are natural and healthy.
- This pain is only morbid if denied.
- Information alone [about the state of the earth] is not enough.
- Unblocking repressed feelings releases energy, clears the mind.
- Unblocking our pain for the world reconnects us with the larger web of life.

(Macy 1983: 22–3)

Denial of pain can feed into a denial of responsibility. In other words, the denial of our pain for the world, or any feelings that surface for us in the face of living on an ailing planet, may produce a denial of our responsibility, our *ability to respond* to the situation. A cycle of denial and an inability to respond may look something like this:

I cannot feel it. I do not recognize my feelings. I do not feel my feelings. I am not responsible. How can I be responsible for something I cannot feel?

I believe that recognizing our complicity, feeling our despair and owning it, can move us from a place of denial to a place of empowerment. This is what despair work sets out to offer.

## ○ **Despairwork and ecofeminism**

So what does despair-and-empowerment work have to do with ecofeminism? To me the very question underlies the aches of a society trying to come to grips with social and ecological breakdown. To question this work denies that the issues which we face involve feeling pain. As an academic, and in the true spirit of objectivity, I am taught to remove myself from feeling anything about what I write, which involves ignoring my pain. Yet when I see clearly and honestly what is happening to the earth and to the peoples of the earth my heart goes out to them. It's as if I can feel the pain of our planet and our planet's people move through me. Moreover, I believe that feeling pain for our world is a measure of our humanity. It is proof that we are awake and alive.

Recently, I had a moving experience. As an ecofeminist, the focus of my personal and planetary work revolves around nuclear issues. I am particularly interested in radioactive waste: how it is produced and what to do with it. After taking part in a weekend conversation entitled 'The moral challenge of radioactive waste', I was feeling rejuvenated to the cause. I had a sense that the work that I do is vital. The weekend, which consisted of 13 people from various backgrounds – activist, religious, academic – left me feeling recharged and hopeful in the face of impossible odds. After we formally ended and closed the final session on Sunday, one participant came forward with a video she wanted to share. It was about the children of Chernobyl. Three Irish women have set up a project which funds one to two-month holidays for the children with local families in County Cork. (It has recently come to my attention that the benefits of such a trip to Ireland can increase a child's life expectancy upwards of two years.) I decided to watch the program.

From the first frame of the video, I began to cry. Unbeknownst to the toddlers and babies themselves, they possess the very monster-like qualities indicative of mutagenic effects caused by radiation exposure. All cloaked in their beautiful innocence, unselfconsciousness and even joy of life, there they were staring at me with missing limbs, fingers protruding where a forearm might be, cleft palates, no noses. Hundreds of children, many of whom will die before reaching adulthood, are the victims of *one accident at one nuclear power station*. I began to wonder what it would be like, as a child, not to be able to run and play for lack of breath, and to some day know that I was the result of a cruel twist of fate, an object of human pity and ignorance.

As I sat watching the video, I found myself reflecting on my own life and future. I am a young woman. It is difficult for me to witness the lives of such children, victims before birth of exposure to radiation. At 27 years of age, I often turn my thoughts to having children, but as I have lived most of my life in close proximity to both nuclear weapons and power facilities, the very reality of motherhood has been robbed from me. What would I do if I gave birth to a child like the one looking at me from the TV monitor? Would I feel responsible for his or her deformity? Would I be able to cope? Would I turn in on myself and lead an embittered life? These questions were closing in on me. What was an incomprehensible problem for children thousands of miles away from me in Belorussia had become my very own predicament; my grief and rage had brought me home. After the video was over I found a wise beech tree and took shelter and cried some more. I cried for the children. I cried for myself. I cried for the future ones yet to come. I cried for the mindlessness that sanctions such abuses of knowledge and power. When my tears had dried up, I found myself once again recommitting to the work of responsible care for radioactive materials and the cessation of nuclear weapons and power production.

My intention in sharing this experience is to underline again that when we can be with our pain, *instead of being paralysed by it*, we can move back into a place of action. If I allowed my pain to build up inside of me and stay unexpected, I would find the task at hand too large, too overwhelming to even think about. Although the problem, in my case relating to nuclear issues, doesn't cease in size or import, my ability to feel that I can make a difference comes alive.

I would like to conclude with a quotation from bell hooks, as her words are pertinent when choosing to take action in a changing world. She entreats humanity to begin to work with the following understanding:

that we all (irrespective of our race, sex or class) have acted in complicity with the existing oppressive system. We all need to make a conscious break with the system. Some of us make this break sooner than others. The compassion we extend to ourselves, the recognition that our change in consciousness and action has been a process, must characterize our approach to those individuals who are politically unconscious. We cannot motivate them to join feminist struggle by asserting political superiority that makes the movement just another oppressive hierarchy.

(hooks 1984: 161–2)

It is true that we cannot *make* people take action or even feel their own feelings. We can, however, offer ecofeminism as a theory and practice, and continue to build a movement of resistance fuelled by creative change in our communities and in our own lives. The challenge lies within each of us, to move forward with the flow of radical interdependence or to stagnate in our skin-encapsulated egos. It is powerful to know, however, that the choice is ours.

○ **Questions and exercises**

1 Do you feel on a profound level that you are connected with the earth? If yes, why? If no, why?

2 Can men be ecofeminists? If yes, why? If no, why?

3 Think of a personal or planetary problem that is present for you now. Explore the feelings that arise for you by writing a poem or short story in which the problem is recognized and people change their lives in order to deal with it.

4 Organize a consciousness raising group with people you trust. Gather together and ask participants to share their feelings about 'what on earth is happening' and how this affects them on a personal level. Talk about ecofeminism as a responses to personal and political crisis. Remember to share speaking space and enable each other to talk openly. Have tea together. See what develops.

○ **Further reading**

For a wonderful collection of women's prose and poetry about the earth, and the joy and pain that they find there, see Anderson (1991). For an inclusion of pornography in an ecofeminist debate, see Griffin (1981) where she pulls apart typical notions of pornography and offers a profound critique of modern society. Macy (1991a) explores

ecological selfhood in a moving collection of essays, stories and practical action, overlaid with an historical context of Buddhist philosophy.
The wisdom of years of experience in feminism, peace and justice, and
poetry circles is shared in Rich (1993). It is a true gem and a 'must'
read for engaged, compassionate people. For new concepts of power
and how we can effect change creatively, as well as structures for
building community, tools for working in groups and an inspired
explanation of earth-based spirituality, see Starhawk (1982). For a
good look at essentialism in feminist theory see Daly (1978, 1984).
For further exploration of systems theory see Bateson (1972), Capra
(1982) and Macy (1991b).

For continued reading into issues of feminism, politics, ecology and
spirituality I highly recommend *woman of power*. Each issue has a
theme, such as 'the living earth', 'woman as warrior', 'women and
community', expressed in written articles, poetry, art, photo essays
and much more. Published by woman of power, Inc. which is a non-
profit organization, this magazine is virtually advertisement-free.
Address: woman of power, PO Box 827, Cambridge, MA 02238 USA.

For more information on activism and ecofeminism contact: The
Women's Environmental Network, Aberdeen Studios, 22 Highbury
Grove, London N5 2BR, tel: (0171) 490 2511. For experiential work-
shops involving despair-and-empowerment work contact: The Insti-
tute for Deep Ecology Education, 36 Broomfield Lane, Palmers Green,
London N13 4HH. For information on the Chernobyl Children's
Project contact: Adi Roche, 8 Sidneyville, Bellview Park, St. Lukes,
Cork, Ireland. All donations are tax-deductible and cheques may be
made payable to the Chernobyl Children's Project, Ltd.

## References

Anderson, L. (1991) *Sisters of the Earth*. New York: Vintage Books.
Bateson, G. (1972) *Steps to an Ecology of Mind*. New York: Ballantine Books.
Biehl, J. (1991) *Rethinking Ecofeminist Politics*. Boston, MA: South End Press.
Capra, F. (1982) *The Turning Point: Science, Society and the Rising Culture*. London: Flamingo.
Carson, R. (1962) *Silent Spring*. Boston, MA: Houghton Mifflin Company.
Collard, A. (1988) *Rape of the Wild*. London: The Women's Press.
Daly, M. (1978) *Gyn/Ecology: The Metaethics of Radical Feminism*. Boston, MA: Beacon Press.
Daly, M. (1984) *Pure Lust: Elemental Feminist Philosophy*. Boston, MA: Beacon Press.
Diamond, I. and Orenstein, G. F. (1990) *Reweaving the World: The Emergence of Ecofeminism*. San Francisco, CA: Sierra Club.
Enloe, C. (1989) *Bananas, Beaches and Bases: Making Feminist Sense of International Politics*. Berkeley, CA: University of California Press.
Griffin, S. (1978) *Woman and Nature: The Roaring Inside Her*. New York: Harper and Row.

Griffin, S. (1981) *Pornography and Silence: Culture's Revenge Against Nature*. San Francisco, CA: Harper and Row.

hooks, b. (1984) *Feminist Theory: From Margin to Center*. Boston, MA: South End Press.

Macy, J. (1983) *Despair and Personal Power in the Nuclear Age*. Philadelphia, PA: New Society Publishers.

Macy, J. (1991a) *World as Lover, World as Self*. Berkeley, CA: Parallax Press.

Macy, J. (1991b) *Mutual Causality in Buddhism and General Systems Theory*. Albany, NY: State University of New York Press.

MacKinnon, C. (1989) *Toward a Feminist Theory of the State*. London: Harvard University Press.

Merchant, C. (1980) *The Death of Nature: Women, Ecology, and the Scientific Revolution*. San Francisco, CA: Harper and Row.

Merchant, C. (1992) *Radical Ecology: The Search for a Livable World*. New York: Routledge.

Millet, K. (1969) *Sexual Politics*. New York: Simon and Schuster.

Plant, J. (1989) *Healing the Wounds: The Promise of Ecofeminism*. Philadelphia, PA: New Society Publishers.

Rich, A. (1993) *What Is Found There: Notebooks on Poetry and Politics*. New York: W. W. Norton & Company.

Shiva, V. (1989) *Staying Alive: Women, Ecology and Development*. London: Zed Books.

Stanley, L. and Wise, S. (1983) *Breaking Out: Feminist Consciousness and Feminist Research*. London: Routledge.

Starhawk (1982) *Dreaming the Dark: Magic, Sex and Politics*. Boston, MA: Beacon Press.

Walsh, V. (1995) Eyewitnesses not spectators – activists not academics: feminist pedagogy and women's creativity, in K. Deepwell (ed.) *New Feminist Art Criticism: Critical Practices*. Manchester: Manchester University Press.

*woman of power* (1991) Spring issue, Cambridge, MA.

# Index

## POWER IN STRUGGLE
FEMINISM, SEXUALITY AND THE STATE

## Davina Cooper

What is power? And how are social change strategies shaped by the ways in which we conceptualize it? Drawing on feminist, poststructuralist, and marxist theory, Davina Cooper develops an innovative framework for understanding power relations within fields as diverse as queer activism, municipal politics, and the regulation of lesbian reproduction. *Power in Struggle* explores the relationship between power, sexuality and the state and, in the process, provides a radical rethinking of these concepts and their interactions. The book concludes with an important and original discussion of how an ethics of empowerment can inform political strategy.

*Special features*:
- brings together central aspects of current radical, political theory in an innovative way
- offers a new way of conceptualizing the state, power and sexuality

### Contents
*Introduction – Beyond domination?: productive and relational power – The politics of sex: metaphorical strategies and the (re)construction of desire – Multiple identities: sexuality and the state in struggle – Penetration on the defensive: regulating lesbian reproduction – Access without power: gay activism and the boundaries of governance – Beyond resistance: political strategy and counter-hegemony – Afterword – Bibliography – Index.*

192pp     0 335 19211 4 (paperback)     0 335 19212 2 (hardback)

**GENDERED WORK**
SEXUALITY, FAMILY AND THE LABOUR MARKET

**Lisa Adkins**

*Gendered Work* contributes to current debates on the labour market via an exploration of the significance of sexual and family relations in structuring employment.
Through detailed studies of conditions of work in the British tourist industry, it
shows how men and women are constituted as different kinds of 'workers' in the
labour market not only when segregated in different occupations but also even
when they are nominally located in the same jobs.

This differentiation is shown to be connected to two key processes: the sexualiz-
ation of women workers which locates women as sexual as well as 'economic'
workers, and the operation of family work relations within the sphere of employment when women work as wives rather than waged-labourers in the context of
the contemporary labour market. These two processes are then drawn together to
show the ways in which labour market production is gendered. This book therefore makes an important contribution to the growing feminist literature which is
exposing the deep embeddedness of gender within labour market processes and
practices.

*Special features*:
• New empirical material on the terms and conditions of typical contemporary jobs
  for women.
• New ways of understanding the gendered structure of the labour market.
• Reviews a range of analyses (feminist and sociological) in a constructively critical way to throw light on change and continuity in employment in the consumer
  society.

**Contents**
*Introduction – Sexuality and the labour market – Family production in the labour market –
Sexual servicing and women's employment – The condition of women's work – References –
Index.*

192pp     0 335 19296 3 (paperback)     0 335 19297 1 (hardback)

## WOMEN IN BRITAIN TODAY

### Veronica Beechey and Elizabeth Whitelegg (eds)

In recent years the impact of feminist approaches has revolutionized almost all aspects of the study of women's role in society, challenging previous assumptions about the nature of gender roles. This book draws on a wealth of current materials to provide an introduction to and an analysis of women's situation in British society. In a series of coordinated essays, the authors examine four key issues – the family, employment, education and health – challenging existing stereotypes of women's role, discussing contemporary research and providing alternative explanations.

Adapted from the popular and innovative Open University course U221: *The Changing Experience of Women*, this book is an invaluable introduction to feminist analyses which will be relevant to students and teachers of women's studies and to all others interested in the position of women in contemporary Britain.

### Contents
*Introduction – Women in the family: companions or caretakers? – Women's employment in contemporary Britain – State education policy and girls' educational experiences – Women, health and medicine – Index.*

### Contributors
Madeleine Arnot, Veronica Beechey, Lesley Doyal, Mary Ann Elston, Diana Leonard, Mary Anne Speakman.

224pp      0 335 15137 X (paperback)